THE SEARCH FOR
THE ANCIENT ORDER

A History of The Restoration Movement
1849-1906

BY

EARL IRVIN WEST

Vol. 1
1849-1865

We have heard with our ears, O God,
  Our fathers have told us,
What work thou didst in their days,
  In the days of old.
                              —Psalms 44: 1.

DEDICATION

*To my wife, Lois Louise,
and to the wives of all gospel
preachers who alone know the toils,
anxieties, and joys of their husbands,
this volume is affectionately dedicated.*

ALEXANDER CAMPBELL

CONTENTS

ACKNOWLEDGMENTS

The publication of a book of this size and nature necessarily demands the assistance of interested people to make it possible. Many have been a help to the author, whose assistance he wishes to acknowledge.

Our appreciation is, therefore, expressed to the following: C. E. W. Dorris of Nashville, Tennessee for the use of many valuable books, and for his assistance in reading the manuscript. B. C. Goodpasture for assistance on the manuscript. Enos Dowling, librarian for Butler University School of Religion, Indianapolis, Indiana; for use of the many valuable books in this library. Ada Mosher, librarian of the United Christian Missionary Society, Indianapolis, Indiana for use of the minutes of the early Society meetings. Minnie Mae Corum of Winter Haven, Florida for original letters which have been used in this writing. Central Church of Christ, Nashville, Tennessee for use of valuable periodicals. My father-in-law, Horace Hinds of Los Angeles, California, for assistance on the index.

FOREWORD

This work, "The Search for the Ancient Order," is monumental. It will take its place along with Richardson's "Memoirs of A. Campbell" and Hayden's "Early History of the Disciples in the Western Reserve" as a "source book" for Restoration material. In the preparation of this work the author had at his command sources of valuable information not accessible to the average reader.

The author is a young man. He was born in Indianapolis, Indiana on May 18, 1920. After finishing his high school work in Indianapolis, he entered Freed-Hardeman College, Henderson, Tennessee, in the fall of 1938, and was graduated from that institution two years later. In the fall of 1940 he entered Abilene Christian College, Abilene, Texas, with the purpose of receiving his B.A. degree from that institution. But in the spring of 1941 the Broadway and Walnut Streets Church of Christ in Santa Ana, California, extended him an invitation to become its co-preacher. This invitation he accepted, and continued his college studies in George Pepperdine College, Los Angeles, California, receiving his B.A. in June, 1943. After being graduated from Pepperdine, he was invited by his home congregation, the Irvington Church of Christ, in Indianapolis, to "do local work." He accepted this invitation and still labors with this faithful congregation. During these years he has done graduate work in the School of Religion at Butler University where he received the M.A. and B.D. degrees; but he does not parade his degrees.

Those who read this work will desire to read anything he may hereafter write.

B. C. GOODPASTURE.

GENERAL INTRODUCTION

Shortly after the turn of the nineteenth century various forces were at work in American religious circles pointing toward a restoration of apostolic Christianity. Few religious groups escaped the plea for reformation within their ranks. Among the Methodists there was James O'Kelley; among the Baptists, Abner Jones and Elias Smith; among the Presbyterians, Barton W. Stone; and in both the Presbyterian and Baptist ranks a little later, there was Alexander Campbell. In the popular mind Stone and Campbell are much better known as leaders in the plea for the return to the ancient order of things.

This religious movement spread rapidly until the 1850 census showed it to be the fourth ranking church in the nation. In the decade from 1850 to 1860 its ranks increased far more rapidly than any other group. But after the Civil War an ominous note began to be sounded. The Missionary Society had been introduced as early as 1849 and sporadic opposition was engendered, but this warfare began to increase tremendously in that era following the Civil War. Too, the instrument of music began to be popularly used in the worship. From here on other practices and attitudes began to multiply, and as they did, the opposition grew. A division within the ranks of this religious movement began to be inevitable. Wherever the society was introduced and the organ came into the worship, groups who could not work and worship with these were forced out to start over again. For the most part these groups that had to leave were in the minority. But they went to work in earnest to rebuild upon what they considered to be the original plea for restoration:

The story of this restoration movement has many times been written, but the story, from the viewpoint of this minority, has never been told. Yet it needs to be. This minority in many parts of the nation is now the majority. It is rapidly growing in many other localities. Many are optimistic enough to believe that within the next quarter of a century not a city or town of any size will be without congregations knowing the plea for a return to New Testament Christianity.

The division within the ranks of those who began pleading for the primitive order was given its first census recognition in 1906.

The churches of Christ and the Disciples of Christ or Christian Church were for the first time listed separately. The report for the churches of Christ was compiled by J. W. Shepherd, and begins with a history of the churches followed by the statistics. Because of the difficulty of getting congregations to report, this census was never regarded as being over a third of the total figures that should have been given. At any rate, the report states there were 2,649 congregations located in thirty-three states and territories. 1,979 of these churches were located in the south central states with Tennessee leading, and Texas coming second. Tennessee had six hundred and thirty-one congregations and Texas had six hundred and twenty-seven. There were 159,658 members among the churches of Christ, according to the report. The church had 1,974 buildings with property valued at $2,555,372. Six hundred and ninety-three churches were using rented halls for meeting places. The report also shows that there were 2,100 preachers that year among the churches.

There were eight Christian colleges employing seventy-three teachers and having an enrollment of 1,024 students among the churches of Christ in 1906. Value of all school property was listed at $170,500. In addition, there was a normal and business college with ten teachers, three hundred and fifty students and property valued at $40,000. There was a classical institute employing six teachers and having eighty students enrolled. The value of this property was listed at $20,000. Included was also an orphan school with six teachers and sixty pupils and property valued at $75,000. Of these, there were three schools in Tennessee, four in Texas, and one each in Kentucky, Alabama, Missouri and Oklahoma, according to the report.

The Disciples of Christ on the other hand had 8,293 local congregations. Missouri led that year with 1,424 churches. The total report shows 982,701 members and 6,641 preachers.

The significance of this year's report lies not in the numbers presented but in the fact that it is an outward expression of division which had been wrought within the ranks of those who were pleading for a return to New Testament Christianity. The fact that the religious periodicals of the two groups paid so little attention to the report can largely be explained on the ground that it came as no surprise to either group. For several years the division had been recognized. For at least twenty years before 1906 there had been little fellowship remaining between the two groups. Down to the present day each has continued to go its own separate way.

To discover the underlying causes of this break which the census report then recognized after the turn of the century presents at once a complicated but most valuable study. The study is complicated because these causes are at once varied. Environmental and social causes are at work. Personal or temperamental causes are at work. In a measure political causes are at work. But, in the main, the causes, we think, narrow down to an interpretation of the plea, and a fundamental attitude toward the scriptures. On the other hand, the study is valuable because of the historical background it furnishes to present-day issues, and the inspiration it affords to those who are continuing at this late date the plea for a return to the ancient order.

The basic problem we face, then, is to seek to know the issues that caused this break in fellowship, and to try to go beneath them to discover the underlying philosophy of each group that made these outward issues so important. This, we realize, is a large order. But yet, this is the real problem which presents itself in a study of the restoration and without some conception, the movement is only partially understood. It would be useless to attempt any study which ignores the basic problem in it.

There are a number of factors to be taken into consideration in answering these problems. First and foremost of these is the men in the movement. These issues were realized in the men who championed them. The temperaments, dispositions, environmental background will be highly important. Yet with this, we recognize at once a danger of drifting into a purely humanistic conception of the whole movement, and attribute everything to background and natural causes. This mistake we do not propose to make. In view of that a second factor presents itself: an analysis of the issues upon the basis of the scriptures themselves. Whatever attitudes the men in the movement took, they did so because of convictions that here is what the Bible teaches. Our method, then, shall be to discover in the events and persons of the period what factors of environment, personal temperament and Bible teaching helped to bring these issues into the open and make them serious enough to have caused the division which came into the brotherhood.

Every historical study must start somewhere and end somewhere. We have set the dates of our investigation for this study to begin with 1849, the year of the establishment of the American Christian Missionary Society, and to end with 1906, the year when the Religious Census for the first time gave recognition to a division. These dates we have purely arbitrarily set; maybe other dates would have suited the purpose just as well. We shall not be dogmatic in these dates, but they seem preferable to others which might be suggested.

The reader is, therefore, asked to remember that this is not intended to be a complete history of the restoration movement. By the year, 1849, the movement was well on its way. Its growth had been phenomenal. Generally speaking, brethren were pretty much united. But over this period of growth, the reader may find any number of books which will give him a good conception of what took place. Robert Richardson's, "Memoirs of Alexander Campbell" is still unsurpassed. One may find in Barton W. Stone's autobiography or in the later "Barton Warren Stone" by C. C. Ware much material to give a general knowledge of the Stone movement. Literature on the New England movement is, of course, much more scarce, but the reader will find M. T. Morrill's "A History of The Christian Denomination in America" very helpful. On the other hand, there has been relatively little research done on the restoration movement from 1849 on down to the turn of the century. It is during this time that the cause is at the crossroads. For the churches of Christ here is the really important part of the movement. It is upon this part that we propose to give the major portion of our attention.

Our first two chapters will deal in a general way with the early part of the restoration movement. This material, we include for two reasons. First, many of our readers will have little or no knowledge of this part of the restoration, and little or no opportunity to read the books which give it. This may supply in part their deficiency. Second, a knowledge of the latter phase of the restoration will depend upon an understanding of the plea and principles which guided the movement in its earlier years. We shall hope to use this understanding of the earlier years as a platform from which to launch our investigation in a more critical and minute manner during the last half of the nineteenth century.

And so we begin.

CHAPTER I

EARLY BEGINNINGS

Although the political implications far overshadowed the religious, yet the revolt of the American colonies against the tyranny of George III was as much for religious freedom as for political. It was only logical that England should bring her religion to the New World as well as her politics, and it was equally natural that these should partake of the same characteristics on this side of the Atlantic as on the other. Consequently, in the pre-Revolutionary War days the most popular and well-known church was the Established Church, the Church of England. All other groups were looked upon with disfavor, and persecution against them in one form or another was seldom absent.

The clergy of the Established Church ruled affairs in the colonies with an iron hand. An assembly held in March, 1624, in Virginia provided that all must attend divine services on Sunday. Whoever missed once without an allowable excuse was fined one pound of coffee; a month's missing caused a fine of fifty pounds. Every person was told to conform to the "canons of England" and "to yield readie obedience to them under paine of censure." No man was allowed to sell his tobacco until the preacher gave permission. Each year at the tobacco harvest, a man was appointed to visit each plantation to collect the minister's portion "out of the first and best tobacco."[1] By 1632 the laws were revised to some extent but contained the same spirit. Non-attendance at services cost the guilty party one shilling instead of one pound of tobacco.

In the main, however, one might conclude that these clergymen were kept busy hunting and punishing all types of heresy. The Act of Uniformity of 1642 enacted in order to preserve the "puritie of doctrine and the unitie of the church, that all ministers whatsoever, which shall reside in the colony are to be conformable to the orders and constitution of the Church of England, and the laws therein established, and not otherwise to be admitted to teach or preach publicly or privately."[2] The same act directed the Governor

---

[1] W. W. Bennett, *Memorials of Methodism in Virginia* (Richmond: Published by author, 1871), pp. 16, 17.

[2] W. W. Bennett, *Memorials of Methodism in Virginia,* p. 19.

1

and counsel to enforce the law rigidly against "all non-conformists, compelling them to depart the colony with all convenience."

Particularly did the clergymen turn against the Quakers. The legislative authorities described them as an "unreasonable and turbulent sort of people, who contrary to the laws, daily gathered assemblies and congregations of people, teaching and publishing lies, miracles, false visions, prophecies, and doctrines tending to destroy religion, laws, communities, and all bonds of civil society."[3] Captains of ships were fined one hundred pounds of sterling for bringing Quakers into the state of Virginia. All Quakers were imprisoned without bail.

Persecution also raged against the Baptists. The first Baptists came to Virginia in 1714. Fifty years later, on the eve of the Revolutionary War, they were relatively numerous. But they would not be put down. In January, 1768, John Waller, Lewis Craig, James Childs and some other Baptists were arrested. They appeared before three magistrates who charged: "These men are great disturbers of the peace; they cannot meet a man on the road, but they must ram a text of scripture down his throat."[4] The magistrates offered to let them go if they would consent not to preach in that county for a year and a day. They refused and they sang as they marched down the streets of Fredericksburg to jail. After serving some time, they were released. They were later tried again. At this trial the fiery Patrick Henry rode fifty miles to defend them. He was sublime in his theme and dramatic in his actions. "These men," he said, "are charged with—with—what?" In low, measured tones he continued, "preaching the gospel of the Son of God." He paused; waved the indictment above his head. The silence was painful. Then lifting his head and hands to the sky, he exclaimed, "Great God!!" The men were immediately dismissed.[5]

In spite of opposition from the English clergy the non-conformists continued to increase. They grew more and more in favor with the colonists. All the while the Established Church was becoming more distasteful. By the time of the Revolutionary War two-thirds of the people favored the Dissenters, yet they were forced by law to pay the clergy. The people complained bitterly

---

[3]W. W. Bennett, *Memorials of Methodism in Virginia*, p. 22.
[4]W. W. Bennett, *Memorials of Methodism in Virginia*, p. 38.
[5]W. W. Bennett, *Memorials of Methodism in Virginia*, pp. 38, 39.

but to little avail. The Bill for Religious Freedom failed to pass in the Assembly in 1779. It was seven years before Thomas Jefferson's Bill for Religious Freedom passed, but it was 1801 before this final vestige of Church and State union was abolished.[6]

One might get an additional view of the condition of the church in New England in these days by a letter written by James Madison, later president of the United States. Madison writes:

> Poverty and luxury prevailed among all sects; pride, ignorance and knavery among the priesthood, and vice and wickedness among the laity. That is bad enough, but it is not the worst I have to tell you. That diabolical, hell-conceived principle of persecution rages among some, and to their eternal infamy, the clergy furnish their quota of imps for such purposes. There are at this time in the adjacent counties, not less than five or six well-meaning persons in close jail for publishing their religious sentiments, which, in the main, are very orthodox.
> . . . I have neither patience to hear, talk nor think of anything relative to this matter, for I have squabbled, and scolded, abused and ridiculed so long about it to no purpose, that I am without common patience. So I must beg you to pity me and pray for the liberty of conscience to all.[7]

Meanwhile, a leaven was at work among the colonial churches of the Established order. As early as 1729 this leaven had begun working in England when John Wesley, noting the formality and tyranny of the Church, proposed forming societies within the church dedicated to the purifying of the corrupt elements. Wesleyan preachers were still Anglicans. Wesley himself lived and died a member of that church and was buried in his Anglican robes. "Wesleyan Societies" came to be established by persons demanding a holier life on the part of the members of this church. It was natural that Wesleyan preachers should come to the New World and should tirelessly preach. These Societies were formed throughout the colonies. It was also natural that the American clergymen should look with disfavor upon the Wesleyan Societies and the Wesleyan preachers. As the time of the Revolutionary War period drew on, it was evident that these Wesleyan Societies were becoming a force with which to reckon. The political upheaval aggravated this situation. The fires of liberty burned fiercely in the hearts of the colonists. Meanwhile, the clergy looked to the

---

[6]W. W. Bennett, *Memorials of Methodism in Virginia*, pp. 42-46.
[7]W. E. MacClenny, *The Life of Rev. James O'Kelley* (Raleigh, N. C., Edwards & Broughton, 1910), pp. 23, 24.

English crown for orders and for protection. The clergy became the object of scorn, as their lot was cast among the Tories. On the other hand, the Wesleyan Societies in America were made up of colonists, crying for liberty. So the feeling of resentment continued to increase.

The question of ordaining preachers was to be a great problem during these years. This was inescapable. The idea prevailed that a man could not preach funerals, administer the sacraments, baptize, or perform marriages unless he was duly ordained. The common belief of apostolic succession prevailed among Anglican clergymen in those days. No preacher could be ordained unless he was ordained by a duly ordained minister who himself was ordained by another duly ordained person on back to the apostolic era. The Wesleyan preachers were not ordained preachers. Not a single preacher in America could be found possessing the right to perform these functions. The Anglican clergymen who were ordained refused to ordain these preachers. The whole matter, then, became one of grave concern, for in time, the distinct existence of these Wesleyan Societies within the Anglican Church was threatened. The question of what could be done in such a crisis was raised on both sides of the Atlantic, and considerable anxiety prevailed.

By the close of the American Revolution, the English clergy in America had fled to their native country, and the colonies were left far short of preachers. The Wesleyan preachers stayed in the colonies but continued to raise questions about church government and the ordination of bishops. In Europe, John Wesley himself was no less concerned about the welfare of these American churches. In the fall of 1784 Wesley wrote in his *Journal:*

Wednesday September 1.—Being now clear in my own mind, I took a step which I had long weighed in my mind, and appointed Mr. Whatcoat and Mr. Vasey to go and serve the desolate sheep in America. *Thursday, September 2.*—I added to them three more, which I verily believe, will be much to the glory of God.[8]

The next day Wesley ordained Thomas Coke as the superintendent in America and Richard Whatcoat and Thomas Vasey as presbyters to be sent with Coke.

---

[8]John Wesley, *Wesley's Journal,* Vol. II (New York: Hunt & Eaton, n. d.), p. 602.

Six weeks later, on November 3, 1784 these three men landed in New York. In the possession of Thomas Coke was a document, written by John Wesley, and destined to be known as the "Magna Charta of American Methodism." The document reads:

To all to whom these presents shall come, John Wesley, late Fellow of Lincoln College in Oxford, Presbyter of the Church of England, sendeth greetings:

Whereas, many of the people of the southern provinces of North America, who desire to continue under my care, and still adhere to the doctrine and discipline of the Church of England, are greatly distressed for want of ministers to administer the sacraments of baptism and the Lord's Supper, according to the usage of the same church: and, whereas, there does not appear to be any other way of supplying them with ministers:

Know all men, that I, John Wesley, think myself to be providentially called at this time to set apart some persons for the work of ministry in America. And, therefore, under the protection of Almighty God, and with a single eye to his glory, I have this day set apart as a Superintendent, by the imposition of my hands and prayers (being assisted by other ordained ministers), Thomas Coke, Doctor of Civil Law, a presbyter of the Church of England, and a man whom I judge to be well qualified for that great work. And I do hereby recommend him to all whom it may concern, as a fit person to preside over the flock of Christ. In testimony whereof I have hereunto set my hand and seal, this second day of September, in the year of our Lord, one thousand seven hundred and eighty-four. [9]

Two weeks after landing in New York, Coke and his company were at the famous Barrett's Chapel in Delaware. It was a Quarterly meeting and fifteen preachers were present, along with five hundred others. Here Coke and Asbury first met. Asbury at the time had been in America thirteen years and was now about forty years of age. Coke himself was prepared to use his powers of ordination to make Asbury a superintendent here in New England. Asbury insisted, however, that a conference be called for the ordination. At the famous Christmas Conference in Baltimore in 1784, Asbury was ordained as Superintendent of the church in America. It was at this conference that the discipline for the Methodist Episcopal Church was accepted, and here, too, for the first time, the title, Methodist Episcopal Church, was accepted as the name for the Wesleyan Societies. The Societies were now trying

[9]Ezra Squier Tipple, *Francis Asbury, The Prophet of the Long Road* (New York: The Methodist Book Concern, 1916), pp. 134, 135.

to bridge the gap between being mere Societies and becoming a Church separate and distinct from the Church of England. The name chosen did not set well with many of the preachers. Nor did this type of government suit many. Even John Wesley had admitted it was not apostolic, but most practical under the circumstances. A compromise was reached which denied the doctrine of apostolic succession. The Methodist Episcopal Church was now born.

The government of this Church may be seen to owe its origin to natural causes rather than a view of doing what the scriptures taught. The background of Methodism was to be found in the Anglican church. But, whereas the Established Church in America grew into disfavor owing to its English leanings during the Revolutionary War days, it was natural that the Methodists should modify their government just enough to nullify this disadvantage. In consequence, its government became a mixture of monarchial and democratic principles. The democratic principles satisfied the freedom-loving colonies. The monarchial phase was carried over from the Established Church. Qualben says:

This final and permanent organization of the Methodist Episcopal Church was a mixture of monarchial and democratic principles. The bishops were given more administrative power than the bishops of England had enjoyed; yet, the legislative power was vested in regular conferences, which were soon almost completely controlled by the lay people. Thus the system was unlike that of any previously known system of church government.[10]

Scarcely had the Methodist Church started, until its first serious internal conflict began to rage. The cause was over a disagreement as to the type of government chosen for the church. There were those who looked upon this government as contrary to the scriptures. Too, they saw in it what they thought was the greed of Francis Asbury who wanted to place himself in the top position at the head of a new church. For a time the opposition was very intense. Its interest to us lies in the fact that it presents the first major attempt of any people to go back to New Testament Christianity.

Opposition to Asbury was mainly led by James O'Kelley. O'Kelley as a leader was hardly second to Asbury. He was said

---

[10]Lars P. Qualben, *A History of the Christian Church* (New York: Thomas Nelson & Sons, 1940), p. 437.

to be "laborious in the ministry, a man of zeal and usefulness, an advocate of holiness, given to prayer and fasting, an able defender of Methodist doctrine and faith, and hard against negro slavery, in private and from the press and pulpit."[11] Asbury and O'Kelley had first met in North Carolina in 1780. Asbury wrote in his journal: "James O'Kelley and myself enjoyed and comforted each other; this dear man rose at midnight and prayed very devoutly for me and himself. He cries, 'Give me children or I die.' "[12]

The date of O'Kelley's birth is not exactly known. It is put anywhere from 1735 to 1757. The former date, however, has been generally accepted since O'Kelley's death was on October 16, 1826 at which time it was believed he was ninety-two years of age. Records of O'Kelley's birth are not to be had. It is generally agreed that he was born in Mecklenburg County, Virginia although some say, Wake County. MacClenny disagrees with both and puts his birth in Ireland. At any rate, there is little question that he was of Irish descent. Shortly before 1760 O'Kelley married Elizabeth Meeks and to them two sons were born—John and William. After this the real story of James O'Kelley begins.

O'Kelley's son, William, was twelve years old when the first Methodist preachers came into the Cedar Creek country of Virginia in 1775. William and his mother were converted, and William immediately began to seek the conversion of his father. So zealous was he that William began thinking about being a preacher but his father discouraged him. Shortly afterward, William left home and moved into the New Hope Valley in Chatam County. In years to come he got into politics and was, for several years a member of the State Legislature of North Carolina.

O'Kelley, however, was not long in getting interested in religion. He listened to the preachers, and read the sermons they brought which had been delivered by Wesley. O'Kelley was struck by the fact that they gave all-sufficiency to the Bible. Wesley said, "We will be downright Christians," and this pleased O'Kelley. He writes:

They (certain ministers) come to us under direction of John Wesley, whose name to me is of precious memory. His writings magnified the Bible, and gave it preference and honor; he declared he regarded the authority of no writings but the inspired. He

---

[11]W. W. Bennett, *Memorials of Methodism in Virginia*, p. 315.
[12]W. W. Bennett, *Memorials of Methodism in Virginia*, p. 315.

urged the sufficiency of the Scriptures for faith and practice, saying, "We will be downright Bible Christians."[13]

About the middle of the Revolutionary War O'Kelley began preaching. He was continually traveling. The influence of Francis Asbury was everywhere seen, and in southern Virginia and North Carolina where O'Kelley traveled, the general impression was that Asbury was a religious tyrant. Fires of opposition were smoulder-ing. His rule to "pay, pray, and obey" which he expected of all his laymen did not set well. As far as O'Kelley was concerned there was too much English in the system and too much Irish in the man to accept Asbury's rule. Tension then mounted.

A crisis was reached by the time the Virginia Conference met on May 18, 1779 at Brokenback Chapel, in Fluvanna County. O'Kelley that year was traveling the New Hope circuit. Preachers attended the conference expecting something to be done to end their servile dependence upon Episcopalian clergy. But Asbury fought the move. He insisted that Wesley was opposed to any such drastic move of separation from the Established Church. The Episcopacy as a form of church government such as the Angli-cans had pleased Asbury very much. A deadlock ensued.

It was clear to Asbury that he must get the support of Northern preachers if he were to get over his ideas. Of the preachers south of the Potomac River almost all were opposed to Asbury. Asbury strengthened his position by an appeal to these Northern preachers.

O'Kelley might have gone further with some of his ideas except for the untenable positions he took at times. At this conference there came up the question of sprinkling or immersion for baptism. O'Kelley dogmatically maintained that sprinkling was baptism, and remained with this belief until his death. Moreover, a measure was passed through the Conference which said: "All preachers were to make it a matter of conscience to rise at four or five in the morning, and it was declared a shame for a preacher to be in bed at six."[14] Preachers, being what they are, have never liked this, and it brought O'Kelley a measure of disrepute.

For the next five years, O'Kelley found himself at odds with Asbury continually. By the time of the famous Christmas Con-ference in Baltimore, O'Kelley was generally recognized as against

---

[13]J. Pressley Barrett, *The Centennial of Religious Journalism* (Dayton, Ohio: Christian Publishing Association, 1908), p. 19.
[14]W. E. MacClenny, *Life of Rev. James O'Kelley*, p. 36.

Asbury's views. A week after this conference, O'Kelley and twelve others were ordained elders by Thomas Coke. Returning from the Conference, O'Kelley began to marshal his forces for a show down battle with Asbury.

According to the Methodist government at this time, the power of appointing preachers rested in the hands of the superintendent, in this case, Francis Asbury. The preacher took the circuit appointed to him and had little he could do about it. The southern preachers didn't like the idea. In 1790 O'Kelley wrote Asbury, complaining that the latter had misused his episcopal powers and threatened Asbury with opposition if he didn't check his course. In South Virginia O'Kelley turned most of the churches against Asbury. But, Asbury was not of the disposition to change his actions and so the trouble mounted.

Another crisis was reached when the General Conference met in Baltimore on November 1, 1792. O'Kelley introduced the motion that a preacher be given the right of appeal to the Conference if he didn't like his appointment. This was a blow at Asbury, who immediately retired from the Conference, leaving the meeting in charge of Thomas Coke. The debate that followed was intense and raged for three days. But finally O'Kelley lost. When this happened, O'Kelley and his followers served notice they were through with the Conference.

Standing by O'Kelley were Rice Haggard, John Allen, John Robertson and William McKendree. McKendree later went back to the Methodists. Allen became a physician and gave up preaching. In the end, O'Kelley and Rice Haggard were the two to carry through with their principles of reform.

Shortly after the General Conference was dismissed on November 14, O'Kelley and his followers met at Reese Chapel in Charlotte County, Virginia. Petitions were sent to the Methodists, asking for union, and stipulating certain amendments. But the Methodists turned these down. Another meeting was held at Piney Grove in Chesterfield County, Virginia on August 2, 1793. They petitioned Asbury to meet them in a Conference to examine the government of the Methodist Episcopal Church by the scriptures. Asbury refused to meet. Another conference was held by the group at Manakintown in Powhaton County, Virginia on December 25, 1793. The group decided to officially sever all relations with the Methodist Episcopal Church. They took the name, "Republican Methodists."

"Theirs was to be a Republican—no slavery—glorious Church, free from all the evils of misgovernment."[15]

The next general meeting of the O'Kelley group was perhaps its most important. The meeting was held August 4, 1794 at Old Lebanon in Surry County, Virginia. A committee of seven had been appointed to devise a plan of church government. Finally, they decided to lay aside every manuscript and go by the Bible alone. Rice Haggard stood up and said:

Brethren, this is a sufficient rule of faith and practice. By it we are told that the disciples were called Christians, and I moved that henceforth and forever the followers of Christ be known as Christians simply.[16]

Following Haggard's suggestion, a Brother Hafferty of North Carolina stood up and moved that they take the Bible itself as their only creed.[17] From these two motions the O'Kelley movement devised what became known as the "Five Cardinal Principles of the Christian Church."

1. The Lord Jesus Christ as the only Head of the Church.

2. The name Christian to the exclusion of all party and sectarian names.

3. The Holy Bible, or the Scriptures of The Old and New Testament our only creed, and a sufficient rule of faith and practice.

4. Christian character, or vital piety, the only test of church fellowship and membership.

5. The right of private judgment, and the liberty of conscience, the privilege and duty of all.[18]

In 1801 the "Republican Methodists" changed their name to the Christian Church.

The significance of O'Kelley's action lies in the main, in the direction he was looking. Theirs was a movement to overthrow human elements in religion and go only by the scriptures. That weaknesses appear in their five cardinal principles is evident, but that they were on the high road back to the ancient order is equally evident.

While the leaven of restoration was working among the Methodists in Virginia and North Carolina, it was also working among

[15]W. E. MacClenny, *Life of Rev. James O'Kelley,* p. 116.
[16]J. Pressley Barrett, *The Centennial of Religious Journalism,* p. 264.
[17]W. E. MacClenny, *Life of Rev. James O'Kelley,* p. 117.
[18]W. E. MacClenny, *Life of Rev. James O'Kelley,* pp. 121, 122.

the Baptists in Vermont and New Hampshire. Here the movement was led by Elias Smith and Abner Jones. So significant are these two men that both must be given special attention.

Elias Smith was born June 17, 1769 at Lyme, Connecticut, in the County of New London. His father was Stephen Smith and his mother was Irene Ransom. His mother was the second wife of Stephen Smith and thirteen years younger than he. She was only nineteen years old when Elias was born. Of his parents Smith writes: "Although my parents were never rich, yet they were industrious, and maintained by their righteous lives, the honorable character of Christians."[19] Stephen was a Baptist until just one year before his death when a church was formed at Woodstock, Vermont which "was called by the ancient name recorded in Acts 11: 26, Christians."

The name, Elias, was given to Smith by his paternal grandmother. She had a son who died in the French and Indian War by the name of Elias, and preferred the name for this reason. Smith himself never did learn to like the name.

Smith was a boy while the Revolutionary War was going on. His family lived within sight of Long Island Sound. He could see the cannons on the British warships belch their flames of death. He was six years old the day the Battle of Bunker Hill was fought. It was natural that as a child he should learn to have great dislike for Tories, and that his heart should have a burning love for freedom. This desire for liberty soon extended itself to religion, and compelled Smith to oppose the tyranny of human creeds.

As a child Smith worried considerably over his sins. His spelling book had a form of prayer in it, and Smith would take this and sneak off to the barn and weep and pray. His mother was a "Newlight" Congregationalist, who believed in sprinkling. She had her three children sprinkled, and Elias shared this fate, although he rebelled against it. His uncle chased him, threatened him, and brought him back, and compelled him to receive the "seal of the covenant."

In the spring of 1780, when Elias Smith was eleven years of age, Stephen Smith moved his family to Hebron, thirty miles away. Here, Smith got his last schooling. He could read the Bible some,

---

[19]Elias Smith, *The Life and Conversion of Elias Smith* (Portsmouth, N. H.: Beck & Foster, 1816), p. 14.

and knew how to write a little. His youthful mind was fed on bad news from the war which gave him a feeling of the uncertainty of life. Groton Fort fell; the British burned New London, and Royalton, Vermont was taken by the Indians.

In May, 1779, while Smith was living in Connecticut, he became greatly concerned over the subject of baptism. He gave himself to considerable study upon the subject, and finally convinced himself that believers were the only people to be baptized, and that immersion was the proper method. The Baptist Church in Woodstock, Connecticut was holding a monthly meeting and William Grow was preaching. Having expressed his desire to be immersed, Smith was taken by Grow to Queechy River, near the house of Ichabod Churchill and was immersed in the name of the Father, Son and the Holy Spirit.

According to Baptist teaching, Smith was now a Christian although he wasn't a Baptist. Four things were required of him to get into the Baptist Church. First, give a reason of his hope in Christ. Second, he must be baptized. Third, he must give his consent to the articles of faith and the church covenant. Fourth, he must be voted in. All of this Smith did and soon became a member of the Second Baptist Church in Woodstock, Connecticut. Yet Smith was not quite sure about his belief in the Articles of Faith. Later he writes:

The articles of faith to which I then assented, contained what the Baptists call particular election; or that Christ died for the elect, and that such a number should be saved, etc. These *articles* I did not understand for they had never been read to me before; and being read but once, it was not possible for me to remember much of them. I assented to them, because the minister and church thought they were true. Since that time, the minister and the members have rejected that abominable doctrine of partiality, and now stand in gospel liberty.[20]

That summer of 1789 Smith began to think of becoming a preacher. He weighed the thought. Meanwhile, he heard several Baptist preachers and turned away in disgust for they appeared to be men of little ability. Smith said: "If I could not make out better than that, I would never try again."[21] So, he made up his mind he would never speak without, first, having evidence of a call from

---

[20]Elias Smith, *The Life and Conversion of Elias Smith,* p. 131.
[21]Elias Smith, *The Life and Conversion of Elias Smith,* p. 133.

God, and second, doing all he could to adequately prepare himself for the gospel ministry. He began, therefore, an intensive study of the Bible. In November that year, he went to Elder William Grow and asked for books that would help him learn to preach. He was given a book of sermons and a Cruden's concordance. It is thus that Smith found himself gradually working his way into becoming a preacher in the Baptist Church.

In the early fall of 1801 Smith moved to Salisbury, New Hampshire. By now he had begun to have some misgivings about certain doctrines in the Baptist church particularly that of Calvinism. He had not hesitated to preach his views and before long found himself in disrepute among many Baptists. In his reaction against Calvinism, he for a time, almost went into Universalism. As was his practice, he went into an intensive study of the scripture and thus was prevented from going to the other extreme.

A man cannot study the Bible long intelligently and independently without coming to some definite convictions about the truth. So, Smith writes:

When in my twenty-fourth year, I believed there would be a people bearing a name different from all the denominations then in this country; but what would they be called, I then could not tell. In the spring of 1802, having rejected the doctrine of Calvin and universalism, to search the scriptures to find the truth, I found the name which the followers of Christ ought to wear; which was *Christians.* (Acts 11 : 26) My mind being fixed upon this as the right name, to the exclusion of all the popular names in the world, in the month of May, at a man's house in Epping, N. H. by the name of Laurence, where I held a meeting and spoke upon the text, Acts 11 : 26, I ventured for the first time, softly to tell the people, that the name, *Christian* was enough for the followers of Christ without addition of the words, *Baptist, Methodist,* etc.[22]

At this meeting Smith spoke against the catechism as being "an invention of men." Opposition grew, and in the main, came from the clergy. Smith gradually became convinced that the clergy were not in agreement because they had a system of their own invention contrary to the New Testament. But, nevertheless, Smith was not to be discouraged, and his work continued. At Portsmouth, New Hampshire in October, 1802 the friends of Elias Smith rented a hall called "Jefferson Hall" over the market and began holding regular meetings here every Sunday morning. Arrangements were

---

[22]Elias Smith, *The Life and Conversion of Elias Smith,* p. 298.

made for Smith and his family to move there, which they did early the following December.

Unfortunately, the hall burned down on December 26, and the few people were left without a meeting house. There were only five members of the church, but they began meeting to discuss ways and means of organizing themselves into a church. These meetings were held in a school house. During them, the determination was expressed to follow the New Testament order and wear the name, Christian, "without any sectarian name added." By the first of March the number had increased to ten. Smith writes:

When our number was some short of twenty, we agreed to consider ourselves a church of Christ, owning him as our only Master, Lord, and Lawgiver, and we agreed to consider ourselves Christians, without the addition of any unscriptural name.[23]

And so the group grew. The last of March, 1803, they were holding meetings in the courthouse. On the first Sunday in April they held their first communion service. By now there were twenty-two members. One year later, there were one hundred and fifty members. By this time the church purchased a lot with a small building on it, and here they continued to meet.

"In June, 1803, about the time of this difficulty, Elder Abner Jones, from Vermont, came to visit me, and was the first free man I had ever seen," writes Smith. In some ways, Smith admitted, Jones had gone beyond him in his thinking. At any rate, the meeting was heartening, for Smith up to this moment had the feeling he was alone.

The brethren, meanwhile, had been meeting to draw up church articles. This meeting, they referred to as a "Christian Conference." But, in 1805 when this Conference met, it was agreed that their articles were useless and so they abandoned them, taking the New Testament as the "only and all-sufficient rule for Christians."

On September 1, 1808 Elias Smith issued from Portsmouth, New Hampshire the first issue of the *Herald of Gospel Liberty*. He had only two hundred and seventy-four subscribers. This was the first religious paper, according to Smith's claim, ever to be published in the world. The name, itself was significant. Smith writes in the first issue:

It may be that some may wish to know why this paper should be named, *Herald of Gospel Liberty*. This kind of liberty is the

---

[23]Elias Smith, *The Life and Conversion of Elias Smith*, pp. 313, 314.

only one which can make us happy, being the glorious liberty of the sons of God which Christ proclaimed; and which all who have are exhorted to stand fast in, being that which is given and enjoyed by the law of liberty; which is the law of the spirit of life in Christ Jesus, which makes free from the law of sin and death.[24]

The *Herald of Gospel Liberty* was to have a stormy existence through the years ahead. The first issue came from the press dated Thursday evening, September 1, 1808. Thereafter, the paper was published every other Thursday from the home of Elias Smith on Jeffrey Street in Portsmouth, New Hampshire. The cost was $1.00 a year. Each issue had four pages and each page was nine by eleven inches in size, three columns to a page. On March 31, 1809, the time for publication was changed to Friday morning. A year later Smith moved to Portland, Maine and from April, 1810 to July, 1811 the paper was published from here. Early in the summer of 1811 Smith moved to Philadelphia and the issue of July 5 appears from there. Here Smith got hopelessly in debt, and to free himself he moved back to Portland. This was on February 4, 1814. By now the subscription list reached one thousand five hundred, a sizable number for those days.

As the months bore on, Smith found his financial burdens unrelieved. In the spring of 1816 he moved to Boston. He began making appeals to his subscribers to send him money or else the paper would go under. As a desperation move, he changed it to a monthly. This helped but little. Finally, in August, 1817 he announced that he would drop the paper immediately unless those who owed him would pay.

Meanwhile, Smith had more misgivings coming up about his beliefs. His old problem of Calvinism still bothered him. In running from it once he had gone into universalism. There seemed to Smith for a time to be no other alternative—it was either Calvinism or universalism. This problem continued to bother him. On October 1, 1817 Smith published in his paper that he had gone into universalism, and this was the last number of the paper that he ever published.

In May, 1818 the *Christian Herald* succeeded the *Herald of Gospel Liberty*. The relationship between the two papers is not altogether clear, but one thing is certain: the *Christian Herald* did consider itself the successor of the *Herald of Gospel Liberty*. But

---

[24]J. Pressley Barrett, *The Centennial of Religious Journalism,* pp. 33, 34.

the new paper was not to last long. On January 15, 1835 the *Christian Herald* announced that it was to become the property of the Eastern Publishing Association. Thereafter, the *Christian Journal* became its successor.

In its own day the *Herald of Gospel Liberty* served well the purpose of pointing men back to the New Testament. On the whole it followed well the motto which it carried across the top of the first issue:

> From realms far distant, and from chimes unknown;
> We make the knowledge of our King your own.

But what were the convictions the *Herald* professed? On the whole they were about the same as those espoused by James O'Kelley. On December 18, 1808 William Guiry of Virginia wrote:

After we became a separate people, three points were determined on. First. No head over the church but Christ. Second. No confession of faith, articles of religion, rubric, canons, creeds, etc., but the New Testament. Third. No religious name but Christians.[25]

On the question of fellowship the *Christian Journal* states:

They (the Christians) hold that the only proper test of Christian fellowship is sincere piety, evidenced by an upright walk and meek deportment. Thus they extend the hand of fellowship to all who have the "fellowship of the Father and the Son." They own all as their brethren whom they have evidence that God owns as His children. They are free to commune with all whom God communes with.[26]

Of hardly less significance than Elias Smith was Abner Jones, who has been accredited with the honor of establishing the "first free Christian Church" in New England.[27] Here the members called themselves just Christians.

Jones was born at Royalton, Massachusetts on April 28, 1772. When he was eight years old, his parents moved to Bridgewater, Vermont. Until he was twenty years old he lived an irreligious and reckless life. For a time he taught school in Granville, New York. In the spring of 1793 he was converted and baptized into the Baptist Church by Elder Elisha Ransom, a Baptist preacher.

[25]J. Pressley Barrett, *The Centennial of Religious Journalism*, p. 46.
[26]J. Pressley Barrett, *The Centennial of Religious Journalism*, p. 60.
[27]C. C. Ware, *Barton W. Stone* (St. Louis: The Bethany Press, 1932), p. 154.

Shortly afterwards, Jones began to study and preach some. He became very much concerned with what to preach, and he determined to study the scriptures and find out. He was soon led to dissent from Calvinism and the result was the Baptist Church gave him the cold shoulder. He became more determined than ever to study the Bible and preach just what it taught.

Meanwhile, Jones had given much attention to medicine. In 1797 or 1798 he began to practice medicine in Lyndon, Vermont. About this same time, he married Demaris Prior. Lyndon now became his permanent home. About this time too, a revival took place, and thoughts of the gospel ministry began to race through his mind. He ceased his practice of medicine and went entirely into preaching. It was in the fall of 1801 that he organized this "free church" in Lyndon, which rejected human names, members insisting solely upon the name, Christian. In 1802 he organized churches at Hanover and Piermont, New Hampshire. From here on, his life is connected with that of Elias Smith in establishing these "free" churches in New England.

This New England movement, as we have said, owes its primary significance to the fact that men and women were looking in the direction of the New Testament order of things, and away from sectarianism. That they did not go far enough is only to be expected when one considers the natural tendency. For those days they were traveling an uncharted course. They were thinking their way along. It was to take time to get those thoughts developed, and for the most part, it remained for others to carry on with them from here.

Chapter II

THE STONE MOVEMENT

To Barton Warren Stone and Alexander Campbell has gone most of the credit for the restoration movement. Of the two, the latter has overshadowed the former in the popularity and recognition he has received for services rendered in the cause of the ancient order. Whether this popular opinion be justified or not is a mooted question, but that both Stone and Campbell deserve outstanding credit for the move to return to apostolic times is readily admitted. Each made his valuable contribution to the movement, and neither should be forgotten.

In 1772 Port Tobacco Creek wound through Charles County in Southern Maryland often with small boats carrying produce back and forth between towns. The Port Tobacco Creek of today is only a shadow of the former glory of this stream. The small town of Port Tobacco was in those early days of the American nation the chief port on the creek. Near this town on Thursday, December 24, 1772 Mary Warren Musgrave Stone, wife of John Stone, became the mother of a son whom she named Barton Warren, in honor of her father.

The first seven years of Stone's life were spent in this region of Maryland. His father died when he was only three years old, and his mother made the living after that. In 1779 the widow packed her belongings and with her children, moved over into the Dan River country on the border of North Carolina. The Revolutionary War was now on, and the youthful mind of Barton W. Stone began to pick up impressions that he was to carry on through life. In 1781 General Green and Lord Cornwallis met in a battle not far from Stone's home, at Guilford Courthouse. The British were making a strong bid to defeat the colonies. Stone could hear the distant roar of guns as the battle continued. Here as a lad he got to see war, and he learned to hate it. Fires of liberty were kindled in his soul that in years to come were to find expression in a violent dislike for creedalism in religion. Stone himself says:

From my earliest recollection I drank deeply into the spirit of liberty, and was so warmed by the soul-inspiring draughts, that

I could not hear the name of British or Tories, without feeling a rush of blood through the whole system.[1]

Every person sooner or later faces the thought of religion and wonders what to do about it. Stone's interest was only slightly awakened in his earlier years. It was only natural that his mother should have had him sprinkled into the Church of England when he was an infant, for the Established Church had become the State Church of Maryland as early as 1692. But when the Revolutionary War was ended, the clergy's salaries were largely abolished owing to the fact that the church was no longer state supported from taxation, and most clergymen had gone back to England. The people then were left in spiritual destitution. The Lord's Day became a day of pleasure, and most meeting houses were deserted. Other preachers started coming, among these Samuel Harris and Dutton Lane, two Baptist preachers. Harris lived on Strawberry Creek, twenty-five miles north of Stone's home. Lane lived on Sandy Creek, a tributary of Bannister River, thirty miles from Stone's home in Virginia. From these men Stone first learned of immersion, but when he listened to the experiences which their converts showed, he couldn't quite fathom it. The Methodists came, and Stone liked them for their piety and sincerity, but he observed that both the Episcopalians and Baptists fought them for their doctrine of "salvation by works." Stone listened to the religious controversies, got somewhat disgusted, and soon lapsed into total religious indifference.

Not without some cause did the state of Virginia, where Stone now lived, come to be looked upon as the "Mother of Presidents." Not far from Stone's home the fiery eloquence of Patrick Henry had helped to bring on the war. The very atmosphere was charged with themes on politics, and Stone naturally turned his attention to thinking of a career as a statesman. He was nearing eighteen years of age, when in 1790, his father's estate was divided up, and he got his share. Stone wisely decided to invest his share in an education.

Down in North Carolina, thirty miles southwest of Stone's home, was the famous school of David Caldwell. Twenty-three years before Caldwell had built himself a two story log cabin. He had

---

[1]Barton W. Stone, *Biography of Elder Barton Warren Stone* (Cincinnati: J. A. & U. P. James, 1847), p. 3.

lived in the top and conducted school below. In 1790 the school had about fifty students. When Stone came to the school on February 1st that year, he found Caldwell to be a man in his sixty-fifth year. Caldwell, born and reared in Lancaster, Pennsylvania, had graduated from Princeton in 1761, and four years later was ordained to the Presbyterian ministry. In 1767 he had come to preach at Buffalo and Alamance, North Carolina near Greensboro. He had opened his school soon after his coming, but made his living by farming.

When Stone arrived, he was not long in sensing that the dominant influence in the school was religion. Students were getting religious, and Stone became concerned. James McGready, one of the popular Presbyterian preachers of the day, came and thirty students "got religion" and joined the Presbyterian Church. Stone didn't want to get overly interested himself for fear he would forget his career at the bar. He determined to go to Hampden-Sidney over in Prince Edward County, Virginia. He set the time for leaving North Carolina, and that day it stormed, and he couldn't leave. What a difference there might have been in Stone's life were it not for that storm!!

Shortly afterwards, Ben McReynolds, his roommate, asked him to go with him to hear McGready. Stone went. The message was enthusiastic and powerful and Stone was profoundly impressed. For a year he struggled, then he heard McGready again. He began to have an intense interest in his soul. Meanwhile, his mother wept over him. She sent for him and asked him to come home and join the Methodists. Amidst this anxiety, Stone went in the spring of 1791, to Alamance and heard William Hodge of Hawfields, North Carolina, and joined the Presbyterian Church.

Stone's associates in the school were all preachers, and before long he cast his lot with them. He was given a text and told to prepare a sermon to be delivered before the Orange Presbytery which was to be a part of his examination to get license to preach. In addition, he was given the subject, "The Trinity," and told to write a thesis. He had never heard or read a sermon on this subject, so he went to work studying Isaac Watts, "Glories of Christ," and devoured this. Through much effort he finally managed to pass the course and received his license to preach from the Orange Presbytery.

The license to preach, however, didn't come until the next session of the Presbytery. According to prevailing practice, a man was examined at one session, and given his license at the next. Sessions were held six months apart. During this six months, Stone had time to think. He began to doubt if the theology he had studied was really in harmony with the scriptures. In the spring of 1796 there were three licentiates who were seeking licenses: Stone, Robert Foster and Robert Tate. Henry Patillo was the leader in the Presbytery. He was a liberal Presbyterian who held, not the Westminster Confession of Faith, but the Bible before Stone to be accepted.

After getting his license, Stone went into eastern North Carolina to a very barren wilderness to do mission work. Here he soon grew discouraged. For a short time thoughts of ceasing to preach entered his mind, and while these were playing at his conscience, he decided on a move into Virginia. On Reed's Creek, near Wytheville was located a Presbyterian meeting house called "Grimes Meeting House." Here on May 15, 1796 Stone spoke again, and the response was overwhelming. He was persuaded to stay, but did so only until July that same year. At that time he moved to Fort Chisiwell. Fort Chisiwell was right on the frontier. Wagon trains moving into the west went through here, and before long, Stone got the fever to move west. By the middle of August, he was in Knoxville and still headed west toward the Cumberland River. Fifteen miles west of Knoxville was Campbell's Station, and west of this was the badlands of the Cherokee Indians. The route from Campbell's Station was through West Point, twenty-five miles from the Station, at the Junction of Holston and Clinch Rivers, near the present Kingston. From here, Bledsoe's Lick in Sumner County, Tennessee was one hundred and twenty miles. Bledsoe's Lick is the present Castalian Springs, five miles east of Gallatin. Stone made this journey, often in danger of Indians, and approached Nashville, "a poor little village hardly worth notice," as Stone put it. But Tennessee was not long to hold Barton Stone. A friend, John Anderson, told Stone of Kentucky, and the latter began to make plans to move near Lexington where a friend, John Blythe, was then living.

Robert Finlay, a Presbyterian preacher, had moved into the Lexington region of Kentucky a short time before. Five miles out of Paris, Kentucky Finlay had opened a log cabin seminary at Cane Ridge, about a quarter of a mile east of the Cane Ridge meeting house. Finlay here trained about ten or twelve Presbyterian preachers, among them Richard McNemar, John Dunlavy and John Thompson. But Finlay was a recalcitrant preacher for his day, and on October 6, 1796 was deposed by the Synod for "insubordination."

Ten miles northeast of Cane Ridge was the Concord meeting house. Here Barton W. Stone preached more or less regularly for two years. During this time, he was a licentiate; he had yet to be ordained. The thought of his ordination led him to re-examine the Westminster Confession of Faith. He had some doubts and misgivings, but was still in the process of thinking matters through. When the Transylvania Presbytery met in 1798 at Cane Ridge, Stone was asked: "Do you receive and adopt the Confession of Faith, as containing the system of doctrine as taught in the Bible"? He replied: "I do, as far as I see it consistent with the Word of God."[2] One might well judge that Stone's respect for the Bible was increasing while his respect for human creeds was decreasing. His face was turned in the right direction.

Kentucky at the turn of the century, was on the verge of a great revival, and Stone felt it coming. One thing which led to this conviction was the work of James McGready in Logan County. McGready, who had powerfully influenced Stone while the latter was a student in Caldwell's school in North Carolina, had come to Logan County. He was a great evangelist. He had located with the Gasper River, Red River and Muddy River churches— all near Russellville, and great revivals had ensued. McGready could dangle people over the fires of hell, causing great anxiety. But at such preaching, Stone was greatly concerned. According to Presbyterian doctrine, man was totally depraved, and had no ability to believe. Yet, how could this doctrine be reconciled with the persuading of men to repent and believe? Why preach to men to believe if they were totally depraved and couldn't? For the next few years this dilemma was to cause Stone no little anxiety.

In the fall of 1800 Stone left Kentucky to go to Virginia and North Carolina. Coming back, he began to show some concern for a general state of religious apathy around Cane Ridge. In the spring of 1801 he went to Logan County and saw one of McGready's great revivals out on a prairie. Stone was given the impetus to preach on the universality of the gospel and of faith as a condition of salvation. Plans of a great revival around Cane Ridge now began to come before him, but he had something else to do first. He hurried over to Virginia again and on July 2, 1801 married Elizabeth Campbell, daughter of Colonel William Campbell. As soon as the wedding was over, he headed back for Cane Ridge.

On Thursday or Friday before the third Lord's Day of August, 1801, the roads around Cane Ridge were crowded with carriages, horses and wagons with people hurrying to meeting. It has been estimated that from twenty to thirty thousand people were in attendance at this Great Revival at Cane Ridge. There were eighteen Presbyterian preachers plus some Methodist and Baptist preachers. Meetings were held on the Ridge at various spots and generally there were five or six preachers holding meetings at once.

Today, looking back upon the Revival, there is a note of humor in the way it was conducted, but in those days, it was a serious affair. Conversion was quite literally a convulsion. Converts went through a series of bodily agitations There were about five general types of these physical contortions: (1) the falling exercise, this was the most common. The subject would cry out in a piercing scream, then fall flat on the ground and lay for several minutes as though dead; (2) the jerks, in this exercise, various parts of the body would jerk violently to one side and then the other; (3) the dancing exercise, this would begin with the jerks and then pass on to dancing. Usually they would dance until they fell exhausted to the ground; (4) the barking exercise, this was really the jerks, but when a person's body jerked suddenly and violently, it caused a big grunt, which appeared to be barking to the observer; (5) the laughter and singing exercise was just what the terms signify.[3]

Stone's doctrine of the universality of the gospel and faith as a condition of salvation could not fail to get him in trouble with the Presbyterian Church as a whole. At first in Kentucky there

---

[3]Barton W. Stone, *Biography of Elder Barton Warren Stone,* pp. 39-42.

was only the Transylvanian Presbytery, but in 1799 two others were added: the West Lexington Presbytery and the Washington Presbytery. This latter covered northeast Kentucky and southwest Ohio. It wasn't long until the Presbytery began opposing the doctrines of the Cane Ridge Revival. The orthodox Presbyterians considered Stone a heretic. Their creed must be upheld at all costs. There were five men who came under their critical eye, men who substantially agreed in Stone's teaching. These were Barton W. Stone, Robert Marshall, Richard McNemar, John Dunlavy, and John Thompson.

The first sign of trouble centered itself around Richard McNemar. The Washington Presbytery had condemned him for his "Arminian views." The case then came before the Synod of Kentucky which had been formed in 1802 and which held its first meeting September 6-13, 1803. The Synod examined the report of the Washington Presbytery and sustained it. In the midst of the proceedings, Stone and his colleagues retired to formulate a proceeding of their own, knowing that McNemar's fate would soon be theirs. On Saturday, the tenth of September, they submitted their objection to the Synod because of the treatment of McNemar and declared themselves withdrawn from it. The report added that the Confession of Faith was an impediment to Revival.

Thus came Stone's break with the Presbyterian Church. Stone, in his autobiography, commenting on the views which he and his colleagues had, says:

The distinguished doctrine preached by us, was, that God loved the world—the whole world, and sent His Son to save them, on condition that they believed in him—that the gospel was the means of salvation—but that this means would never be effectual to this end, until believed and obeyed by us—that God required us to believe in His Son, and had given us sufficient evidence in His word to produce faith in us, if attended by us—that sinners were capable of understanding and believing this testimony, and of acting upon it by coming to the Saviour and obeying him and from him obtaining salvation and the Holy Spirit.[4]

The Calvinism of the day declared that a man was depraved and man could do nothing to be saved; he had to wait and if God saw fit to call him, He would do so, but if God didn't see fit, the man was lost to the glory of God. Stone and his group said that God

----

[4]Barton W. Stone, *Biography of Elder Barton Warren Stone*, p. 45.

loved man, and wanted all men to be saved. The gospel is God's power to save for it contains sufficient evidence to produce faith to the honest inquirer, and if the sinner will believe and obey this gospel he can be saved. This, in 1804, was as far as Stone appears to have gone in his thinking, but it was far enough to make the Calvinistic Presbyterians consider Stone a heretic.

When these five men withdrew themselves from the Synod of Kentucky, they set up a Presbytery of their own which they called the Springfield Presbytery. Meanwhile, they sent letters to the churches, telling them of their views. The document telling of their views became known as the "Apology of The Springfield Presbytery." It expressed their total abandonment of all authoritative creeds except the Bible. Stone called the congregation together where he had been preaching and informed them he could no longer preach for the Presbyterian Church. He stated that he would continue to preach among them, but not as a Presbyterian. In taking this stand Stone sacrificed the friendship of two large congregations in addition to a large salary. Under the new Presbytery, in less than a year, fifteen congregations were established—seven in Ohio and eight in Kentucky. But it took also less than a year for them to see that this Presbytery "savored of a party spirit," and was a handicap to their work. Plans were immediately begun to dissolve the organization, and on June 28, 1804 there was issued, "The Last Will and Testament of The Springfield Presbytery."

The Last Will and Testament contains less than eight hundred words, but it is one of the classical documents coming out of the restoration movement. It showed the sincerity and honesty which characterized Stone in wanting to give up everything of human origin in religion and take only the Bible. Once having planted their faith upon the Word of God they found themselves led farther and farther from human elements in religion. Stone writes:

When we at first withdrew, we felt ourselves free from all creeds but the Bible, and since that time by constant application to it, we are led farther from the idea of adopting creeds and confessions as standards, than we were at first; consequently to come under the jurisdiction of that church now is entirely out of the question.[5]

---

[5] C. C. Ware, *Barton W. Stone*, p. 145.

Since the average reader of this book will not likely have the "Last Will and Testament of The Springfield Presbytery" easily accessible, we insert it at this point.

The Presbytery of Springfield, sitting at Cane Ridge, in the county of Bourbon, being, through a gracious Providence, in more than ordinary bodily health, growing in strength and size daily; and in perfect soundness and composure of mind; but knowing that it is appointed for all delegated bodies once to die: and considering that the life of every such body is very uncertain, do make, and ordain this our last Will and Testament, in manner and form following, viz.

Imprimis. We *will,* that this body die, be dissolved, and sink into union with the Body of Christ at large; for there is but one Body, and one Spirit, even as we are called in one hope of our calling.

Item. We *will,* that our name of distinction, with its *Reverend* title, be forgotten, that there be but one Lord over God's heritage, and his name One.

Item. We *will,* that our power of making laws for the government of the church, and executing them by delegated authority, forever cease; that the people may have free course to the Bible, and adopt *the law of the Spirit of life in Christ Jesus.*

Item. We *will,* that candidates for the Gospel ministry henceforth study the Holy Scriptures with fervent prayer, and obtain license from God to preach the simple Gospel, *with the Holy Ghost sent down from heaven,* without any mixture of philosophy, vain deceit, traditions of men, or the rudiments of the world. And let none henceforth take *this honor to himself, but he that is called of God, as was Aaron.*

Item. We *will,* that the church of Christ resume her native right of internal government—try her candidates for the ministry, as to their soundness in the faith, acquaintance with experimental religion, gravity and aptness to teach; and admit no other proof of their authority but Christ speaking in them. We will, that the church of Christ look up to the Lord of the harvest to send forth laborers into his harvest; and that she resume her primitive right of trying those *who say they are apostles, and are not.*

Item. We *will,* that each particular church, as a body, actuated by the same spirit, choose her own preacher, and support him by a free will offering, without a written *call* or *subscription*—admit members—remove offences; and never henceforth *delegate* her right of government to any man or set of men whatever.

Item. We *will,* that the people henceforth take the Bible as the only sure guide to heaven; and as many as are offended with other books, which stand in competition with it, may cast them into the fire if they choose; for it is better to enter into life having one book, than having many to be cast into hell.

Item. We *will,* that preachers and people, cultivate a spirit of mutual forbearance; pray more and dispute less; and while they behold the signs of the times, look up, and confidently expect that redemption draweth nigh.

Item. We *will,* that our weak brethren, who may have been wishing to make the Presbytery of Springfield their king, and wot not what is now become of it, betake themselves to the Rock of Ages, and follow Jesus for the future.

Item. We *will,* that the Synod of Kentucky examine every member, who may be *suspected* of having departed from the Confession of Faith, and suspend every such suspected heretic immediately; in order that the oppressed may go free, and taste the sweets of gospel liberty.

Item. We *will,* that Ja————, the author of two letters lately published in Lexington, be encouraged in his zeal to destroy *partyism.* We will, moreover, that our past conduct be examined into by all who may have correct information; but let foreigners beware of speaking evil of things which they know not.

Item. Finally we *will,* that all our *sister bodies* read their Bibles carefully, that they may see their fate there determined, and prepare for death before it is too late.

Springfield Presbytery } L. S.
June 28th, 1804

Robert Marshall
John Dunlavy
Richard M'Nemar   } Witnesses.
B. W. Stone
John Thompson
David Purviance

THE WITNESSES' ADDRESS

We, the above named witnesses of the Last Will and Testament of the Springfield Presbytery, knowing that there will be many conjectures respecting the causes which have occasioned the dissolution of that body, think proper to testify, that from its first existence it was knit together in love, lived in peace and concord, and died a voluntary and happy death.

Their reasons for dissolving that body were the following: With deep concern they viewed the divisions, and party spirit among professing Christians, principally owing to the adoption of human creeds and forms of government. While they were united under the name of a Presbytery, they endeavored to cultivate a spirit of love and unity with all Christians; but found it extremely difficult to suppress the idea that they themselves were a party separate from others. This difficulty increased in proportion to their success in the ministry. Jealousies were excited in the minds of other denominations; and a temptation was laid before those who were connected with the various parties, to view them in the same light. At their last meeting they undertook to prepare for the press a piece entitled Observations on Church Government, in which the world will see the beautiful simplicity of Christian church government, stript of human inventions and lordly traditions. As they proceeded in the investigation of that subject, they soon found that there was neither precept nor example in the New Testament for such confederacies as modern Church Sessions, Presbyteries, Synods, General Assemblies, etc. Hence they concluded, that while they continued in the connection in which they then stood, they were off the foundation of the Apostles and Prophets, of which Christ himself is the chief corner stone. However just, therefore, their views of church government might have been, they would have gone out under the name and sanction of a self-constituted body. Therefore, from a principle of love to Christians of every name, the precious cause of Jesus, and dying sinners who are kept from the Lord by the existence of sects and parties in the church, they have cheerfully consented to retire from the din and fury of conflicting parties—sink out of the view of fleshly minds, and die the death. They believe their death will be great gain to the world. But though dead, as above, and stript of their mortal frame, which only served to keep them too near the confines of Egyptian bondage, they yet live and speak in the land of gospel liberty; they blow the trumpet of jubilee, and willingly devote themselves to the help of the Lord against the mighty. They will aid the brethren, by their counsel, when required; assist in ordaining elders, or pastors—seek the divine blessings—unite with all Christians—commune together, and strengthen each others' hands in the work of the Lord.

We design, by the grace of God, to continue in the exercise of those functions, which belong to us as ministers of the gospel, confidently trusting in the Lord, that he will be with us. We candidly acknowledge, that in some things we may err, through human infirmity; but he will correct our wanderings, and preserve his church. Let all Christians join with us, in crying to God day and night, to remove the obstacles which stand in the way of his work, and give him no rest till he make Jerusalem a praise in the earth. We heartily unite with our Christian brethren of every name, in thanksgiving to God for the display of his goodness in the glorious work he is carrying on in our Western country, which we hope will terminate in the universal spread of the gospel, and unity of the church.[6]

---

[6]Charles A. Young, *Historical Documents Advocating Christian Union* (Chicago: The Christian Century Co., 1904), pp. 19-26.

The noblest intentions are often perverted by enemies. Stone and his group were looking toward New Testament Christianity, but friends of orthodoxy could not tolerate this. Documents containing evil reports were scattered about them. The name, "New Lights" was hurled at them. This name was long used in religious circles at that time to denote any off-brand group. in any religious sect. But the name stuck, and for years Stone's group was designated as the "New Light Christian Church." Added to this trouble was that which soon came up from within the group and which was more grievous than any other.

Three missionaries from the Shakers soon made their appearance in the group—Bates, Mitchum and Young. They were neat, grave and very unassuming. They urged the people to confess their sins to them; taught marriage was wrong; and urged men to forsake the marriage state. About this time David Purviance began to notice the utmost pride in Richard McNemar and John Dunlavy. When the Shakers came, they stopped at Cane Ridge, but made no converts, and so they moved on into Ohio. John Thompson was at Springfield, but they could not move him. They went to Turtle Creek and here converted Richard McNemar, and at Eagle Creek, they converted John Dunlavy. Stone labored night and day to save his ranks from these preachers, but to little avail. To make matters worse John Thompson and Robert Marshall went back to the Presbyterian Church and Stone found himself standing for a time practically alone.

Meanwhile, the subject of baptism became agitated, and Stone found himself greatly unsettled. Robert Marshall, who had been studying the question, became convinced that the Baptists were right on immersion. Stone became concerned for fear Marshall would go to the Baptists, so he wrote Marshall, seeking to convince him of his error. Marshall's reply argued against pedobaptism and in favor of immersion. Stone, while not at first convinced on immersion, nevertheless, favored the view that pedobaptism was wrong. Very shortly the brethren came together and generally agreed that immersion was scriptural baptism. The preachers went to work and immersed each other. Many others also were immersed.

Stone's investigation of the subject of baptism continued. Soon he convinced himself that immersion was for the remission of

sins and should be administered to the penitent believer. At a
great revival, about this time, when mourners were praying, Stone
reflected upon Acts 2: 38. He got up and spoke his thoughts.
However, he admitted, as he wrote about the occasion, "into the
spirit of the doctrine I was never fully led, until it was revived
by Brother Alexander Campbell, some years after."[7] His ret-
icence to press the point must be understood in the light of the
times. He was greatly persecuted on every side, and being by
nature a peaceful man, he would likely be hesitant about taking
such an important step without slow, careful deliberation. Of the
feelings at this time, Stone writes:

The floods of earth and hell are let loose against us, but me
in particular. I am seriously threatened with imprisonment, and
stripes I expect to receive for the testimony of Jesus. Kentucky is
turning upside down. The truth pervades in spite of man . . .
the scribes, the disputers of this world are gnashing upon us.[8]

Again he says:

God knows I am not fond of controversy. A sense of duty has
impelled me to advance it. In the simplicity of truth is all my
delight. To cultivate the benevolent affections of the gospel shall
employ my future life.[9]

For a number of years Stone's mind was unsettled on the whole
subject of baptism. There seemed to be little question with him
that the design of baptism was for the remission of sins,
yet, he hardly feels sure enough to press the point too violently.
Samuel Rogers, as late as 1821, attended a meeting which Stone
conducted at Millersburg, Kentucky. The audiences were large
and interest at a high pitch. After laboring with the mourners
until late at night, Stone arose and said:

Brethren, something must be wrong; we have been labouring
with these mourners earnestly, and they are deeply penitent; why
have they not found relief? We all know that God is willing to
pardon them, and certainly they are anxious to receive it. The
cause must be that we do not preach as the apostles did. On the
day of Pentecost those who were "pierced to the heart," were
promptly told what to do for the remission of sins. And "they

---

[7]Barton W. Stone, *Biography of Elder Barton Warren Stone*, p. 61.
[8]C. C. Ware, *Barton Warren Stone*, p. 208.
[9]C. C. Ware, *Barton Warren Stone*, p. 210.

gladly received the word and were baptized; and the same day about three thousand were added unto them."

Rogers admits that he thought Stone was beside himself.[10]

The questions of baptism were not alone in Stone's mind, but were found in the minds of brethren everywhere who were looking toward the ancient order. B. F. Hall, who was ordained to preach by Stone, on May 15, 1825, was one to have such a conflict. During the summer of 1825, Hall held many camp meetings. Very often meetings would close, without the mourner's having found relief. Hall became dissatisfied and felt that something was wrong with the way of preaching. A year later, Hall found the conviction that he wanted. He went to the home of a Brother Guess on Line Creek, which divided Kentucky and Tennessee. In the cabin he found the first copy of the Campbell-McCalla debate he had ever seen. He read quickly, but took the time to follow carefully Campbell's speech on the design of baptism. Suddenly he sprang to his feet, dropped the book to the floor, and cried: "Eureka! Eureka! I have found it, I have found it!!" The whole plan of salvation now became clear to him. When he spoke of the matter to Stone that fall, Stone had replied that he had been preaching that, but found it chilled his audiences, and so had dropped it.[11]

Meanwhile, Stone had kept himself busy in the Lord's work. In 1819 he established the church at Georgetown, Kentucky; in 1823, he established the Union Church in Fayette County; and in 1828, he established the church at Cynthiana. During a part of this time, he kept himself busy teaching school. On November 2, 1819 he purchased a farm on the waters of North Elkhorn, near Georgetown, and began teaching in Rittenhouse Academy. A part of the time also, he spent in publishing his religious periodical, the *Christian Messenger*. The *Messenger* began as a monthly in November, 1826 with twenty-four pages. Its motto was: "Let the Unity of Christians Be Our Polar Star."

It was inevitable that Barton W. Stone should come in contact with Alexander Campbell, for unquestionably the two were the foremost religious thinkers of their times. Stone and Campbell first met at Georgetown, Kentucky in 1824, and each received fav-

---

[10]John I. Rogers, *Autobiography of Samuel Rogers* (Cincinnati: Standard Publishing Co., 1880), pp. 55, 56.

[11]John I. Rogers, *Autobiography of Samuel Rogers,* p. 59,

orably the views of the other.   Stone was ever an admirer of Campbell.   He writes of Campbell:

I will not say there are no faults in Brother Campbell; but, that there are fewer, perhaps, in him, than any man I know on earth; and over these few my love would throw a veil, and hide them from view forever.   I am constrained, and willingly constrained to acknowledge him the greatest promoter of this reformation of any man living.   The Lord reward him![12]

As to the similiarity of their views Stone writes:

The Reformed Baptists have received the doctrine taught by us many years ago.   For nearly thirty years we have taught that sectarianism was anti-Christian, and that all Christians should be united in one body of Christ—the same they teach.   We then and ever since, have taught that authoritative creeds and confessions were the strong props of sectarianism, and should be given to the moles and bats—they teach the same.   We have from that time preached the gospel to every creature to whom we had access, and urged them to believe and obey it—that its own evidence was sufficient to produce faith in all that heard it, that the unrenewed sinner must, and could, believe it unto justification and salvation—and through the Holy Spirit of promise, and every other promise of the New Covenant was given. They proclaim the same doctrine. Many years ago some of us preached baptism as a means, in connection with faith and repentance, for the remission of sins and the gift of the Holy Spirit—they preach the same and extend it farther than we have done.   We rejected all names but Christian—they acknowledge it most proper, but seem to prefer another.[13]

Up to now Stone's group had insisted upon the name, Christian, to the exclusion of all others.   Followers of Alexander Campbell took the name, Reformers or Reformed Baptists.   The two groups would exist side by side in various towns, especially in Kentucky, and slowly understanding and agreement would be reached between them bringing about a union of forces.   At Millersburg, Kentucky near Cane Ridge, the two groups were to be found.   Occasionally they communed together.   Finally, seeing there was little difference between them in faith and practice they united on April 24, 1831. But the union was soon to become larger in its scope.

In 1831 Stone made the friendship of John T. Johnson.   Each was fervently interested in unity.   But there were others of great influence in Kentucky who were also as interested.   There were

---

[12]Barton W. Stone, *Biography of Elder Barton Warren Stone,* p. 76.
[13]Barton W. Stone, "Union," *Millennial Harbinger,* Vol. II, No. 9 (September 5, 1831), p. 385.

men like John Rogers and "Raccoon" John Smith just as interested. These men arranged a joint meeting of the "Christians" and "Reformers" for Christmas, 1831. This came on Sunday, so they arranged a series of meetings to last all week. This was the beginning of a series of joint meetings which lasted until 1835. The Oldham Cotton Factory, 168 N. Broadway, was rented, swept and garnished for the meeting. Speeches were to be spontaneous. John Smith was the first to speak. He concluded by saying:

Let us, then my brethren, be no longer Campbellites or Stoneites, New Lights or Old Lights, or any other kind of lights, but let us come to the Bible and to the Bible alone, as the only book in the world that can give us all the light we need.[14]

Concerning the general spirit which prevailed at the meeting, John Rogers wrote in 1844, twelve years later:

No one ever thought that the Reformers, so called, had come over to us, or that we had gone over to them; that they were required to relinquish their opinions or we ours. We found ourselves contending for the same great principles of Christianity, and we resolved to unite our energies to harmonize the church, and save the world . . . I entered into it upon principle. I think immense good has grown out of it, that had it never taken place, our cause in Kentucky would be far in the rear of the position it now occupies.[15]

How easy it is to forget the passing of time when discussing the events which come before us! Many important items of interest cry for attention while studying the life of Barton W. Stone. Yet, with the passing of these events, we forget so easily that Stone is slowly reaching out for his three-score years and ten. Stone was in his sixty-second year when in 1834, he moved to Jacksonville, Illinois, the land of the Kickapoo Indians in the "far west." Here he gave his time to preaching tours. But he was slowing down. At his home out on the Diamond Grove Prairie near Jacksonville in the fall of 1836 he lay seriously ill. Three years later, his hearing went bad, and two years after that, he suffered a stroke of paralysis, and almost died.

Stone's death came on Saturday, November 9, 1844 at four o'clock in the morning. He was at Hannibal, Missouri, at the home of his son-in-law, Captain Samuel Bowen, who had married his

---

[14] John Augustus Williams, *Life of Elder John Smith* (Cincinnati: Christian Standard Publishing Co., 1904), p. 454
[15] C. C. Ware, *Barton Warren Stone*, p. 247.

daughter, Amanda. Only a few days before Stone had attended an annual meeting in Boone County near Columbia. At the meeting he had had an attack but presided anyway on Monday, and delivered a discourse which he regarded as his last.

On Thursday, Nov. 7, he sent for Jacob Creath, Jr., but Creath was sick and couldn't arrive until later. He and Stone sang a song and had prayer. Creath asked Stone if he had any fear of death. Stone's reply was, "O, no, Brother Creath, I know in whom I have believed and in whom I have trusted, and I am persuaded that he is able to keep that which I have committed to him. I know that my Redeemer lives. All my dependence is in God and in His Son Jesus Christ." Then Stone quoted scripture, commenting upon them at the same time. Then he added, "But my strength fails, but God is my strength and my portion forever."

Stone turned for a moment to his family and exhorted them to be faithful. Turning back to Creath, he said, "Brother Creath, if so great and so holy a man as Paul was afraid that he might be a cast-away, may not so frail and poor a man as I fear too? But my God is good and merciful, and my Saviour is strong and mighty to save me." In a moment Creath had to leave. Stone called after him, "God bless you, my brother. I hope to meet you in heaven."

Stone was put in a chair by his friends. Dr. David Morton asked him what he thought of the doctrine he had been preaching. He replied that he believed it on the whole to be true although some mistakes had been made. The rest of the time he spent in smoking his pipe and conversing upon the love of God. Presently, he reclined his head upon the shoulder of his son, Barton, and went to his eternal sleep.[16]

He was buried at Hannibal, but later his body was re-buried at Cane Ridge. A monument today beside the old Cane Ridge meeting house marks the place of burial of one of the greatest of the pioneers—Barton Warren Stone.

It is not likely that Tolbert Fanning overstated the case, when, upon receiving news of Stone's death, he wrote:

The history of Brother Stone would be the history of the most important religious movements in the United States, for nearly half a century. . . . To be sure his talent was not, perhaps, quite so brilliant as some others; but his acquaintance with the Scriptures

---

[16]Jacob Creath, "Obituary," *Millennial Harbinger*, Third Series, Vol. I, No. 12 (December, 1844), p. 621.

was extensive and critical, and a more humble, conscientious and pious man cannot be found. If justice is ever done to his memory, he will be regarded as the first great American reformer,—the first man, who, to much purpose, pleaded the ground that the Bible, without note, commentary or creed, must destroy antichristian powers, and eventually conquer the world. Although I have heard Father Stone slandered, and his views grossly perverted, yet never did I hear mortal man utter a syllable derogatory to his moral worth. A man more devoted to Christianity, has not lived nor died, and many stars will adorn his crown in a coming day.[17]

---

[17]Tolbert Fanning, "A Good Man Has Fallen," *Christian Review*, Vol. I, No. 12 (December, 1844), p. 288.

CHAPTER III

THE CAMPBELL MOVEMENT

In September, 1850, a young twenty-three year old man by the name of John F. Rowe arrived for the first time in the little community called Bethany, Virginia to begin college under the tutorship of one of the most illustrious of religious leaders to live within the past century—Alexander Campbell. In Rowe's pocket was a letter from J. H. Jones, preacher for the church in Wooster, Ohio, addressed to President Campbell on behalf of the youth. Accordingly, the first person Rowe wanted to see was Campbell, so out to Campbell's famous study he went. Stepping into the study, Rowe saw at once there were no other chairs besides the one Campbell occupied. Campbell immediately piled up some books and pointing to them, said to Rowe: "Please, Sir, take a literary seat."[1] The words were spoken and the inward tension ceased, for Rowe had come with hero-worship in his heart for such a man whose reputation was known throughout the nation. Throughout the rest of the conversation Rowe felt perfectly at ease.

This unusual devotion which Rowe felt toward a man he had never seen, but about whom he had heard much, was a very common thing, for Alexander Campbell, president of Bethany College, was no usual man. In personal appearance Campbell was tall, vigorous and athletic. His hair was light and his complexion moderately fair. His face had no straight lines, and his aquiline nose was arched as John Smith said, a "little to the north." Few ever saw him when his countenance was not cheerful. Men came from miles to drink at this fountain of knowledge. The saints of the age had beaten a path to his door.

Scarcely can a man be found who does not have some one trait more pronounced in his make-up than others. While in Campbell there was a rare combination of many of the nobler traits, yet the outstanding quality seemed to be his power of concentration which gave to him a rich store-house of knowledge. His mind was keen and logical, and his arguments were generally well arranged. Friend and foe alike spoke in praise of this man, and even the

---

[1] John F. Rowe, "Reminiscences of the Restoration," *American Christian Review*, Vol. XXIX, No. 18 (April 29, 1886), p. 141.

worldly great recognized in Campbell no common man. General Robert E. Lee spoke of Campbell in the following words:

He was a man in whom were illustriously combined all the qualities that could adorn or elevate the nature to which he belonged. Knowledge, the most various and extended virtue that never loitered in her career nor deviated from her course. A man who if he had been delegated as the representative of his species to one of the superior worlds, would have suggested a grand idea of the human race. Such was President Campbell.[2]

At the time of the debate with N. L. Rice in 1843 Alexander Campbell was at the height of his power. Certainly in no period before or after was he any more active. Tolbert Fanning, one of Campbell's great admirers, writes of Campbell at this period of his life in the following words:

Alexander Campbell is about sixty years old; has been blessed by nature with a fine constitution; has led a most active life, and consequently enjoys remarkable good health for one of his age, and his intellect is as vigorous as it was at twenty-five. In personal appearance, there is no man like him. His scholarship is admired by both friends and foes; and in logical powers, the world, in my humble opinion, has not his equal. As a declaimer, he is not generally admired by the multitude; but men of the best order of mind are always delighted with his addresses. He is most chaste, pointed, and dignified, in all his public exhibitions; knows not how to take advantage of an opponent, and will not condescend to little tricks for the sake of applause. His arguments are always well arranged, and are generally full and satisfactory on every point he touches. It is scarcely probable any man has ever become truly distinguished, who has not attained his pre-eminence for some one particular trait, and evidently Alexander Campbell owes his greatness to his powers of *concentration,* and his habit of presenting the greatest subjects in a few *pointed* and *palpable propositions.* His doctrine is that the universe is ruled by a few general laws, and to illustrate the most important truths, a few leading points only need be discussed. For logic, scriptural knowledge, genuine criticisms, dignity of manner, fairness and Christian courtesy, it is barely probable Alexander Campbell has an equal living. . . .[3]

These are strong words and one might well ask if it might be possible that Fanning overstated the case. Friends of Alexander Campbell do not think so. There has never been a great question

---

[2] Robert E. Lee, "The Late R. E. Lee's Letter," *Apostolic Times,* Vol. III, No. 4 (May 4, 1871), p. 27.

[3] Tolbert Fanning, "Campbell and Rice's Debate," *Christian Review,* Vol. I, No. 5 (May, 1844), pp. 115, 116.

to them but that Campbell was one of the foremost thinkers in
the nation, and that his religious influence has been on the whole
a precious enlightenment to those inquirers after the truth of God's
word. Nevertheless, such strong testimonials of the greatness of
the man lead naturally into investigation of his life, his work, and
the secret of such a lasting influence. Such a story takes us back
nearly two centuries and off to a country for its beginning far away
from America.

The story begins in Northern Ireland in the year 1786. A
better place to begin could not be found, for the people of Northern
Ireland are a people as distinct and different from the usual Irish
as are the Hindus from the Chinese. Here in the northeastern
corner of the Emerald Isle where Alexander Campbell was born
the people were predominantly Anglo-Scottish in blood and
Protestant in religion. Settled in the early seventeenth century by
Presbyterian Scots, this section of Ireland has long struggled with
Catholic Ireland to the south of them, but in their own independent
way they have declared their liberty even down to the present day.
Perhaps the geography has lent some to this fierce passion of independence, for northeast Ireland is a land of fertile valleys, stony
mountain moorland and bold rocky shores washed by the North
Channel and Irish Sea. This section comprises the heart of the
commercial and industrial regions of Ireland today, and in Campbell's day those rich valleys were an agriculturalist's dreamland.
Here the people had their own living. There was an air of financial
and economic independence, and so the people of northeastern Ireland lifted their proud heads in defiance of Catholic Ireland.

The exact date of Alexander Campbell's birth will probably never
be settled to the satisfaction of every interested party. Records of
this date were lost in a shipwreck, and so nothing authoritative remains by which to go. From Campbell's day on down differences
of opinion have existed. Richardson places the date as September
12, 1788. W. K. Pendleton, twice the son-in-law of Campbell,
placed the date in June, 1786. Moses E. Lard placed the date 1787.
Tolbert Fanning thought Campbell to be older than any of these
men put it. In March or April 1835 Campbell and Fanning were
on an extended tour into the northeastern part of the United States
and on the way stopped in Georgetown, Kentucky to visit in the
home of John T. Johnson. They were dining together and Richard

N. Johnson was present. Campbell and R. N. Johnson, in the course of their conversation, discussed their ages. There was, says Fanning, no doubt in the minds of either that they were the same age, and Johnson was fifty-four.[4] In which case, the birth of Campbell is put back to 1781. Charles V. Segar, who wrote the biographical sketch of Campbell in the book, "Lectures on The Pentateuch," uses the date of Campbell's birth the same as W. K. Pendleton. Segar declares that this is the date Thomas Campbell gave to him in 1847 and the one which the family generally considered most correct.[5] While it is well to recognize that the date can never be definitely set, yet the greater weight of evidence seems to point toward Segar's date, viz., that Alexander Campbell was born in June, 1786.

As one looks northward on a map of Ireland, the rocky shores of Lough Neagh which border on County Antrim in northeastern Ireland suddenly take a sharp turn westward near the city of Antrim and continue so over into the county of Armagh before turning again southward to form the northern coast line for the Lough. Here, only a few miles from where the Lough makes that first turn, on the north shores of the Lough, stands Shane's Castle. Northward from here about a mile, over into County Antrim, stood a little village called Ballymena. Only a short distance from this village was a little cottage, surrounded by a few acres of ground, where in 1786 there lived a preacher in the Seceder Church by the name of Thomas Campbell with a bride of less than a year, Jane Corneigle Campbell. Here their first son, Alexander, was born.

Thomas, James, Archibald and Enos were the four sons of Archibald Campbell, Thomas being the elder. He was born on February 1, 1763 in County Down Ireland. Thomas had a bright intellect and determined to be a teacher. His first excursion into teaching took him into the south of Ireland, into the County of Connaught. But his father was dissatisfied, and summoned him back home. He then settled down for a time to teach at Sheepbridge, near Newry in the southern part of County Down.

Before many months Campbell had the customary experience which lead him to believe he was called of God to preach. He belonged to the Anti-Burgher group of the Seceders. Through the

[4]Tolbert Fanning, "Sketches in the Life of Alexander Campbell, No. 1," *Gospel Advocate*, Vol. VIII, No. 20 (May 15, 1866), pp. 306, 307.
[5]Charles V. Segar, *Lectures on the Pentateuch* (Cincinnati: Bosworth, Chase & Hall, Publishers, 1871), p. 12.

help of John Kinley who promised to pay his expenses, Campbell attended Glasgow University for three years, finishing the pre-scribed course, and then went to Whitburn where he studied under Professor A. B. Bruce in the Anti-Burgher School. Finishing his course, he took an examination, and was given a license to preach under the Synod. His first preaching was done near Sheep-bridge. After his marriage to Jane Corneigle, he moved to Market Hill in the county adjoining Down on the west, County Armagh. He moved to Ahorey in 1798 in the same county, in a community called Rich Hill. It was near here that the youthful days of Alexander Campbell were spent.

The greatness of Alexander Campbell can in no small measure be traced to his noble parents. Thomas Campbell was a severe critic, a kind disciplinarian, and a devoted scholar. Alexander's mind was very early to be filled with large selections of literature. He read extensively, and memorized many choice items in literature and in scripture. It was the rule in the Campbell family that each child should sometime during the day, memorize a verse of scripture to recite at evening worship. Almost daily the boy studied the Bible along with Brown's catechism. He memorized rich passages in Greek, Roman, French and English literature. In later years many marvelled at the knowledge which Campbell possessed. Fanning says of him:

Hence, we never saw a man so perfectly familiar with the most important events recorded in the Sacred oracles, particularly the Old Testament, and also in Greek, Roman and English history. Singular as it may appear, Alexander Campbell could recite and fully appreciate more of the English poets, especially Milton, Shakespeare, Thompson and Young, than any one with whom we have had the satisfaction of associating.[6]

Campbell, in his literary tastes, seems to have had little desire for the more modern productions. Everything from the Reformation movement on back to ancient history, he knew extensively. But the more modern writings of his time did not challange his atten-tion.

Campbell's religious background is very interesting. Thomas Campbell had a high regard for the Bible, and this fact very early made an impression upon Alexander's mind. He would come into

---

[6]Tolbert Fanning, "Sketches in the Life of Alexander Campbell, No. 1," *Gospel Advocate,* Vol. VIII, No. 20 (May 15, 1866), p. 307.

THOMAS CAMPBELL

his father's library and notice frequently the Bible and a Concordance upon the stand while many other books were in the library shelves untouched. Gradually his father was turning more to the Bible as a pure fountain of living water and away from creeds and doctrines of men.

The church to which the Campbells belonged, as previously stated, was the Seceder branch of the Presbyterian Church. Its history is long and complicated, but the full story of the Campbells cannot be told without a brief sketch of it.

There are often many strange ironies in history! In Scotland in 1559 there was a large class of insurgents, Calvinistic in belief, who opposed the regent. Elizabeth, queen of England, hated them;

yet politics makes strange bedfellows, and Elizabeth found herself fighting on their side. She won out and the Treaty of Edinburgh was signed in 1560 providing that the government of Scotland should be turned over to a council of Lords. In August that same year, the Scottish Parliament made Calvinistic Protestantism the Established Religion of Scotland.[7] But, for a few years, Calvinism was not to have an easy time. Much credit can be given to John Knox for withstanding Mary Stuart, regent of Scotland and an ardent Catholic, and thus preventing the nation from going into Catholicism. Before long Mary became unpopular, and was forced to abdicate the throne in 1566.

In 1578 the "Second Book of Discipline," embodying the full Presbyterian organization was drawn up. The General Assembly was made supreme. It worked through the provincial synods and presbyteries down to the local parish. The book of devotion which Knox had composed at Frankfort for use in the church at Geneva formed the substance for the "Book of Common Order" for the Scottish Church.

Notwithstanding these events it was not until 1690 that Presbyterianism in Scotland could sit on a more secure throne. Various attempts were made by the English to plant the Episcopalian religion in Scotland. In 1638 the Scots adopted the National Covenant of the Scots to defend the Presbyterian Church. The English king, Charles I, called shortly after, a parliament to handle the Scots. The result was a war which began in 1640. Eventually Scotland was subdued by Cromwell in 1640, but still little peace was found. It was not until the Westminster Confession of Faith was ratified in 1690 and Presbyterianism again reinstated in Scotland that peace was to be known.

Scottish Presbyterianism found a fundamental weakness in its close tie-up with the civil government. After the Presbyterian system had been established by the assembly, the old polity of the church was retained by law. In 1572 a compromise was reached between ecclesiastical and civil officers that old names and titles, such as bishops and abbotts should continue, but that the incumbents were subject to the General Assembly in spiritual things and to the king in temporal. By the turn of the eighteenth century, the General Assembly had begun to show a dictatorial spirit. This was

---

[7]George Park Fisher, *History of the Christian Church* (New York: Charles Scribners Sons, 1946), p. 365.

in keeping with the general spirit of secularism which became characteristic of the times.

This secularism in Scotland began to assert itself after 1707 with the union of English and Scottish parliaments. Deism began to assert itself in the country, and the church of Scotland became saturated with the secular spirit of the times. Ultimately two parties came to the front—the Moderates and the Evangelicals. The former fell in with the spirit of the times and the latter stayed loyal to the old orthodoxy.

The bulk of the people belonged to the Evangelical group, but the leadership in the church was going the way of the Moderates. Dissension was fomenting, which was enhanced in 1712 when the Union Parliament took away the right of the people to select their preachers and restored patronage. On the same issue the General Assembly took action in 1731 with an act declaring that when a vacancy was to be filled by a presbytery, the election should lie with the "heritors, being Protestants and the elders." The Evangelicals considered this a virtual surrender of their rights, and so, led by Ebenezer Erskine and three others, they strongly objected. Erskine was promptly expelled from the ministry of the church. The next year he and others formed an Associate Presbytery and thus the Secession Church was born.

The people were behind the new movement. The Assembly announced in 1765 that the Seceders had one hundred and twenty meeting houses and a hundred thousand members who formerly belonged to the Established Church of Scotland. By 1800 there were two hundred Seceder Congregations in Scotland. But the good fortune of the Seceders was not to last long, for division was to be characteristic of them. In 1789 the Seceders divided into Burghers and Anti-Burghers on the question of the burgesses taking an oath. The burgesses of the towns required oaths binding the people to support the religion practiced in that realm. Those who considered the oath unlawful were the Anti-burghers. In 1799 both branches of the Seceder Church divided again into New Lights and Old Lights on the question of whether the Solemn League and Covenant should be made a term of communion. Thomas Campbell was an Old Light Anti-Burgher in the Seceder Presbyterian Church. Thus he was well acquainted with religious division.

Amidst this religious division, Thomas Campbell worked for

unity and sought to bring himself and his family closer to God. He was led more and more to depend upon the Bible, and made firmer attempts to follow its leadings. Once the Governor-General of Ireland offered him a position as private tutor with a large salary and a luxurious home, but Campbell knew that to move there would place his family in an environment of worldly pride and fashion, and so he refused.[8] As a preacher, he worked hard, and before long developed a stomach trouble that gave him considerable pain. The doctors could do him no good, so finally recommended a trip abroad.

Several families around Rich-Hill had already come to America. Thomas Hodgens had sold his land and come. His daughter had married James Foster, a Scotch Independent, and they, too, had come. Alexander had already told his father he was coming when he got old enough, so Thomas Campbell, when faced with the necessity of a trip overseas, naturally turned to America. For thirty-five days, then, in 1807 his ship plowed the waves of the Atlantic, finally to arrive in Philadelphia. It was early spring. Fortunately, the Synod of North America was in conference at Philadelphia, and here, Campbell presented his credentials, only to be assigned to work under the Chartiers Presbytery in western Pennsylvania.

The next two years of Thomas Campbell's life can be fairly easily traced through the records of the minutes of the Chartiers Presbytery, for often was Campbell's name before them. The minutes of Saturday, May 16, 1807 tell that Campbell was received for the first time into the fellowship of this group. At the session of June 30, and July 1, 1807, Thomas Campbell was given appointments at Buffalo on the second and third Sundays of July; at Mount Pleasant on the fourth; and on the first Sunday of August, at Pittsburgh. Thus Campbell was kept busy, preaching Sunday after Sunday.

A man who reads the Bible with an open and intelligent mind will sooner or later absorb much to make him dissatisfied with the human elements in religion. That man, if he has faith and courage, will dare to speak out sooner or later against what is wrong. As Campbell filled his appointments, he found himself teaching things contrary to the creed of the church, but things which he felt were

[8]Thomas W. Grafton, *Life of Alexander Campbell* (St. Louis: Christian Board of Publication, 1897), p. 20.

in harmony with the scriptures. It was only a matter of time until earnest opposition would arise.

The first sign of antagonism came at the regular meeting of the Chartiers Presbytery held at the Mt. Hope meeting house on October 27, 1807. The order of business came around to the question of filling appointments, and it was found that a Mr. John Anderson had not kept his appointment at Buffalo on one recent Sunday at which time he was to assist Thomas Campbell in administering the Lord's Supper. When Anderson was called upon to give an account of his action, he replied that he knew Campbell to be a teacher of false doctrine in that he had heard him say before that there was nothing but human authority for creeds and confessions of faith. The Presbytery asked if anyone else had known of Campbell teaching these doctrines, and a Mr. William Wilson responded that he did.

Both Anderson and Wilson were typical protectors of orthodoxy. Anderson was short and stocky in stature, having the appearance of having no neck. His voice was weak, and his temper irascible, although he tried to appear humble and meek. With the people as a whole he was a very unpopular preacher. Anderson had become professor of theology for the Associate Churches in the Presbytery of Chartiers on April 21, 1794. Less is known of Wilson. He was born in 1770, got his training at Glasgow University, came to America in 1791 or 1792, and was ordained a preacher in the Seceder church in 1800.[9]

Although Thomas Campbell objected to Anderson's charges, it did him little good. The Presbytery promptly penalized him by taking away his appointments for the next two months. Early in 1808, the Presbytery met again, but the matter only became worse. On February 9 the meeting was at the Buffalo meeting house. Charges were read against Campbell. He was asked then to speak for himself. Campbell replied:

With regard to faith I believe that the soul of man is the subject of it; the Divine Spirit is the author of it; the Divine Word the rule and reason of it; Christ and Him crucified the object of it; the Divine pardon, acceptance and assistance, or grace here and glory hereafter, the direct, proper and formal end of it. . . .

With respect to Confessions of Faith and Testimonies I believe that the church has all the Divine warrant for such exhibitions of

---

[9]W. H. Hanna, *Thomas Campbell, Seceder, and Christian Union Advocate* (Cincinnati: The Christian Standard Publishing Co., 1935), pp. 38, 39.

the truth, that our Confession and Testimony adduce for that purpose; and that it is lawful and warrantable to use them as terms of
communion insofar as our testimony requires; in which sense 1
have never opposed them.[10]

This meeting at Buffalo appears to have lasted down to Saturday,
February 11, 1808. It resulted in suspending Thomas Campbell
from the ministry in the Seceder Church. Nevertheless, at their
next meeting at Mt. Hope meeting house on March 8, Campbell
tried to get them to suspend their judgment, but they refused.
He was now ready to appeal his action to the Synod.

The Synod of the Associated Churches met on May 18, 1808 in
Philadelphia and Thomas Campbell was present. It was on Friday,
May 20 that it got to the case of Campbell. Papers were read
containing the charges and Campbell's answer. Consideration of
the affair was postponed until the next day, and continued from
then on over to Monday, May 23. The result was that the Synod
upheld Thomas Campbell in many particulars but concluded by
saying his answers on the first two articles were "evasive," "un-
satisfactory" and "highly equivocal."[11] And so, Campbell, much
against his will, was forced to submit.

Throughout June and July, 1808, Campbell preached by appointment in Philadelphia. When the Chartiers Presbytery met again
on September 13, 1808 at Burgettstown, Campbell was there. He
found no assignment waiting for him, and asked the reason. There
were sharp words of controversy, charges of falsehood, and Thomas
Campbell denounced the authority of the Presbytery, the Synod,
and all their courts. The next day he was suspended from his
ministerial office. This day, September 13, 1808, can be taken as
the day when Campbell formally made his separation from Seceder-
ism.

Campbell saw the evils of division, and it became evident to him
that the trouble lay with human creeds. Nevertheless, he wanted
to be as charitable as possible. Alexander Campbell writes of his
father's attitude:

He objected not so much to the doctrines of the Secession creed
and platform, as a doctrinal basis, but to the assumption of any
formula of religious theories or opinions, as the foundation of the
church of Christ; alleging that the holy Scriptures, Divinely in-

---

[10]W. H. Hanna, *Thomas Campbell*, pp. 45-47.
[11]W. H. Hanna, *Thomas Campbell*, p. 83.

spired, were all sufficient and alone sufficient for all the purposes contemplated by their Author, in giving them.[12]

Meanwhile, near Washington, Pennsylvania where Thomas Campbell lived, some friends from Scotland also lived. There was "General" Thomas Achesons, a Lieutenant-Colonel of the twenty-second Regiment of the Pennsylvania militia; James Foster and Thomas Hodgens, each of whom had come from Ireland. In the houses of these friends Campbell continued to preach. His voice was heard in Maple Groves where open air services were held. In due time it became evident that many of these hearers were in sympathy with Campbell's views. He proposed to some of the principal ones among them to have a meeting at some home to give more definite form to the movement. The House of Abraham Altars between Mt. Pleasant and Washington, Pennsylvania was chosen, and here, one of the most famous meetings of the restoration was held. Campbell's speech closed with the famous motto: "Where the Bible speaks; we speak; where the Bible is silent, we are silent."

The idea which Campbell embodied in this motto was not new. Many years before in 1659, Edward Stillingfleet, who later became Bishop of Worcester, had said: "For the church to require more than Christ himself did, or make the condition of her communion more than our Saviour did for discipleship, is wholly unwarranted."[13] Chillingworth had written his book, "The Religion of Protestants, a Safe Way to Salvation" in 1637, and had argued that the Bible was the sole authority in matters of salvation. His conclusion, "The Bible, I say, the Bible only, is the religion of Protestants" purported to be the claim of all Protestant bodies. Yet notwithstanding the idea Campbell presented in his motto was not new, it nevertheless was revolutionary in one phase: a few people now applied it to Protestant creeds and confessions of faith whereas, the Prostestant bodies had almost exclusively applied it to Roman Catholic traditions. For the first time there were some who realized that the motto struck with equal force against human creeds as it did against Catholic traditions.

Quite naturally then, when Campbell first spoke these words, and

---

[12]Alexander Campbell, *Memoirs of Elder Thomas Campbell* (Cincinnati: H. S. Bosworth, 1861), p. 11.
[13]A. C. Watters, *History of British Churches of Christ* (Indianapolis: Butler University, 1948), p. 2.

paused, there was a solemn hush that fell across the assembly that showed the intensity of the emotions of the hour. Campbell sat down. A Scottish bookseller, Andrew Munro, a rather sentimental person, was the first to break the silence. "Mr. Campbell," he said, "if we adopt *that* as a basis, then there is an end of infant baptism." Campbell replied: "Of course, if infant baptism be not found in the scriptures, we can have nothing to do with it." Thomas Acheson then arose and cried: "I hope I may never see the day when my heart will renounce that blessed saying of the Scripture, 'Suffer little children to come unto me and forbid them not, for of such is the kingdom of heaven.'" Saying that he burst into tears. James Foster, who even in Ireland had been opposed to infant baptism, arose and cried out: "Mr. Acheson, I would remark that in the portion of Scripture you have quoted, *there is no reference whatever to infant baptism.*"[14]

The anxiety which these men expressed must not be construed as division within their ranks. On the contrary their various statements show an earnest seeking after the way of the Lord. They were as men stepping out of intense darkness into light, and the light blinded them for a spell. These men were coming out of the darkness of partyism and stepping forth into the glorious light of revealed truth, and they staggered for a moment to get their bearings. But from here on, their activities were to be stepped up, and their ideas were taking on more definite form.

At a meeting at the headwaters of the Buffalo held on August 17, 1809 this small band of men formed themselves into the "Christian Association of Washington." This Association was not to be recognized as a Church, but was a society for the promotion of Christian unity. If the idea appears to be related more to denominationalism than apostolic Christianity, it can be explained on the ground that these men had not as yet fully come to a knowledge of the ancient order, but were step by step going in that direction. Richardson explains:

Neither Thomas Campbell himself, however, nor those associated with him, had a full conception of all that was involved in these principles. They only felt that the religious intolerance of the times had itself become intolerable, and that a reformation was imperiously demanded.[15]

---

[14]Robert Richardson, *Memoirs of Alexander Campbell* (Cincinnati: Standard Publishing Co., Vol. I, 1897), p. 238.
[15]Robert Richardson, *Memoirs of Alexander Campbell*, Vol. I, p. 245.

At any rate, as soon as the Association was formed, it was seen immediately that a building in which to meet was needed. Accordingly, a log cabin was erected on the Sinclair farm, three miles from Mt. Pleasant on the road to Washington. For a time this building was used for a school and Campbell renewed his teaching career here. Near this building was the residence of a Mr. Welch, a man friendly to the views of the Association. Welch fixed up a room for Thomas Campbell and here Campbell spent much of his time in studying and writing. Here Campbell wrote the Declaration and Address. When it was finished, Campbell called a special meeting of the Association and read it before them. The document met their general acquiescence, and was ordered printed on September 7, 1809.

The Declaration and Address is another of the famous documents to come out of the movement to restore primitive Christianity. It is divided into three parts. The "Declaration" gives the purpose and plan of the Association. The "Address" goes more into detail, giving the forces at work in the religious world which necessitated a restoration movement. The third part is the "Appendix" which is designed to answer questions and refute arguments against the purpose of the Association. Campbell's plan for unity was, in brief, a re-statement in different words of Rupertus Meldinius famous maxim: "In essentials unity; in non-essentials liberty; in all things charity." Campbell uses the terms, faith and opinion. The former is based upon the expressed declarations of the Bible and the latter, upon things about which the Bible is silent. Unity, Campbell believed, could be realized upon the express teachings of the Bible, and in opinions, there should be liberty. The important and timely enunciations of the Declaration and Address have given it a deserved place among the classics in restoration literature.

Meanwhile, back in Ireland, the family of Thomas Campbell waited patiently for news from Campbell that would call them to follow him to America. In March, 1808, the letter came, urging them to hurry to join him. So the family prepared to leave. But misfortune struck in the form of a smallpox epidemic which caused considerable delay. It was September 20 before they set out for Londonderry to get a ship to America. On September 28 the ship weighed anchor at Lough Foyle in her attempts to put out to sea. But the ship had a hard time, and didn't get started until

October 1. But hopes were short lived for the wind was bad and the ship didn't get out of the Lough. Finally the ship got into the sea.

In the calamities of the world sometimes the believer can see the hand of God at work. It appears to have been an act of providence that the ship didn't go well, and before long was wrecked. Campbell used the time for meditation, and then and there decided to devote his life to preaching. When youthful Alexander Campbell stepped from the sea on to the rugged coastland of Scotland after that wreck, he was a youth now determined to devote himself to God.

On November 8, Campbell entered Glasgow University where his father had gone many years before. Campbell sat under Professor Young in Greek; Professor Jardin in Logic and Belles Lettres and Professor Ure in Experimental Philosophy. The latter two had taught Thomas Campbell twenty-five years earlier.

Many students of Campbell have sought the answer to Campbell's thinking in those intellectual factors which influenced him during this time in Scotland. Just how far this influence went may be a hard matter to determine. That he came in contact with Scottish philosophy, and particularly the "Common Sense" School of Scottish philosophy is evident. That traces of this philosophy show in his thinking in later years is equally evident.

Thomas Reid, the founder of the Common Sense School of Scottish philosophy, died in 1796, twelve years before Campbell came to Glasgow. Since 1763 Reid had been professor of moral philosophy at Glasgow where for a century following him his teachings were followed. Intellectual centers like Aberdeen, Glasgow and Edinburgh were effected. Protestant thinkers both in Europe and America were influenced. Hamilton, Jefferson, Madison and many other leading figures in colonial America were philosophical disciples of Thomas Reid. Reid had been educated at Aberdeen, and had followed Adam Smith, author of "The Wealth of Nations" as professor of Moral Philosophy at Glasgow in 1763. The honor probably came to him because of his rebuttal of the skepticism of David Hume. Hume was once the literary lion of Scotland, but Reid more than Immanuel Kant, calmed him down by the application of "Common Sense" or "Universal Reason". Reid in his philosophy did believe in God and did also believe that man had a soul. His was not the skepticism common in philosophical circles of that day.

While in Glasgow, Campbell also came in contact with the various independent movements in the church which doubtlessly influenced him profoundly. Here he had met Grenville Ewing, formerly minister of Lady Glenorchy's in Edinburgh, who had founded the theological school at Glasgow. Ewing was connected with the independent movement led by James and Robert Haldane. The Haldane brothers had left the church of Scotland because of the cold formalism of the church. Both were relatively wealthy, and Robert devoted his money to educating missionaries for work in India. James was the preacher of the two who was more outstanding. He was tireless in his efforts to preach. In 1799 the Haldanes had organized an independent church in Edinburgh. Within nine years they had organized eighty-five churches. It was while Ewing was connected with their theological school that Campbell became acquainted with him, and the two became the closest of friends. An Independent Church had been established at Rich Hill in Ireland, and James Haldane had preached here while Thomas Campbell was yet there.

Another movement, led by John Glas and Robert Sandeman also was prevalent in Scotland, and doubtlessly, Campbell learned extensively of these views. John Glas, minister of Tealing, had been deposed from the Church of Scotland in 1730 and had organized independent churches in Dundee, Perth and Edinburgh. These churches were congregational in government. They denied that creeds or confessions of faith were worth anything. Glas taught there were two classes of officers: the "extraordinary" consisting of Apostles, Prophets and Evangelists, and the "Ordinary" consisting of elders and deacons. Robert Sandeman adopted Independent views in 1755. Sandeman believed that faith was a simple assent to the testimony of Christ. He advocated the weekly observance of the Lord's Supper and a plurality of elders in one local congregation. The Independent movement led by Glas and Sandeman differed from that led by the Haldanes by the spirit which characterized them. Haldane was free from a controversial spirit, but Sandeman was of the opposite temperament. Alexander Campbell, much later, writes of Sandeman and Haldane:

Concerning Sandeman and Haldane, how they can be associated under one species, is to me a matter of surprise. The former a Paido-baptist, the latter a Baptist; the former, as keen, as sharp, as censorious, as acrimonious as Juvenal; the latter as mild, as charitable, as condescending as any man this age has produced. As authors I know them well. The one is like the mountain storm that roars among the cliffs; the other like the balmy zephyrs that breathe upon banks of violets. . .[16]

From Grenville Ewing, Campbell's close friend, the latter borrowed an intensely independent spirit. At once, he began to examine for himself, the claims of the Seceder Church as a religious group. Slowly, he was led to doubt them. The crucial hour came at the semi-annual communion service, near the close of his stay in Glasgow. It was the custom to give all who were to partake of the Lord's Supper a metallic token to shut out the unworthies from partaking. As Campbell had come from Ireland without any letter or recommendation, it was necessary for him to take an examination before the elders on Saturday to determine his worthiness. He took the examination and passed. But the next day, his conscience hurt him. He put his token in the plate that morning and refused to partake of the communion.[17] Campbell had now crossed the rubicon; he was no longer with the Seceder Church.

On July 31, 1809 Campbell left Glasgow for Greenock. Four days later, he and his family were on the ship, *Latonia,* headed for America. This time the trip went smoothly, and the ship landed at New York on Friday, September 29. The following Thursday, they left New York for Philadelphia where they arrived on Saturday. The following Monday, they started on that westward trek across Pennsylvania in the direction of Washington. Thomas Campbell, who had learned of their coming, had left his home in Washington, going toward Philadelphia. On the way, the two parties met. Thomas Campbell fondly embraced his family, and they, in return, had their spirits renewed within them by this reunion.

There was much to talk about—much that would leave its effect upon the future turn of events.

----

[16]Alexander Campbell, "Reply," *Christian Baptist,* Vol. III, No. 9 (April 3, 1826), p. 228.

[17]T. W. Grafton, *Life of Alexander Campbell,* pp. 40, 41.

CHAPTER IV

A MOVEMENT CRYSTALLIZES

It was early fall of 1809 that Thomas and Alexander Campbell met again in Pennsylvania. The Christian Association of Washington was a very young organization. The Declaration and Address had just been printed. The events of the previous two years had hurried by in the anxiety which Thomas Campbell had felt. So he had much to tell his son. The son listened patiently and thoughtfully, and then related to his father his own experiences which had led him out of the Seceder Church. Each was saddened with the conditions that prevailed in religious partyism, but each felt confident that the answer lay in a more complete return to the Scriptures. Thoughtfully did Alexander Campbell read the Declaration and Address through. Handing it back to his father, he expressed his approval of it, and his determination to devote his life to proclaiming the principles contained in it. He furthermore explained his determination to retire to his chamber, and spend six months in a careful study of the Bible. Then he announced that he would spend his life preaching the Divine Word, and for that preaching, he would never accept financial compensation. His father replied: "Upon these principles, my dear son, I fear you will have to wear many a ragged coat."[1]

It is said that soon after "Raccoon" John Smith of Kentucky began preaching, some of his friends came to him, advising him to cease preaching so strongly, or else his "Baptist brethren" would become angered, and not pay him, and he would never be able to get out of debt. To this Smith replied: "Conscience is an article that I have never yet brought into market; but should I offer it for sale, Montgomery County, with all its lands and houses, would not be enough to buy it, much less that farm of one hundred acres."[2] When John Calvin was studying at Strassburg one cold winter, his financial circumstances were so bad that he went days at a time without food, and was often without heat. A Cath-

---

[1]Richardson, *Memoirs of Alexander Campbell*, Vol. I, p. 275.
[2]John Augustus Williams, *Life of Elder John Smith* (Cincinnati: The Standard Publishing Co., 1904), pp. 158, 159.

olic offered him good financial means if he would cease his opposition to Catholicism, but Calvin refused. Such is the material of which great men are made. It is the lot of great men to put the cause of truth first and foremost in their hearts, then be loyal to their conviction despite whatever else may be involved.

He who would seek to understand the greatness of Alexander Campbell must study him in this light. There was one object always before the man: Truth. He wanted the Truth more than he wanted anything else. He himself writes:

Often have I said, and often have I written, that *truth,* truth eternal and divine, is now, and long has been with me the *pearl of great price.* To her I will, with the blessing of God, sacrifice everything. But on no altar will I offer her a victim. If I have lost sight of her, God who searcheth the hearts knows I have not done it intentionally. With my whole heart I have sought the *truth,* and I know that I have found it.[3]

On another occasion he wrote:

Numbers with me count nothing. Let God be true, and every man a liai. Let truth stand, though the heavens fall. When contending with thirty millions of Lutherans, I feel myself contending with but one man. In opposing seventy millions of Greek and Eastern Professors, I am in conflict with but one leader. When one hundred millions of Baptists assail me, I feel myself in a struggle with but one mind. In all the Methodists I see but John Wesley; in all the Calvinists, John Calvin; and in all the Episcopalians, one Cranmer. Names, numbers, circumstances weigh nothing in the scales of justice, truth and holiness.[4]

When Campbell opened his debate with McCalla, he said:

Men, Brethren and Fathers:
Through the goodness and mercy of God, I appear before you, at this time and in this place, for the purpose of contending for a part of that faith, and an item of that religious practice, once delivered to the saints. My prayer to God is, that for the sake of his Son Jesus Christ I may speak as I ought to speak; that in the spirit of the Truth I may contend for the truth; that with humility and love, with zeal according to knowledge and unfeigned devotion, I may open my lips on every occasion when I address my fellow mortal and immortal creatures on the subject

---

[3] Alexander Campbell, "A Demand for Justice from Editors in General, and Mr. Brantley in Particular," *Millennial Harbinger,* Vol. 1, No. 3 (March 1, 1830), p. 97.

[4] Alexander Campbell, "The Christian Organization—No. XXV," *Millennial Harbinger,* New Series, Vol. VII, No. 7 (July, 1843), p. 307.

of religion.   Expecting that they and I will soon appear before
the judgment seat of Christ, may I speak in such a way that I may
not be ashamed nor afraid to meet them there.   May I ever act
under the influence of that "wisdom which cometh from above,
which is first pure, then peaceable, then gentle, easy to be entreated,
full of mercy and of good fruits, without partiality and without
hypocrisy."   And may you, my friends, examine and "prove all
things and hold fast that which is good."[5]

In Campbell's search for Truth, he made the Bible the ultimate
source of all his authority.   He loved to study the Word itself, and
it can be safely said that few men ever attained to the knowledge
which he had of the Divine Word.   Campbell expresses his attitude thus:

For the last ten years I have not looked into the works of
these men; and have lost the taste which I once had for controversial reading of this sort, and during this period my inquiries into
the Christian religion have been almost exclusively confined to
the Holy Scriptures.   And I can assure you that the Scriptures,
when made their own interpreter, and accompanied with earnest
desires to the author of these writings, have become, to me, a
book entirely new and unlike what they were when read and
consulted as a book of reference—.[6]

He who would undertake to put Truth first in his heart must
find himself sooner or later facing the problem of what to do
with the messages of other men who purport to be harbingers of
truth.   It is all too easy to become slaves to other men's thinking.
A man who can disregard the person of other men, and still pursue patiently the Truth is a rare commodity; his is the genius of
greatness.   Campbell did read extensively from other men, but he
thought independently, and took from other men what he conceived
to be in harmony with the truth.   Time and again on this point
he expresses his attitude.   In the article alluded to above, he
also says:

I call no man master upon the earth; and although my own
father has been a diligent student, and a teacher of the Christian
religion since his youth; and, in my opinion, understands this
book as well as any person with whom I am acquainted, yet there
is no man with whom I have debated more, and reasoned more,

---

[5]Alexander Campbell, *A Debate on Christian Baptism* (Buffalo: Published
by Campbell & Sala, 1824), pp. 41, 42.
[6]Alexander Campbell, "Reply," *Christian Baptist*, Vol. III, No. 9, (April
3, 1826), p. 229.

on all subjects, than he—I have been so long disciplined in the school of free inquiry, that, if I know my own mind, there is not a man upon the earth whose authority can influence me, any farther than he comes with the authority of evidence, reason, and truth. To arrive at this state of mind is the result of many experiments and efforts; and to me has been arduous beyond expression. I have endeavored to read the Scriptures as though no one had read them before me; and I am as much on my guard against reading them today, through the medium of my own views yesterday, or a week ago, as I am against being influenced by any foreign name, authority or system whatever.

Yet, Campbell was always on the look-out for Truth. He never hesitated to read the writings of others for it, and to accept what Truth they had.

I was some fourteen years ago a great admirer of the works of John Newton. I read them with great delight, and I still love the author and admire many of his sentiments. He was not a staunch Episcopalian, though he died in that connexion. In an apology to a friend for his departure from the tenets of that sect in some instances, he said, "whenever he found a pretty feather in any bird, he endeavored to attach it to his own plummage, and although he had become a very speckled bird, so much so that no one of any species would altogether own him as belonging to them, he flattered himself that he was the prettiest bird among them." From that day to the present I have been looking for pretty feathers, and I have become more speckled than Newton of Olney; but whether I have as good a taste in the selection, must be decided by connoisseurs in ornithology.[7]

It was therefore Campbell's custom to take from the writings of men only what he conceived to be the truth, and to reject all else. This policy he followed unswervingly through his long life. Nowhere does this attitude come out more than in the great religious debates which he held. As a debater, Campbell showed himself always interested in the cause of truth. He debated, not for the joy of polemics, but for the desire to know and dispense the Truth. His opponents, he insisted, must be the giants of the opposition. He would not lift his gun save at the champions of error, and when he did, he sought earnestly for the Truth. Campbell's attitude can thus be seen in his discussion with Rice in these words:

I care nothing for triumphing over Mr. Rice or any other mortal. It is no pleasure to expose human weakness or human folly,

---

[7]Alexander Campbell, "Reply," *Christian Baptist*, Vol. III, No. 9 (April 3, 1826), p. 228.

only in so far as the cause of the truth and mission of the Messiah, and the interests of humanity may require it. There is a higher tribunal in my eye, than human approbation, or the plaudits of my poor fellow-mortals.[8]

But aside from Campbell's independence of mind, another quality of his life contributed to his greatness: his tireless application of his energy to the work ahead. "An ounce of pluck," said James A. Garfield, "is worth a pound of luck." Beecher said: "The elect are 'whosoever will'; the non-elect are 'whosoever won't'." Alexander Campbell was a worker. Arising every morning at four o'clock, he worked steadily until ten at night. His health was excellent; his disposition cheerful. He was almost never sick. When not in his study, he was busy at some manual labor. He was rarely idle. Tolbert Fanning writes of him:

We do not deny that blood will always tell in man as well as in beast, but any one at all familiar with the every day life of this unequalled man, can but account satisfactorily for his great powers of endurance and his almost more than human executive abilities. In addition to his iron frame-work, his habits were studied, and, of course regular. He was rarely sick, complained of few aches, was no dispeptic maintained a cheerful temper, and, of course, yielded to no melancholic temptations. He rose at early dawn, ate and drank as a philosopher, and exercised in the open air as a man of common sense. When on journeys he exercised considerably in early walks, and at home, we have frequently seen him, and can almost see him now, with coat off and spade in hand, pitching about mother earth in a manner which seemed to say, "it is good for both soul and body." He was a farmer of a high order, an admirable mechanic, and loved dearly the shrubbery which he had planted with his own hands about his premises, and especially that upon which he could look from his own quiet little office, in which he did his best thinking. We never saw Alexander Campbell idle. This is the main key to his greatness. He worked with his hands to qualify himself for studying to advantage, and when not writing or preaching, he was busy in conversation with some one, as he often said he was no respecter of persons, but took men as they came, great and small, and he ardently labored to profit all. There was a work of physical majesty, self-possession and independence of appearance about Alexander Campbell, of which he was as unconscious and innocent

---

[8]Alexander Campbell, *Debate on Christian Baptism* (Lexington: A. T. Skellman & Son, 1844), p. 456.

as a child, that said to the passer-by: "this is one of nature's noble-men."[9]

And so Campbell, determined to independently study the Bible, and to work tirelessly in an effort to know the truth, began his long career which was destined to overshadow the influence of his father in years to come. Meanwhile, Thomas Campbell had been preaching in groves and in the houses of friends. But, it was seen that many members lived near Buffalo Creek, so it was de-cided to build a meeting house. A site was chosen on the farm of William Gilchrist, in the valley of the Brush Run, two miles above its junction with Buffalo Creek. Here, Alexander Campbell preached his first sermon on September 16, 1810.

As a preacher, Campbell developed great power. In his de-livery he had a decided Scotch brogue. He never moved about in the pulpit, and made few gestures. His voice never descended below a lofty conversational tone, or arose to strain his vocal cords.[10]

Before long, the subject of infant baptism began to trouble Campbell. He read the third proposition in the Declaration and Address: "That (in order to church union and communion) nothing ought to be inculcated upon Christians as articles of faith, nor required of them as terms of communion, but what is expressly taught and enjoined upon them in the word of God. Nor ought anything to be admitted as of divine obligation, in their church constitution and management, but what is expressly en-joined by the authority of our Lord Jesus Christ and His apostles upon the New Testament Church; either in express terms, or by approved precedent."

"Upon reading this," says Alexander Campbell, "I asked my father in what passage or portion of the inspired oracles, he could find a precept or expressed precedent for the baptism or sprink-ling of infants in the name of the Father, Son and the Holy Spirit."[11]

Campbell's thinking about infant baptism was also occasioned by another circumstance in his life. This was the birth of his

---

[9]Tolbert Fanning, "Sketches on the Life of Alexander Campbell—No. 2," *Gospel Advocate,* Vol. VIII, No. 21 (May 22, 1866), pp. 321-325.
[10]W. C. Morro, *Brother McGarvey* (St. Louis: Bethany Press, 1940), pp. 56, 57.
[11]Charles V. Segar, *Lectures on the Pentateuch,* p. 19.

BRUSH RUN CHURCH.

first child, a tiny girl named Jane, who was born on March 13, 1812. Campbell's marriage had taken place a year earlier, almost to the day, March 12. His wife was Margaret Brown, daughter of John Brown, one of the most successful business men found in that region of Virginia. He lived eight miles from Charleston in the valley of the Buffalo on a rich farm. He was a carpenter and millwright. He owned a gristmill and a saw mill. But, wherever Brown was known, he was spoken of as the man who lived in "The Mansion," a house to become famous for being the one that Alexander Campbell later lived in.

Most houses in Brooke County, Virginia were log stockades, built to serve the double purpose of furnishing a home and a fortress from Indian attacks. But this one was different. It was a pretentious thing three stories high, constructed of oak timbers and hand cut walnut weather boarding, painted dark red and put together with wooden pegs. In the parlor on March 12, 1811 Alex-

ander Campbell and Margaret Brown kneeled on two prayer
benches of black walnut trimmed in gold and took their wedding
vows.

So, after the birth of their first child, Campbell began to want
to investigate the subject of baptism. He asked Andrew Munro
to get him some books on the subject, and Munro did. Campbell
studied the word baptize in Greek to see that it meant immersion.
He concluded there was nothing in the scriptures favoring infant
baptism, so he began making immediate plans to be immersed.
He finally contacted a preacher by the name of Matthias Luse who
agreed to immerse him. But Campbell by now found others that
wanted immersion. His sister, Dorthea, also wanted to be immersed. On Wednesday, June 12, 1812, Campbell went to a
deep pool in Buffalo Creek. Several were there. Before the
baptizing was finished, Thomas Campbell, his wife, James and
Sarah Henon and James Foster—in all, seven persons—were immersed. Before long, practically the whole Brush Run church had
followed suit.

This bold venture of immersion immediately made the Baptists
in the neighborhood lift an eyebrow. Campbell began to receive
invitations to preach for them. Yet he was reluctant to accept.
Alexander Campbell's opinion of the Baptist preachers of that day
was not complimentary to them, for he thought of them as "little
men in big offices." He writes:

I had no idea of uniting with the Baptists more than with the
Moravians or the mere Independents. I had unfortunately formed
a very unfavorable opinion of the Baptist preachers as then introduced to my acquaintance, as narrow, contracted, illiberal, and
uneducated men. This, indeed, I am sorry to say, is still my
opinion of the ministry of that Association at that day; and
whether they are yet much improved, I am without satisfactory
evidence.[12]

Nevertheless, in the fall of 1812 Campbell learned that the Redstone
Baptist Association was having a meeting at Uniontown,
Pennsylvania, and Campbell determined to go as a spectator.
They insisted he preach, but he refused. He came home thoroughly

---

[12]Alexander Campbell, "Anecdotes, Incidents, and Facts," *Millennial Harbinger*, Third Series- Vol. V, No. 6 (June, 1848), p. 349.

disgusted. He said later, "I returned home, not intending ever to visit another association."[13]

On his way home, however, he learned much to his surprise that the Baptist people themselves had no more use for their preachers than Campbell did. They too, looked upon them as defenders of partyism rather than proclaimers of the gospel. So Campbell decided to lay the matter before the members of the Brush Run Church.

East of Washington, Pennsylvania, along the Monongahela River, there were numerous Baptist Churches who had banded together in the Redstone Association. Redstone was the name of an old Indian fort on the river about sixty miles above Pittsburgh. Their doctrinal belief was found in the Philadelphia Confession of Faith, adopted by the Baptist Churches in 1742. The Philadelphia Confession was substantially the same as the Westminster Confession which the churches of Scotland had adopted in 1690. The Philadelphia Confession was, accordingly, thoroughly Calvinistic, and was changed only in those points that suited Baptist practices.

Campbell and the Brush Run Church had little confidence in creeds and confessions of faith. But the Baptists continued to insist that Brush Run join their association. When Campbell laid the matter before the church, it was decided that the church would draw up a statement of its beliefs and lay it before the association. This statement remonstrated against all human creeds and expressed a willingness to cooperate under the condition that the church could preach and teach what it believed the Bible taught. And so, the Brush Run Church was admitted in 1813 to the Redstone Association with only a small objection from a minority element.

In the long run, neither the Baptists nor Campbell were satisfied. The minority continued to work against Campbell for his heterodoxy. Campbell himself felt that he was a Baptist in name only. He writes to an uncle in Ireland in 1815:

For my own part I must say that, after long study and investigation of books, and more especially the Sacred Scriptures, I have through clear convictions of truth and duty, renounced much

---

[13]Alexander Campbell, "Anecdotes, Incidents, and Facts," *Millennial Harbinger,* Third Series, Vol. V, No. 6 (June, 1848), p. 346.

of the traditions and errors of my early education. I am now an Independent in church government; of that faith and view of the gospel exhibited in John Walker's *Seven Letters to Alexander Knox,* and a Baptist so far as regards baptism. What I am in religion I am from examination, reflection, and conviction, not from "ipse dixit" tradition or human authority.[14]

The establishment of the church in Wellsburgh added little to Campbell's favor among the Baptists. Campbell's father-in-law John Brown and his family were converted from the Presbyterian Church and became members of the Brush Run Church. Soon it was found that many members of this church were gradually moving westward, so it was decided that the whole church should move together to Zanesville, Ohio. Brown didn't like the idea of losing Alexander Campbell. As an inducement to make him stay, he gave to him his rich farm, together with the "mansion." Campbell changed his mind. Meanwhile, Brown had moved to Wellsburgh and set himself up in business. Campbell came occasionally and preached in the court house. Two or three other families lived here who were members of the church. Out from Wellsburgh was a Baptist Church of the Regular Baptist order on Cross Creek. Here Brown went to church most of the time. Finally, it was decided to put up a church building in Wellsburgh, and Campbell volunteered to spend four months of his time, visiting the country and raising money.

When the Wellsburgh church was erected, Campbell, contrary to his expectations, was in much disfavor. Elder Pritchard, who preached for the regular Baptist Church out at Cross Creek, became extremely jealous. He became bolder in his accusations as to Campbell's heterdoxy, so the tension between Campbell and the Baptists mounted. It reached its height when Campbell delivered his famous "Sermon On The Law" before the Redstone Association which met that year (1816) at Cross Creek.

For some time Campbell had been thinking upon the relation of the two covenants in the Bible. Baptists were accustomed to disregard the covenants, and to quote one as freely as the other to a sinner. In 1812 Campbell had written to his father:

How many disciples of Moses are to be found in the professed school of Jesus Christ! and how few among the teachers of the New Testament seem to know that Christ's ministers are not

[14]Richardson, *Memoirs of Alexander Campbell,* Vol. I, p. 466.

able ministers of the Old Testament, but of the New! Do they not, like scholars to their teacher, run to Moses to prove forms of worship, ordinances, discipline, and government in the Christian Church, when asked to account for their practices?[15]

Campbell had come to the conviction that much of the error in religious practice was due to the lack of understanding of the relation of the covenants. This idea was enveloping his mind at the time the Redstone Association met at Cross Creek on August 30, 1816.

Campbell came to the Association meeting as a messenger of the Brush Run Church. There was a clamor among Baptist people to hear him. But Elder Pritchard was the host, and he refused. His excuse was that Campbell was too close, that someone farther should be the speaker. He accordingly arranged for Elder Stone of Ohio to speak. Providentially, Stone suddenly became ill. Pritchard was forced then, due to public desire, to ask Campbell to speak. Campbell, not having expected to speak, took only a few minutes to collect his thoughts, and then delivered his sermon. Still, Pritchard would not give up. A woman fainted in the audience, and Pritchard left with her. In the middle of the sermon, he called out many Baptist preachers, and a private council was taken against Campbell. Pritchard wanted Campbell publicly condemned. One of the Baptist preachers replied to Pritchard: "Elder Pritchard, I am not yet prepared to say whether it be or be not Bible doctrine, but one thing I can say, were we to make such an annunciation, we would sacrifice ourselves and not Mr. Campbell."[16]

The Sermon on The Law has become one of the most famous of Campbell's speeches. In it Campbell showed that the law of Moses was abrogated, and therefore, not binding upon Christians. The effect of the sermon was like a bombshell in the Baptist camps. A movement started to charge Campbell with heresy and have him excluded from the Baptist fellowship. The next regular meeting of the Redstone Association at Peter's Creek in 1817 brought the subject up, but through the intervention of some friends, it was dropped. Nevertheless, for the next number of

---

[15]Richardson, *Memoirs of Alexander Campbell,* p. 448.
[16]Alexander Campbell, "Anecdotes, Incidents, and Facts," *Millennial Harbinger,* Third Series, Vol. V, No. 6 (June, 1848), p. 349.

years, the feelings which the Baptists entertained toward Campbell were never cordial.

Meanwhile, Campbell continued to study and to grow, and to use his influence to spread the cause of restoration. In accordance with this desire he made plans to open a seminary in his home which he called "Buffalo Seminary." This was in January, 1818. He wanted the school to instruct young men in religion, but here he felt a disappointment. Most students came from neighborhood farms and studied English and Language for professional services. Nor were these students inclined toward religion. Tuition was five dollars a quarter and board, one dollar and a half a week, so the price was attractive to this group. Campbell's disappointment caused the Seminary to be short-lived.

During this time, Campbell had never thought seriously of entering a religious debate. As a matter of fact, debates were particularly odious to him. They breathed the spirit of partyism, and Campbell noticed that in many cases the disputants strove for personal victory rather than a victory for the truth. Therefore, when, in the winter of 1819, Campbell began to receive letters from John Birch, a Baptist preacher in Mt. Pleasant, Ohio, to come and debate John Walker, a Presbyterian preacher on baptism, Campbell was reluctant to go. Birch had gone to Mt. Pleasant that fall and had succeeded in baptizing an unusual number of people. The ire of Walker was aroused, and he soon issued a challenge for a discussion. Birch wrote Campbell twice and received no reply. He wrote his third letter saying,

Dear Brother: I once more undertake to address you by letter; as we are commanded not to weary in well-doing, I am disposed to persevere. I am coming this third time unto you. I can not persuade myself that you will refuse to attend to the dispute with Mr. Walker, therefore, I do not feel disposed to complain because you have sent me no answer. True, I have expected an answer, signifying your acceptance of the same. I am as yet disappointed, but am not offended nor discouraged. I can truly say it is the unanimous wish of all the church to which I belong, that you should be the disputant. It is Brother Nathaniel Skinner's desire; it is the wish of all the brethren with whom I have conversed, that you should be the man.[17]

Campbell finally agreed and the debate took place near Mount Pleasant on June 19, 20, 1820. The debate was on the subject

[17]Richardson, *Memoirs of Alexander Campbell*, Vol. II, p. 15.

and mode of baptism. Walker opened and Campbell closed it. Walker contended that baptism came in the room of circumcision, and therefore, infants had a right to it. Campbell, who for the past eight years had dwelt on the subject of the covenants, was thoroughly acquainted with his ground, and answered by a general reflection upon the place, purpose, and relationship of the two covenants. The two contenders traversed the usual ground on the mode of baptism, Campbell frequently going out of his way to state the ground on which he proposed a restoration of the church.

At the close of the debate, Campbell issued a challenge to "any Pedobaptist minister of any denomination" to debate with him the subject of infant baptism. In May, 1823, he heard from his challenge. W. L. McCalla of Kentucky, a Presbyterian preacher, responded that he was willing to accept the challenge. A correspondence took place which lasted up into the summer. Finally, it was agreed that the debate should be held in a grove near Washington, Kentucky in October.

Campbell rode horseback to the debate, accompanied by Sidney Rigdon, then a popular Baptist preacher in Ohio. Jeremiah Vardeman, a well-known Kentucky Baptist preacher, was Campbell's moderator. The topic was the same as with Walker: the subject and mode of baptism. The two men went over the same ground on the covenants, but when it came to infant baptism, Campbell injected the argument that baptism was for the remission of sins, and therefore, could not be for infants since they had no sins. This thought was revolutionary for its day, and Campbell knew the Baptists were against it. He says to them,

My Baptist brethren, as well as the Pedobaptist brotherhood, I humbly conceive, require to be admonished on this point. You have been, some of you, no doubt, too different in asserting this grand import of baptism.[18]

Campbell had come to see that baptism was a way into the church, and so declares "that baptism was never designed for, nor commanded to be administered to, a member of the church."[19]

By now Campbell was convinced that debating was really valuable. Throngs of people had come to hear him. His reputation as

---

[18]Alexander Campbell, *Debate on Christian Baptism* (Buffalo: Published by Campbell & Sala, 1824), p. 144.
[19]Alexander Campbell, *Debate on Christian Baptism,* p. 195.

a speaker spread far and wide. Campbell could now see that debate
was worth while. He writes:

There are not a few who deprecate religious controversy as an
evil of no small magnitude. But these are either ill-informed, or
those conscious that their principles will not bear investigation.
So long as there is good and evil, truth and error in this world,
so long will there be opposition; for it is in the nature of good and
evil, of truth and error, to oppose each other. We cheerfully confess that it is much to be regretted that controversy amongst
Christians should exist; but it is more to be regretted that error,
the professed cause of it should exist.[20]

Indeed, these two debates convinced Campbell that "a week's debating is worth a year's preaching."

Meanwhile, Campbell's trouble with the Redstone Association
was continuing, and became increasing clear that something was
going to need to be done. Fortunately, in the summer of 1823,
while preparations were being made for the debate with McCalla,
an opportunity presented itself to do something. The opportunity
came from the Western Reserve, in northeastern Ohio, in the form
of an invitation for the Wellsburgh Church to join the Mahoning
Baptist Association. The leading spirit behind this Association
was Adamson Bentley, a Baptist preacher of Warren, Ohio who
had within more recent years found a decided similarity in his
views and those of Alexander Campbell.

Bentley, after reading the Campbell-Walker debate in 1820, became a great admirer of Campbell's. At this time, he was using
his influence on the Western Reserve to hold annual "minister's
meetings" among the Baptist preachers to discuss the scriptures.
At his suggestion, the Mahoning Baptist Association was born on
August 30, 1820.[21] There was a noticeable difference between
this Association and others of that day. Its general policy was less
tyranical, allowing more freedom among churches than was usual
for that day. Its constitution declared that it did not have authority
over the churches, but that it would recognize the independence
of the congregations. The association claimed to act in an advisory
capacity only, at the same time disclaiming any superiority, jurisdiction or coercive right.

Fortunately, the original records of the Mahoning Baptist As-

[20] Alexander Campbell, *Debate on Christian Baptism*, p. vi.
[21] A. S. Hayden, *History of the Disciples in the Western Reserve* (Cincinnati: Chase & Hall, 1875), p. 25.

sociation are still in existence. The original records were given by John Rudolph in the winter of 1875-76 to B. A. Hinsdale, president of Hiram College. Hinsdale turned them over to the college on September 17, 1888 where they are still kept. We give below the first six articles in the constitution that the general policy and character of the Association may be seen.

First. Our object is to glorify God. This we would endeavor to do by urging the importance of the doctrine And Precepts of the gospel in their Moral and evangelical nature commending ourselves to every man's conscience in the sight of God—not Pretending to Halve Atharity over any man nor over the churches whose representatives form this Association. But we act as an advisory council only. Disclaiming all Superiority, Jurisdiction, coersive Right and Infallibility and acknowledging the Independence of every church which has received Authority from Christ to Perform all Duties enjoined respecting the government of His Church in this world—

Second. The utility of an Association Appears in many respects as the obtaining a more general acquaintance with the State of the Churches and giving advice in cases of difficulty: supply destitute churches; and guarding ourselves against innovations which the churches of Christ may expect always to be troubled with, by those who Ly-In Wait to deceive; Acts 15: 2; 6: 24—

Third. The Messengers chosen, and sent to the Association by the Churches, should be judicious, well versed in the scriptures, prudent, men of integrity, and sound in the faith. It is therefore expected that the churches will respect such qualifications, in order that they may be benefitted by the consultation of their Messengers. No church is to send more than three Messengers.

Fourth. With the Messengers the churches are to send letters to the Association. Those letters are to contain the Names of the Messengers from each church, the State of the churches respecting their continuance in the faith, their Number baptised, received by letter, Dismissed, Restored, Excommunicated, Deceised, and their latest number. When any church wants council of the Association, they shall state their cases by Query in their letter by which they may expect the Judgment—

Fifth. The Association to meet annually at such place, and times as shall be determined at their Preceding Session, and continue until the business is finished. The Association to be opened with divine service, after which the letters are to be given in, and read; then a Moderator and Clerk selected. Due care should be taken that a Person of a cool temper be chosen Moderator. Then Business is to be attended to and Minutes thereof made, circular prepared and signed, and a coppy of it sent with the Minutes of the Association to each church in the Union.

Sixth.   All matters are to be determined by a majority of the votes of the Messengers present.

Seventh.   Churches are to be received into the Association by Petetion, setting forth their desire to be admitted, their faith order and willingness to be conformable to the rules of this associated Bobby.   When it is read and the matter ripened for note.   They being found to correspond to the faith and practice of this body of the petition the Moderator declares that such a church is received into the association.   In token of which he gives the Messengers presenting the Petition the right hand of fellowship and bids them take his seat.

From here on, the constitution sets forth the beliefs of the Association.   Article ten declares that baptism is by immersion and not sprinkling or pouring.   Article eleven shows that the proper subject of baptism is the believer.   The thirteenth article shows the first day of the week to be the Lord's Day, the day of worship.

In the summer of 1821 Adamson Bentley and Sidney Rigdon, who at that time was the outstanding orator and preacher for the association, happened to go to Kentucky, and on the way back they stopped by to visit Campbell at Bethany.   They discussed the scriptures all night and the next day Rigdon said that if he had within the last year taught and promulgated from the pulpit one error he had a thousand.[22]

During the summer of 1823, when Campbell saw that the Redstone Association was ready to take action, he became interested in going into the Mahoning Association.   There was also the fact that the McCalla debate was soon coming up, and if Campbell allowed the Redstone Association to take action, it would hurt his influence in this coming discussion.   Accordingly, Alexander Campbell, John Brown and George Young were appointed messengers from the Wellsburg Church to the Mahoning Association.   A statement of belief was drawn up, peculiar in its independence and freedom from creedal verbiage. In August, 1823 the Association meeting was held at Hubbard in Trumbull County, Ohio.   Bentley preached a sermon based upon John 3 : 16, 17.   Following this, the application of the Wellsburg Church was considered and Campbell's group was voted in.

In the fall of 1822 Campbell began to think of giving up Buffalo Seminary.   The published debate with Walker had taught him the

---

[22]A. S. Hayden, *History of the Disciples in the Western Reserve*, p. 19.

power of the press to disseminate his views. So he began thinking of printing a paper. About this time he made the acquaintance of a young preacher from Pittsburgh by the name of Walter Scott. Campbell, in discussing the idea of the paper with Scott, suggested that he wanted to name the paper, "The Christian," but Scott objected. He thought it would be a means of disarming prejudice to call it "The Christian Baptist." In the spring of 1823, Campbell published his "Prospectus" for the proposed paper. In this Campbell said:

"The Christian Baptist" shall espouse the cause of no religious sect, excepting the ancient sect, "called Christians first at antioch." Its sole object shall be the eviction of truth and the exposing of error in doctrine and practice. The editor, acknowledging no standard of religious faith or works other than the Old and New Testament, and the latter as the only standard of the religion of Jesus Christ, will, intentionally at least, oppose nothing which it contains and recommend nothing which it does not enjoin. Having no worldly interest at stake from the adoption or reprobation of any article of faith or religious practice, having no gift nor religious emolument to blind his eyes or to pervert his judgment, he hopes to manifest that he is an impartial advocate of truth.[23]

Campbell bought the type, presses, etc., and erected a building near the creek fording at the base of the cemetery hill. Here, he began publication of the *Christian Baptist,* the first issue of which appeared August 3, 1823.

For seven years the *Christian Baptist* breathed the spirit of iconoclasm. He was harsh and very often bitter in his denunciations of prevalent religious practices. Campbell sought to expose the pride, worldliness and paganism in the churches. He turned his attack against the "kingdom of the clergy," for he believed that the Protestant clergy was as guilty as the Romanish of deluding the people, and holding from them the words of life. Robert Semple, a Virginia Baptist preacher, wrote to Campbell under the title, "Robert Cautious," asking Campbell not be immoderate in his condemnation of evil and reminding him of the danger of "running past Jerusalem, as one hastens out of Babylon."

In spite of his extremities, Campbell's *Christian Baptist* exercised no small influence for good for the restoration. The pages of the paper vibrate with the call for a return to the "ancient order of things." Creeds, confessions of faith, and authoritative councils of

[23]Richardson, *Memoirs of Alexander Campbell,* Vol. II, p. 50.

men are repudiated and the editor launches out alone in his quest
for the way of truth.   Many of his plans began to take more permanent and tangible form.   He saw that partyism, creedalism, and
the power of the clergy must fall. He pled for a return to the church
of the New Testament, and for the destruction of denominationalism.   He writes :

I have no idea of adding to the catalogue of new sects.   This
game has been played too long.   I labor to see sectarianism abolished, and all Christians of every name united upon the one foundation on which the apostolic church was founded.   To bring
Baptists and Paido-baptists to this is my supreme end.   But to
connect myself with any people who would require me to sacrifice
one item of revealed truth, to subscribe any creed of human device,
or to restrain me from publishing my sentiments as discretion and
conscience direct, is now, and I hope ever shall be, the farthest
from my desires, and the most incompatible with my views.[24]

While Campbell did not intend to start a new sect, yet it was not his
idea to bring all the sects together in one group.   He writes :

I have no idea of seeing, nor one wish to see, the sects unite in
one grand army.   This would be dangerous to our liberties and
laws.   For this the Saviour did not pray.   It is only the disciples
of Christ dispersed among them, that reason and benevolence would
call out of them.   Let them unite who love the Lord, and then we
shall soon see the hireling priesthood and their worldly establishments prostrate in the dust.[25]

If the question be asked just how Campbell proposed to restore
the ancient order, it can be answered by saying that he advocated
that men drop things of human origin in religion, and go by the
sacred scriptures.   Accordingly, Campbell writes :

To make a move in the business of restoration, and in returning
to the covenant is, I confess, quite a different thing from speculat-
ing or talking about it ; and yet it only requires an intelligent mind
and a willing heart.   These will direct and embolden every effort.
The people must abandon the language, customs and manners of
Ashdod.   For this purpose they will meet, and read, and examine
the New Covenant writings.   They will also look to Heaven for
wisdom and courage, and as soon as any item of the will of Heaven
is distinctly apprehended, it will be brought into their practice.[26]

[24]Alexander Campbell, "Reply to 'T. T.,'" *Christian Baptist,* Vol. III, No.
7 (February 6, 1826), p. 217.
[25]Alexander Campbell, "A Restoration of the Ancient Order of Things—
No. III," *Christian Baptist,* Vol. II, No. 9 (April 4, 1825), p. 140.
[26]Alexander Campbell, "Reply to Faithful," *Christian Baptist,* Vol. III,
No. 2 (September 5, 1825), p. 185.

Again Campbell says,

But a restoration of the ancient order of things, it appears, is all that is contemplated by the wise disciples of the Lord; as it is agreed that this is all that is wanting to the perfection, happiness, and glory of the Christian community. To contribute to this is our most ardent desire—our daily and diligent inquiry and pursuit. Now, in attempting to accomplish this, it must be observed that it belongs to every individual and to every congregation of individuals to discard from their faith and their practice everything that is not found written in the New Testament of the Lord and Saviour, and to believe and practice whatever is there enjoined. This done, and everything is done which ought to be done.[27]

The *Christian Baptist,* in a few years made many friends, but also many enemies. In spite of the fact Campbell did not want to be a sect his enemies continued to push every way possible to christen him and those of like mind as a sect. Campbell observes,

Some religious editors in Kentucky call those who are desirous of seeing the ancient order of things restored, "the Restorationers," "the Campbellites," and the most reproachful epithets are showered upon them because they have some conscientious regard for the Divine Author and the divine authority of the New Testament.— This may go down very well with some; but all who fear God and keep his commandments will pity and deplore the weakness and folly of those who either think to convince or to persuade by such means.[28]

By 1829, Campbell began to be concerned lest the name "Christian Baptist" be applied as a party name to those advocating restoration. He determined at once to drop the paper, and put this name out of existence. Moreover, his spirit had been bitter, and many of his friends had encouraged him to be more moderate in his condemnation of evil. It was believed best to cease publication of the *Christian Baptist* at the close of 1829, and begin another paper. So, on January 4, 1830 Campbell became the editor of the *Millennial Harbinger.*

The name of this new periodical was particularly significant. Campbell believed in the millennium. His view was that the millennium was a period of time when "the nations of this world are all to become the kingdoms of our King—they are all to submit to his government, and to feel the benign and blissful in-

[27]Alexander Campbell, "A Restoration of the Ancient Order of Things— No. II," *Christian Baptist,* Vol. II, No. 8 (March 7, 1825), p. 133.
[28]Alexander Campbell, "A Good 'Christening,'" *Christian Baptist,* Vol. IV, No. 4 (November 6, 1826)), p. 288.

fluence of his sceptre."[29]   Campbell believed that eventually Christianity would triumph over the whole world and the influence of Christ would be preeminent.   But, Campbell also believed that "the sectarian establishments could not admit of this spread and triumph of Christianity."   Therefore, the only way to have the millennium was to restore the ancient order, and in addition, to destroy sectarianism in all its forms.   In view of this Campbell wrote in the "prospectus" for the *Harbinger:*

This work shall be devoted to the destruction of Sectarianism, Infidelity and Antichristian doctrine and practice.   It shall have for its object the development, and introduction of that political and religious order of society called THE MILLENNIUM, which will be the consummation of that ultimate amelioration of society proposed in the Christian scriptures. . .[30]

Campbell announced that each number of the *Millennial Harbinger* was to have forty-eight pages.   It was to be printed on "super royal paper," and published on the first Monday of each month.   The cost was two dollars and fifty cents a year.

Meanwhile, step by step the advocates of restoration found themselves being driven farther and farther from Baptist ranks.   Some had begun to doubt the propriety of having such associations.   In Kentucky, the North District Association found Elder John Smith guilty of preaching "Campbellism."   At the meeting of 1827 three charges were veiled at Smith.   He was charged with using Alexander Campbell's translation called "Living Oracles," of saying, "I immerse you," instead of "I baptize you," and of administering the Lord's Supper in a way that he allowed the communicants to break the loaf for themselves.   Without waiting for himself to be singled out, Smith arose and said: "I plead guilty to them all."[31]   Much debating went on and the matter was tabled for another year, but at that time, the majority was favorable to Smith.   Finally, however, in 1830 the Association divided, and those advocating restoration soon dissolved themselves.   J. A. Williams gives this account of the dissolution:

But the main question, which had been held in reserve was now solemnly propounded: "Is there any authority in the Word of God

[29]Alexander Campbell, "Millennium—No. I," *Millennial Harbinger,* Vol. I, No. 2 (February 1, 1830), pp. 53-58.
[30]Alexander Campbell, "Prospectus," *Millennial Harbinger,* Vol. I, No. 1 (January 4, 1830), p. 3.
[31]Errett Gates, *The Early Relation and Separation of Baptists and Disciples* (Chicago: The Christian Century Co., 1904), pp. 70, 71.

for this Association to meet at all?" After some debate, in which nothing was said or done to give offense, they finally, and with much unanimity, resolved:

No church requesting the next Association to be appointed at any of their meeting houses, and this body not having authority to force it upon any; and every church which appeared here by her letter and messengers unanimously agreeing that the word of God is the only rule of faith and practice for Christians—on motion and second, that the Constitution of the North District Association of Baptists be dissolved—after consultation among the brethren, when the question was put, it was carried in the affirmative; and the said Association was thereby dissolved. Upon after consultation, the brethren agree to attend at Sharpsburg, at the request of her messengers in the name of the church, on Friday before the third Saturday, and the days following, in August, 1832, and there communicate with one another, either by letter or otherwise, such information respecting the progress and affairs of each church as they may think of sufficient importance of interest to communicate.[32]

Within the Bracken Association, the Licking Association and that of Boones' Creek, the story was the same: the Regular Baptists would become "corrupted" by the influence of the teachings of Campbell. The Association would divide, and that part made up of the Advocates of restoration would soon dissolve itself.

In 1830 the Mahoning Association met in the church edifice in Austintown on the Western Reserve. The meeting opened with songs, exhortations, and prayers. John Henry, one of the preachers, stood up and said: "I charge you to look out what you are about to do here: we want nothing here which the word of the Lord will not sanction." He sat down and in a moment suggested the resolution that the Association be dissolved, and it was carried. Commenting later, Campbell said:

Such a meeting was not witnessed in the memory of any present, as was the late meeting of churches in Austintown. The first day, Friday, was spent in declaring the wonders which God had wrought in various portions of the Western Reserve by the restoration of the ancient gospel. Songs of praise and tears of joy mingled with these reports, translated us nigher the regions of bliss than we had ever before approached. The next day, finding no business to transact, no inquiries to answer, nothing to do but "to love, and wonder, and adore," it was *unanimously* agreed that the Mahoning Association as "an advisory council," as "an ecclesiastical tribunal,"

---

[32]John A. Williams, *Life of Elder John Smith* (Cincinnati: Christian Standard Publishing Co., 1904), pp. 416, 417.

exercising any supervision or jurisdiction over particular congregations, should never meet again. This Association came to its end as tranquilly as ever did a good old man whose attenuated thread of life, worn to a hair's breadth, dropped asunder by its own imbecility

"Night dews fall not more gently to the ground,
        Nor weary worn out winds expire more soft,"
than did this Association give up the ghost.[33]

Few men were capable of doing as much work as Campbell during his years of the prime of his life. He was constantly traveling, preaching and speaking before clubs and societies. His reputation as a speaker spread far and wide, and his services were in demand. Added to this is the activity which occasionally arose of engaging in debates upon his views.

In February, 1828 Campbell received a letter from an individual in Canton, Ohio, bewailing the advances of infidelity. The man asked Campbell to come and meet a person who was spreading the tenets of Skepticism in that city. Campbell refused saying he would not draw a bow until he could shoot at the king of the skeptics himself. That opportunity was soon to present itself, for Robert Owen, champion of Skepticism, had delivered a series of lectures in New Orleans, and challenged the clergy for a debate. Campbell published the challenge in the *Christian Baptist* and announced his acceptance of it. In a few weeks Owen came to Bethany to make plans for the discussion.

Robert Owen was a brilliant man, born at New Wales in 1769. At the age of eighteen he had become a partner in a cotton mill. He was successful and arose rapidly in the business world. He became head of the New Lanark Mills of Glasgow, employing over two thousand persons. He entered upon many benevolent projects to improve the working classes, and soon himself became quite wealthy. He began visiting foreign countries, delivering speeches. Unfortunately, the good he advocated was mixed with evil, for in addition to wanting to improve the social system, he fought Christianity, as standing opposed to all progress.

Campbell met him in debate in the largest Methodist church house in the city of Cincinnati. Campbell's moderators were judge Jacob Burnet, former mayor of the city; Major Daniel Gano, and

[33]Alexander Campbell, "Mahoning Association," *Millennial Harbinger,* Vol. I, No. 9 (September 6, 1830), pp. 414, 415.

Col. Samuel W. Davis. The debate started on Monday, April 13, 1829, and with the exception of Sunday, continued over the twenty-first. The attendance was so large that many couldn't get in, and had to return home. On the last day there were twelve hundred present.

Eight years later Campbell spoke before the College of Teachers at Cincinnati. This was really an association of those who either were teachers or had been. The group met on October 3, and Dr. Joshua L. Wilson spoke, recommending the Bible as a universal text-book. In a subsequent lecture, Bishop Purcell of the Roman Catholic diocese in the city spoke and denied this. Campbell spoke on "Moral Culture," connecting the rapid march of modern improvement with the Spirit of inquiry produced by the Protestant Reformation. Purcell took exception, saying the Protestant Reformation was the cause of all the infidelity in the world. Campbell told Purcell if he wished a discussion, that he, Campbell, was prepared. At the same time he announced that he would speak on Monday evening at the Sycamore Street Church on the subject. The evening following, he spoke at Wesley Chapel, and gave six propositions which he declared he would defend against Purcell. The debate began on Friday night, January 13, 1837.

The next of Campbell's great debates was with N. L. Rice in the fall of 1843. While in Kentucky in 1842, the Presbyterians greeted Campbell, appearing to be favorable to a debate. A long correspondence was held, and, in August, 1843, final arrangements were made for the debate. Campbell's opponent was to have been Professor Young of Centre College, but he became ill, and N. L. Rice of Paris, Kentucky was chosen. Campbell, knowing something of Rice's bitter spirit, did not like the selection, but was forced to comply. The debate began on Wednesday, November 15, 1843 in the Reformed Church at Lexington, and lasted for sixteen days.

In the year, 1841, Campbell added to his busy program that of becoming president of a College. Bethany College opened its doors that fall. Campbell was president of a college, editor of a paper, preacher, lecturer, and in a short time, president of a missionary society.

Of Campbell's later activities there shall be occasion to give a more detailed account later. It is enough to get this brief background before launching into the details that will follow.

Chapter V

EARLY PIONEER PREACHERS

Theatrical performances, dramas and plays must necessarily be preceded by an introduction to the characters who will perform. Across the stage of Time the drama of the restoration movement was enacted through most of the nineteenth century. The characters of this drama likewise need to be introduced to prepare our minds for the story they so well enacted. There is a romance about their lives and an inspiration gained from them. Their names adorn the pages of the history of the church and add a glorious lustre to the events of the previous century. One may well imagine that he is entering a great "Hall of Fame" of the restoration. All around the side there stands in imagination men like Walter Scott, W. K. Pendleton, David S. Burnet, Tolbert Fanning, Benjamin Franklin, Jacob Creath, Jr. Being dead, yet they speak, but their story can only be briefly told here.

Next to Thomas and Alexander Campbell the most celebrated leader of the restoration was Walter Scott, the announcer of the "Golden Oracle" whose eloquence stirred the Western Reserve in 1827 and 1828 as nothing else had ever done. In personal appearance, in pulpit speaking, in type of mind Scott was the antithesis of Campbell, yet he supplemented Campbell in many ways. Campbell was tall, vigorous and athletic whereas Scott was of average height and slender. The disposition of Campbell was always cheerful, but Scott was meditative and sad very frequently. Campbell's face had no straight lines. His nose was arched a little to the right. His hair was light in color. Scott, on the other hand, had a straight nose, full lips, dark eyes and hair as black as a raven's wing. Campbell's mind loved to dwell upon great principles. Scott's mind was analytical. It would take Scott's mind, not Campbell's, to think of the gospel as containing facts, commands, promises. But it would take Campbell's mind, not Scott's, to see in the promise of God to Abraham the germ of the two covenants with all their implications.

Walter Scott was a great preacher, but withal had many eccentricities, as the following account will show:

76

WALTER SCOTT

Brother Walter Scott took great care of his voice. His mind was greatly under its influence. If the instrument was in perfect tune, how admirably he could play upon it! When out of tune, he was as weak as Sampson when shorn of his hair. Dear Walter! he was a great dyspeptic; and like all such persons, at times eccentric. He would change his diet to keep his voice, and consequently, his mind, in working order. Sometimes he would drink coffee, and then tea, and then water; and now and then milk. He was taking supper once with a good sister who had heard of his fondness for milk (he had just laid aside the lacteal diet and had gone back to coffee and tea), when she said, "Brother Scott, will you have a glass of milk?" "I thank you, sister. There is no music in a cow," said Walter, in his blandest way. Of course he thought that milk was injurious to his voice.[1]

[1] James Challen, "Memorabilia," *Christian Standard,* Vol. V, No. 15 (April 9, 1870), p. 113.

Robert Richardson, Campbell's biographer, compares Scott and Campbell in the following words:

Thus, while Mr. Campbell was fearless, self-reliant and firm, Mr. Scott was naturally timid, diffident and yielding; and, while the former was calm, steady and prudent, the latter was excitable, variable and precipitate. The one like the North Star was ever in position, unaffected by terrestrial influences; the other, like the magnetic needle, was often disturbed and trembling on its centre, yet ever returning or seeking to return to its true direction. Both were nobly endowed with the powers of higher reason—a delicate self-consciousness, a decided will and a clear perception of truth. But, as it regards the other departments of the inner nature, in Mr. Campbell the understanding predominated, in Mr. Scott, the feelings; and, if the former excelled in imagination, the latter was superior in brilliancy of fancy. If the tendency of one was to generalize, to take wide and extended views and to group a multitude of particulars under a single head or principle, that of the other was to analyze, to divide subjects into their particulars and consider their details. If the one was disposed to trace analogies and evolve the remotest correspondences of relations, the other delighted in comparisons and sought for the resemblancies of things. If the one possessed the inducive power of the philosopher the other had in a more delicate musical faculty and more active ideality, a larger share of the attributes of the poet. In a word, in almost all those qualities of mind and character which might be regarded differential or distinctive, they were singularly fitted to supply each other's wants and to form a rare and delightful companionship.[2]

William Baxter, Scott's biographer, compares Campbell and Scott in the following words:

Campbell was always great and self-possessed; Scott subject to great depression, and, consequently, unequal in his public efforts: but at times he knew a rapture, which seemed almost inspiration, to which the former was a stranger. Campbell never fell below the expectations of his hearers, Scott frequently did; but there were times when he rose to a height of eloquence which the former never equalled. If Campbell at times reminded his hearers of Paul on Mars Hill, commanding the attention of the assembled wisdom of Athens; Scott, in his happiest moments, seemed more like Peter on the Memorable Pentecost, with cloven tongue of flame on his head, and the inspiration of the Spirit of Truth in his heart, while from heart-pierced sinners on every side rose the agonizing cry, "Men and brethren, what shall we do?"[3]

[2]Robert Richardson, *Memoirs of Alexander Campbell* (Cincinnati: Standard Publishing Co., 1897), Vol. I, pp. 510, 511.
[3]William Baxter, *Life of Elder Walter Scott* (Cincinnati: Bosworth, Chase & Hall, 1874), pp. 338, 339.

On another occasion, Baxter made the following comparison:

Scott's power, however, was over the hearts of men, of the masses; his dark eyes seemed to penetrate the secrets of the soul, and his voice was soothing or terrible as he gave utterance to the promises or threatenings of the word of God. Multitudes were awakened under his preaching to the peril of their souls, and pointed successfully to the Lamb of God, and on some occasions bitter enemies and violent persecutors were changed, almost as suddenly as Saul of Tarsus, and became not only faithful Christains, but firm and life-long friends of the preacher whom they once had threatened and reviled.

Campbell's greatness and strength may in a great measure be realized by a careful study of his writings; but the noblest efforts of his worthy fellow-laborer, as far as the expression is concerned, perished almost at their birth, they could not be reproduced by either speaker or hearer; the impression made on the minds and hearts of those who heard him, will never fade until all things else shall fade. But the tablets on which those memories dear and sweet are written, are perishable, and when the present generation passes, or rather when the remnant of those who heard him in his prime which yet lingers shall have passed away, the world will not know anything save by dim and imperfect tradition of the wonderful eloquency of this gifted, the princely man. I claim not to have set him faithfully as he seemed to me and the thousands who heard him, but these few fragments, imperfect as they are, will give some idea of the man; and while we can safely entrust the fame of Alexander Campbell to the proofs which his writings afford of his great, his eminent abilities, yet, at the same time, we cannot forbear laying this humble, heartfelt tribute upon the tomb of Walter Scott.[4]

Walter Scott was born in Moffat, Dumfriesshire, Scotland on October 31, 1796. His father was John Scott, a man of fine character, noble culture, whose occupation was that of a music teacher. His mother, Mary Innes Scott, was a gracious lady of great piety whose highest ambition for her son, Walter, was that he should be a minister in the Scotch Presbyterian Church of which she was a devoted member. She was a tender-hearted lady. In June, 1821 when her husband took a trip to Annan and suddenly died there, the grief of Mary Innes was so great that she followed him within a month in death.

Mary Innes had a brother, George, who had left Scotland a few years before to seek his fortune in America. George was ambitious

---

[4]William Baxter, "Alexander Campbell and Walter Scott as Preachers," *Christian Standard*, Vol. IV, No. 24 (June 12, 1869), p. 185.

that all of his relatives should follow him, and to this end, he worked and saved his money. One day, he wrote his sister to send him one of her sons. The parents considered and decided to send Walter. There was a reason for this decision. Walter Scott had proved to be alert and capable, and accordingly had been sent to the University of Edinburgh. He had the better education and was more capable of making a success in America. So it was decided to send Walter. George was working in New York City for the government in the customs house. Walter prepared to go to his uncle. He sailed from Greenock in the late spring of 1818 and landed in New York on July 7, 1818.

Soon after landing in New York, Scott secured a position as a Latin teacher in a classical academy at Jamaica, Long Island. But Scott was not destined to stay long in New York. The "West" was beckoning, and immigrants were continually moving from New York to the new lands and new opportunities out along the Ohio River. Scott caught the fever, and before long he prepared to go. He, with a companion, walked the distance from New York to Pittsburgh in the spring of 1819 and arrived in the city on May 7, 1819.

After his arrival in Pittsburgh, Scott first turned his attention toward a position for livelihood. Naturally he thought of teaching. He learned of a George Forrester who was a preacher and a principal of an academy. Before long, he had secured a position teaching under Forrester. Both Forrester and Scott were devoutly religious. Forrester, it appeared to Scott, was a peculiar person in that he rejected all human creeds, and purported to take the Bible alone for his religious guide. This appealed to Scott. With Forrester as his teacher Scott sat for hour after hour examining the holy oracles to come to a fuller knowledge of the word of God. Gradually the light dawned, and Scott began to see in some measure the glory and beauty of the ancient religion of the New Testament Church. He was convinced. But what should he do about baptism? He would study and see. It did not take him long to see that infant baptism was unauthorized in the scriptures, and that sprinkling or pouring were unknown to the Bible. Accordingly, Scott was immersed by Forrester.

The church for which Forrester preached met in those days in the courthouse. Most of the members were of Scotch descent and

carried with them much of the Scotch strictness. While the church
wanted to hold fast the form of sound words, yet in many ways it
went to extremes. The "holy kiss" was regularly practiced as well
as feet washing. In matters of discipline, they were most strict.
Any young lady who appeared in worship wearing costly apparel
or jewelry and ornaments could expect a public rebuke. The elders
of the church looked upon marriage outside of the church as a
scandal. If a man married a wife, no matter how good she might
be morally; if she were not a member of the church, the man was
rebuked in the presence of his wife and compelled to confess he was
sorry for the marriage. It probably was some comfort to the wife
to hear him say he would never do such a thing again.

At any rate, to this little church Scott went regularly to hear
Forrester. This went on until Forrester drowned while bathing in
the Allegheny River, and Scott had to take his place as public pro-
claimer. Meanwhile, Scott had taken over the Academy. Robert
Richardson and Samuel Church were two of his illustrious students.
His rules for the classroom were obedience, order, accuracy. He
believed in exercising as little discipline as possible, but continued
to keep his rules ever before his students, trusting their honor to
keep them.

Scott, in the meantime, had continued studying the Bible. His
mind was toying with the subject of baptism. He felt there was a
significance attached to it that he had not yet discovered. A tract
on the subject came suddenly into his hands from a Scotch Baptist
Church of New York City. Scott was impressed, so much so that
he left Pittsburgh for New York to study the matter further. But
he was disappointed. In Pittsburgh, meanwhile, his absence was
felt. The wealthy Richardson family wanted Scott back at the
academy and sent letters urging him to return, and return he did.

His mind was yet unsettled on some points, so he continued to
study. Soon after returning to Pittsburgh the idea took hold of
him that the great central idea of the Christian religion was the
Messiahship of Christ. Jesus is the Son of God! This idea Scott
soon called the "Golden Oracle." He continued to study the Bible
diligently, and made the vow that if God would give him a comprehensive view of the Bible, he would subordinate all other work
to the preaching of the gospel.

The winter of 1821-22 Scott was still teaching in Pittsburgh.

It was at this time that Scott first met Alexander Campbell. He and Campbell soon began to discuss their religious views, and both were surprised to find they occupied very similiar ground. Each recognized in the other qualities of superior nature. Through Alexander Campbell Scott became acquainted with Thomas Campbell.

During this time, both Campbell and Scott were pondering the purpose of baptism as set forth in the Scriptures. Both of them had arrived at a conclusion radical for the day that baptism, as set forth in the New Testament, was for the remission of sins. Campbell, in his debate with Walker in 1820, only hinted at the idea there. Scott could not help but have the same conclusion, but neither man was disposed to push the matter until it was necessary. That necessity was supplied in 1823 when Campbell received a challenge from W. L. McCalla of Washington, Kentucky for a debate. Soon after getting the challenge, Campbell resolved to go over the whole subject again. But, at this time, Scott paid a visit to Bethany, and Thomas Campbell brought up the subject for them to discuss it. Alexander Campbell tells of the occasion in his own words:

Immediately on receiving a challenge from Mr. Wm. L. M'Calla, of Kentucky, May 17, 1823, I resolved to settle the true meaning of baptism before I ever debated the subject again. To examine this matter I went to my Testament with the zeal of a freshman. Mr. Thomas Campbell and myself discussed this matter at considerable length for some months. It was not named to a third person till July or August following, when brother Walter Scott made his first visit to my residence. During his stay my father informed him, in my presence, of the contemplated debate, and stated at considerable length the views of baptism which we had agreed to offer on the occasion. As it had not been divulged to any other person, I was anxious for the judgment of one whom I so highly esteemed on account of his knowledge of the Holy Scriptures, and waited for his opinion with much interest. He gave it upon the whole in favor of the views offered; and more than once during his stay recommended the importance of giving such a view in the approaching discussion.[5]

By the spring of 1823 Campbell had determined to publish a paper. He was prone to call it, "The Christian," but Scott convinced him of the lack of wisdom in this decision. It was Scott's

---

[5] Alexander Campbell, "Events of 1823 and 1827," *Millennial Harbinger,* New Series, Vol. II, No. 10 (October, 1838), p. 468.

view that to call it "The Christian Baptist" would disarm prejudice among the Baptists. Campbell acquiesced, and the new periodical took this name. Scott himself agreed to present articles for publication. He conceived of his relation to Alexander Campbell as the same Philip Melanchthon bore to Martin Luther in the Reformation. Under the title of "Philip" Scott wrote his articles. The first one to appear was "A Divinely Authorized Plan of Teaching the Christian Religion."

On January 3, 1823 Scott had married Miss Sarah Whitsett who lived a few miles from Pittsburgh. Scott was now twenty-six years old. He was rather handsome, but a meditative and melancholy youth. Three years later, he determined to move his family from Pittsburgh to Steubenville, Ohio. The purpose of this move is uncertain; perhaps it was to get close to Bethany, the home of his friend, Alexander Campbell. That same summer he attended the meeting of the Mahoning Baptist Association held on the Western Reserve. He went only as a visitor and an observer, but on Lord's Day was invited to speak. So eloquently did he present his lesson that many thought he was Alexander Campbell. Scott probably did not imagine that in just one year he would be chosen as Evangelist for the Association.

Soon after arriving in Steubenville Scott opened up an Academy. In the summer of 1827 Alexander Campbell was on his way to New Lisbon on the Western Reserve to attend the annual meeting of the Mahoning Association. He went by Steubenville on the way to convince Scott to accompany him. Campbell, through young Jacob Osborne, had an idea that an Evangelist was to be appointed. To him Walter Scott was the logical man for that work. Campbell writes:

In 1827 I had the pleasure of prevailing upon brother Scott, then engaged in teaching a school in Steubenville, Ohio, to accompany me to the Western Reserve, where, by my frequent visits in that direction, the Mahoning Association were almost to a man on the side of going forward to the ancient and primitive order of things. The churches had, however, as yet done nothing but change their theory and resolve to go forward. A request to have an Evangelist appointed, came, if I remember right, from the before mentioned brother Osborne, then a resident in that district, or from a church which he had induced to make such a

request. We all went to work in good earnest, and brother Scott
was appointed and accepted of the work.[6]

After becoming the Association's Evangelist, Scott's first sermon was delivered in the Baptist Church at New Lisbon in Colum-
biana County. When he arrived on Sunday, every seat in the
meeting house was taken. Soon many were standing and the
aisles and the door were jammed with people. Scott preached on
Matt. 16: 16. A very peculiar circumstance occurred. A devout
man in the community, William Amend, had long before come to
the conclusion that repentance and baptism were essential to salvation, as announced by Peter in Acts 2: 38. He had further
declared his intention to obey the gospel the first time he heard
a man teach that way. On the day Scott was preaching, Amend
was late arriving. Outside the packed door, he suddenly heard
Scott's first sentence which was a quotation of Acts 2: 38. Amend
pushed his way through the crowd and went down to the front
and made known his intentions to obey the gospel. This was
November 18, 1827.

Scott's work on the Western Reserve thus got off to a great
start. Amend's conversion soon influenced more. Many heard
the gospel for the first time and obeyed it. Opposition was aroused.
A woman requested baptism, but her son threatened to shoot
Scott if he baptized her. The sects were aroused, names were
called, challenges were issued. There was great excitement.
Scott was in demand everywhere. New Lisbon, Deerfield, Austintown, Warren—Scott traveled and conversions were rapidly
made. Scott, to get closer to his work, moved to Canfield.
Thomas Campbell came to observe Scott's work, and report on it
to Alexander Campbell. For two years this work went on and
the people were stirred up as nothing had stirred them before.

In 1831 Scott paid a visit to Cincinnati which was then the
"Queen City" of the west. James Challen was then the preacher
for the church. Challen was disposed to make a move, and it
it was agreed that Scott should follow him. While in Cincinnati,
Scott became ill with dyspepsia. His pulpit efforts were on the
whole very inferior. The church didn't grow. Scott grew discouraged. He wrote to Louisiana asking Challen to come back.

---

[6]Alexander Campbell, "Events of 1823 and 1827," *Millennial Harbinger,*
New Series, Vol. II, No. 10 (October, 1838)), p. 469.

Challen came back, and for a time, he and Scott worked together in Cincinnati.

January, 1832 Scott began the publication of a paper he called, "The Evangelist." About this time he moved to Carthage, Ohio, and began preaching for the small church. There were few results, and Scott grew discouraged. He blamed himself, and thought the people didn't like him. He determined to find out. John T. Johnson, Benjamin Finnell, John O'Kane, Love H. Jameson, and B. U. Watkins were invited to come to Carthage and help out in a gospel meeting. They came. Johnson and O'Kane did the preaching. For several days the meeting dragged on, and there were few responses. Finally Scott stood up and spoke. He told the people that he had preached as best he could and there were no responses. Concluding it was his fault, he had gotten others to preach, and still they would not respond. He wondered how they could sit back and listen to the preaching they had without being touched. What was the matter with them? Some of the visiting preachers thought Scott had ruined the meeting, but he didn't. Conversions started coming and there were thirty or forty before the meeting closed.

In 1835 Scott discontinued publishing the *Evangelist* in order to give himself time to write the book, the "Gospel Restored" which he published in 1836. In January, 1838 he resumed publishing the *Evangelist*.

Scott moved back to Pittsburgh in 1844 and found himself soon appointed an elder in the church. He set to work to publish another paper which he called the *Protestant Unionist*. A great fire swept through Pittsburgh on Thursday, April 10, 1845 and burned up his printing office. For the next few years, however, Scott continued his preaching in Pittsburgh.

On April 28, 1849, Scott's wife died, and the next year he married Annie B. Allen of Mayslick, Kentucky. About this time, the Baptists moved out of a school in Covington, Kentucky and Walter Scott started a Female Academy. This Academy he kept going for several years. In July, 1855, Tolbert Fanning visited Cincinnati and with Benjamin Franklin went to see Scott at Covington College "of which he is at present proprietor."[7]

---

[7]Tolbert Fanning, "Tour North," *Gospel Advocate,* Vol. I, No. 3 (September, 1855), p. 71.

Scott's second wife died in 1854, and Scott married a rich widow, Eliza Sandige, of Mason County, Kentucky. This marriage was never congenial. Scott had no appreciation of money. He was so tender in heart that he gave away nearly all he ever made. Often he would go to a store for a basket of groceries, and give them all away before he got home. Once he had two cows and he gave a neighbor one cow, because the neighbor had none. Scott's third wife was not accustomed to such handling of funds. Overlooking the greatness in Scott's soul, she would storm at him and run him out of the house. Often he spent the night sitting on the door step of a neighbor. Once she ran him off from home. Several days later he was found walking the streets of Cincinnati in a daze.

About this time Scott began work on a new book which he was to call "The Messiahship, or Great Demonstration." This was his most elaborate effort at writing and was the last attempt he made. Scott explained the book in a letter addressed to Ben Franklin:

Dear Sir: Today I initiated the stereotyping of a volume to be entitled, "The Messiahship, or Great Demonstration." It will contain four hundred pages, more or less—the page containing 1705 ems which will give a great deal of reading in the whole book. It will be sold in retail at one dollar per copy.

The volume is intended to convey the reader into a field of thought and meditation lying somewhat beyond the domain of first principles, and I hope it has a freshness that will make it acceptable to him.

It can be brought out only at great expense, and as it is the fruit of much labor, much thought and some research—above all, as it has been got up for the particular benefit of my brethren, it would afford me unspeakable pleasure would they purchase it. . .[8]

While many widely praised the book, in reality it was a disappointment to both Scott and the brotherhood. Moses E. Lard's appraisal of Scott as a writer may appear to be harsh, but probably it is the most accurate appraisal of all. Lard wrote:

As a writer, we must in candor say we think Bro. Scott simply a failure. Such, at least, is the opinion we have felt compelled to form of the work which he evidently intended to be his masterpiece—The Great Demonstration. As a book, it is too common

---

[8]Walter Scott, "A New Book," *American Christian Review*, Vol. II, No. 5 (February 1, 1859), p. 18.

for the learned reader, and too learned for the common reader. It clearly disappointed both its author and the brotherhood.[9]

Walter Scott was now growing old. On October 31, 1860, he passed his sixty-fourth birthday. Since becoming a citizen of the United States, he had always had a great interest in his country's welfare. In politics he was a democrat yet he did not fail to see the good in men of the other party. With a heavy heart in the fall of 1860 Scott watched the trend toward Civil War. He had friends in both the North and the South that he knew would be affected. That summer he had written an essay called the "Crisis" which was an effort to check the feelings coming up between the states. Scott went to church, but the burden of a divided land and the hatred that existed between brethren was such that he refused to take the communion. What good was the Lord's Supper in a land torn by such strife? During the last quarter of 1860, Scott refused all efforts to get him to speak. Only once did he respond, and that was on Lord's Day, January 27, 1861. His few remarks were upon the state of the nation, and then he encouraged brethren to try to avoid the conflict. He very quickly sat down. In the fall of 1860 he addressed a letter to his oldest son, John, then thirty-seven years of age and expressed his tremendous grief at the state of the nation. When the news of the fall of Fort Sumter reached him, he wrote again of his terrible remorse at such a catastrophe.

Broken badly in heart and soul with the country's evils, Scott, on Tuesday, April 16—three days after the fall of the federal fortress in 1861—became seriously ill. The doctor called it typhoid pneumonia. Quickly it grew worse, and by the next Sunday, Scott realized that the end was now in sight. Elder John Rogers was in the vicinity and stopped by to converse with his old friend. L. P. Streator, another of the preachers nearby, came to pay him a visit. Scott was dwelling in the land of memory, reliving the moments when he preached the gospel with such force and success on the Western Reserve. He spoke of the great honor which God had bestowed upon him to let him develop the kingdom of God among men. On Tuesday night at ten o'clock, he passed quietly away.

---

[9]Moses E. Lard, "A Monument to Walter Scott," *Lard's Quarterly*, Vol. II, No. 2 (January, 1865), p. 133.

John Rogers and L. P. Streator preached the funeral, and then Streator immediately wrote to Alexander Campbell the news. His letter, dated April 25, two days after Scott's death, told of the severe attack of typhoid pneumonia which in seven days brought on the termination of Scott's life. Campbell received the news with great sorrow and wrote:

No death in my horizon, out of my own family, came more unexpectedly or more ungratefully to my ears than this of our much beloved and highly appreciated brother Walter Scott; and none awoke more tender sympathies and regrets. Next to my Father, he was my most cordial and indefatigable fellow laborer in the origin and progress of the present reformation. We often took counsel together in our efforts to plead and advocate the paramount claims of original and apostolic Christianity. His whole heart was in the work. He was, indeed, truly eloquent in the whole import of that word in pleading the claims of the Author and Founder of the Christian faith and hope; and in disabusing the inquiring mind of all its prejudices, misapprehensions and errors. He was, too, most successful in winning souls to the allegiance of the Divine Author and Founder of the Christian institution, and in putting to silence the cavilings and objections of the modern Pharisees and Sadducees of Sectariandom.

He, indeed, possessed, upon the whole view of his character, a happy temperament. It is true, though not a verb, he had his moods and tenses, as men of genius generally have. He was both logical and rhetorical in his conceptions and utterances. He could and he did simultaneously address and interest the understanding, the conscience, and the hearts of his hearers; and in his happiest seasons constrain their attention and their acquiescence. . . .

I knew him well. I knew him long. I love him much. We might not, indeed, agree in every opinion nor in every point of expediency. But we never loved each other less, because we did not acquiesce in every opinion, and in every measure. By the eye of faith and the eye of hope, methinks I see him in Abraham's bosom.[10]

But of all words written about Walter Scott by his contemporaries there perhaps was no encomium truer and more beautiful than that penned by Moses E. Lard. Lard writes:

We have not yet met the man of earth we loved more tenderly than gentle Walter Scott. He was himself a poem, great and small, sublime and tame; but with a spirit as pure and aims as

---

[10]Alexander Campbell, "Elder Walter Scott's Demise," *Millennial Harbinger,* Series V, Vol IV, No. 5 (May, 1861), p. 296.

high as ever fall to the lot of men. With a mind singularly formed for large generalization, he yet combined traits strangely weak, while with an utterance rich even up to a gorgeousness, he would still mingle sayings insipid as those of a housemaid. In two respects only did Walter Scott never become a common man—in profound, exhausting admiration for the Saviour, and in the love of truth. Here he will never be excelled. In thought he was strong, eccentric, and not always safe; in expression, antithetic and unnatural, but at times tender and sweet as the genius of Burns. As a preacher, he was generally to a high degree instructive and pleasing; at times positively enchanting; then again common-place as a plodding field-hand. He affected new modes of combining old truths, and new forms of speech for familiar thoughts, to an extent that lent a frequent charm to oratory, which, otherwise, would have been pronounced inelegant. . . [11]

WILLIAM KIMBROUGH PENDLETON

One of the most influential of the pre-Civil War preachers and pioneer leaders was W. K. Pendleton. Certainly there were few more talented than he. He had a broad cultural background and an educated mind that enjoyed to its fullest the finer productions in literature and learning. J. W. McGarvey once spoke of Pendleton as "one of the clearest headed men he had ever known."[12] McGarvey had met Pendleton when the former entered Bethany College in 1847. Very often did he have private counsels with his teacher. Consequently, McGarvey said that on a great many of the important questions he had been forced to consider he had been influenced by Pendleton's private counsel more so than that of any man. Pendleton, in his manners was always dignified, courteous and graceful. He was rarely known to get unduly excited. His broad knowledge and calm, deliberate consideration of every issue made him a natural leader in the earlier days of the restoration.

Pendleton was born of the old Virginia aristocrats. His father was Edmund Pendleton and his mother was Unity Yancey Kimbrough. His ancestral history reads of heroic achievements and strong courageous leadership. His mother was an Episcopalian, but his father claimed no religious affiliation until about 1833 when

[11]Moses E. Lard, "A Monument to Walter Scott," *Lard's Quarterly,* Vol. II, No. 2 (January, 1865), p. 133.
[12]J. W. McGarvey, "W. K. Pendleton," *Christian Standard,* Vol. XXXV, No. 37 (September 16, 1899), p. 1193.

W. K. PENDLETON

he became intensely interested in the writings of Alexander Campbell. After being baptized, he continued to plead the cause of restoration. When young Pendleton was an infant, his parents moved from Yanceyville out to a home built by his great grandfather, Henry Pendleton. The name of this old home was, oddly enough, "Cuckoo."

When W. K. Pendleton was thirteen, he and his younger brother entered the school of Jeremiah C. Harris who in those days was looked upon as the "prince of the pedagogues." After finishing here, Pendleton went to a classical academy conducted by W. G. Nelson. After a few sessions here, he entered the school of David Richardson, a teacher of mathematics and astronomy. From here, Pendleton enrolled in the University of Virginia to put the finishing touches on his education.

Across the front of one of the stateliest buildings at the University of Virginia were printed these words: "You shall know the truth and the truth shall make you free." Pendleton was one of two hundred and sixty-five students who looked at these words in the fall of 1836 upon enrolling in school. He began a study of law as he dreamed of becoming one of Virginia's great statesmen.

Two years before Pendleton attended the University, his father and mother, and his older brother, Madison, all had become interested in the writings of Alexander Campbell and were baptized. They formed the nucleus of a small congregation near Cuckoo called Mount Gilboa in Louisa County. It was only natural that while W. K. Pendleton was in the University, he should devote some of his time to reading the *Millennial Harbinger* as well as some of the older copies of the *Christian Baptist*. These, along with the Bible, gave him his religious instruction. Until the spring of 1840, then Pendleton continued his study of law at the University, and his search for truth religiously.

It was the custom of Alexander Campbell to travel extensively and preach in addition to editing the *Millennial Harbinger*. His tours took him over a wide range of territory, and very frequently they took him to Virginia. Quite often, Campbell would take one of his daughters with him on these trips. Campbell's daughter, Lavina, was a young lady of great beauty and an unusual buoyant personality. She came with her father to Charlottesville, Virginia in 1838. Pendleton, while a student at the University there, lived with an aunt, Mrs. Lucy Pendleton Vowles. When Campbell and his daughter made their first public appearance in town, Pendleton was at home in bed sick. The boys at the University attended and saw Campbell's daughter. They came to Pendleton's bedside and joked with Pendleton and told him of her beauty. Pendleton joked back, assuring the boys he would get well, meet Lavina, and beat them all out yet. He lived to accomplish this feat.

Pendleton left the University in the spring of 1840 and came back to Louisa County. In June that year he listened to Campbell preach, and was baptized by Campbell near the Mount Gilboa Church. Meanwhile, he had won Lavina's heart and the two were making plans to marry. On October 14, 1840, they were married. The ceremony took place in the Campbell mansion at Bethany—in the same room where Alexander Campbell later died. Warwick Martin performed the ceremony.

By now, Pendleton had reached a crisis in his life. All of his plans and his education pointed toward a career in politics. Too, he had bright prospects in that field. He belonged to the Whig party. In 1840 he acted as a delegate to the Young Men's National Ratification Convention in Baltimore. This convention followed the Whig Convention and was to endorse the nomination of Harrison and Tyler as leaders on the party ticket. Here, Pendleton met and heard Henry Clay and Daniel Webster who were both present. Yet, notwithstanding bright political prospects, Pendleton was feeling the pull from the Campbells. Alexander Campbell recognized the ability of Pendleton. Plans had already been announced that Campbell was to establish a college at Bethany, and Campbell was anxious to have his son-in-law associated with him in this work. And so for a time Pendleton pushed his political interests in the background although he never quite freed his soul from a desire for a place in the political world.

Bethany College opened its doors in the fall of 1841 and Pendleton, along with Robert Richardson, was elected as a teacher in physical sciences. Meanwhile, Pendleton and his wife had moved to their home in Bethany. On Sept. 2, 1841, their first daughter, Campbellina, was born. This is the daughter who in later years was affectionately known as "Miss Cammie." Around his house in Bethany Pendleton cared for his flowers, and in the college, taught his classes. His wife was of frail health, and undoubtedly brought many anxious hours to Pendleton. A few years passed, and she grew worse. On May 29, 1846 she died. The doctors called her trouble consumption. She was twenty-nine years old. Her body was borne to the cemetery at Bethany and laid to rest. On a slab over her remains were inscribed the words:

Beautiful in person, pure in heart, warm in her affections, ardent in her mind and ever ready to do good, her friends might well have prayed the good Lord to lend her a little longer to soothe and lighten the sorrows of earth; but He has taken her where there is fullness of joy, and though we raise this stone to her memory, we know she sleeps not here, but rejoices as an angel in the presence of God.[13]

The Trustees of the College met on August 13, 1845 and elected Pendleton to the office of vice-president. Campbell was gone frequently and the need of someone to take his place in his absence was evident. But during this time, Pendleton himself was sick often with dyspepsia. This, in addition to his wife's illness and his duties around the college, made the passing days more and more difficult. Early in 1846 Pendleton went to Philadelphia to consult a physican, and was advised to take an ocean voyage. Lavina's death that spring probably made the voyage seem more necessary so during that summer, Pendleton went to England. With him went Clarinda, another of Campbell's daughters, and a Mr. and Mrs. Semple of Pittsburgh. He returned from his trip somewhat refreshed.

Pendleton wanted to be released from some of his duties, but found more and more put upon him. In July, 1846, he offered his resignation to the Trustees of Bethany College, but it was promptly refused. Moreover, he was now acting as co-editor of the *Millennial Harbinger,* which position he began in January, 1846. During the months of May to October, 1847, Campbell was in England, and the editing of the *Harbinger* was left entirely to Pendleton. Pendleton now entered a period of intense activity. The paper and the college together allowed him little freedom. Moreover, plans were now developing for the establishment of the American Christian Missionary Society and Pendleton was to figure some in that. He attended the first convention in the fall of 1849 in the absence of Campbell who was sick.

In the summer of 1848 Pendleton had married his second wife. Again he chose a daughter of Campbell—Clarinda. In looks Clarinda was similiar to Lavina, but was quieter and more reserved. This marriage, too, did not last long for in 1850 Clarinda

[13]F. D. Power, *Life of W. K. Pendleton* (St. Louis: Christian Publishing Co., 1902), p. 78.

also died.   Pendleton's third wife was Catherine Huntington King
of Warren, Ohio, whom he married on September 19, 1855.

His work with the college and the paper continued and
as Campbell grew more feeble, Pendleton stepped into his place.
In 1864 Campbell turned the *Harbinger* over to Pendleton who
continued its publication until 1870 when the press of college
duties made it imperative to cease its publication.   After Campbell's
death in 1866, the Trustees elected Pendleton president of the
college which position he held until he was too feeble to continue
it.   From 1869-1870 he served as associate editor with W. T.
Moore of the *Christian Quarterly*.   During a part of this time, at
the request of Isaac Errett, he wrote some for the *Christian
Standard*.   About 1875 he became president of the General Christian Missionary Convention.   In 1884, with advancing age making
the proper fulfillment of his duties impossible, Pendleton resigned
as president of Bethany College.   He was asked, however, to
allow his name to stand as president.   This he did and B. C.
Hagerman was appointed chairman of the faculty for a year.   At
the end of the next year, however, he requested the Trustees to
elect a president, which they did.   W. H. Woolery was elected
and thereafter, Pendleton was listed as president, *emeritus*.

Meanwhile, Pendleton's political interests never lagged.   In 1855
he ran for Congress but was defeated.   In the political campaigns
of 1860 he supported Bell and Everett and ever after was a Democrat.   After the War between the States, when the state of West
Virginia was formed, Pendleton was called upon for active political services.   Both the Democratic and Republican conventions of
his district nominated him to be their representative in the state's
Constitution Convention in 1872.   The following year he was State
Superintendent of Public Schools, which office he held for years.
While Pendleton was acting as State Superintendent of Public
Schools, the Governor of West Virginia requested him to select
and suitably inscribe the West Virginia Memorial Stone for the
Washington Monument in Washington, D. C. This stone may be
found at the two hundred foot landing of the monument.

Pendleton's last years were spent in Florida, although he continued to make trips to Bethany.   In March, 1886, he moved to
Deland.   Shortly after this, he bought an orange grove and small
farm near Eustis.   Here he continued to enjoy his books and

visit with friends who stopped by. It was while he was on a trip back to Bethany that he passed quietly and peacefully away. It was September 1, 1899.

DAVID STAATS BURNET

Another of the influential pre-Civil War preachers was D. S. Burnet. In personal appearance Burnet was a small man, but strong and healthful. His manners were very formal and stiff. He was really a humble man, but his aristocratic dignity often made many think he was proud and haughty. In nature, he was very sensitive. These qualities made him have many enemies that otherwise he might not have had. As a speaker, Burnet was outstanding. He was easy and graceful on the platform and his voice was rich and melodious. But as a writer, he was almost a failure. Although he was for a number of years in the editorial chair, he could not be considered greatly successful. It was as a speaker, and as an organizer that he gained his greatest reputation. In the latter ability he had few equals. He was the leading figure in organizing the Societies that sprang up among the brethren. On February 28, 1867—less than five months before his death—he wrote to W. T. Moore: "I consider the inauguration of our Society system, which I vowed to urge upon the brethren, if God raised me from my protracted illness of 1845, as one of the most important acts of my career."[14] Only a few years before his death he wrote the following: "From the time I urged the scheme of associated evangelical action upon the brethren, in 1845, to the present, the work has commanded my heart, my best energies, and my means."[15]

Burnet was born in Dayton, Ohio on July 6, 1808. When Burnet was eight years of age, however, his parents moved to Cincinnati. In these early days, Isaac G. Burnet, D. S. Burnet's father, was active in political circles. In 1821 he was elected mayor of Cincinnati, an office which he held for many years. D. S. Burnet, although only thirteen years of age, became his father's clerk. Thus Burnet's background is to be found less among the common people of life and more in the political and aristocratic circles.

---

[14]W. T. Moore, *The Living Pulpit of the Christian Church* (St. Louis: Christian Publishing Co., 1867), p. 45.
[15]D. S. Burnet, "Resignation of Brother D. S. Burnet," *Millennial Harbinger,* Fifth Series, Vol. VII, No. 4 (April, 1864), p. 185.

D. S. BURNET

From an early age Burnet was interested in religion. He had
been sprinkled and belonged to the Presbyterian Church in Cincinnati. When he was only sixteen, he was teaching a Sunday-
School class which compelled him to study scriptures. Before
long his investigations soon convinced him that sprinkling was
wrong. On December 26, 1824, he was immersed into Christ and
became a member of the Enon Baptist Church. At this time the
cause of restoration was comparatively young. Aside from the
Campbells there were few who entirely embraced his views. In
Kentucky that number probably included only two—P. S. Fall
and Jeremiah Vardeman. Fall had gone to Cincinnati at the request of the Enon Baptist Church and had witnessed the immersion

of D. S. Burnet. [16] Whether Fall baptized Burnet or not is not entirely clear. At any rate, shortly after being immersed, Burnet began preaching and became known as the "boy preacher."

In 1827 Burnet and William Montague of Kentucky established the Sycamore Street Baptist Church in Cincinnati with eighty members. A short time later, when Alexander Campbell's views became known in the congregation, the church divided into the Ninth Street Baptist Church and the famous Christian Chapel, located at the corner of Walnut and Eighth Streets.

On March 30, 1830 Burnet was married to Mary Gano, the youngest daughter of Major-General John S. Gano of Ohio. Mary had been immersed in 1827 by Jeremiah Vardeman, and was, therefore, already in sympathy with the views that Burnet entertained.

Burnet's life was divided between writing, preaching, and teaching. During the year, 1833, he was busy in full-time evangelistic work. From 1836-40 he published the *Christian Preacher,* a monthly periodical. In 1846 he published the *Christian Family Magazine.* At various times he edited the following papers: *Christian Age, The Reformer, The Monthly Age,* and the *Sunday School Journal.* Late in 1839 Burnet tried teaching. He purchased a farm from O. M. Spencer on the Hamilton turnpike, eight miles northwest of Cincinnati. Here, he opened a "female" institution, as schools for girls then were popularly called. He named this institution "The Hygeia Female Atheneum." Campbell seems to have doubted the wisdom of Burnet's running such a school, for upon the announcement of the opening of the institution, Campbell wrote:

Brother Burnet's character, intellectual, literary, and moral, is so well and so favorably known, not only to our brethren, but very generally throughout the community of our widely extended readers, as to need no commendation. I am only sorry that one so eminently qualified to be useful on a large scale as an Evangelist, either in Europe or America, should be confined to the labors of either a public or a private Academy. [17]

In 1845 Burnet inaugurated the American Christian Bible Society, a Society which never was popular among any of the breth-

---

[16]Robert Richardson, *Memoirs of Alexander Campbell* (Cincinnati: Standard Publishing Co., 1897), Vol. II, p. 122.

[17]Alexander Campbell, "The Hygeia Female Atheneum, Near Cincinnati," *Millennial Harbinger,* New Series, Vol. IV, No. 1 (January, 1840), p. 48.

ren. Campbell was critical of Burnet. It seems that, while Campbell greatly admired the character and ability of D. S. Burnet,
he frequently called in question the latter's judgment. Campbell
believed the inauguration of this Society was premature. Campbell's attitude stung Burnet, but the whole matter eventually blew
over. Burnet was present at the first convention of the Missionary Society in 1849, and was, until his death, one of the leading figures in it. For about a year in 1859 and 1860 Burnet was
Corresponding Secretary. After the death of Campbell, Burnet
was elected as the Missionary Society's president, but in this office
he never served due to his own death.

Burnet's death came at 11:30 A. M. on July 8, 1867 in Baltimore, Maryland. He had gone to Baltimore from Cincinnati in
1860, and was preparing to move to Louisville when his death
came. He possessed a very malignant form of dysentery which
caused him much suffering, although his last few hours were quiet
and peaceful. Tuesday morning before his death, although a
sick man, Burnet went to the church building to baptize a person.
The Sunday before he had preached his farewell sermon, and had all
his belongings packed when death came.

His body was borne from Baltimore to Cincinnati for burial.
W. T. Moore, who then preached for the Walnut and Eighth
Streets Church in Cincinnati for which Burnet had formerly
preached, read an appropriate hymn at the funeral service. L. L.
Pinkerton led the prayer. Isaac Errett gave the address after
which the body was taken to the cemetery at Spring Grove for
burial.

Thus did Burnet live and die. His name shall appear often in
this study of the restoration movement.

CHAPTER VI

OTHER EARLY PIONEER PREACHERS

It is not exaggerating in the least to say that after the death of Alexander Campbell in 1866 the most prominent man in the brotherhood was Benjamin Franklin. When Franklin died, David Lipscomb wrote:

The cause loses its most able and indefatigable defender since the days of Alexander Campbell, and his loss is simply irreparable.[1]

Still the influence of Franklin goes back as early as 1845. Ten years prior to this Franklin had been preaching the gospel, but his influence then was limited to the places where he had labored. His labors broadened in 1845 when he first came before the brotherhood in the capacity of an editor. From then until his death in 1878 his pen was seldom still. He was one of the greatest champions of truth since apostolic days.

Joseph Franklin, the father of Benjamin Franklin, was born in Providence, Rhode Island in 1783. Early in life he moved into eastern Ohio and settled in Belmont County. About 1811 he married Isabella Devold, and to this union Ben Franklin, their eldest son, was born. The date of his birth was February 1, 1812. While Ben was still an infant, his parents moved on a stream called Salt Run in Noble County, Ohio, and here they lived until 1833. Seven children were born here—six sons and a daughter.

Joseph Franklin's brother, Calvin, had moved into Henry County, Indiana, and shortly afterward, in 1832, Ben Franklin, Calvin's nephew, came to live with his uncle. That year Calvin and a man by the name of William Stewart built the first mill south of Middletown on Deer Creek. Ben Franklin was employed by his uncle. When Calvin decided to build a grist-mill of a better type, Ben digged the millrace. Middletown, where the Franklins now came, was located in the northwest corner of Henry County. The town was laid out in 1829 by Jacob Koontz, and the first sale of the lots took place on Christmas day of that year. Deer Creek was south of the town in what was then a great wilderness. A part of the winter of 1832-33 Ben Franklin went to

---

[1]David Lipscomb, "The Death of Benjamin Franklin," *Gospel Advocate*, Vol. XX, No. 43 (October 31, 1878), p. 677.

BEN FRANKLIN

Knightstown to help construct the National Road which was then being built through Indiana. Ben Franklin bought an eighty acre tract of wilderness and spent a part of his time erecting a cabin and clearing the land. Meanwhile, he "wooed and won" Mary Personett, a neighbor girl two and one-half years older than himself.

The Joseph Franklin family moved into Henry County in May, 1833. Up until this time, none of the family had shown the slightest interest in religion. As the manner of the community was, the boys drifted into profanity and general religious indifference. All of this was changed when, in 1833, Samuel Rogers moved with his family into Henry County.

Rogers set to work immediately and opened a school. All of the Franklin boys attended except Ben. Meanwhile, Rogers also established a church by preaching in a school house. On one occasion when Rogers was forced to discipline and expel a member, the schoolhouse then was denied the church, so they met in houses and out in the groves when the weather permitted.

Joseph Franklin, who was a neighbor of Samuel Rogers, had a Methodist background and did not believe in immersion. Rogers went to work to convert him. Of Joseph Franklin Rogers wrote:

Old Brother Franklin was not the best balanced man in the world; he was too much like myself in disposition, with a quick and impulsive nature, he was easily exasperated, easily excited. He suddenly became very happy, and as suddenly very unhappy. Sometimes he was lifted to the third heaven in transports of joy, and would then relapse into a state of despondency and gloom almost bordering on despair. We used to say he either lived in the garret or the cellar. Withal, however, he was a good and pure man; earnest in the advocacy of truth; and as far from making compromises with error as any living man. He stood upon principle; was ever ready to sacrifice personal interest and the praise of men for what he believed to be the truth.[2]

Ben Franklin's mother had a different disposition, Rogers declared.

She was always cheerful, and hoping for the best. While he was apt to look upon the dark side of things, she was always looking on the bright side; her sky was a cloudless one. There were very few women in her day who had a better acquaintance with the Bible than she, or who had so bright an intellect. . . . When we consider the character of this woman, we are not surprised that four of her six sons became ministers of the gospel of Christ.[3]

Samuel Rogers and Joseph Franklin agreed to meet in each other's cabins on Saturday afternoon and study the Bible through. They studied honestly, agreeing to mark each passage on which they could not agree and come back to it. They avoided every sign of discussion or prejudice. When they finished, they found that not a passage had been marked. Before long the Franklin family, including Ben, had been baptized.

Ben Franklin went zealously to work studying his Bible and preparing himself to preach. To the average listener in those early days he doubtlessly appeared to have little prospects as a preacher. His education had been very limited, and consequently, his grammar was poor. His form of delivery showed his backwoods cul-

---

[2]John I. Rogers, *Autobiography of Samuel Rogers* (Cincinnati: Standard Publishing Co., 1880), p. 144.

[3]John I. Rogers, *Autobiography of Samuel Rogers,* pp. 144, 145.

SAMUEL ROGERS

ture. John Longley, one of Indiana's early pioneer preachers, often
went to hear Franklin, and was one of his severe critics. Franklin
had unconsciously formed the habit of saying, "My dear friends
and brethering" and he always had the "ing" on it. Longley took
a piece of paper and a pin at one meeting and made a hole for
every time Franklin repeated this phrase. At the conclusion of the
sermon, he counted one hundred and fifty holes.

Yet, despite this early handicap Ben Franklin developed into
one of the most powerful proclaimers of the ancient gospel ever
known on American soil. While Franklin gained wide fame as
an editor and a debater, yet in the pulpit he came as near repre-

senting perfection as a gospel preacher that could be found. He quoted scripture voluminously. He did not pretend to be a philosopher, a politician, a teller of stories, or anything of the kind. He was a *gospel preacher* in everything the term implies.

In 1890 Joseph Franklin, son of Ben Franklin, was preaching for the church in Bedford, Indiana. One day Alfred Ellmore stopped at Bedford and spent some time with Joseph. During his stay, he on one occasion looked through the old family album. He came across a picture of Ben Franklin. Ellmore writes:

While looking through the album, my eyes rested upon the picture of Benjamin Franklin which brought to my mind the scenes of other days, when I sat under the mighty ministrations of the greatest preacher I ever listened to. And even now, after having listened to many men of varied abilities, I am firm in the conviction that Benjamin Franklin was the greatest gospel preacher I ever heard.[4]

When Samuel Rogers grew old, and Ben Franklin had become famous as a preacher, Rogers found a great satisfaction in the knowledge of the fact that he had introduced Franklin to the gospel. Rogers writes:

I have ever felt, in looking back over those times and considering that work, that, if I had done no more for my Master than to be instrumental in giving to the world Benjamin Franklin, I would have no reason to be ashamed; but would feel that I had by no means lived and labored in vain. Ben Franklin may, in common with his race, have faults and foibles: but, to my mind, he is one of the most direct and powerful gospel preachers and writers of this age. He indulges very little, if any, in speculation, but lays down his proposition, and proceeds with proofs that carry conviction to the mind almost irresistibly. He is emphatically a gospel preacher. Christ is his theme, first, midst and last. We may have scores of men among us more learned, in the popular sense, and more refined and elegant in manners and address; but it is my judgment that we have not a man among us who can preach the gospel with less admixture of philosophy and speculation, and with greater force, than Ben Franklin.[5]

Shortly before Franklin's death, he visited Nashville on a tour into the South. Here, David Lipscomb heard him preach. Commenting on Ben Franklin's preaching, Lipscomb wrote:

---

[4]A. Ellmore, "Wheat and Chaff," *Christian Leader,* Vol. IV, No. 16 (April 22, 1890), p. 4.

[5]John I. Rogers, *Autobiography of Samuel Rogers,* p. 149.

Earnestness, clearness, simplicity, with a strong reverence for and determination to know nothing in religion save what the Bible teaches, were the striking characteristics of his discourses.[6]

J. W. McGarvey, commenting upon Franklin's power as a debator and preacher, said:

His power lies in two peculiarities. First. His close and constant dependence upon the very words of the English Bible, which he has richly treasured up in his memory. Second. His earnest and vehement manner of pressing home upon the hearts of his audience any advantages which his position or his argument may have given him . . .

Brother Franklin has another peculiarity as a debatant of which I must speak, and which I cannot too highly commend to the imitation of all the brethren. He is preeminently an evangelist, and his whole soul seems to be wrapped up in the desire to convert souls to Christ. This thought never forsakes him in discussion. His speeches are therefore characterized by the same tender solicitude for his audience, the same solemnity of manner, and almost the same pathos, as when he is preaching for the conversion of sinners. It is not an uncommon occurrence for him to draw tears from the eyes of a large portion of his audience.[7]

Daniel Sommer was preaching in Clark County, Kentucky in 1874 and was discussing Ben Franklin with an old elder in the church. The old elder said that he was with Ben like Pat Caldwell was with the North Star at Newbern, North Carolina in 1833. That year, there was a great meteor shower, and stars were falling everywhere. Many thought the world had come to an end, and crowds of people were terror stricken. But Pat Caldwell was calm. He cried out, "Be aisy, boys. I've got my eye on the North Star, and if that don't fall, we are safe." The elder had his eye on Ben Franklin, and to him the cause of restoration was not lost as long as Franklin lived.[8]

It is not likely that a greater, nobler, truer, purer preacher of the gospel lived since apostolic times than Ben Franklin.

In 1835, shortly after his conversion, Franklin wrote his first article for the press. It set forth the plan of salvation, and was published in the *Heretic Detector,* a paper published in Middleburg,

---

[6]David Lipscomb, "Benjamin Franklin," *Gospel Advocate,* Vol. XX, No. 48 (December 5, 1878)), p. 758.

[7]J. W. McGarvey, "The Chillicothe Debate," *American Christian Review,* Vol. III, No. 23 (June 5, 1860), p. 91.

[8]Daniel Sommer, "A Neat Compliment," *American Christian Review,* Vol. XVIII, No. 24 (June 15, 1875), p. 189.

Ohio by Arthur Crihfield. Meanwhile, Franklin earned a living by working at the mill which he owned and farming. In 1842 he moved to New Lisbon, ten miles southeast of Newcastle, Indiana. He stayed here for two years. A part of this time he preached for the church at Bethel, twelve miles north of Richmond. In 1844 he moved his family to Centerville, county seat of Wayne County, Indiana.

Daniel K. Winder had started a paper in 1843 which he called *The Reformer*. But a year later he dropped it. Ben Franklin liked the name and beginning in 1845, started a paper by this same name. For a year Franklin's paper was published by Samuel C. Meredith, who also published a county paper in Centerville. In the spring of 1846 Franklin obtained some printing material for himself. *The Reformer* was a monthly and had three hundred subscribers the first year. In November, 1846 he enlarged the paper and put it out for $1.00 a year. About 1847 Franklin moved to Milton, Indiana, and changed the name of the paper to *The Western Reformer*.

During this time, Franklin found himself getting into several religious discussions. In 1843 he debated George W. McCune, a Universalist preacher. In October, 1847, he held a four days' discussion with Erasmus Manford, a Universalist preacher again. This was his first published discussion. A month later he debated a Methodist preacher by the name of Henry R. Pritchard.

Alexander Wilford Hall, meanwhile, had begun publishing a paper which he called *The Gospel Proclamation* from Loydsville, Ohio. In January, 1850, Franklin negotiated with Hall to merge the two papers, and so *The Proclamation and Reformer* was born. Alexander Hall and William Pinkerton were co-editors. But Ben Franklin's editorial career through this period was rather uncertain. He was a popular editor and writer but appeared to lack the means to get himself as well established as he would like.

The next of Franklin's editorial attempts came as a co-editor with D. S. Burnet on *The Christian Age*. In 1844, shortly after he had moved back to Pittsburgh, Walter Scott began publishing *The Protestant Unionist*. In 1848 he moved it to Cincinnati. At the close of this year George Campbell and others purchased the paper and emerged it with *The Christian Age*. At this time the *Age* was edited by Dr. Gatchell and T. J. Melish. Gatchell, shortly after, sold his interest to George Campbell and Melish sold his to

D. S. Burnet. In the spring of 1850 Campbell sold his interest to Ben Franklin and so, Franklin and Burnet came to be co-editors of *The Christian Age*. Meanwhile, Franklin attempted to publish both the *Age,* which was a weekly, and the *Proclamation and Reformer,* which was a monthly.

The five years between 1850-55 were years of disappointment and struggle for Ben Franklin. His publishing interests proved a financial loss, and often he was without sufficient money to buy the necessities for his family. Moreover, Franklin had moved his family near Cincinnati to Hygeia where he could be closer to his publishing interests and to his co-partner, D. S. Burnet, who operated the Female School at Hygeia. During this time, Franklin divided his time preaching for the Clinton Street Church in Cincinnati and the church in Covington, Kentucky. His family attended church at Mt. Healthy and most of his children there obeyed the gospel. Burnet was an aristocrat and Franklin was of little financial means. Franklin's wife was discontented. But perhaps Franklin's greatest disappointment came after 1853 when he and Burnet agreed to turn *The Christian Age* over to the American Christian Publication Society. Franklin saw himself pushed into the background. His independent spirit exerted itself and he broke all relations with the paper, giving his word to the Society that he would not publish another paper for at least two years.

Franklin, however, had fully determined to remain before the people as an editor. Immediate plans were made for a new periodical so on January 1, 1856 the first issue of the *American Christian Review* came off the press. At this time the paper was a monthly, but on January 5, 1858 the first issue of the weekly *American Christian Review* came off the press. Moses E. Lard, C. L. Loos, John Rogers, Isaac Errett and Elijah Goodwin were then listed as contributing editors. For many years the *Review* was to be the most influential paper in the brotherhood. It wielded an influence not equalled by any other.

The years between 1856 and 1878 found Franklin appearing in a diversity of ways. After the establishment of the American Christian Missionary Society in 1849, the influence of Ben Franklin went wholly behind that organization. For a short time in 1856 and 1857 he was the Corresponding Secretary. In his one speech before the Society Convention, he deplored the lack of interest in the Society, and urged men to get behind it. Yet, as time went on, his ardor for the Society cooled and by 1866, he turned solidly against it. Too, in 1869 when the Louisville Plan was accepted by the brethren, Franklin threw his influence behind that, but in slightly over a year, he had again turned against that plan. There is therefore an enigma about Franklin that is hard to explain. What is the explanation? Shortly after Franklin's death, David Lipscomb wrote an article evaluating his life and work. Lipscomb writes that Franklin was ordinarily a man of great firmness, but at times was influenced by others against his own judgment. It would seem, then, that the great heart of Ben Franklin was torn between two great desires. On the one hand he had a passion for unity among the brethren and on the other, he had a passion for an independent stand for the truth. It grieved Franklin deeply when his own passion for the truth conflicted with his desire for unity, but in the end, he was always faithful to his conviction. Lipscomb points out that Franklin was persuaded, even at times against his better judgment, that the adoption of societies would bring about better unity and activity. When he saw they failed, he returned to "always trust the primitive and divine methods." Back in the earlier days, while Franklin was advocating the societies, he had paid a visit to Franklin College, and spent a night with Tolbert Fanning. They talked of the societies "that were then engulfing the brotherhood." Both of them agreed they were wrong. At the end of their conversation each gave the other his right hand as a pledge to "resist them and to walk in the good old ways."[9] About the same time, Franklin paid a visit to Jacob Creath, Jr., and Creath remembered Franklin's promise that he was going to get out of the societies and "wash his hands of them as soon as possible."[10] At heart Franklin was convicted that the societies were unscriptural, but he patiently waited to see if there was any way he could harmonize his convictions with the existence of the societies before he spoke out.

Franklin was bitterly opposed to the use of instrumental music in the worship. He regarded the instrument as an innovation and refused to preach where the instrument was used.

It will be unnecessary to detail here the chronicle of Franklin's

---

[9]David Lipscomb, "Benjamin Franklin," *Gospel Advocate,* Vol. XX, No. 48 (December 5, 1878), p. 758.

[10]Jacob Creath, "Brother Franklin's Death and Services," *American Christian Review,* Vol. XXII, No. 10 (March 4, 1879), p. 73.

activity through the remainder of his life. That story is largely the story with which these further chapters shall deal. Until that Tuesday afternoon of October 23, 1878, Franklin was a busy man in the kingdom of his Master. Even when that day dawned upon the home of James Plummer near Anderson, Indiana where Franklin was staying, the editor of the *Review* was in a jovial mood. All that morning he wrote his editorials for his paper. After lunch, he complained of a heavy load on his stomach and a severe pain around his heart. His daughter and wife tried to put him to bed, but he wouldn't go, for it was too painful to attempt to move. They continued to insist but each time Franklin would stretch forth his hand and say, "Don't touch me, my time has come." He remained seated in a chair. The doctor was brought in, but he could do nothing. At four o'clock in the afternoon Franklin was unconscious. One hour later, he breathed his last—still sitting in the chair. W. W. Witmer and M. T. Hough preached the funeral for Franklin two days later in the Franklin home. The worn body of this sixty-seven year old gospel preacher was laid reverently in the grave near Anderson.

Franklin's death was a severe blow to the aging Jacob Creath who looked upon Franklin as the saviour of the restoration. Creath wrote:

If our own brethren believed in canonizing men, he could soon be placed in the front ranks on the roll of canonization among our great men, and if their mantles ever fell upon any man, that man was Benjamin Franklin. His death is universally regarded by the readers of the *Review* as a great loss to our restoration. He has left no one who can fill his place, and we shall not see his like soon again.[11]

TOLBERT FANNING

Unquestionably, the most influential preacher in the Southland before the War Between the States was Tolbert Fanning. There were other great men, of course. Among these were J. B. Ferguson, Sandy E. Jones, J. K. Speer, John Mulkey, J. M. Barnes and W. H. Wharton, but for lasting influence Tolbert Fanning towers above them all.

In personal appearance Fanning had much to his advantage. Although he was far from being handsome, yet he was a giant of a

---

[11]Jacob Creath, "Brother Franklin's Death and Services," *American Christian Review*, Vol. XXII, No. 10 (March 4, 1879), p. 73.

TOLBERT FANNING

man, weighing between two hundred and two hundred and fifty at
all times. Most of the time he weighed two hundred and forty.
He was a tall man and in no sense of the term was he fat. This
extremely good physical condition made it possible for Fanning to
do as much work as most any two men would do. It was nothing
unusual for him to spend all day at school or on the farm, and then
write or study at night until 2:00 A.M. The next day he would
continue his usual program. Fanning possessed a powerful brain,
a strong will, an indomitable courage, great self-reliance and perseverance. He was of an intensely independent frame of mind and

was absolutely unyielding in anything he set out to accomplish. It was Fanning's custom to decide slowly what was right and then to throw everything he had into what he believed. Some people considered him overbearing and selfish, and even his friends admitted this was one of his few weaknesses.

Fanning always maintained a great interest in the farm. He loved good stock. A large part of his time was devoted to the outdoors. By hard work and the practice of economy Fanning managed to have a considerable amount of this world's goods on hand when he died. Some of his critics claimed he had his heart too much on money. This was hardly true, although the best friends Fanning had thought that at times he devoted so much of his interest to the farm that he neglected his preaching. The following letter, written by William Lipscomb, elder brother of David Lipscomb, and co-editor of the *Gospel Advocate* from 1855-1861, to W. C. Huffman, a preacher of Sumner County, Tennessee, will illustrate the point.

Franklin College
May 13, 1857

Dear Brother Huffman,

Your remittance came safe to hand and we can but return you our sincere thanks for your continued kindness. Brother Fanning has been much engaged in stock business but I hope he is pretty well through. I think an occasional word of admonition from abroad might be of service in calling his thoughts to more important matters. And I trust now he will labor abroad more than he has done. The cause I know demands his service and I think the brethren ought to be more urgent upon him to devote his time to the work. All are well.

Yours in the truth,
W. LIPSCOMB

Fanning himself was conscious of his great love for farm life. In another letter, preserved for us by Minnie Mae Corum, W. C. Huffman's granddaughter, now living in old age at Winter Haven, Florida, Fanning writes to Huffman:

Franklin College
May 25, 1868

Brother Huffman:

It is said "we are twice a child, but once a man." I love fine animals, fine people, fine horses, fine cattle, fine sheep, fine dogs and fine hogs. Now I am at the point. Have you the growing birkshires that are all right in shape? If so, I want some two

sows and a boar if I can get them. I would like a young sow
that will have pigs towards fall, and then a pair or two of pigs.
Have you got them? Tell me exactly what you can spare, young or
old and the prices. If you have not birkshires, who has the
genuine? Health good. Would like to hold a meeting with you.
Write.

Truly,

T. FANNING

Tolbert Fanning was born May 10, 1810 in Cannon County,
Tennessee. His parents were William and Nancy Bromley Fanning, who had come to Tennessee a short time before from Virginia.
William Fanning died in Texas in 1865. Around 1818 the family
moved from Tennessee into Lauderdale County in northern Alabama. Here Fanning grew up amidst the poverties of pioneer
life and early learned the value of hard work and economy.

Methodism was the predominant religion in Fanning's community although his mother was a Baptist and his father made no
religious profession at all. Nevertheless, Fanning himself had a
deeply religious soul and always desired to do the will of God at
all times. When he was a lad seventeen years old, he heard the
gospel of Christ and obeyed its commandments. It was September,
1827. B. F. Hall had gone from Kentucky into Lauderdale County
to preach. On Lord's Day evening he preached on Cyprus Creek.
Tolbert Fanning was present and heard the discourse. When the
invitation was given, Fanning came forward and made the confession. The next morning, James E. Matthews, a Mississippi
preacher, baptized him.*[12]

No sooner had Fanning been immersed, than he began to try
to preach. He spoke in school houses and in groves, and for a
short time, for the church at Cyprus Creek. There were few people who heard Fanning speak who believed he would ever make
a preacher. He was a tall overgrown youth of six feet and six
inches. His clothes were the homespun garments of the pioneers.
Most of his early sermons lacked polish and organization. An
elderly lady thought she would do Fanning a favor and so she

---

*In 1904 H. R. Moore of Huntland, Tennessee, delivered an address in
memory of Tolbert Fanning and stated that Fanning was baptized by E. D.
Moore. The address is recorded in "Franklin College and Its Influences,"
p. 123. This is obviously an error. When James E. Matthews died, Fanning
printed an account of it in the *Advocate,* stating at the time that Matthews
had baptized him.

[12]John I. Rogers, *Autobiography of Elder Samuel Rogers* (Cincinnati:
Standard Publishing Co., 1880), p. 60.

said to him, "Brother Fanning, you never can preach, and will always run your legs too far through your breeches. Do go home and go to plowing." Rees Jones, an early pioneer preacher, said to him, "I do not think you will ever make a preacher. It might be well for you to go at something else." Both of these people lived to see the day when Fanning could address an audience for three hours and hold it in rapt attention. Fanning developed into a powerful speaker. His utterances were clear and distinct and his voice was pleasant and clear. His English was always the purest.

Great respect was paid to the preaching of Fanning by T. B. Larimore, who was a student of Fanning's in 1867. Larimore writes:

Tolbert Fanning was, in some respects, a preacher without a peer. His preaching possessed some strikingly strange peculiarities. He evidently believed, without distressing, disturbing doubt or mental reservation, the gospel to be "the power of God unto salvation"; and he never tired of preaching it, in its peerless, primitive purity and sweet, sublime simplicity, without much variety or phraseology, but with a power and pathos that carried conviction to the hearts of those who diligently heard him.[13]

Fanning loved the gospel and believed with all his heart it was the power of God unto salvation. He would never tolerate any deviation from its precepts. While he was a man of great firmness, he was also humble and kind. On one occasion Fanning was getting ready to hold a debate in Lebanon, Tennessee. His opponent was delivering his first speech and in the course of the speech quoted bombastically:

> "I'm monarch of all I survey,
> My right there is none to dispute.
> From the center, all round to the sea,
> I am lord of the fowl and the *brute*."

The speaker made the word, brute, defiantly point at Fanning. Without saying a word, Fanning got up and walked out. The debate ended then and there and to the thinking part of the audience Fanning won a quick and decisive victory.

Three years after his conversion Fanning left his home and crossed the Tennessee River to take up the work of preaching the

---

[13]T. B. Larimore, *Franklin College and Its Influences* (Nashville: McQuiddy Printing Co., 1906), p. 412.

gospel. The date was October 1, 1830.[14] For the next year Fanning preached in middle Tennessee. In November, 1831 he entered the University of Nashville, and graduated in 1835. During this time he preached in and around Nashville. In the spring of 1835 Fanning took an extended tour with Alexander Campbell, visiting points through Kentucky and the East. During the time Fanning was in Nashville, Phillip S. Fall preached for the church there. In 1837 Fanning married Fall's sister, Charlotte. The same year he opened a Female Seminary at Franklin, Tennessee. For the next two years Fanning taught in this Seminary and preached in the vicinity. On January 1, 1840, Fanning moved to a farm five miles southeast of Nashville. He taught another Female Seminary here until 1842.

Tolbert Fanning was now making quite a reputation for himself. His ability was everywhere recognized. At the time Fanning was with Campbell, Campbell wrote of him:

The church (in Nashville) now counts about six hundred members, and employs brother Fanning as its evangelist. This devout, and ardent, and gifted brother, about finishing his academic studies in the University of Nashville, under the presidency of the justly celebrated Doctor *Lindsley,* one of the most talented, learned and liberal of American presidents, cannot make full proof of his ministry and therefore, only labors occasionally in the word and teaching. He expects to graduate next September, and is desirous of fitting himself for permanent and extensive usefulness.[15]

On January 30, 1844, the legislature of the state of Tennessee granted the charter for the building of Franklin College. The first session of the school began on January 1, 1845. Tolbert Fanning was president of the college. In another chapter Franklin College will be more fully discussed, so further mention of it would be out of place here. Suffice it to say, Fanning continued as the president of the school through most of its existence and influenced profoundly many of the young men who later became some of the Southland's greatest preachers.

Fanning never gained the reputation in religious polemics that many other preachers did. Yet, occasionally he did debate. In 1842 he held a discussion at Perryville, Kentucky with N. L. Rice,

---

[14]Tolbert Fanning, "Notes on a Tour"—No. 3," *Christian Review,* Vol. I, No. 11 (November, 1844), p. 244.

[15]Alexander Campbell, "Sketch of a Tour of Seventy-Five Days," *Millenial Harbinger,* Vol. VI, No. 6 (June, 1835), p. 280.

the man who, a year later, debated Alexander Campbell.* Fanning afterward regretted the debate for he feared Rice had used him for the purpose of getting ready for Campbell.

Another phase of Fanning's versatility needs to be mentioned. In addition to being a preacher and teacher Fanning was an editor. One might well judge, however, that with Fanning, editing a religious periodical was purely a secondary matter. In January, 1844, he began publishing the *Christian Review*. Four years later, he turned this paper over to J. B. Ferguson, then a popular preacher in Nashville, who changed its name, and published it under the name, *Christian Magazine*. In the summer of 1855 Fanning, together with William Lipscomb began editing the *Gospel Advocate*. The War Between the States cut Fanning's editorial work short, but when the war ended, Fanning was again publishing the paper, using David Lipscomb as co-editor. After 1867 Fanning's name disappears from the *Advocate* editorial corps. For two years, beginning in 1872, he edited the *Religious Historian*.

From the first Fanning was a critic of the missionary society. However, his attitude toward the society shows the greatness of his mind. Fanning very early formed the conviction that the Society was an unscriptural institution. However, his objections were by and large held in abeyance. The great men in the brotherhood promoted the Society. Alexander Campbell, D. S. Burnet, Benjamin Franklin, W. K. Pendleton, John T. Johnson and a host of others favored the Society. For a time Fanning appears to have assumed the attitude that he himself might be wrong. He gave himself every opportunity to discover his error. He went to the first convention of 1849 as an observer, thinking he might learn something to cause him to change his mind. In 1855 he started the *Gospel Advocate* intending to use its columns for open discussion on the question in the hope unity would be achieved. As he became more convinced that the Society was an evil, he spoke out more boldly against it. E. G. Sewell wrote of Fanning: "He never had much confidence in human plans and human schemes in

---

*A mistaken impression has cropped out regarding this debate. H. Leo Boles, *Biographical Sketches of Gospel Preachers*, p. 152, states that Fanning debated a Methodist preacher named Rice. Boles doubtlessly copied this from E. G. Sewell's article written in the *Advocate* upon the death of Fanning. Sewell's article shows, however, that it was written hastily and from memory. Fanning informs us in the first volume of the *Christian Review* that it was N. L. Rice, a Presbyterian.

religion by which to do the work of the church, and as he advanced in life, and studied the scriptures more, he had less and less."[16]

For two years prior to his death Fanning had taken on the appearance to his friends of being a tired and rapidly-breaking man. His strong voice was weakening, and his body was beginning to stoop a little. The last week of April, 1874 began for Fanning with a bit of complaining about rheumatism and dyspepsia. But he went ahead working until Thursday evening, April 30th. He left home to walk to a shop not far from his house, and no sooner did he arrive until a terrible pain hit him in his side. He was assisted to the house, but found no relief there. A physician was called and he seemed to think the trouble was inflammation of the liver. Slowly, Fanning got worse until the next Lord's Day which was May 3rd. At the usual hour for worship, he asked the brethren to come to his room and break bread with him. He asked them also to sing, but such an effort on this occasion was difficult, but amidst tears, they did the best they could. At 12:30, shortly after noon of that Lord's Day, he breathed his last.

JACOB CREATH, JR.

One of the most colorful characters of the entire restoration movement was Jacob Creath, Jr. He was fearlessly independent in his thinking and an oddity in almost all the deportments of his life. Typical of his idiosyncracies were the events surrounding his death. Two years before he died, he wrote out his own obituary. Since Jesus and the apostles all died without a funeral sermon being preached for them, there would be none for Jacob Creath, Jr., either. He requested that he be buried in a plain, cheap coffin, with his pocket Bible placed under his head and a copy of Campbell's *Living Oracles* under that. He had lived and fought with his Bible in one hand and the *Living Oracles* in the other. Nothing would suit him better than that they should be the pillow for his head until Time crumbled them to dust together. Jacob Creath, the "Iron Duke of the Restoration," as John F. Rowe called him, was quietly laid to rest on Monday morning, January 11, 1886. His death had taken place just two days before at seven o'clock in the morning at his old home in Palmyra, Missouri.[17]

[16]E. G. Sewell, "Brother T. Fanning," *Gospel Advocate,* Vol. XVI, No. 21 (May 21, 1874), p. 493.
[17]John F. Rowe, "Death of Jacob Creath," *American Christian Review,* Vol. XXIX, No. 5 (January 21, 1886), p. 29.

JACOB CREATH

Men like Jacob Creath are what make the restoration movement breathe the atmosphere of romance. Not often has the world known such men, and less often has it appreciated those few it has known. "In the person of Jacob Creath we have stalwart Christian manhood, solidity of character, sternness of purpose, invincible will-power, a disposition that tolerates no wrong, a sense of justice that knows no relenting."[18] Rowe once called him the John Knox of the restoration.

[18]John F. Rowe, "Jacob Creath," *American Christian Review*, Vol. XXI, No. 49 (December 10, 1878), p. 393.

The father of Jacob Creath, Jr., was William Creath. He was born on December 23, 1768 while his parents were on a trip from Dublin, Ireland to Nova Scotia. William Creath's father, Samuel, declared himself in favor of the colonies during the Revolutionary War and was imprisoned for seven years by the British because of this. William was a Presbyterian, the same religion that his parents espoused, but in 1787 he was immersed by Elder Henry Lester and became a member of a Baptist congregation in Granville County, North Carolina. After his baptism, William studied theology under Elder John Williams, a Calvinistic Baptist. Very shortly he became an outstanding Baptist preacher. On one occasion a deist said there were only two things that could make him cry—shaving with a dull razor and hearing William Creath preach. A member of Congress once remarked that William Creath was the only man he ever heard preach who could deliver a three hours' sermon and not say something *not* worth hearing.

William Creath married Lucretia Brame, a young lady of English descent. She gave birth to sixteen children. Since William Creath was away most of the time preaching, the care of the family fell almost entirely upon his wife. She was very devout and required her children to read the Bible and commit large portions of it to memory. Five of her nine sons became ministers. The home of William Creath was the home of Baptist preachers from Maine to Georgia.

When William Creath's second son was born, naming of the infant was left to William's younger brother, Jacob. Accordingly, Jacob gave the babe his own name. In years to come William's brother, Jacob was called Jacob Creath, Sr. William's son, Jacob, was called Jacob Creath, Jr. It was January 17, 1799 that Jacob Creath, Jr., was born. The place was a log cabin on Butcher's Creek, in Mecklenburg County, Virginia, six miles from Boydtown, the county seat. When Jacob Creath, Jr. was quite young, his parents moved on Taylor's Creek in the lower part of the county. Creath, Jr., went to a school taught by Joshua Stanley located three miles from his father's house. Later he went to school to Jones Gee under whom he learned the art of writing. He became thoroughly acquainted with his New Testament by reading it in the light of a blazing brush pile at night and in the day time, during brief periods when the horses were resting.

Since Creath's father was a Baptist preacher, it was only natural that he should think of the welfare of his soul and of conversion in terms of Baptist teaching. Baptists espoused the doctrine of "experimental religion." A man could do nothing to be saved, but yet something had to happen before he could be saved, according to the doctrine. Creath tried to get an experience, and at times, thought he had one, but the emotion subsided, and he was left destitute of any hope. Soon he became disgusted and for a brief period tried to be an infidel, but found he couldn't honestly believe infidelity. Creath writes:

I never saw the day when I did not desire to be good and please God, my Maker. I often withdrew to retired places, and prayed to him that I might see a great light shining around me, like Saul of Tarsus; or hear a voice informing me that my sins were pardoned. Under these circumstances nature sometimes gave way and I went to sleep on my knees, overwhelmed with the dreadful consideration that I was forever lost.[19]

In April, 1817 a meeting of the Meherrin Baptist Association was held at Ready Creek meeting house in Brunswick County, Virginia. William Creath and some other prominent Baptist preachers were expected to be present. Jacob Creath decided to go. After the last address, an invitation was given for all who wanted prayer on their behalf to come to the altar. Creath thought this to be a good opportunity to be saved, so he went. The preachers prayed, and Creath felt some temporary relief for his anxious soul. The Baptists readily declared him saved. Accordingly on the third Lord's Day of May, 1817 Creath was immersed by his father at the Baptist meeting house on Wilson's Creek. When he came up from the water he felt a measure of peace.

Creath by disposition was of a serious mind. He got more pleasure out of associating with the old than with the young. He boasted that he never read a novel. In years to come this seriousness gave him a saturnine temperament. He had an irascible temper that he found it almost impossible to control. David Lipscomb once wrote of him:

He would rebuke and scold an audience on slight provocation, with severity, but present to them the gospel of the Son of God with the simplicity, and tenderness of child-like faith in the Saviour. I have heard but few preachers that could present the gospel with more simplicity, tenderness and love than Brother Creath. He

---

[19]P. Donan, *Memoirs of Jacob Creath, Jr.* (Cincinnati: Chase & Hall, 1877), p. 49.

had by nature an irritable temper to contend with: he made manful efforts to master it.[20]

Creath preached his first sermon on the third Lord's Day in June, 1817. The circumstances were rather peculiar. The Baptist preacher who was to do the preaching could not be present for the service at the meeting house because of high water. The Methodist preacher, James Nolly, was invited to speak. Nolly stood up and then spoke to Creath. "Jacob, can't you preach for us today?" he asked. Jacob replied: "No sir, I can not. What led you to ask me that question?" "Oh," said Nolly, "I think you *will* preach and you had as well begin today." Creath refused to preach and Nolly delivered a sermon. At the conclusion of Nolly's address, he asked Creath to close the service. Creath preached a sermon on Gal. 3:10. After the service, an old lady told him that he could word a good prayer, but would never make a preacher.

Creath had a mind to agree with the old lady and so for two years he labored on a farm, not trying to preach. But the desire to preach the gospel got the better of him. In January, 1819 Creath went to see William Dossy at Society Hill to get some assistance through the Charleston Baptist Association for an education. He then attended the University of North Carolina at Chapel Hill and studied under Abner W. Clopton. He stayed in the university until the fall of 1820. Clopton moved to Caswell County and Creath went along. During this time he became an ordained minister in the Baptist Church. The ordination took place on September 23, 24, 1820 at the Mill Creek Meeting House in Caswell County. In November, 1821 Creath entered Columbia College in Washington, D. C. and worshiped with the First Baptist Church in Washington.

After leaving Washington, Creath went back to North Carolina, but stayed there only a short time, and moved to Kentucky. While he was in Kentucky, the churches in Louisville and Lexington offered him positions. Most of his time up to the late summer of 1826 was spent with the Baptist Church at Great Crossing in Scott County. In October, 1826 he moved from Kentucky to Natchez, Mississippi, and from there to New Orleans. All the while he continued to preach. On the way he spent several days at the Hermitage near Nashville, having letters of recommendation

[20]David Lipscomb, "Death of Jacob Creath," *Gospel Advocate,* Vol. XXVIII, No. 3 (January 20, 1886), p. 38.

from Col. Richard M. Johnson, brother of John T. Johnson, who was a prominent army official. Creath had as his companion Albert Gallatin Creath, son of Jacob Creath, Sr. In Nashville they visited Col. Robert Foster, lieutenant-governor of Tennessee. At Natchez Creath so enraged the Methodists, Episcopalians and Presbyterians that they burned him in effigy.

In the fall of 1827 Creath contacted yellow fever. At times he almost died. The disease caused him to leave the deep south, so early in 1828 he took a steamer from New Orleans and went to Louisville and from there to Bethany, Virginia. Before long, he was back in Kentucky and preached at Versailles, Cane Run and South Elkhorn.

One of the most trying circumstances of his life came when the Great Crossings Baptist Church tried him for heresy. Creath, through reading the *Christian Baptist,* had become acquainted with restoration principles. He denounced creeds and taught that the word of God was the instrumentality through which conversion took place and that to be converted a man had simply to obey the word of God. Silas M. Noel, a strongly partisan Baptist, was then preaching at Great Crossings. The church sent Creath a letter dated May 17, 1829, demanding he give an account of himself. Hearing of the letter, Creath's uncle, Jacob, Sr., came immediately to see him. Creath told his uncle he intended to stand by his convictions.

At the trial by the Great Crossings Church Creath read Paul's defense before Agrippa and Festus. John T. Johnson, who was later one of the leading pioneer preachers in Kentucky, was present. After the trial, Johnson said: "Absolutely, if they don't let that man alone the stones of the street will cry out against them."[21] Later Johnson told Creath that he would never have been connected with the restoration except for Creath.

When the Elkhorn Baptist Association convened in August, 1829 in Lexington, an effort was made to adopt a resolution to exclude all of those from the Baptist Church who believed in taking the "Bible alone." Through the efforts of Johnson, the purpose was thwarted and for another year, the preachers remained free to preach.

At the close of the year 1829, Creath took a trip with Alexander Campbell to Nashville. On this trip Campbell encountered Oba-

[21]P. Donan, *Memoirs of Jacob Creath, Jr.,* p. 82.

diah Jennings, a very biased Presbyterian preacher. Most of the controversy later appeared in the *Millennial Harbinger*.

[margin note: Not clear should be developed left out]

As the time drew near for the annual meeting of the Elkhorn Association in 1830, Jacob Creath, Jr., and his uncle became anxious to know what would happen. The Baptist church at Lexington a year before had invited young Creath to be their preacher, a fact which estranged Creath and Jeremiah Vardeman. Vardeman thence used his influence against Creath. Indicative of what was to take place at the Elkhorn Association was the pronouncement of the Franklin Association which met a month earlier at Frankfort, Kentucky. This latter association prepared charges against Elkhorn for not having previously dismissed those in its number who held the heretical doctrine of the work of the Holy Spirit through the word in conversion. The Elkhorn Association, then, was "on the spot" when it did meet, for it had to do something or face criticism from other Baptist associations in Kentucky. At the meeting of the Elkhorn Association came Raccoon John Smith, Jacob Creath, Sr. and Jacob Creath, Jr. Charges were made and passed upon and not any of the three was allowed to speak in his own defense. Thus, these three men were expelled from Baptist fellowship in Kentucky.

[margin note: not very explicit]

In September, 1831 Creath married Mrs. Susan Bedford, widow of Sidney Bedford of Bourbon County, Kentucky. For the next few years Creath farmed and then preached on Saturday and Sundays. In 1834 he held a debate with Lewis Green, professor of Ancient Languages in Danville College. The debate was held in July in Lincoln County. For the next three years Creath entered more extensively into preaching. He and John T. Johnson were almost continual companions. In 1835 they held a meeting in Fayette County, Kentucky. The same year they preached at Versailles and baptized a hundred and forty. For the next three years they preached continuously until the sects became alarmed for fear the whole country was going to the "Campbellites."

The year 1838, marked the beginning of Creath's domestic troubles. His wife was thrown from her horse and permanently injured. She was with child at the time. The child was born but was always delicate and died early in life. Creath's wife was now a permanent invalid. She felt she would die and so requested Creath to move to Missouri so she could die near her

people.   In 1839 Creath moved to Lewis County, Missouri.   A
year later he moved near Monticello on the Fabius River.

After the death of his wife on July 16, 1841, Creath had considerable trouble.   His wife, as has been mentioned, was the widow
of Sidney Bedford.   She had one son, Creath's stepson, Sidney
Bedford, Jr.   His wife's first husband had left considerable property and this had been willed to the stepson of Creath.   Creath
had been appointed his guardian.   Meanwhile, Sidney Bedford,
Sr.'s sisters and brothers wanted the property.   They lured the
boy away from Creath and they instituted proper court proceedings
and secured the guardianship from Creath.   The boy died underage
in Washington, Pennsylvania, and the elder Bedford's relatives got
the possessions.   Creath himself was ruined financially in the whole
transaction.

In October, 1841, Creath moved to Palmyra, Missouri, where he
lived until he died.   In March, 1842, he married Mrs. Prudence
Rogers of Bowling Green.   Just what made Creath always prefer
widows for wives has never been explained.   Apparently he was
always happy with them.

It is needless to follow through the next years of his life.   The
story would read more like a diary than a detailed history.   From
Palmyra, Missouri, he traveled continually preaching the gospel and
establishing congregations.   His work took him over Illinois,
Missouri, Louisiana, Kentucky, Indiana, Tennessee.

In Creath's many trips over Missouri in preaching, he rode an
old horse he called Jack.   He was very much attached to this horse.
On one occasion he stopped with a brother in a village, and the
man sent the horse to the tavern stable.   The tavern was owned
by a member of the church that knew Creath well.   Frequently,
Creath would send someone over to see if Jack had been fed, then
watered, and bedded.   The lady became annoyed finally and sent
word back to Creath: "Go tell Brother Creath that I have done
everything for his horse I can think of, except to give him a cup
of coffee, and I am getting that ready."

As the years slowly came upon Creath, his physical frame began to gradually give way, but his mind remained active.   In 1877
John A. Brooks held a meeting in Palmyra.   Creath was then
seventy-eight.   Brooks writes:

In his person and carriage, he reminds me much of Brother
Campbell.   He is a man of magnificent proportions, and under

the weight of nearly eighty years, stands as erect as an Indian. His physical frame is wearing out, but his mental faculties know no failure yet.[22]

In 1884 John F. Rowe was on a trip west and at seven o'clock one evening stopped by Palmyra to see Creath. Creath was just going to bed but upon seeing Rowe for the first time stayed up and talked with him for three hours. Creath did almost all of the talking. The cause of Zion was heavy on his heart. It must have been a touching scene to listen to such a man talk. Rowe writes of this meeting:

But he has about finished his course, he has fought the good fight, and, with his beloved companion, he soon expects to pass the shores of mortality, and receive his crown of righteousness. He fully comprehends the present crisis of the churches, many of which he was instrumental in bringing into life; and though cheered by the prospect of a home in heaven, he mourned over the desolation of Zion, as Jesus lamented the desolation of Jerusalem. We assured him that all was not lost, but that the heart of the great brotherhood, when not misdirected by the "kingdom of the clergy" rising up in our midst, still beats responsive to the loud call of the gospel, and still throbs with pulsations of renewed life and vigor.[23]

When Rowe stood up to leave, both he and Creath recognized that this was probably their last meeting together on earth. Creath stood up to walk to the doorway with Rowe. He was a large man —at least six feet tall. He had a large high forehead, a sharp aquiline nose, penetrating blue-grey eyes, a firmly set mouth, and a deep sonorous voice. In general appearance Creath looked a great deal like Alexander Campbell. But, as Rowe and Creath moved to the door, Creath smothered the younger man in his large arms. They stood in the doorway like that, and Creath lifted his wrinkled face to the darkened skies, and there prayed fervently and deeply as only Creath could pray that God would guide and bless this godly brother.

When Creath prayed, it was as though one was standing in the presence of someone divine. One Saturday in June, 1854, L. B. Wilkes went to Lagrange, Missouri to preach. His appointment was to preach on Saturday night, Sunday morning and Sunday evening. When he arrived and had gone to the home of a Brother

---

[22]John A. Brooks, "Jacob Creath," *Gospel Advocate,* Vol. XIX, No. 5 (February 1, 1877), p. 67.

[23]John F. Rowe, "Beyond the Mississippi," *American Christian Review,* Vol. XXVII, No. 7 (February 14, 1884), p. 52.

Gill, he found Jacob Creath there. About eight o'clock that evening it started raining, and it rained almost all night. But the next morning was the Lord's Day. The rain had stopped, the sun was shining brightly, and from the distant trees the birds were warbling merrily. Creath and Wilkes came down to breakfast. Creath was very meditative and silent. After breakfast he said to Wilkes, "Let us take a walk."

They walked for a quarter of a mile. Not a word was spoken. Finally Creath pointed to the right and said, "This way." They walked two hundred yards further into a woods. There was no path or road, and Creath was so silent that Wilkes was afraid to speak. "Yonder is a good place" said Creath in a moment. They walked over beside a fallen tree, and here both bowed down while Creath prayed.

Here beneath the tall trees, the air full of the music of glad birds and redolent with the odors of thousands of flowers, all praising God, Brother Creath said: "Let us pray." We fell on our knees and O such a prayer! The earth had drunk up the rain and all nature seemed to be refreshed and happy. Every leaf and flower and bird and being in nature around us seemed to be striving its utmost to magnify God. All this Brother Creath mentioned in his prayer, and then called upon his soul and all that was within him to bless the Lord. My soul trembled with excitement. Brother Creath talked so to God that I voluntarily felt for the moment that if I should open my eyes I should certainly see him upon whom no one can look and live. I never heard such a prayer before, and now thirty years have passed since that remarkable experience, and yet I have heard no such prayer since. At the close of his lengthy prayer, he asked me to pray. I did. During the second prayer, he would every few moments break forth in expressions of thanksgiving and praise. "Oh bless the Lord, my soul. Give thanks unto his name. His mercy endureth forever."[24]

On one occasion, during the War Between the States, a company of troops was encamped near Palmyra, intending to capture the city. Creath went out to the grove to pray and the leader of the troops happened to be near. He edged closer to the grove and listened as Creath prayed for his neighbors, his town and for peace. The next day the troops withdrew without any attempt to capture the town.

Creath was of the firm conviction that around 1849 a great

---

[24]L. B. Wilkes, "no title," *American Christian Review,* Vol. XXVII, No. 17 (April 24, 1884), p. 131.

change came over the restoration movement, and over Alexander Campbell. The *Millennial Harbinger* of these years was not the same paper that it was before. He believed that Campbell was easing out of the picture, and that his corps of younger teachers and friends were influencing him in the wrong direction. In 1857 Dr. Robert Richardson published in the *Harbinger* some articles on "German Neology and French Philosophy." Neither Creath nor Tolbert Fanning liked it. Both wrote Campbell a protest. Creath wrote that if what Richardson was printing was the gospel, ninety-nine out of one hundred readers of the *Harbinger* did not know what the gospel was, and he added, "I am one of that number." Creath believed that Richardson would kill the *Harbinger* if that were allowed to go on. Campbell soon stopped Richardson, but it made the latter look with great disfavor upon Creath. Consequently, when Richardson wrote his "Memoirs of Alexander Campbell," he mentioned every other pioneer with whom Campbell had been connected, but brought in Creath's name only when it was un-avoidable, and then stated only points to his disfavor. After pub-lication of the "Memoirs," Creath wrote to Richardson, asking why this was done. His letter received no answer.

Creath avowed that in the last fifteen years of the life of the *Millennial Harbinger,* it was as different from the earlier *Harbinger* as day and night. When Campbell died, Creath wrote to W. K. Pendleton, asking that his subscription to the paper be discon-tinued. Pendleton wrote back urging that he continue, and Creath did for one more year. But after that, he wrote to have it dis-continued. Pendleton wanted his reasons. Creath's reply was that he disagreed with the attitude of the *Harbinger* toward the South in those days of the War Between the States. The *Harbinger* had spoken of "justice" being on the side of the North, and of the South's being "conquered." Such expressions were not right in a paper devoted to the spread of the gospel, Creath thought and so expressed himself. The effect was that now he was looked upon with disfavor both by Richardson and Pendleton.

I mention this fact to show that my discontinuance of the *Harbinger* after Bro. Campbell's death was another cause why I was treated as I was by the author of the last years of the Harbinger, and by the author of his Memoirs, and that the breth-ren and posterity may know the reasons of the treatment I received that whosoever writes the history of this Reformation may do me more justice than did the author of the Memoirs. [25]

No one more bitterly opposed missionary societies and other human organizations to supplant the church than Jacob Creath, Jr. He was the first great opponent of human organizations. By nature he could not refrain from speaking out against practices he believed to be wrong. Likewise he was an opponent to the use of instrumental music in the worship. Throughout most of this study the work of Jacob Creath will be further noted. Truly he was a mighty prince in Israel.

---

[25]Jacob Creath, "The Bible Alone Rejected by the Conventions," *Gospel Advocate*, Vol. XIX, No. 47 (November 22, 1877), p. 724.

CHAPTER VII

THE PROGRESS OF THE CAUSE

Before launching directly into the historical events of the years to be covered in this study, it would be well to get a general view of the progress of the cause up to the pre-Civil War days. To what extent had the church grown? What were the problems that it met? What was its general condition? To see this general condition will furnish a background on which to paint the events that are soon to be pictured, and will add interest and enchantment to the intensely thrilling story of the restoration movement.

The "reformation" first attracted men of the middle class. These men were not highly cultured but they were men for the most part of fair education. Moreover, most of them were men of independent turn of mind and of great courage. They loved liberty and were willing to sacrifice everything for what they believed to be true. To be sure there were many men of prominence in politics, medicine and business who accepted the views of pioneers. At first their views were peculiar to most hearers. Consequently, they invoked study. Moreover, with the clergy of the day they were greatly abhorred. Nobody accepted then, the gospel message because it was popular, for it wasn't. There was that courageous love for the liberty of the gospel, free from human creeds and from the authority of council that gave the impetus for men to submit to the living oracles. Once converted, they worked intensely to convert others. They were convinced they were right and would have others to be. The whole restoration movement soon took on the color of beligerency and aggressiveness. These pioneers believed in their cause, and they pressed on, wilting before no tribunal, but with the profound conviction they had the truth and that the truth, under God, would triumph.

Referring to these pioneer preachers, Champ Clark, one-time Speaker of the House of Representatives in Congress, said in a centennial address delivered at Pittsburgh, Pennsylvania:

First in the field, they set the compass and fixed the chart by which our ship has sailed, and by which it will sail till Gabriel's trumpet summons the quick and dead to the judgment-bar of God.

Their names live forevermore and their works do follow them. If the spirits of just men made perfect on high take cognizance of the affairs of this world, as I have no doubt they do, the souls of these masterful pioneers must be filled with amazement and delight as they contemplate the results of the first hundred years of the movement which they started.

As these early preachers went out, they relied solely upon their Bibles. Most of them knew little about philosophy, although there were exceptions to this rule. Their preaching was almost entirely expository and any other kind was tabooed. They freely underwent sacrifices, satisfying themselves with the conviction that at their worst, they had more material prosperity and ease than their Lord. In their presentation of the gospel, their phraseology was charged with scripture quotations or references. Oratory was the order of the day, and sermons less than an hour long were never head of—most of them running two and a half hours. Concerning the preaching of these days Morrill says:

This preaching was powerfully emotional and thoroughly spontaneous. A single text-book, the Bible, provided preachers with their whole stock in trade. It must be confessed that in these latter days we have very superficial ideas about the sermon preparation of a hundred years ago. Given a man dead in earnest, with a book like the Bible, viewed as it was in those days, a book read and re-read and largely committed to memory; and given a man whose mind, thoroughly awakened, was charged to the brim with scripture, and solemnized by prayer vigil and lonely meditation; and given the motion and fire of delivery prevalent in those days, and you have a generator of tremendous sensations and impressions. The sermon might be fanciful and extemporaneous, but it could not be unprepared. The exegesis was faulty no doubt, but the application was direct and pointed. Many a sermon abounded in oratorical grace and fascination, and contained a residium of homely truth that was wholesome and palatable. Notes were tabooed and regarded as a stigma. . . .[1]

Down to the year 1827, the Campbells had established only two churches—Brush Run and Wellsburgh. The years from 1809 to 1827 were for the most part formative ones. Step by step, the Campbells were thinking their way along, trusting to the revealed word for guidance. By 1823 when Campbell started the *Christian Baptist,* his mind on all essential points of doctrine was made up.

---

[1]Milo True Morrill, *A History of the Christian Denomination in America* (Dayton: Christian Publishing Co., 1912), pp. 103, 104.

Creeds and Confessions of Faith had kept men away from the word of God. Consequently, Campbell pointed his guns toward the ramparts of the clergy and let loose with an unrelenting barrage that shook the kingdom of the clergy as it had never been shaken. Such teaching had its effect, but it was not strongly evangelistic. Campbell was planting the seed, but up to 1827, he saw little evidence of a harvest. That year when Walter Scott was sent as evangelist to the Western Reserve and kept the baptismal waters stirring, Campbell grew concerned for he had never known the cause to prosper in such a way before. The evangelistic fever took hold, and the restoration was on its way.

By 1836 D. S. Burnet remarked that the disciples numbered over one hundred thousand and ranked as the fourth largest body of religious people in the nation.[2] Ten years later Campbell wrote:

We little expected, some thirty years ago, that the principles of Christian union and a restoration of primitive Christianity in letter and spirit, in theory and practice, could have been plead with such success, or have taken such deep hold of the consciences and of the hearts of multitudes of all creeds and parties, of all castes and conditions of society, as we have already lived to witness. We must say that it is, "the Lord's doing, and marvelous in our eyes."[3]

By 1850 a writer in the *Ecclesiastical Reformer* reports the total number of disciples to be over two hundred thousand, but others put the number as high as three hundred thousand. A year later, Campbell writes:

The territory over which the doctrine of the reformation has been more or less diffused, within one quarter of a century, is unprecedented in any age known in history and to me. It is preached or read in books, not only in all the United States of America, and in all the British provinces of North America, from St. Johns to San Francisco, and from Oregon to the Neuces: it has also been preached or read in England, Scotland, Ireland, Wales, and the Isle of Man. It has crossed the Pacific to Australia and New Zealand, and visited Liberia, on the coast of Africa. At some of these points it has, indeed, touched but slightly but even there, like a little leaven hid in a large measure of meal, it must work, as the Messiah said, until the mass be leavened.[4]

---

[2] D. S. Burnet, "Progress of the Present Reformation," *Christian Preacher,* Vol. I, No. 1 (January, 1836), p. 21.
[3] Alexander Campbell, "Preface," *Millennial Harbinger,* Third Series, Vol. III, No. 1 (January, 1846), p. 1.
[4] Alexander Campbell, "The Cause of Reformation," *Millennial Harbinger,* Series IV, Vol. I, No. 10 (October, 1851), p. 590.

Some years later, Isaac Errett reports that based upon the rate of increase, the disciples were first in the decade from 1850 to 1860. By 1870 it was the fifth largest religious body in the United States.[5]

Although this picture is somewhat bright, there is a darker side to it. The strong evangelistic appeal, with its emphasis upon first principles, naturally left the church in need of some teaching that it was not getting. What was the nature of the New Testament church? How was it to be organized? Because there was a lack of the proper conception of the church, Tolbert Fanning undertook to write many articles on "Church Organization." As early as 1845 Fanning wrote of the glorious progress of the cause, yet he paints a darker picture, citing examples to show that in many cases the church was degenerating into a sect. Was this church about which the pioneers preached to be the New Testament Church, and would its leaven work effectively throughout Babylon to call men back to Jerusalem, or would the product of their efforts be the erection of another sect in Christendom? To men of vision and foresight this question was of grave concern. A few warnings begin to appear. Fanning wrote:

No other proof is necessary to establish the fact, that an apostacy has commenced. The preachers and churches in many places, have evidently stopped at first principles, and have, from ignorance of the spiritual organization, practices and enjoyments of God's empire, and from an ambition to have a name amongst men, grown weary, and desire peace with the conflicting parties. . . . There are tens of thousands, who will sacrifice all that is earthly, before they will "strike hands" with the drunken captives of Baby- lon. Indeed, while we profess, a belief of the scriptures, and obedi- ence thereto, are essential to Christianity, and compromise with factions is yielding the whole apostolic ground. . . .

The crisis has come. . . . The churches are not generally walking blamelessly, and some of the leading preachers begin to talk of their clerical *"brethren"* amongst the sects, and are really taking more pleasure in seeking popularity amongst parties, and worldly gain and honor, than in teaching the disciples the whole truth.[6]

In 1846 *The Reformer*, edited by Benjamin Franklin, came out with a picture of this darker side. Franklin was then a young editor, but his influence was already being felt. He bemoans the

---

[5]Isaac Errett, "How We Stand in the Last Census," *Christian Standard,* Vol. VIII, No. 2 (January 11, 1873), p .12.

[6]Tolbert Fanning, "The Crisis," *Christian Review,* Vol. II, No. 10 (Octo- ber, 1845), pp. 217, 218,

fact that the restoration has come to a dead halt, an observation which doubtlessly was overstated. Franklin gave five reasons for this lack of progress: (1) Great political excitement. (2) Second advent excitement. (3) Lack of faith among disciples. (4) Many good preachers had left the field. (5) Preaching lacked zeal, scriptural argument, as in the former years. But, what was the answer?

Under these circumstances, what is to be done? We answer, let every Disciple of our blessed Lord determine to read the Scriptures some every day, with the most devout and prayerful attention possible. . . . That the cause in which we are engaged is emphatically the cause of God, whether our actions are always the best calculated to promote it or not, we have never entertained one doubt since we first acknowledged the authority of the great King. . . . Let us, then, brethren, make one mighty effort to save the church from corruption, lukewarmness, speculation, and sin of every kind, that it finally may be presented to the Lord, "a glorious church, without spot, or wrinkle, or any such thing," and ascribe all the glory to God and the Lamb forever and ever.[7]

Franklin had the utmost faith in the cause he espoused. He believed thoroughly it was from God. As long as men were true to this cause, God would bless them, and the cause would triumph. Upon the inauguration of the *American Christian Review* in 1856, Franklin states in his "Introductory Address":

We have seen the workings of this cause during the last twenty years and have carefully considered its history since the first effort in the United States, to call the attention of the people to original Christianity, as well as the rise of Christianity in Jerusalem at the beginning. We have also carefully considered the means employed to oppose it, and impede its progress, and we are well prepared to say that it is the cause of God, and that it can be successfully maintained, defended, and extended, in defiance of all opposition. There is no cause on earth that can stand before it.[8]

Only a short while before his death, John T. Johnson views the cause of Christ and expresses his amazement.

Taking a bird's-eye view of the field before us, what most prominently strikes the eye? Congregations have sprung up as by enchantment; the land has been dotted over with houses of

---

[7] Joseph Franklin and J. A. Headington, *The Life and Times of Benjamin Franklin* (St. Louis: Christian Board of Publication, 1879), pp. 91, 92.
[8] Benjamin Franklin, "Introductory Address," *American Christian Review,* Vol. I, No. 1 (January, 1856), p. 4.

worship; evangelists have been sustained in the field beyond any former example; schools, male and female, and colleges, are rising in every direction. . . .'[9]

If one were to step into the worship service of one of these churches in the early restoration movement, what would he find? How were the services conducted? One might find himself well able to understand this picture by considering the description given of the church at Noah Springs in Kentucky. The church was established in 1828 with twenty-eight members. Two years later there were ninety. They met at first only monthly, and generally connected a meeting on Saturday with that of the Lord's Day. In 1830 their service is described as follows:

They have done away their monthly Saturday meetings, and now meet every first day of the week. Their order is as follows: After meeting early, say between nine and ten o'clock, they engage in singing hymns of praise to their exalted King. Next, as appropriate prayer is offered by one of the Elders or Bishops (for they have four selected from among themselves), an opportunity is then afforded to anyone who wishes to make a profession of their faith in Jesus as the Messiah. If any come forward upon such profession, they are immersed into the name of the Father, Son, and Holy Spirit; and then they are received into the congregation as fellow disciples. One of the elders then instructs the congregation from some portion of the Holy Oracles, afterwards an exhortation by one of the others is delivered. The Deacons then prepare and furnish the table. One of the Elders, after singing an appropriate hymn, prays and then breaks the bread. In like manner the wine is poured; and all who have been legally naturalized, and deport themselves as disciples, are authorized to participate, without regard to any human *theory* or *ism,* to commemorate and show forth the Lord's death. A hymn is then sung, and the brethren greet each other as fellow disciples, by a shake of the hand, and then retire.[10]

With this statement of the general condition of the church before the War Between the States a more detailed description of the advancement of the cause in the various states now must come before us. Yet, this picture must necessarily be brief. Large books have been written on the church in various states, so it cannot be expected that more than a brief outline of brother-

[9]John T. Johnson, "Communication from Elder J. T. Johnson," *American Christian Review,* Vol. II, No. 1 (January, 1857), p. 27.

[10]Stephen, "News from Kentucky," *Millennial Harbinger,* Vol. I, No. 9 (September, 1830), p. 425.

hood activities can be given in a single chapter. No attempt, then, can be undertaken to describe the state of the church in the various sections of the country in anything like completeness, but a briefer sketch will at least portray the extent to which the plea for a return to the ancient order of things had gone.

One finds in New York City in 1842 a congregation with one hundred and thirty members meeting on Green Street. The church had Silas E. Shepherd as its preacher. Another congregation in New York City met on Lawrence Street with seventy-five members. Both churches were predominantly made up of Scotchmen, and both had had considerable trouble. A new congregation was established in Brooklyn in 1842, but apparently was never successful. By 1845 one finds congregations at Manchester, Amsterdam, Pittstown and Troy in the state of New York. By 1850 the church in New York City was meeting on Seventeenth Street about thirty yards from Sixtieth Avenue. By 1855 there were four congregations in the one county of Onandoga.

In Philadelphia before the war the church was small and hard pressed to grow. In 1848 Dr. B. F. Hall moved to Philadelphia. He reports that there were a few members meeting in a poor building which itself was poorly located. Hall writes:

Almost everything flourishes here, but pure, primitive Christianity; it has a hard struggle to keep its holy head above the proud waves of sin, sectarianism, and infidelity.[11]

When Alexander Campbell visited Philadelphia in 1842, he found the church had one hundred and thirty members and met on Fifth and Gaskill Streets. There was another small congregation meeting on Race Street. After B. F. Hall left Philadelphia, James Challen moved there from Cincinnati, and the church perhaps had her greatest growth under Challen.

The first statistics for the state of Pennsylvania were compiled in 1851. At that time it was discovered there were fifty-five congregations in the state with a little over two thousand members. The largest congregation met at Allegheny City. Here, Samuel Church, "the walking Bible," lived and preached.

The church in Baltimore, Maryland, fared better. When Alexander Campbell visited here in 1842, he found the church in

[11]B. F. Hall, "Letter from Dr. B. F. Hall," *Christian Magazine*, Vol. I, No. 7 (July, 1848), p. 204.

a healthful condition and meeting on St. Paul's Street. Seven years later, a meetinghouse was put up at the cost of six thousand dollars. It was here D. S. Burnet preached later and here that he died.

The church in the nation's capital was established in 1843 by Dr. James T. Barclay, who later was the first missionary sent out by the new society to Jerusalem. The church at first met in his home, but after Barclay went to Jerusalem, it met in the home of R. G. Campbell, one of the deacons. In the spring of 1850 it had only eighteen members. Until after the war, the church was kicked about from one place to another, never securing a permanent building of its own until the war had ended.

In Virginia the church fared well. One could find thriving congregations in Antioch, Jerusalem, Newton, Smyrna, and Richmond as early as 1845. At Fredericksburg the church had serious internal conflicts that prevented a large growth and influence. James Henshall and R. L. Coleman were perhaps the two outstanding Virginia preachers before the war.

In the Carolinas the churches were few and far between. Joshua K. Speer established a church in Dobson, Surry County, North Carolina, in 1856. There were some churches of the O'Kelley movement there much earlier in the restoration movement. In South Carolina, the most famous congregation was at Erwintown. Dr. Erwin pioneered the cause here. Erwintown was not really a town but a "Christian neighborhood." It consisted of a post office, a male and female academy, and a congregation.[12] There was a church at Evergreen in Anderson district and one at Union in Barnesville district.

Perhaps no state, however, enjoyed greater growth of the church before the war than Ohio. By 1852 the state had over twenty thousand members. The southwest district of the state had sixty-seven congregations with over five thousand members. There were ten thousand members on the Western Reserve and five thousand more in the remainder of the state. Yet, by 1852, there were in Ohio twelve cities with over six thousand population, and churches in only four of these. There were eighty-seven county-seat towns, and only twenty-one had congregations.[13] One of the

---

[12] J. J. Trott, "Evangelizing in the South," *Christian Review,* Vol. IV, No. 4 (April, 1847), pp. 133-136.
[13] T. J. Melish, "Our Cause in Ohio," *The Disciple,* Vol. I. No. 9 (April, 1852), pp. 272, 273.

oldest churches in the state was the Antioch Church in Clinton County, established by Samuel Rogers. The churches on the Western Reserve were largely established by Walter Scott when he preached under the direction of the Mahoning Association in 1827. In Cincinnati, the church came over from the Baptists very early in the restoration.

In Michigan, one finds congregations to be less numerous than in Ohio. A church met in Detroit early in the 1850's, and by 1856 one reads of plans to erect a building. Isaac Errett moved to Lyons, in Ionia County, that year and organized a church with twenty-four members. Thereafter, the churches in Michigan seemed to grow much faster.

No state enjoyed greater growth than Indiana. Very early did the cause reach this state, and the progress was phenomenal. The cause began in southern Indiana very early after the turn of the nineteenth century. The city of Vincennes on the Wabash River in Indian Territory fell to the small army of George Rogers Clark on February 24, 1779. The legislature of Virginia, in recognition of his victory, gave him nearly one hundred and fifty thousand acres of land in what is now southern Indiana which was called "Clark's Grant," afterwards known as Clark County. Toward this plot of ground in the summer of 1799 came the family of Absolem Littell. He had two sons, Absolem, Jr., aged eleven, and John T., aged nine.

At that time Clark's Grant knew but one church, a small Baptist Church having been organized the year before by Isaac Edwards of Kentucky. A few years passed, and by 1819 John T. Littell was recognized as the pastor of the church. For thirty years this little church grew, and in 1829 it numbered a membership of two hundred and fifty. On July 24, 1812, it led in the formation of the Silver Creek Baptist Association. When the first issues of the *Christian Baptist* began to be read, it profoundly influenced the members. By 1828 the majority in the church had adopted the views of Alexander Campbell. The next year the Baptist Articles of Faith were voted out, and a division in the church resulted. Of this history, James M. Mathes writes:

Before the Reformation was preached in Indiana, a very large and respectable Baptist Association called the "Silver Creek Association" held its annual meetings in this county. Elders Absolem Littell, Mordecai Cole, and J. T. Littell were the leading men in this body; but these beloved brethren, together with others, embraced the reformation at an early period and boldly contended for union upon the Bible alone. The result of their self-denying and zealous efforts in favor of the ancient gospel was that a large majority of the "Silver Creek Association" also embraced the reformation. And if I am not mistaken, as early as 1827 or 1828 they had exchanged the name "Regular Baptist" for CHRISTIAN, and the "Confession of Faith" and "Rules of Decorum" for the Bible alone, and accordingly the churches were reorganized upon the ONE FOUNDATION.[14]

Among the early pioneer Indiana preachers were such men as John Wright, Joseph Hostetler, Elijah Goodwin, Benjamin Franklin, James M. Mathes, John P. Thompson, Beverly Vawter, Ovid Butler, John O'Kane, S. K. Hoshour, and John Longley, John O'Kane established the first church in Indianapolis as early as 1833 in the home of Benjamin Roberts, who lived in a log cabin on the northeast corner of Illinois and Market Streets. The first state-wide meeting of the churches was held in 1839, a full report of which was sent to the *Millennial Harbinger*. The report showed that Indiana then had a total of one hundred and fifteen churches with seven thousand, seven hundred and one congregations identified with the restoration.[15] Four years later, the *Christian Record* reports more than twenty thousand members in the entire state.

With the establishment of Northwestern Christian University in 1855 in Indianapolis, this city took on greater importance as a radiating center for the gospel. Famous preachers over the brotherhood found their way to the city, and in no place was the cause more prosperous in the days before the war. Yet, despite this fact, there was a temptation to ease the struggle, as Benjamin Franklin observed when he visited the city in 1856:

In Indianapolis, there are some fifteen or eighteen preachers— some of them old and experienced men, some in the prime of life, and others young—aiming to perfect their education and knowledge for a more useful life. In a place like this, where the professors in the college are all preachers, where there are other able and eminent men, and where the characters of young men are forming for the ministry, those from abroad will expect to find a model church. . . . Such an expectation is natural and right. In

---

[14]James M. Mathes, "Notes on a Tour to the South Part of the State," *Christian Record*, Vol. II, No. 4 (October, 1844), p. 84.

[15]F. W. Emmons, "Statistics of Indiana," *Millennial Harbinger*, New Series, Vol. III, No. 7 (July, 1839), pp. 355-357.

view of it, there should be an effort, as far as possible, to show forth Christianity in this church. At present, the church has no preacher whose business it is to look after its interests and take the special oversight. It certainly cannot succeed in this way.[16]

The church likewise got an early start in Illinois. The first congregation appeared to have started in Wabash County. Seth Gard and James Pool organized Barney's Prairie Christian Church on July 17, 1819. Gard, who was a member of the Convention that framed the State Constitution, was an elder in this church. The second congregation in the state was established a month later on Coffee Creek in Wabash County. Small country congregations multiplied for the next ten years. In 1832 a congregation was established in Jacksonville by people who moved in from Kentucky. At Old Union, ten miles west of Clinton, a church was organized October 13, 1832, under a white oak tree. Hughes Bowles preached here. His son, Walter P. Bowles, was perhaps the best known preacher in Illinois at this time. Young Bowles and Abraham Lincoln were the closest of chums. One day Lincoln said to Bowles: "Wat, if I could preach like you, I would rather do that than be president."

Kentucky, too, saw the advancement of the restoration movement. Perhaps no state was in the heart of the movement more. Men like Jeremiah Vardeman, P. S. Fall, and Raccoon John Smith were the early advocates in the state. John T. Johnson, John Rogers, and Jacob Creath were among the later preachers. Kentucky received its first impetus toward restoration from the Barton W. Stone movement which has already been recounted. After the appearance of the *Christian Baptist,* many Kentucky Baptists started the return trip to Jerusalem, and so the movement went forward at a rapid pace. Big meetings were the order of the day. John Allen Gano had forty-one additions in December, 1848, at Paris, Kentucky. By 1844 the *Christian Journal* reports fifty thousand members in the state, although it is likely that this number is somewhat exaggerated. Twenty-five to seventy-five additions, however, were frequent in meetings especially under such preaching as that done by John T. Johnson and Raccoon John Smith.

Some idea of the size of the church in Kentucky can be gotten by the report of S. M. Scott, who was sent to visit all the congre-

---

[16]Benjamin Franklin, "Affairs About Indianapolis," *American Christian Review,* Vol. I, No. 3 (March, 1856), pp. 90, 91.

gations in the state in 1845. He reports three hundred and eighty congregations with a membership of thirty-three thousand, eight hundred and thirty. This number is much more likely than the fifty thousand previously mentioned. There were one hundred and ninety-five preachers in the state. One hundred and thirty-six congregations had been established in the past year.[17] By 1858 it was estimated that there were fifty thousand in the state, which is probably an accurate estimate.

From Kentucky and the North our attention now turns toward the Southland with a view to a sketch of the extent to which the churches had grown here. General reports coming from the South before the war indicate that the church had known only a slow growth, much slower than in the North. The reports indicate a general wave of religious indifference that swept the whole Southland. A. Paden reports:

I should be glad were it in my power to give quite an extended history of the church in the South, but at present I cannot. I can say, however, as far as I can learn, that our members are very few, and are almost destitute of proclaimers. In all my travels I do not think that I have seen so great a field for evangelical labor as South Mississippi and Louisiana. . . .[18]

On another occasion J. A. Butler reports:

There is an onward steadfastness in the brethren here, which shows strength. And if the spirit of the world could be cooled down, and the spirit of Christ increased, I think our vessels, cargoed with the waves of eternal life, would sooner outride the storm of sectarianism and safely anchor on the shores of everlasting deliverance. The energy is here, but we lack concentrated effort. But we make fair promises; if we *fail of compliance,* we will do better in the future.[19]

In 1838 and 1839 Alexander Campbell made an extended tour into the South. He writes to R. L. Coleman of the conditions he found in the following words:

Disciples of Christ are not numerous in the South. . . . We are disabusing the public mind of false impressions and presenting definite views of first principles. The Baptists are exceedingly

---

[17]S. M. Scott, "Christian Statistics of Kentucky," *Christian Review,* Vol. II, No. 11 (November, 1845), p. 238.
[18]A. Paden, "Religious Intelligence," *Christian Magazine,* Vol. I, No. 3 (March, 1848), p. 96.
[19]J. A. Butler, "Prospects in Mississippi," *Christian Review,* Vol. II, No. 5 (May, 1845), p. 118.

opposed through the decrees of their Associations, who have forbid the opening of their meetinghouses to me and the brethren. . . . Favourable impressions have been made in all places, and a few converted. But our population in the South is much more ignorant than in Virginia. We have a few educated, intelligent men, as we have a few rich and powerful; but the majority are poor, ignorant, and uneducated. . . . The brethren are of the best class of citizens and of very respectable attainments. But it will require many sermons and labors, or much reading, to achieve much in these regions.[20]

It can be dangerous to speak too broadly in terms of generalizations, for these can be easily misunderstood. Yet there are values which must not be overlooked. To say that a general wave of indifference swept the South before the war is not to say that there were not religious people there, for there were. Some of the most devoted people in the nation were there, but the general picture of the Southland as a whole is that of indifference toward religion. During this time, the cause of the restoration progressed slowly. But in the North the picture was different, and here the church became deeply implanted. The war left the people of the South in poverty and desolation so that, when the war ended, a general wave of religious enthusiasm came across the people, which made the South a fertile field in which to plant the seed of the New Testament Christianity. By the war's end, the issues of the society and the instrument of music had been frequently discussed. Through the influence of men like Tolbert Fanning and David Lipscomb, together with Franklin College and the *Gospel Advocate,* this seed began to be sown in what was almost virgin soil. These men had already been <u>convicted</u> that societies and instruments were wrong. New churches that were planted soon were indoctrinated against all innovations. Consequently in the matter of time the churches of the South stood rigidly against these innovations. In the North where the bulk of the brotherhood resided, there were enough teachers who believed in societies and instruments to swing the churches in line. Perhaps the South in particular, and the present-day churches of Christ in general, owe much to these prewar conditions.

In another chapter a lengthy discussion will be found on the church in Tennessee. Nothing comprehensive will be attempted

_____

[20]Robert Richardson, *Memoirs of Alexander Campbell,* Vol. II, pp. 453, 454.

at this point.   In East Tennessee the churches were very scarce.
G. C. Metcalf wrote Fanning in 1846 saying that next to "midnight darkness reigns in this section of the country."[21]   J. J. Trott
held a meeting at Hamilton in 1845 in the home of a Brother Price
and established the "church of God in Hickory Valley."   In 1844
there were eleven congregations in East Tennessee.   As late as
1855 there was no church in Chattanooga.   The most influential
church in middle Tennessee, if not in the whole South, was in
Nashville.   This congregation had been formed in 1828 from the
Baptist Church in the city.   In West Tennessee the picture is
somewhat optimistic.   John R. Howard resided at Paris, and was
undoubtedly a very influential preacher.   In Obion County there
were three congregations as late as 1855.   That year a church of
ten members was established at Dyersburg.   At Memphis there
was a thriving congregation before the war.

Likewise were there few members in Alabama, although many
congregations were being established.   The strongest church in
Alabama before the war was at Marion where Alexander Graham
resided.   Marion, in Perry County, was often referred to as the
"Eden of the South" and by others as the "Athens of the South."
"It is the cradle of science, and the home of scholars."   Here was
located Howard College, Judson Institute, and Marion Female
Seminary.   This congregation took the lead in spreading the gospel throughout the state.

Another strong Alabama church before the war was located at
Russellville.   This congregation was established in 1842 under
unusual circumstances.   Tolbert Fanning left Nashville on January
20, 1842, on a tour to the South.   He visited Franklin and Columbia
in Tennessee and found these churches nearly dead.   He went on
to Florence and Tuscumbia, Alabama, and from here to Russellville.   At the latter place he met Dr. Sevier, son of a former
governor of Tennessee, who was the only member of the church
then in the city.   Fanning spent a night in the city and preached
on the importance of searching the scriptures.   The next morning
he started to leave town.   About a mile from the city the slender
carriage gave way.   He was informed that it would take several
days to repair it.   He and his wife walked back to town through
the mud, and here again he began an extended gospel meeting.

---

[21]Tolbert Fanning, "Church Intelligence," *Christian Review,* Vol. III, No.
1 (January, 1846), p. 22.

He preached a week, and twenty were baptized. But Fanning was tired. He went to Tuscumbia, and W. H. Wharton came down to help. Before the meeting ended, Fanning baptized two doctors, one lawyer, the clerks of the county, circuit, and chancery courts with their families, the wife of the postmaster, the jailer and his household, and the wife and daughter of the sheriff. The meeting ended with seventy-four additions.[22] Later, Fanning reported one hundred and five additions, indicating that others soon came in as a result of the meeting.[23]

Before the war one finds churches at Lafayette, Clinton, Bluff Creek, Fayetteville, Cedar Plains, Florence, Moulton, in addition to the other places already mentioned.

The strongest church in Mississippi before the war appeared to be at Columbus. This church was established in 1842. They built a new brick building in 1845, and by that time had ninety members. By 1847 the church had one hundred and fifty members, most of whom were young people. At Jackson there was no church in 1844, but five years later one reads of T. W. Caskey baptizing twelve persons there. When Fanning visited Jackson in 1847, he found but few members. A brother, General Clark, lived there. So did James E. Matthews, who was an outstanding preacher of the gospel in Mississippi before the war. Fanning preached in the Baptist meetinghouse and then in the state house. He immersed three persons, and from this beginning, it appears, the church in Jackson, Mississippi, started.[24]

On this tour to Mississippi, Fanning makes the following observation regarding the church generally throughout the South:

Through all parts of Alabama, Mississippi, and Tennessee we passed, there is a great lack of godly intelligence and godly piety. The people are generally intelligent on other matters, and friendly disposed; but the blessings of the pure and spiritual religion of the Bible are but imperfectly enjoyed. A hundred able and humble preachers are needed where there is one to be found at present.[25]

---

[22]Tolbert Fanning, "News from the Churches," *Millennial Harbinger,* New Series, Vol. VI, No. 4 (April, 1842), p. 186.

[23]Tolbert Fanning, "The Church at Russellville, Alabama," *Christian Review,* Vol. II, No. 1 (January, 1844), p. 47.

[24]Tolbert Fanning, "Observations on a Tour to the South," *Christian Review,* Vol. IV, No. 2 (February, 1847), pp. 37-45.

[25]Tolbert Fanning, "Notes on a Tour—No. 4," *Christian Review,* Vol. I, No. 12 (December, 1844), p. 269.

P. B. Lawson was another Mississippi preacher. In 1855 he resided at Crawfordsville, a city renowned for "wealth, wickedness, and mud." He complains that people are so completely engrossed in politics that they care nothing for spiritual interests.[26]

The restoration movement in Georgia in some ways antedates that led by the Campbells in other states. There were men in Georgia pleading for restoration who had never heard of Alexander Campbell or Barton W. Stone. Christian Herman Dasher was one such man. Dasher's parents had fled Salzburg, Germany, to escape persecution by the Roman Catholics. They were Lutherans religiously. Dasher himself was very much dissatisfied with religious division and began to search the scriptures on all subjects, but especially upon the subject of baptism. While studying the Bible, he chanced to meet a Mrs. Threadcraft of Savannah, who told him of a preacher in her city by the name of S. C. Dunning, who had formerly been a Baptist but who was now pleading for the Bible religion. Dasher went to Savannah, talked to Dunning, and was baptized. After returning home, Dasher baptized his wife, his wife's sister and her husband. This group began holding services as early as 1819. Later Dasher moved from Effingham County, where he had been residing, to Lowndes, near where Valdosta now stands. Most of the little congregation went with him. Dasher died in 1866, but the congregation, though small, lived on.[27]

The most influential church in the state of Georgia before the war appears to have been at Augusta. No preacher traveling through the state would have wanted to miss this congregation. Most of the wealth and talent in the church was found here. A rich widow, Sister Tubman, lived here. She at one time donated ten thousand dollars to endow a chair at Bethany College. Frequently she gave money to the erection of meetinghouses in the brotherhood. She gave eight thousand dollars to erect a house of worship in Augusta. When Alexander Campbell visited Georgia in 1845, he stayed with Sister Tubman. He found in the church men like Dr. D. Hook, former mayor of the city, and an influential worker pressing the cause of Christ. While in Augusta, Campbell

---

[26]P. B. Lawson, "Report from P. B. Lawson," *Gospel Advocate,* Vol. I, No. 4 (October, 1855), p. 126.

[27]James A. Harding, "The Church of God at Valdosta, Georgia," *Gospel Advocate,* Vol. XXV, No. 7 (February 15, 1883), p. 102.

visited with Ex-Governor Schley. Schley almost became a Christian and expressed to Campbell after their conversation that all doubt had now been dispelled from his mind. Unfortunately we have no way of knowing whether this man ever acted upon his convictions or not. After Campbell left, Dr. Hook decided to devote his time to being an evangelist. For the next few years he and N. W. Smith planted small congregations in Georgia.

Late in 1848 Samuel J. Pinkerton went to Augusta to preach. J. S. Lamar also came shortly after. A. G. Thomas and P. F. Lamar became prominent in the work. But in 1855 Pinkerton left the church and joined the Episcopalians, and this did the church no small amount of harm. The next year J. S. Lamar and A. G. Thomas began publishing a paper called *The Christian Union*. It is doubtful if this paper ever had a wide influence, but it probably did much to stabilize the church in those early, critical days.

In the western side of the Mississippi River the cause of restoration moved forward, although, in the case of Louisiana, its progress was much slower. Few congregations were to be found in the state before the war. At Baton Rouge, John T. Johnson held a meeting in 1849 and baptized thirty-eight. In New Orleans the church fared well until the speculations of J. B. Ferguson set it back. In 1845 the New Orleans congregation met at 82½ Julia Street. Five years later a new house of worship was built at the corner of Camp and Melpomere Streets, and J. B. Ferguson delivered the dedication sermon. Shortly before the war the theories of Ferguson crept into the church and divided it.

The plea for restoration made its inroads into Arkansas very early. At Little Rock, the state capital, this was particularly true, and, like Nashville, the church owed its origin to the Baptists. In 1824 Silas T. Toucray established the Baptist Church in the city. This congregation was strongly Calvinistic. On July 4, 1832, led by B. F. Hall, this church renounced its creed and took its stand upon the Bible alone. Less than three weeks later, W. W. Stevenson, a preacher for the Cumberland Presbyterian Church, renounced denominationalism and took his stand for the truth. His preaching and work with the congregation in Little Rock helped it tremendously. In 1845 John T. Johnson and R. C. Ricketts came to the city and conducted a five weeks' evangelistic meeting, baptizing eighty-three and having ninety-seven additions in all.[28]

There were other smaller congregations in the state, but their progress for the most part was slow. Stephen Strickland, a Baptist preacher, was converted by reading the *Christian Baptist* and the *Millennial Harbinger*. He founded one of the first congregations in the state at West Fork in Washington County in June, 1836. By 1847 one finds David S. Pyle laboring in Carroll County where he organized a congregation of thirty-one members in August, 1847. Nathan Polly and William H. Stewart were among the other early Arkansas preachers.

But, undoubtedly, the most influential congregation in the state was found at Fayetteville, and was largely the work of Robert Graham. Graham had graduated from Bethany College in July, 1847, and by December that year was in Arkansas. He held a week's meeting in Little Rock, and was urged to locate there. Refusing, he went on to Fayetteville. He arrived at the latter place February 2, 1848. At this time John T. Johnson was in Arkansas, so Johnson and Graham preached in a two weeks' meeting. The usual order was, Graham preaching and Johnson exhorting. Their services were held in the Methodist church building on West Center Street. Before the meeting closed they had converted a preacher, a doctor, and four lawyers. Among the lawyers converted was Lafayette Gregg, who, in 1886, was a candidate for governor of the state on the Republican ticket. The preacher converted was William T. Larimore of the Cumberland Presbyterian Church. When Graham and Johnson arrived in Fayetteville, they found seven members of the church already there, among whom were Dr. Thomas J. Pollard and Judge Jonas M. Tebbetts, who were the pillars of the church.

Graham's main purpose in going to Arkansas had been to act as an agent for Bethany College and the *Millennial Harbinger*. After his meetings at Fayetteville, he continued on his itinerary, later coming back to Fayetteville to locate with the church. For a while the church met in the courthouse and then in the Masonic Hall. It enjoyed a steady growth. But Graham had visions of a school. On December 14, 1852, a charter was granted for a college. The school opened at the corner of Dickson and St.

---

[28]W. W. Stevenson, "News from the Churches," *Christian Review,* Vol. II, No. 5 (May, 1845), p. 119.

Charles Street, and the first class to graduate was on July 4, 1854. Meanwhile a lot was purchased on the southwest corner of the public square. By 1859 a commodious building of brick and cut stone had been erected. The war affected the church seriously in Fayetteville, but this will be shown in more detail in another chapter.

The state of Missouri was hardly behind any when it came to the progress of the restoration. Soon after being admitted as a state in 1821 people from Kentucky and Tennessee began over-flowing the land in quest for cheap farms and a more stable financial security. With these people came the story of the restoration plea, and churches were planted rapidly in Missouri before the war. Randolph County was early settled by people coming from Fayette County, Kentucky. They were mostly Baptists, but some had rejected denominational creeds for the Bible alone before coming. A meetinghouse was erected, and Allen Wright came to hold a meeting. The result was the establishment of the Antioch Church, the first in the county. From this congregation came Alexander Proctor, later a famous pioneer preacher.

The most influential preacher in Missouri was undoubtedly T. M. Allen. Allen was born in Virginia in 1797 and moved to Boone County, Missouri, when he was thirty-nine, in the year 1836. Allen had a crippled arm and hand. He had settled on a nice farm, owned several slaves, and was quite wealthy financially for those days. He held meetings throughout Missouri and planted churches over the state.

The church in St. Louis was established February 18, 1837, and at first worshiped in the Sheppard School on Fourth Street. R. B. Fife was the leading spirit that kept the church going before the war. Fife was born in Edinburgh, Scotland, in 1792, and by trade was a gunsmith. He came to Missouri sometime shortly after 1830. When W. H. Hopson's father died, Fife married Hopson's mother. W. G. Fife, his son, also was a leading influence in the St. Louis church. By 1844 the church in St. Louis had one hundred members but no house of worship. They met in the third story of a house at the corner of Vine and Third Streets, but the next year had moved to Sixth Street and Franklin Avenue.

State meetings were held very early in Missouri. Some knowledge of the spread of the restoration can be gained by the reports

T. M. ALLEN

of these meetings. In 1845 it was reported that there were eighteen thousand members in the state. By the war this number had reached hardly less than twenty-five thousand.

As the American frontier pushed westward the plea for restoration moved with it. Pardee Butler went to Kansas, and largely through his efforts the cause began to be preached there. The gold rush to California in 1849 opened up the far west. By 1852 there were three congregations in that state—Stockton, Santa Clara, and San Jose. But by far the cause knew its greatest advancement in the west in the state of Texas.

Congress granted statehood to Texas in December, 1845. Already there were some pleading restoration in the state. E. H. East writes:

It affords me pleasure to be able to say there are a few even in Texas who reject all human creeds and take up the New Testament alone for their rule of faith and practice.[29]

But there were few preachers in Texas. S. B. Giles had moved there in 1837, and was one of the few who devoted his time to preaching. A few school teachers and lawyers preached occasionally. Churches were begging for preachers to move there. A small congregation had been established at Brenham and another at Travis, and both agreed to pay a preacher three hundred dollars a year to move out. From Huntsville, Texas, Robert T. Walker wrote in 1845:

There are but few disciples in this country, and there are no evangelists in this county (Montgomery); there is no church, and I firmly believe, never will be until we are succored by the brethren of the United States. Brethren, help us, *help* us, or many, I fear, will perish! Imagine our situation, bring your Christian minds to bear on our *deplorable situation!* We are here, scattered like lost sheep, tossed to and fro by many melancholy breezes, and are susceptible of many sensual impulses. . . .[30]

B. F. Hall went to the state in 1849 on business and preached as often as he could, although he was sick most of the time. He writes back:

The people of Texas, among whom I have traveled and preached, are hospitable, intelligent, independent, every man claiming the right to believe and act for himself in religion. I have never seen a people more ready to hear and obey the gospel. I know of no country which presents so fine a prospect for usefulness as Texas just now. The people are not yet sectarianized.[31]

With such encouragements preachers did slowly migrate to Texas. Hall went back to Kentucky and then returned to Texas to live the rest of his days. Carroll Kendrick, editor of the *Ecclesiastical Reformer,* moved to Crockett in January, 1851. That year Kendrick reported to the *Reformer* that there were one hundred preachers in the state.

---

[29]Tolbert Fanning, "From Texas," *Christian Review,* Vol. II, No. 8 (August, 1846), p. 191.

[30]Robert T. Walker, "A Call from Texas," *Christian Review,* Vol. II, No. 8 (August, 1845), p. 191.

[31]B. F. Hall, "Things in Texas," *Millennial Harbinger,* Third Series, Vol. VII, No. 2 (February, 1850), p. 103.

There were seven counties in the general vicinity of San Augustine which had no preachers at all during these years. In Austin, S. B. Giles labored with a congregation of thirty members. But the cause grew rapidly. In March, 1852, Kendrick reported that nineteen had been added in the previous two months. Giles went to West Texas in 1855 and in a meeting baptized one hundred and seven persons in five months. This same year the church in Dallas was planted.

The *Gospel Advocate* very early in its existence made much headway in the state. Kendrick, soon after arriving in the state, began publishing a paper which he called the *Christian Philanthropist*. This paper was short-lived, and the subscription list was turned over to the *Advocate*. Tolbert Fanning then requested Kendrick to edit a "Texas Department" in the paper, which he did. The *Advocate* very early became a popular paper in the state, a fact that was to later influence the direction of the cause in the coming struggle over innovations.

With this picture before us of the extent of the spread of the cause before the Civil War, we are prepared to launch directly into the major events of the period. Again it is emphasized that this picture is necessarily far from being complete, the only purpose being in giving it to recount to the neophyte in restoration history the broad extent to which the cause had grown so there may be a more tangible platform from which to observe the coming events.

Chapter VIII

EARLY EFFORTS AT ORGANIZATION

In the northeastern part of Ohio is one of the most interesting geographical areas of the restoration movement. It was here that the first real problem of organization among the brethren began to exert itself. So important to a study of restoration history is this area that a few observations about it are not out of order.

The Western Reserve, as it was called, was bounded on the north by Lake Erie, on the east by the state of Pennsylvania, on the south by the forty-first parallel of north latitude, and on the west by Sandusky and Seneca Counties. It stretched one hundred and twenty miles each and west and fifty miles north and south, in all occupying some three million acres of land. The name, Western Reserve, is of interesting derivation. King Charles II had granted to the colony of Connecticut in 1662 all lands in the new world stretching within certain specified boundaries to the far west. It must be remembered that at this time the knowledge of the lands of America was very imperfect. It was generally supposed that the "South Seas" or Pacific Ocean was but a few miles west of the Appalachian Mountains, so Connecticut was granted all land between the forty-first and forty-second latitude to the Pacific Ocean. After the colonies united themselves into a federal government, these land-grants became a source of conflict. However, in September, 1786, Connecticut ceded to the new federal government her right to all the land she had been granted, except that three million acres between Sandusky and Seneca Counties, Ohio, and the Pennsylvania state line. These lands she reserved for herself. Before long this territory was known as the Connecticut Western Reserve, and finally the Western Reserve.

It has already been recounted that on Western Reserve in 1820 the Baptists formed the Mahoning Association on very liberal terms. The Wellsburgh Church, of which the Campbells were members, applied for membership in the association and was received. Walter Scott became in 1827 the evangelist for the association and through his preaching the apostolic gospel was announced for the first time generally on the Reserve. For three years churches were planted by magic on the Western Reserve, and converts were made by the scores. So singular was Scott's success that Alexander Campbell became anxious whether the truth and the truth alone could convert men that rapidly. Later Campbell wrote:

I was so doubtful of these conversions that, when I visited the Mahoning Association last August, I was asking every person who could inform me both of the means employed in the great conversions in that quarter, and also of the behaviour of the converts. I also was particular in inquiring about the apostasies, and found that they were free from these exceptions, and that in about one thousand conversions in one year, not more than six or seven individuals had turned away from the holy commandment.[1]

Even though the cause was apparently prospering under the work of the Mahoning Association, some brethren became anxious as to whether or not such an organization could be defended by the scriptures. As a vital part of the message of these men was the plea for a return to original ground, it was asked by inquiring minds, "Was there scriptural authority for the existence of such an organization?" Although some were not convinced that such an organization violated any teaching of the word of God, yet there was a general feeling among members that the association ought to be permanently dissolved. Accordingly plans were made to accomplish this at the meeting in Austintown in August, 1830.

This particular historic meeting of the Mahoning Association opened as usual with its songs, exhortations, and prayers. John Henry, one of the preachers, stood up and said: "I charge you to look out what you are about to do here; we want nothing here which the word of the Lord will not sanction."[2] He sat down and in a few moments arose and suggested a resolution to dissolve the association. This resolution was passed and the association was dissolved.

The death of the Mahoning Association indicates that a spirit of unrest was being felt regarding ecclesiasticisms unknown to the scriptures as early as 1830. Many of these early brethren, too, had come to the restoration principles from the Baptists where they had seen the extremes of creedalism and human societies.

---

[1]Alexander Campbell, "Dialogue Between the Editor of the Christian Baptist and Adelphos," *Christian Baptist,* Vol. VI, No. 8 (March 2, 1829), p. 526.
[2]Alexander Campbell, "Mahoning Association," *Millennial Harbinger,* Vol. 1, No. 9 (September, 1830), p. 415.

Many had been ostracized, denounced, and rejected by the various associations, and there was, therefore, an inward fear of such ecclesiasticisms. Yet many others were quick to realize that the danger of a thing does not argue against its existence. There was an attitude of fear and restraint that made it apparent that if ecclesiasticisms were ever to gain much headway among the brethren, they would need to be sold on the idea. Proponents of institutionalism must pursue cautiously or else run the danger of a division within their own ranks. The next twenty years were to find the subject up many times for discussion.

Alexander Campbell was not pleased with the dissolving of the Mahoning Association, but sensing the intense desire on the part of the majority, he silently acquiesced. After the resolution for dissolving the association was passed, Campbell arose and said: "Brethren, what now are you going to do? Are you never going to meet again?" A hush fell over the audience, and then Campbell suggested that the brethren meet annually hereafter for preaching the gospel, mutual edification, and for hearing reports on the progress of the cause. Accordingly, the next meeting of the brethren was held at New Lisbon on Friday, August 26, 1831. William Hayden presided at this meeting, and Walter Scott delivered a sermon on the reason of the Christian's hope.[3] After these discussions, the topic of "Cooperation" was discussed, the beginning of a long discussion of this subject which was to last for years ahead.

The term, cooperation, obviously indicates a working together for some specific purpose. The great question among the pioneers was, how and in what manner can the various congregations work together to convert the world? The scope of this question at first limited itself to districts, then to states, and then to the entire brotherhood. Consequently, district cooperation meetings were among the earliest held, but one soon reads of state meetings and then finally of brotherhood attempts at cooperation which were realized in the formation of the American Christian Bible Society and the American Christian Missionary Society, the latter being the greater of the two.

Brethren who favored the cooperation efforts feared that the nature of their cooperation meetings were much misunderstood.

---

[3] Alexander Campbell, "General Meeting in New Lisbon," *Millennial Harbinger*, Vol. II, No. 9 (September, 1831), pp. 445, 446.

Consequently, frequent articles inform the readers of the various publications of the real purpose and design of these meetings. In Kentucky the brethren who had been under the influence of Barton W. Stone had very early shrunk back from any kind of organized effort between brethren. While Stone's followers looked with some suspicion upon Campbell and the "reformers," still the two groups found themselves coming slowly together. The publication of the *Christian Messenger,* which began in 1826, had something to do with this. It was not long before the subject of cooperation made its appearance in the *Messenger.* Walter Scott, writing under his usual name, "Philip," presented an article to the *Messenger* early in 1827 favoring conferences and cooperation meetings. Scott wrote:

Brother Stone:

As the subject of conference is considerably agitated at present, in the religious community, on the propriety of which there is (as upon almost every other subject) a variety of opinions; and as it certainly is a matter of no small importance, I beg leave to invite your attention to the subject, with a single view of eliciting information and ascertaining, if possible, what is propriety.

The very considerable hostility of many of our good brethren to every convocation in the shape of conference, together with the importance of the subject, renders it necessary that something should be said. For my own part, I have really thought that the most of the opposition to our annual meetings, from the brethren of the Christian Connection, arises from a want of correct information as to the objects of our association. For names I wish not to contend; I care not whether a religious convocation be termed conference, association, or annual meeting; but as to the propriety of the brethren occasionally meeting for religious edification, instruction, and information, from different parts of the community, within proper and limited bounds, there should exist no doubts whatever, particularly when the innocent as well as the useful objects of our meeting are ascertained.

Many are under the impression that we associate for the purpose of legislating or making laws for the rule and government of our churches. Nothing is more foreign from our views. I acknowledge one lawgiver and believe the great Head of the church has left a perfect code of laws for the government of his people; therefore, we stand not in need of human lawmaking to facilitate the prosperity of the Redeemer's cause. . . .

It may then be inquired, what propriety is there in your conference or annual meeting? I answer, simply to worship together and strengthen the bonds of union; to receive and obtain information from the different churches, either from their letters or messengers, and attend to their suggestions, and as far as in our power, comply with their requests; attend to ordination, if thought proper, when required by the brethren; to arrange our appointments so as to supply the destitute churches with preaching; and imitate the primitive church by making such requests only as may be proper to set things in order.[4]

To this article Stone replied that he appreciated the views set forth and agreed with them in the main. Nevertheless, the brethren of the Christian connection had been led away from conferences and cooperation meetings because they saw in them too much similarity to the Baptist Associations which they felt were tremendously despotic.

J. Eichbaum, one of the editors of the *Christian Magazine,* found himself in 1850 trying to put down a rising tide of opposition to cooperation meetings in Tennessee. In answering the question, "What is the design of cooperation meetings," Eichbaum wrote:

1. They are *not* designed to interfere with the perfect and untrammeled independence of any congregation of Christ whatever, whether rich or poor, influential or obscure.

2. They are *not* designed to frame or devise a creed, church covenant, or articles of faith, or in any degree to infringe upon the fullest exercise of the divine right of private interpretation.

3. They do *not* claim the slightest authority to legislate as to any ordinance, custom or usage, that must or must not be observed by the churches of Christ.

4. They do *not* claim any right to excommunicate or in any degree disfellowship any congregation that may think proper to refuse participation in their measures or recommendations.

5. They are *not* designed to establish any tests of Christian character, nor to decide who or who are not evangelists, bishops, or deacons, nor in any sense to interfere with the action of any congregation with reference to sending forth preachers of the word.

6. They do *not* claim any authority to arbitrate the differences that may exist between different members of the same congregation or between distinct congregations.

7. They have *not* authority to enforce any recommendation or plan of expediency, and their resolutions must be regarded, not as decrees or laws, but as simply *propositions* to the churches, with whom resides all power.

---

[4]Walter Scott, *For the Christian Messenger,* Vol. II, No. 3 (January 25, 1827), p. 49.

8. They are not designed to permanently concentrate power and money in the hands of a few. As a matter of fact they have never done so, nor is it possible that they ever can.

9. They are not intended to give a separate and independent existence to any body ecclesiastic.

10. They are *not* designed to divert the means of the brotherhood from necessary and beneficial local operations, but rather to encourage and build up these local efforts.

On the other hand—

1. They *are* intended to ascertain the true condition of the various congregations cooperating, and show the state of the cause in any given section. Without true, reliable knowledge on these matters, it is impossible to know either what *ought* to be done, or what can be done.

2. They *are* designed to secure the training and organization of those brethren who are scattered throughout the country, who do not enjoy Christian instruction, and who are unable to provide for it.

3. They *are* intended to bring the small means of individual congregations together, and to accomplish with these united means what no one congregation could effect.

4. They *are* intended to secure, as far as possible, the accomplishment of the church's mission: "Go ye into all the world, and preach the gospel to every creature."

5. They *are* designed to secure system and efficacy of action in place of irregularity and inefficacy.

6. They *are* designed to be instrumental in setting on foot the best ways and means of carrying out what are confessedly the duties of the church of Christ.

7. They *are* designed, by congregating the talents of the churches, to elicit the truth on such subjects as come up for action, and then to disseminate this truth.

8. They *are* designed to unite the brotherhood, not by a system of consolidation, but by the influence of truth, love, and harmony.

9. They *are* designed to refresh the spirits of the holy brethren, to give words of encouragement to the weary, wisdom to the inexperienced, strength to the weak, humility to the proud, and to shed over all the genial influences of fraternal love.[5]

The only apology needed for such lengthy quotations is that they convey to the reader the purpose and nature of the cooperation meetings. These meetings were but assemblies of the delegated messengers of the congregations, who, when they came together, organized themselves with their presidents, secretaries and

[5]J. Eichbaum, "Cooperation Meetings," *Christian Magazine,* Vol. III, No, 9 (September, 1850), pp. 277, 278.

treasurers. They made it clear that their purpose was not to, in any way, infringe upon the local autonomy of a congregation, or to legislate laws for the churches, but to discuss the progress of the cause and suggest ways and means of evangelizing the particular community where the member-congregations in the cooperation were located. Congregations through their messengers to the cooperation pledged certain specified amounts to finance the preaching of the gospel. Cooperations selected evangelists and assured them their pay and authorized them to preach within a certain area.

Thus cooperation meetings were logical forerunners of the organizations and societies, both state and national, later to be found in the brotherhood. Any defense that could be made for them was the same that could be made for later Missionary and Bible Societies. Cooperations, from all practical intents and purposes, were innocent-looking organizations. They left the churches free and independent. Their resolutions were only recommendations and not laws and legislation. For this reason they found wide acceptance in the brotherhood. On the other hand another group of brethren looked with suspicion upon them. The opposition was spotted, unorganized, and sometimes senseless, and all in all, accomplished little. Campbell, writing of some of these opposers, said:

I have found a large class of men, professors, too, who will sit for a year rather than rise up crooked. They are conscientious men; but they do nothing right lest they should do something wrong.[6]

Nevertheless, the general frame of mind in the brotherhood made it evident that the subject had to have free discussion. The year 1831 found Campbell presenting a series of five essays on the subject through the *Harbinger*. The second and third essays were written by Walter Scott in the absence of Campbell and do not materially affect the issue. The articles were somewhat exhaustive of the theme and pursued the entire subject slowly. Campbell started the series by laying down the general thesis that Jesus left the conversion of the world up to the church, a fact which no one was ready to deny. Next Campbell proceeded to

---

[6]Alexander Campbell, "Cooperation," *Millennial Harbinger,* New Series, Vol. II, No. 6 (June, 1838), p. 269.

another plank in his platform: viz., that the agency for this conversion was the word of God. With these as the beginning points Campbell went on to point out that each member of church was to do the preaching of the word, and, at times where the task was too great for individual members the local congregations must take over. From here Campbell proceeded to point out that where the task was too great for a local congregation, many congregations should go together to perform it. So he wrote: "A church can do what an individual disciple cannot, and so can a district of churches do what a single congregation cannot."[7] Coming then directly to the point Campbell urged that the churches of his day begin taking active steps toward cooperation among themselves.

Agreeably to the reason and nature of things, which must never be lost sight of, and to all that is said or implied in the New Testament, upon this subject, it behooves the churches at this time, to regard their location, as respects states and counties, in their efforts to convert the world. . . .
The only question is, how shall this be done to the best advantage? The New Testament furnishes the principles which call forth our energies, but suggests no plan. . . . The churches in every country, have from scripture and reason, all authority to bring their combined energies home, they may, and ought to cooperate with their weaker neighbors, in the same state, and so on increasing the circle of their cooperations, as they fill up the interior, with all light and goodness, until the knowledge of the glory of the Lord cover the whole earth.[8]

From this one may well see Campbell's viewpoint toward these organizations for cooperation. He believed the New Testament Church was to preach the word to convert the world. But, he believed the New Testament was not a code of laws, and therefore, while it was up to the church to preach the word, since the New Testament offered no plan, any plan within the bounds of reason was permissible on the ground of expediency. On this ground Campbell was ever wont to defend organizations outside of the local congregations doing the work of the church.

Scarcely had Campbell's articles reached the public until opposition came up. A Mr. "A. B. G." replied immediately to the

---

[7]Alexander Campbell, "The Cooperation of Churches—No. I," *Millennial Harbinger*, Vol. II, No. 5 (May, 1831), p. 237.
[8]Alexander Campbell, "Cooperation of Churches—No. IV," *Millennial Harbinger*, Vol. II, No. 10 (October, 1831), pp. 437, 438.

Harbinger that "there never was, and there never can be, any occasion for such a combination of the churches to build up the Redeemer's kingdom."[9] This, of course, was striking directly at the root of the problem. That the church was God's agency to convert the world was evident to all, and that the instrumentality to do the converting was the word of God, was equally evident. That the churches could and should cooperate was also evident. But, did the churches have scriptural authority to organization institutions and ecclesiasticisms separate and apart from the local church to do the work of the church? This was the real problem. Campbell's reply was in the affirmative and was defended on the ground of expediency.

After the discussion of 1831 and 1832 in the *Harbinger* on cooperation, little was written on the subject for a decade. When, in the spring of 1838 Barton W. Stone wrote Campbell informing him that many preachers were going into worldly positions to make enough to live on, Campbell replied with an article urging better cooperation to prevent this.[10] But aside from this little was said until 1841. By this time Campbell was thoroughly convinced that the brethren were not taking full advantage of their opportunities and therefore, better organization was needed. Accordingly, at the close of 1841 Campbell wrote that "our organization and discipline are greatly defective, and essentially inadequate to the present condition and wants of Society." From this Campbell reopens the whole field of study on cooperation. He writes:

From my spiritual observatory, and by means of the telescope of faith in history sacred, ecclesiastic, and political; aided, too, by the accumulating lights of experience, observation and biblical developments, I am so deeply penetrated with the necessity of a more intimate organization, union and cooperation than at present existing among us, that I feel myself in duty bound again to invite the attention of the brotherhood, especially of those who are in heart and life devoted to the honor, dignity and influence of Christianity in the world, to a more thorough and profound consideration of the subject than they have ever yet given to it.[11]

Campbell continues and bemoans the fact that there is no general

---

[9]A. B. G., "Cooperation of Churches—No. V," *Millennial Harbinger,* Vol. III, No. 5 (May, 1832), p. 201.
[10]Alexander Campbell, "Cooperation," *Millennial Harbinger,* New Series, Vol. II, No. 6 (June, 1838), pp. 267-271.
[11]Alexander Campbell, "The Nature of the Christian Organization," *Millennial Harbinger,* New Series, Vol. V, No. 11 (November, 1841), p. 533.

cooperation, no general organization, no coming together for the
support of the gospel. He states the reason that he holds; viz., such
meetings in the past have been converted into legislative halls,
and therefore, brethren had rejected them.

The whole field of cooperation had been opened up again.
Campbell's purpose is now clear: he believes the church stands
in need of a "general organization," a brotherhood-wide organization, through which the churches might cooperate to convert the
world. After hurling the challenge to the brethren to investigate
the subject anew, he proceeds to lay down again certain principles
to which he holds. This time Campbell begins with the conception of the church as a kingdom. He lays down the fact that
a kingdom must have a constitution, organization, joint and common interests, and a community organization. Campbell writes:

Now if Christ's kingdom consists of ten thousand families, or
churches—particular, distinct, and independent communities—how
are they to act in concert, maintain unity or interests, or cooperate
in any system of conservation or enlargement, unless by consultation and systematic cooperation? I affirm it to be, in my humble
opinion, and from years of observation and experience impossible.[12]

It will be necessary to notice at this point a particular concept
which Campbell held which clashed with that held by many others.
Over these concepts considerable division was yet to come. The
church of the New Testament is spoken of in two different senses—
the universal and local. The church universal consisted of all
baptized believers. The church in this sense is spoken of in the
scriptures as the body of Christ, the kingdom of Christ, the
house of God, temple of God, etc. The church universal has
but one officer—Christ who is the Head of the body, the King
plenipotentiary over the kingdom. In New Testament times
this King appointed his special ambassadors to establish the church
and indoctrinate it in its infancy. The apostles, strictly speaking,
were not officers of the church. They existed before the church
did, and were appointed by Christ, not by the church. They were
officers *pro tempore* and with the close of the first century left
the church in the form of individual congregations overseen by
bishops or elders to accomplish the work of converting the world

---

[12]Alexander Campbell, "The Nature of the Christian Organization—No.
II," *Millennial Harbinger,* New Series, Vol. VI, No. 2 (February, 1842),
p. 60.

to Christ. The church universal, as such, was not left with any specific work to do, but all work to be done was left up to the local congregations. Hence, in New Testament times, the only organization of Christians to exist was a local church. It is obvious, then, that the plan of the New Testament by which the world was to be converted was the establishing of local churches in every community of the world, and these local churches, in turn, under Christ, convert those within its reach. From Jerusalem to Judea, thence to Samaria and finally to the uttermost parts of the earth, churches were planted in New Testament times without the aid of any other organization than the local church, and souls were thus converted to Christ.

Ecclessiasticisms unknown to the church owe their origin directly or indirectly to beginning with the church universal. This has been carried to the farthest extreme in Roman Catholicism. Beginning with the consideration of the church universal, they reasoned that an earthly pope must reign in the place of Christ. The apostles must have their successors, and so the bishops became this. On these two major assumptions, both starting with the concept of the church universal, Roman Catholicism has built its structure. The Synods, Conferences of Protestantism all have started from the same premise, but have not gone to the extreme of Romanism. For the brethren of a century ago to begin at this point and work toward general organizations was likewise to start on a false premise, and in these concepts the differences arose.

In 1842 Campbell began a series of essays on "Church Organization" which lasted up through 1848. In his first article on this subject he sets forth five arguments for Church Organization. Actually, there are six, the last two being numbered five each, and in all probability because of a typographical error.

1. We can do comparatively nothing in distributing the Bible abroad without cooperation.

2. We can do comparatively but little in the great missionary field of the world either at home or abroad with cooperation.

3. We can do little or nothing to improve and elevate the Christian ministry without cooperation.

4. We can do but little to check, restrain, and remove the flood of imposture and fraud committed upon the benevolence of the brethren by irresponsible, plausible, and deceptious persons, without cooperation.

5. We cannot concentrate the action of the tens of thousands of Israel, in any great Christian effort, but by cooperation.

5. We can have no thorough cooperation without a more ample, extensive, and thorough church organization.[13]

The next year, 1843, Campbell presents his views on Church Organization by presenting a hypothetical case of a group of evangelists who go to an island called Guernsey. In five years they establish congregations which Campbell calls A, B, C, D, etc. After a while, Campbell says, these churches discover they cannot work efficiently without pooling their resources. A meeting is called at congregation A, and here the churches decided to band together and act in all matters just as one church.[14]

To this hypothetical case there was strong objection, at least from one anonymous individual. He replies:

We do not misapprehend Brother Campbell, then, when we say seven separate churches in the island of Guernsey are in his plan of organizing, to form one "whole church"—the church of Guernsey. Here then, I affirm, is a new organization, a new church, and a new name—a district church—a district name.. I call it new, because no such use of the word church is found in the scriptures.[15]

The writer of these words goes on to point out that Campbell has in mind a political embodiment of Christians that has no foundation in scriptures. He furthermore argues that in no way could this superimposed organization find it necessary to govern itself and the churches but by the iron grasp of a pope or an emperor. He looks upon this suggestion from Campbell as embodying a complete abandonment of New Testament Christianity. Accordingly, he continues:

For instance, some persons, Brother Campbell informs us, wrote to him for an organization, and he propounded the Guernsey case for an answer. I will say of all such applicants that if they are not duped and led astray from the simple organization of the New Testament, they will owe their safety, not to their own prudence, but to the discretion of others totally, for in that they sought an organization at his hands, they gave to all men the most animated demonstration of a disposition lurking in them to associate the fortunes of original Christianity, which we have been these twenty-

---

[13]Alexander Campbell, "Five Arguments for Church Organization," *Millennial Harbinger*, New Series, Vol. VI, No. 11 (November, 1842), p. 523.
[14]Alexander Campbell, "The Nature of the Christian Organization," *Millennial Harbinger*, New Series, Vol. VII, No. 2 (February, 1843), p. 78ff.
[15]Anonymous, "Organization," *Millennial Harbinger*, Third Series, Vol. I, No. 1 (January, 1844), p. 42.

five years seeking to restore, with the wisdom of a human organization. Can it be that such brethren do not know that most of
our churches already possess an organization, and neither require
nor demand another at the hand of any man? What does our
church at Carthage want of Brother Campbell? If he encourages
the brethren to play their part well on the present organization,
he does well.

In November of that year, 1843, the Campbell-Rice debate was
held in Lexington, Kentucky. The subject of cooperation was
being by now considered so much that few brethren could get
together for long without its being discussed. In between sessions
of the debate several brethren got together and discussed cooperation along with the possibility of forming a missionary society.
Jacob Creath, Sr. "by his tears, his prayers and his arguments"
got the brethren to abandon their plan temporarily.

In October, 1844 a meeting was held at Steubenville, Ohio to
exchange views on the subject of cooperation. At the conclusion
a committee of five was appointed to draft some propositions for
a more general meeting at Wellsburg on December 26, 1844.
At this meeting the propositions were discussed, but only a few
congregations were represented. Another meeting at Wellsburg
was held on April 1, 1845. Campbell made it plain that these
meetings were only for the purpose of getting discussion.

No individual or set of individuals has any authority to dictate
to their brethren or enforce upon them any views or rules of action
on any subject connected with their spiritual relations to the Lord
and to one another.[16]

The purpose was to get a discussion on the subject in order that
some recommendations could be made to the brethren as a whole.
The whole procedure was to be democratic, so far as Campbell
was concerned.

If then they prefer disorder to order, no general organization,
to a general organization; if they can prefer what now is, to any
thing that can be substituted for it, of course they must have it.

That year, 1845, Campbell was able to write:

Much has been written, and a great deal said, and little done,
on the whole subject of Christian organization. But there is a
growing interest in the subject manifested, and there is a growing

[16]Alexander Campbell, "Church Organization," *Millennial Harbinger,*
Third Series, Vol. II, No. 2 (February, 1845), p. 60.

need felt for a more scriptural and efficient organization and co-operation.[17]

The very fact that the cause for greater cooperation and for organized institutions outside the church had Alexander Campbell behind it, was enough to put it over. Yet, there was some scattered opposition, as we have already seen. T. M. Henley criticized the prevailing trend toward organizations and suggested a plan of his own.

It does appear to me there is a falling off in some measure from what we set out with—"a restoration of the ancient gospel and order of things, and a pure apostolic speech." If I am mistaken in this, it will give me pleasure to find it to be so. But it seems to me like a departure from the simplicity of the Christian institution to have cooperation meetings with *Presidents* and *Secretaries,* calling for the *Messengers* of churches, and laying off districts. This was nearly the principle upon which the Baptists began in Old Virginia (except their creed) and it has now become the scourge and curse to the peace of society. I am for cooperation too; but cooperation, if I understand the term, implies *weakness.* When any one church wishes to send out an Evangelist, and is unable to sustain him in the field, she may invite her sister congregations to cooperate with her. If the invitation is accepted, when the members visit those inviting them on a set day, they ought to act as if in the *house of another family.* The elders of this congregation preside and state the object for which they were invited and their inability to perform the work themselves, and ask their assistance and the sum of money wanting. This being agreed on, then all concerned can unite in selecting their evangelist or pointing out the most suitable ground to be occupied by him—for one year or the time agreed on. The congregation proposing to cooperate appoints one of its members or elders to receive all moneys and pay over quarterly to their evangelist what they may judge necessary to sustain him in the field. This brother's account to be presented to the churches cooperating annually. Such is our course, and I think there is not the same danger of running into the popish principles and practices of the sects as when we have Presidents and Secretaries—with their anathemas following.[18]

For a number of years Tolbert Fanning watched the efforts at cooperation with grave doubts in his mind. Fanning on all points

---

[17]Alexander Campbell, "Church Organization," *Millennial Harbinger,* Third Series, Vol. II, No. 2 (February, 1845), p. 59.

[18]T. M. Henley, "Cooperation of Churches," *Millennial Harbinger,* Vol. VII, No. 7 (July, 1836), pp. 333, 334.

"hastened slowly." He generally thought a thing through, but in the end came to an independent conclusion and stayed there. In 1855 Fanning wrote:

It is well understood that for many years I have doubted the practical results of the cooperations in Tennessee, and indeed in other states, but I have yielded to my brethren of age and experience, and I should be willing to yield longer, could I conclude it would be to the honor of God.[19]

That year Fanning established the *Gospel Advocate*. One of his chief purposes in doing so was to give the whole subject of cooperation a thorough examination. So he continues:

In establishing *The Gospel Advocate,* I determined, by the help of the Lord, to give the subject of cooperation a thorough examination. I do not pretend to say how it has been wrought about, but I have for years believed that a change must take place in our views of cooperation before we can labor to each other's advantage, or to the honor of God.

The church in Nashville, Tennessee, very early had its own misgivings about these cooperative organizations. A number of brethren met in the church house in January, 1842, to discuss cooperation. They studied the Bible as though they had never seen it before. At the end they reached the following conclusions:

1. That there is positive scriptural authority for every religious work that is well pleasing to God.
2. That the church of Christ is the only divinely consecrated organization on earth for Christian labor.
3. All other organizations through which men propose to perform spiritual labor tend but to obscure, discredit, and subvert the reign of the Messiah.[20]

Encouragements in cooperative efforts were not long in having their effect. Organized efforts sprang up like magic over the nation. In Virginia, around Wellsburgh, district cooperations were begun as early as 1831. At the close of a protracted meeting in Jacksonville, Illinois, in 1834, it was decided to start a cooperation meeting. The Illinois State Meeting was held for the first time two years later. In 1839 a Cooperation Meeting was held in Richmond, Virginia, representing twenty-five congregations. The same year, the first state meeting of the churches in Indiana was

---

[19]Tolbert Fanning, "Cooperation," *Gospel Advocate,* Vol. I, No. 4 (October, 1855), p. 110.
[20]Tolbert Fanning, "The Path of Safety," *Gospel Advocate,* Vol. VIII, No. 6 (February 6, 1866), p. 82,

organized. A convention of South Kentucky churches was organized in 1842. The same year a convention in northern Missouri was organized, and also the same year an organization was formed at Warrensville, Ohio. By 1844 one reads of the General Cooperation of Disciples in Virginia. By 1850 the Kentucky State Missionary Society was organized with John T. Johnson as president. Two years later the Ohio Christian Missionary Society was organized at Wooster. The list could be extended to great length, but these are enough to convey the thought that the general trend in the brotherhood was more and more toward organizations outside the church to do the work of the church.

One major step in this direction needs special attention—viz.: the American Christian Bible Society. It was the first attempt at anything similar to a brotherhood-wide organization yet promoted. It was founded by D. S. Burnet in Cincinnati, Ohio, on January 27, 1845. Soon after its establishment, its constitution was widely published in brotherhood periodicals along with articles urging the support of the brotherhood to this society.

No sooner was the Bible Society organized than opposition poured down upon it. Aylette Raines, editor of the *Christian Teacher,* a Kentucky publication, doubted the practicability of the enterprise. J. J. Goss, editor of the *Christian Intelligencer* of Virginia, thought it would be wiser to cooperate with the American and Foreign Bible Society, a Baptist organization, than to establish another. Campbell himself thought the Bible Society to be premature, thinking the brethren were not yet ready for it. Campbell also felt that the colleges—Bethany, Bacon, and Franklin—should be put on a more substantial financial basis before trying something like a Bible Society.

Burnet seemed to have been stunned by the opposition. For several issues of the *Harbinger* after 1845 he and Campbell defended themselves over the society. Burnet wanted to know if the brotherhood had been sufficiently consulted when Campbell established Bethany College. Campbell's reply was that the nature of the two institutions was entirely different. Bethany College was a private institution, established from the funds of himself and his friends, whereas the Bible Society purported to be a brotherhood organization. Very little of the opposition to the Society came because brethren thought it was an organization, but only because it was inexpedient at that time to start it.

For eleven years the Bible Society existed with very little interest displayed in it. It was off to a bad start and never got much sympathy behind it. In 1856 the Ohio State Convention met and agreed to terminate the Bible Society and turn its funds over to the American Bible Union. This was done, and so ended the first general brotherhood attempt at organization.

Of course that which far overshadowed the Bible Society was the American Christian Missionary Society. It is toward this society that we turn our attention in the chapter that follows.

CHAPTER IX

THE AMERICAN CHRISTIAN MISSIONARY SOCIETY

"The most important event in the history of the Disciples, next to the founding of Bethany College, was the organization of the American Christian Missionary Society."[1]   D. S. Burnet wrote to W. T. Moore in a letter dated February 28, 1867: "I consider the inauguration of our society system which I vowed to urge upon the brethren, if God raised me from my protracted illness of 1845, as one of the most important acts of my career."[2]   These strictures, stating the importance of the founding of the American Christian Missionary Society, are not overdrawn.   The establishment of this society marked the climax of years of intense effort on the part of Alexander Campbell to urge the brotherhood to found some kind of a general organization through which the entire brotherhood could cooperate to evangelize the world.   The society's establishment also was the first real test to which the unity of the brotherhood had been put.   Likewise was it the first real occasion for the airing of internal differences with the church—differences which in the course of time were to create a widening breach within the ranks of those advocating a return to the primitve order of things.

1849!!   This is a year when a rather youthful nation and an equally youthful religious movement were afflicted with "growing pains."   The nation was going through its most critical period. Zachary Taylor was the president, and with the exception of Abraham Lincoln, never was a president faced with such grave problems.   The question of slavery was before the nation, and violent debates were thundering from the halls of Congress.   Gold had been discovered in the Lower Sacramento Valley in 1848. During the next year, eighty thousand immigrants swarmed into the new El Dorado.   The government found itself with laws inadequate to meet the controversies arising.   National expansion

---

[1]Frederick D. Power, *Life of William Kimbrough Pendleton, LL.D.* (St. Louis: Christian Publishing Co., 1902), p .128.

[2]F. M. Greene, *Christian Missions and Historical Sketches of Missionary Societies Among the Disciples of Christ* (St. Louis: John Burns Publishing Co., 1884), p. 172.

key-noted the times. At the very time the Convention of 1849
was meeting to decide the wisdom of establishing a missionary
society, California was seeking entrance into the new-born Union.
These were the days when Webster, Clay, Calhoun, and Benton
were thrilling the people with their glowing eloquence. But their
language painted a horizon of gloom behind the glowing sunrise,
for slavery told the most thoughtful that darker days were yet
ahead. Side by side the nation and the church were headed for
internal chaos whose results would not soon be lost by either.

Campbell's frequent essays on Church Organization between
1841 and 1848 were producing their effects, although in some
cases these effects were not altogether desired. The magic name
of Alexander Campbell behind any idea usually was enough to
discourage any opposition from becoming too effective. On the
other hand, his name frequently caused too ready acquiesence *acquiescence*
from many. The articles in opposition to Campbell's essays on
Church Organization did not discourage him, for Campbell felt
his way along slowly enough to know that he had the bulk of the
brotherhood behind him. Consequently, the opening of the year
1849 gave Campbell the feeling that the groundwork had been
sufficiently laid that some more difinite action should now be taken
to form a general organization for cooperation. He was encouraged, too, by the fact that brethren who agreed with him were
urging him on.

There is now heard from the East and from the West, from
the North and from the South, one general, if not universal, call
for a more efficient organization of our churches. Experience,
than which there is not a more efficient teacher, decides and
promulgates that our present cooperative system is comparatively
inefficient and inadequate to the exigencies of the times and the
cause we plead. . . . [3]

Sensing a wide demand for a general organization, Campbell urges
that some definite attention be given to it. Still, he urges calm
and deliberate action and warns against extremes.

There are extreme views on all subjects as well as moderate
and rational ones. I have always been a pleader for organization;
still organization is not faith, nor humility nor liberality.[4]

---

[3]Alexander Campbell, "Church Organization—No. I," *Millennial Harbinger,* Third Series, Vol. VI, No. 2 (February, 1849), p. 90.
[4]Alexander Campbell, "Church Organization—No. I," *Millennial Harbinger,* Third Series, Vol. VI, No. 2 (February, 1849), p. 92.

Campbell went on to point out that the principles for which he had pleaded were as firmly established as those of the Protestant Reformation. Throughout the land he believed there were a thousand or more local congregations vehemently crying for some means of cooperating their efforts. Many people appeared to believe that if they had such an organization as would unite their combined efforts, they would carry everything before them. While Campbell shared this optimism, he also believed that some sort of organization was necessary to prevent the restoration movement from going into retrograde.

[handwritten marginal note: coordinating]

Two questions presented themselves for consideration. First, Campbell asked: "What shall be the form or character of our organization?" The second was: "How shall it be established?" Campbell suggested that a committee be appointed and investigate the subject and make some report to the brotherhood.

Have we, then, no scriptural model, no divine precedent or authority for any form of church organization and cooperation? and if so, what is it? We must appoint a committee to examine the subject, and to report in our next number.[5]

Two months later Campbell reports that the committee had been able to meet only once, and, therefore, was not ready at that time to give a report. In view of that he decided to set forth again his views on the subject of a general organization for the benefit of those who might yet be unconvinced. After recognizing the independent character of the congregations, he asserts that this independence did not forbid their working together on any great accomplishment. In his next article, Campbell shows that the New Testament usage of the term, church, embodied single congregations, and the church of Christ in the aggregate or the whole is the entire Christian community on earth. That being true, he suggested that the church knows two classes of officers—officers who belong to a local community such as bishops, elders, and deacons; and those who belong to the whole Christian community —the apostles, prophets, and evangelists. Campbell then struck with a very forceful conclusion:

In all things pertaining to public interest, not of Christian faith, piety, or morality, the church of Jesus Christ in its aggregate character, is left free and unshackled by any apostolic authority.

---

[5] Alexander Campbell, "Church Organization—No. II," *Millennial Harbinger*, Third Series, Vol. VI, No. 4 (April 1849), p. 221.

This is the great point which I assert as of capital importance in any great conventional movement or cooperation in advancing the public interests of a common Christianity and a common salvation. My strong proof for this conclusion is that, while faith, piety, and morality are all divinely established and enacted by special agents —apostles and prophets possessed of plenary inspiration; matters of prudential arrangement for the evangelizing of the world, for the better application of our means and resources, according to the exigencies of society and the ever-varying complexion of things around us—are left without a single law, statute, ordinance, or enactment in the New Testament.[6]

This is the heart of Campbell's reasoning on Church Organization. He insists upon beginning with the church in the aggregate or universal sense of the term. It is vital to his viewpoint to ignore, at least for the time being, the local character of the church. It is with the church universal that he begins. Reasoning from the point that the church in the aggregate has the responsibility of converting the world, and that since Christ has given no divine plan for the church, in this sense, to function; therefore, the church is left free to devise its own plan, according to its own wisdom, with only the law of expediency applying. To be sure, any plan the church would devise would be unauthorized in the New Testament, and it would be the height of folly to look for a New Testament example for it. To Campbell, it was expediency pure and simple and on that ground could be defended.

The weakness in Campbell's reasoning was to be found in his beginning point—the church universal. The church universal had but one set of officers—the apostles, and these were the personal ambassadors of Christ sent on a special mission to supervise the work for Christ in the infancy of His Church. Through the apostles the divine word was spoken by Christ, and through the apostles Christ established and confirmed His Messiahship. At the close of the apostolic age, when the last apostle had died, the church was known only by the individual congregations scattered over the world. The work of Christ through the church to evangelize the world was carried on through the influence of the local church in its community. Even in apostolic times the churches felt no need of an organization, devised by human planning, through which the church could cooperate to evangelize the world. They had a

---

[6] Alexander Campbell, "Church Organization—No. III," *Millennial Harbinger*, Third Series, Vol. VI, No. 5 (May, 1849), p. 270.

fervency and zeal, and the history of the church has well shown that the less zeal and devotion there is in the church, the more institutionalism and human organizations are needed.

By the late spring of 1849 Campbell urges his readers to write to him any criticisims, objections, or suggestions they may have. Then Campbell suggested that if his views were agreed upon, "we will dispatch the matter with all speed and concur with them in the call of a general meeting in Cincinnati, Lexington, Louisville, or Pittsburgh."[7]

The Christian Intelligencer, published in Virginia, took up Campbell's plan and suggested the calling of a general convention to meet in Baltimore, but rather in Cincinnati.   There were a number of reasons for this, but the main one was that Baltimore was out of reach of the main bulk of the brethren who lived in the "west."   (Indiana, Illinois, Missouri, Arkansas, and all territory in the Mississippi Valley was then the west.)   Another point of consideration not to be overlooked was that the church had probably had a greater growth by this time in Cincinnati than any other city.   Moreover, it was easily accessible by steamboat, the main method of travel in those days.

The time for this general convention was generally suggested to be the month of October.   The *Christian Magazine* wrote:

We believe in the necessity and propriety of such a meeting. We think Cincinnati the most eligible point for such a meeting, and would make an effort to have the churches of our state represented there.   We would be gratified that the meeting should take place so as to include the fourth Lord's Day in October next.   We are confident our State Meeting, which will convene some ten days prior to that time, will make arrangements to be represented[8]

Campbell, however, opposed October as the time for the meeting and suggested it be called the first Monday of November.   His reason for this suggestion grew out of the fact that an epidemic of cholera was then sweeping the city, and he felt there might be a possibility that it would subside by November.   Needless to say, Campbell's insistence on November was overridden and the meeting was set for October.

-----

[7]Alexander Campbell, "Church Organization—No. IV," *Millennial Harbinger,* Third Series, Vol. VI, No. 5 (May, 1849), p. 273.

[8]Tolbert Fanning, W. H. Wharton, J. J. Trott, J. B. Ferguson, "Meeting for General Consultation," *Christian Magazine,* Vol. II, No. 8 (August, 1849), p. 311.

As the summer of 1849 bore on, Campbell continued to press the urgency of "a more efficient and scriptural organization." He writes:

I am of opinion that a convention, or general meeting, of the churches of the Reformation is a very great desideratum. Nay, I will say, further, that it is all important to the cause of reformation. I am also of the opinion that Cincinnati is the proper place for holding such convention. But the questions are: *How shall such convention be obtained, when shall it be held, and for what purposes?* These I cannot more than *moot,* or propound. I must, however, to suggest considerations to our brethren, say that it should not be a convention of bookmakers, or of editors, to concoct a great book concern; but a convention of messengers of churches, selected and constituted such by the churches—one from every church, if possible—or if impossible, one from a district, or some definite number of churches. It is not to be composed of a few self-appointed messengers, or of messengers from one, two, or three districts, or states, but a *general* convention. I know that neither wisdom nor piety are rated by numbers; still in the multitude of counselors there is more general safety, and more confidence than in a few. The purposes of such a primary convention are already indicated by the general demand for a more general and efficient cooperation in the Bible cause, in the missionary cause, in the education cause.[9]

Up to this time the character of the proposed convention had been very little discussed. By this time Campbell insists that the convention should not be one of bookmakers or of editors, but truly a representative body of the brotherhood at large. He did not use the term, delegate, but messenger, insisting that messengers be sent if possible from all the churches. Moreover, in Campbell's insistence upon a "more general and scriptural organization," he does not use the term, missionary society, as an equivalent of this. The missionary society was but one phase of the organization in which he was interested. He wanted an organization that would be missionary, educational, and benevolent, taking care of all the interests of the church and not limited to any one interest.

Alexander Campbell, because of sickness, was unable to attend the convention when it did meet in October that year. This is a simple statement of fact, and yet there are matters to raise questions in one's mind. There is no evidence of any sickness which

---

[9]Alexander Campbell, "Convention," *Millennial Harbinger,* Third Series, Vol. VI, No. 8 (August, 1849), pp. 475, 476.

Campbell had that was at all serious. Apparently he was not sick enough to stay away from his regular duties. One cannot help but feel—although it is just a feeling—that there were other matters that prevented Campbell from attending the convention. Was it because he feared that his ideas would be rejected and that he himself might possibly be placed in a false light? The question cannot be answered with any degree of certainty, and yet there are indications pointing in that direction.

By the year 1849 there was at least a mild rumble of opposition to Campbell running through many places in the brotherhood. While it is true that these might possibly be caused by misunderstanding, yet they were there. By this time there were not less than twenty to twenty-five publications in the brotherhood, and yet Campbell had, at various times, insisted that these were not needed, but were a waste of money, of time, and of ink. He had opposed a tract society at Cincinnati, and had looked with displeasure upon other schools aside from Bethany College with the feeling they were not needed. It was only natural that Campbell should be accused of being jealous for his own interests. Did he want all other publications to cease being printed merely that the *Harbinger* might enjoy wider reading? Was he jealous of the tract society at Cincinnati for fear that Cincinnati and not Bethany would be the Jerusalem of the restoration? Did he look with disfavor upon other schools than Bethany merely that Bethany might enjoy greater prominence? There were many brethren who thought so, and some seemed to fear that the "general organization" Campbell had in mind was to be an ecclesiasticism to exercise controls over the brotherhood that would favor Campbell. Campbell doubtlessly sensed that many were looking upon him as a dictator, and resolved not to attend the convention, that the organization be the work of the brethren and not of himself. While it is true that no quotation can be given to substantiate the views expressed above in the writings of the day, yet by dipping back into the past and sensing the general feeling, the explanation seems to be highly plausible, and we doubt not, correct.

The Convention met, according to announcement, on Tuesday, October 23, 1849, at Christian Chapel, corner of Walnut and Eighth Streets, in Cincinnati. In Campbell's place came W. K. Pendleton. Writing later of the entire meeting, Pendleton says:

We met, not for the purpose of enacting ecclesiastic laws, not to interfere with the true and scriptural independence of the churches, but to consult about the best ways for giving efficiency to our power, and to devise such methods of cooperation, in the great work of converting and sanctifying the world, as our combined counsels, under the guidance of Providence, might suggest and approve. There are some duties of the church which a single congregation cannot, by her unaided strength, discharge. . . . A primary object being to devise some scheme for a more effectual proclamation of the gospel in destitute places, both at home and abroad, the Convention took under consideration the organization of a Missionary Society.[10]

We are assured that many wild schemes were suggested during the meeting, but that Pendleton headed them off and guided the entire course of the way on "safe" grounds.

He found many prepared to push some wild scheme or another, involving publications, etc., such as some already well-established organization might afford to carry on. He seems to have been the clear-headed, cool-headed one to check the exuberant and speculative, and prove helpful on the side of the more practical; to have been the wise and careful one in counsel, and strong and safe in argument, favoring the adoption of feasible propositions.[11]

The first meeting of the convention in the Walnut and Eighth Streets church building was hardly more than a preliminary one. L. L. Pinkerton was called to the chair, and John M. Bramwell of Indiana was appointed secretary. A group of permanent officers had to be selected. Even though he was absent, Alexander Campbell was elected president. There were four vice-presidents. These were David S. Burnet, John O'Kane, John T. Johnson, and Walter Scott. James Challen, who had labored so long in Cincinnati, was chosen corresponding secretary. A committee was appointed to define the order in which the business should be taken up, and was required to make a report the next morning. With this work completed, the first session of this historic convention closed.

The next morning at nine o'clock the convention held its second meeting. In the absence of Campbell, D. S. Burnet took the chair and presided. He also led the morning's prayer. The first order of business was brought forth from James Challen, who the day

---

[10]W. K. Pendleton, "The Convention of Christian Churches," *Millennial Harbinger*, Third Series, Vol. VI, No. 12 (December, 1849), pp. 689, 690.
[11]F. D. Power, *Life of W. K. Pendleton*, p. 131.

before had been selected as corresponding secretary. Challen now declined the invitation. Two men—Thomas J. Melish and John W. Bramwell—were then appointed to fill the position.

It would be interesting to follow the business procedures in each of the sessions, but yet this would involve many details which would contribute very little to this total study. A knowledge, however, of the general procedure might well give one an idea of how such meetings were ordinarily conducted. When the morning session of Wednesday, October 24, finally got into full swing by settling the men for the office of corresponding secretary, J. J. Moss wanted to know, at the outset, what constituted a delegate, and then followed by suggesting that the name *delegate* be dropped and the word *messenger* used instead. Moss' motion was over-ridden, but for what purpose is not explained. Some discussion then followed as to who should be allowed a member of the organization. J. Young of Kentucky moved that all members of the Christian Churches in North America be invited to participate with the Convention. W. K. Pendleton moved, as an amendment, that each church represented be given one vote. He pointed out that the independence of the churches should be recognized. Elijah Goodwin wanted the convention to be regarded as an experiment, and thought that the largest liberty should be allowed until some future meeting when a definite principle could be adopted. William Begg of Indiana then offered the following resolution: "Resolved, That every properly accredited Christian evangelist and elder of a Christian church present, or that may be present, be, by virtue of their office, invited to a seat with us, as members of this convention." R. G. Fife, of St. Louis, Missouri, strongly objected. He had fears that the adoption of such a resolution would be the beginning of clericalism in the church, and would eventually destroy the equality of the churches. The resolution, then, was tabled. By now the morning session was ready to be closed, so John T. Johnson worded a benedictory prayer.

The afternoon session, which met at two o'clock, was very brief, but yet, was a definite step in the progress of the convention. After a reading of the forty-fifth Psalm by D. S. Burnet and a prayer led by W. K. Pendleton, John T. Johnson offered the following resolution to the convocation: "Resolved, That a missionary society as a means to concentrate and dispense the wealth and benevolence of the brethren of this Reformation, in an effort to convert the world, is both scriptural and expedient." One cannot help but wonder as to the propriety of such a resolution, for certainly the fact that it was passed or declined would effect the issue of whether or not the society was scriptural in no way. A committee was selected to draft a constitution, and with this the afternoon session closed. Those included on the committee were John O'Kane, John T. Johnson, H. D. Palmer, Walter Scott, John T. Powell, and L. L. Pinkerton.

When the convention met that evening at seven o'clock, the scripture was read by D. S. Burnet, who read from the twelfth chapter of Isaiah, and the prayer was led by W. Davenport of Illinois. Nothing of great importance was forthcoming from this session. L. L. Pinkerton very tersely remarked that "our existence as a people is involved in some general cooperation for the conversion of the world." Then followed another resolution which recommended the society to the cordial support of the brethren. This particular resolution was introduced by W. K. Pendleton and read: "Resolved, That the Missionary Society contemplated by this action be presented to the brethren as the chief object of importance among our benevolent enterprises." And so ended the three sessions of Wednesday, October 24, 1849.

The meeting the next morning seemed to concern itself with the interests of the Bible Society. As was customary, the meeting opened with a scripture reading and a prayer. The one hundred and twenty-seventh Psalm was read, and the prayer was led by William Begg. H. Van Tuyl of Ohio recommended a resolution that the American Christian Bible Society arrange her constitution so as to make a missionary department. The motion was laid on the table. T. J. Melish of Ohio made the motion that the Bible Society be resolved into an Evangelical Society for the promotion of both Bible and missionary objects and that the convention drop the Missionary Society idea altogether. He contended that a union of the two would both harmonize the brotherhood and avoid bringing into existence cumbrous machinery. S. S. Church then moved that the American Christian Bible Society change her constitution to read, American Christian Bible and Missionary Society. The question was argued considerably. W. K. Pendleton opposed the union of the two on the ground that this union would prejudice the brethren against both societies. Pendleton's motion that the Missionary Society be considered by the brethren as the

[handwritten marginal note:] L. L. Pinkerton was the first true liberal, arguing for the reception of the unimmersed + against the inerrancy of the Scriptures.

chief work was put to a committee of seven that a resolution might be prepared for it. The committee immediately adjourned and came back in a few minutes with the resolution formed that the Missionary Society be recommended to the support of the brethren, and that the managers of the American Christian Bible Society were requested to furnish the Missionary Society with Bibles. It was a good compromise move, but probably not too well pleasing to the managers of the Bible Society.

By the time of the afternoon session at two o'clock on this Thursday, October 25, the committee which had been appointed to draw up a constitution was ready to report. They read their constitution slowly article by article and discussed each point. The name, upon which they had settled was, Christian Missionary Society. Walter Scott wasn't particularly fond of the name, and suggested a more up to date name by recommending the word, American, be placed in front of the name. Scott's motion was carried, and the name now became, American Christian Missionary Society. Before the session had been dismissed, E. B. Howels of Cincinnati gave one hundred dollars to make Alexander Campbell a life member of the Society.

The next morning, Friday morning, October 26, business was resumed as usual at nine o'clock. A motion was suggested whereby the Convention was asked to recommend to the churches that they not countenance as a preacher any man who was not approved and acknowledged by two or more churches. Another recommendation was suggested to the churches that they call in other men when ordaining their evangelists. Carroll Kendrick objected on the ground this was an unscriptural move. John O'Kane didn't agree. He argued that an evangelist was an officer of several congregations and not of one. Walter Scott agreed, and so went the meeting.

The entire convention lasted four days. There were one hundred and fifty-six delegates who met in all. The constitution which they accepted contained thirteen articles which are here given:

Article 1st. This Society shall be called the American Christian Missionary Society.

Article 2d. The object of this Society shall be to promote the spread of the gospel in destitute places of our own and foreign lands.

Article 3d. The Society shall be composed of annual delegates,

Life Members and Life Directors. Any church may appoint a delegate for an annual contribution of ten dollars. Twenty dollars paid at one time shall be requisite to constitute a member for life, and one hundred dollars paid at one time, or a sum which in addition to any previous contribution shall amount to one hundred dollars, shall be required to constitute a director for life.

Article 4th. The officers of the Society shall consist of a president, twenty vice-presidents, a treasurer, a corresponding secretary, and a recording secretary, who shall be elected by the members of the Society at its annual meeting.

Article 5th. The Society shall also annually elect twenty-five managers, who together with the officers and life directors of this Society, shall constitute an executive board, to conduct the business of the Society, and shall continue in office until their successors are elected, seven of whom shall constitute a quorum for the transaction of business.

Article 6th. Two of the vice-presidents, the treasurer, the secretaries, and at least fifteen of the managers shall reside in Cincinnati or its vicinity.

Article 7th. The executive board shall have power to appoint its own meetings, elect its own chairman, enact its own by-laws and rules of order, provided always that they be not inconsistent with the Constitution; fill any vacancies which may occur in their own body, or in the offices of the Society during the year, and if deemed necessary by two-thirds of the members present at a regular meeting, convene special meetings of the Society. They shall establish such agencies as the interest of the Society may require, appoint agents and missionaries, fix their compensation, direct and instruct them concerning their particular fields and labors, make all appropriations to be paid out of the Treasury, and present to the Society at each annual meeting a full report of their proceedings during the past year.

Article 8th. All moneys or other property contributed and designated for any particular missionary field, shall be so appropriated or returned to the donors, or their lawful agents.

Article 9th. The treasurer shall give bonds to such an amount as the excutive board shall think proper.

Article 10th. All the officers, managers, missionaries and agents of the Society, shall be members in good standing in the churches of God.

Article 11th. The Society shall meet annually at Cincinnati on the first Wednesday after the third Lord's Day of October, or at such time and place as shall have been designated at the previous annual meeting.

Article 12th. No person shall receive an appointment from the executive board, unless he shall give satisfactory evidence of his Christian character and qualifications.

Article 13th. No alteration of this constitution shall be made, without a vote of two-thirds of the members present at an annual meeting, nor unless the same shall have been proposed at a previous annual meeting, or recommended by the executive board.

The chief weakness which later caused so much consternation in the restoration was to be found in Article 3d. This article made membership in the Society dependent upon the payment of money, which many looked upon as definitely a weakness. This will later come to our attention as this study proceeds.

Before closing the Convention, it was necessary to fill in all of the officers required by the Constitution. Alexander Campbell was already elected the president. Twenty vice-presidents had to be found. These were D. S. Burnet, Dr. Irwin, Walter Scott, T. M. Allen, W. K. Pendleton, John T. Johnson, John T. Jones, John O'Kane, Tolbert Fanning, Daniel Hook, E. Parmley, Francis Dungan, Richard Hawley, James T. Barclay, Francis Palmer, J. J. Moss, M. Moberley, William Rowzee, Alexander Graham, and William Clark. The corresponding secretary finally resolved itself upon James Challen. Recording secretary was George S. Jenkins and treasurer was Jesse B. Ferguson.

The managers selected included T. J. Melish, Gerge Tait, S. S. Clark, B. S. Lawson, T. J. Murdock, S. H. Hathway, Andrew Leslie, Lewis Wells, Thurston Crane, C. A. Gould, N. T. Marshall, R. J. Latimer, James Leslie, and W. A. Trowbridge. The foreign managers were Samuel Church, George McMannus, R. L. Coleman, William Morton, P. S. Fall, Elijah Goodwin, S. S. Church, A. Gould, Alexander Hall and Jesse B. Ferguson.

Before the convention closed, a motion was made which would allow each person an opportunity to become Life Members and Life Directors of the Society, according to the terms of the constitution. The brethren promptly responded and in a few minutes fifty-two persons were entered as Life Members by paying twenty dollars each. Eleven were entered as Life Directors by paying one hundred dollars each. All totaled there was $2,140 subscribed, and enough promised to make the finances of the first convention amount to over five thousand dollars.

After the Convention was over, D. S. Burnet addressed a letter to Campbell, informing him that he had been elected as president. Burnet wrote:

When Bro. Pendleton appeared in the convention and informed us that your absence occurred in consequence of illness, we doubly sympathized with you in an affliction, which was also a disaster to us, as it deprived the convention of your society and counsel. The convention over which you were elected president has requested me to assure you of their sympathy and prayers—a duty most genial to my feelings, the more especially as I can, in the same communication, contribute to your joy by announcing a happy issue of our meeting. About five thousand dollars was raised in money and pledges for our various enterprises but especially for the Bible and Missionary Societies, which shared about equally in the munificence. I never knew so fine a meeting. It lasted one week and filled us full of joy and love. The representatives of the churches from abroad amounted to about two hundred.[12]

Campbell himself seemed to be very much pleased with the results of the convention. He wrote:

Denied the pleasure of having been present on this interesting occasion by an unusually severe indisposition. I am peculiarly gratified with the great issues of deliberation. Our expectations from the Convention have been more than realized. We are much pleased with the result, and regard it as a very happy pledge of good things to come. The unanimity, cordiality, and the generous concurrence of the brethren in all the important subjects before them, was worthy of themselves and the great cause in which they were enlisted. Enough was done at one session, and enough to occupy our best energies for some time to come. Bible distribution and evangelical labor—two transcendent objects of Christian effort most essential to the conversion of the world—deserve at our hand a very cordial and generous support.[13]

Whether or not Alexander Campbell was entirely pleased with the results cannot be for certain told. That the American Christian Missionary Society does not appear to coincide in every detail with what he wanted appears evident. Campbell had plead for more of an ecclesiasticism, organized on truly democratic principles, to devise ways and means of operation for the churches in all points of expediency. The Missionary Society was but one phase of the idea, and yet its organizers tried to steer it clear of any ecclesiasticism to direct the churches in order to avoid criticism. C. L. Loos wrote:

In all the discussions and acts of the convention, the strictest and most jealous care was taken never in the least degree to assume

[12]F. M. Greene, *Christian Missions and Historical Sketches*, p. 67.
[13]Alexander Campbell, "The Convention of Christian Churches," *Millennial Harbinger*, Third Series, Vol. VI, No. 12 (December, 1849), p. 694.

any ecclesiastical privileges. That assembly—composed of men who were in heart and soul 'revolutionary soldiers' in the good, early war against all ecclesiastical assumptions, and who were yet fresh and brave as ever in the defence of the cherished principles of freedom from the old fetters of ecclesiastical bondage—would have sprung to their feet to a man at the first attempt to usurp any ecclesiastical authority. Again and again, from the beginning to the end, clear voices were heard repudiating the very thought of such unauthorized purpose or action. This is a most noteworthy fact in the history of this assembly.[14]

Loos, throughout his life, was intimately connected with the Society, and bore a certain bias in favor of it. It is not likely that the Society was ever as completely free from ecclesiasticism as the strength of his words would indicate.

Throughout the year, 1850, Campbell had much to say about the Missionary Society. Early in the year he wrote:

We have an organized Missionary Society—a committee of ways and means—and desire no more, at present, than to notice the foundation laid, on which we may build a glorious superstructure. In our next, we shall consider the field of labor, with our views of the ways and means by which it is to be cultivated.[15]

While in these articles that followed, Campbell appeared to be interested in pushing aside all criticism, yet some was to come, and with the passing of years was to increase. The chief work of 1849 now had been done; the rubicon was crossed; the crisis had come. A glance at the horizon ahead showed the gathering of dark clouds, but to escape them was impossible. Straight toward them the course of events was moving.

---

[14]Charles L. Loos, *First General Convention* (Guide Printing & Publishing Co., 1891), p. 71.
[15]Alexander Campbell, "The Christian Missionary Society," *Millennial Harbinger,* Third Series, Vol. VII, No. 2 (February, 1850), p. 76.

CHAPTER X

ALEXANDER CAMPBELL AND THE MISSIONARY SOCIETY

One of the most mooted questions coming out of this period of the restoration movement relates itself to the attitudes of Alexander Campbell toward the American Christian Missionary Society. The subject forms a great part of the controversy which, in years to come, was to be before the brotherhood. No study of the origin and early activities of the Society can be complete without a discussion of this controversial point.

The heat of such a controversy can be attributed to the high veneration in which Campbell has been held by all adherents to restoration principles. While such veneration is commendable, yet it has its dangers for too frequently is there a temptation to ascribe to Campbell a greatness of which he was not worthy. Indeed, it is the danger of the study of the whole restoration movement, for with many there seems to be a fundamental interest in restoring the restoration rather than the New Testament Church. In the restoration movement no authority of any kind is to be found. No man is qualified to intelligently approach the study unless he recognizes that those who played the important roles were just men, and liable to errors. We lose nothing in admitting that at times they were wrong, for there is only one authority—the New Testament scriptures. This study of the restoration movement is approached, not with the idea of attempting to fit any pioneer leader into a mold, but to study as objectively as possible what they did teach. Where they were wrong, we shall frankly state it; where they were right ,we shall gladly uphold it.

But those who favored and those who opposed the society back in the restoration movement held Campbell in the highest esteem. It was only natural that each should want to feel that Campbell favored his position. But what are the facts? While it is admitted that Campbell, in the period immediately preceding and following the establishment of the Society, favored this organization; yet, opposers of the Society feel that Campbell was then in old age, and was under the influence of younger men who swayed

181

him in favor of the Society. It was only natural that these younger men should deny this charge, and should stoutly defend Campbell as being in favor of Societies. To say the least of it, the problem is great, but yet not an impossible one. To get at all the facts the heart of the controversy which followed these earlier years is laid before us, and from these we draw what we believe are logical conclusions.

Perhaps the leading champion of the view that Campbell changed his position was David Lipscomb, who for years, following 1866, was editor of the *Gospel Advocate*. Lipscomb built this conviction upon two or three facts, the first of which was a statement made by Charles V. Segar that after 1847 Campbell was never again himself. It may be recalled that W. T. Moore undertook the work of gathering up some of Campbell's "Lectures on The Pentateuch" delivered at Bethany College in 1859 for publication. Moore assigned the task of introducing the book with a biography of Campbell to Mr. Segar of Cincinnati. Segar was not a member of the church, and to get his information paid a visit to Bethany to speak to the wife of Campbell. Segar, having Campbell's family as his authority, then wrote:

In 1847, Mr. Campbell made a tour to Europe, partly for his health, and partly to visit the congregations of his church in Great Britain. On reaching London he was the honored guest of our Minister at the Court of St. James, Mr. Bancroft, and through him and through letters from the first men of this country, was the recipient of honors and attentions from the great leaders and molders of political opinion in England. Only in Scotland, in the city of Edinburgh, did any thing occur to mar the influence and pleasure of his trip. His position on the slavery question had been grossly misrepresented by a clergyman who was desirous to engage him in debate, but with whom Mr. Campbell refused to hold any intercourse on account of his questionable character. The refusal, for the cause assigned, led to a recourse before the civil tribunals, on the part of the clergyman, in an action for libel, the final result of which was a verdict in Mr. Campbell's favor. The labors and events of this tour, added to the burden of the college, seemed to have materially affected his mind and general health; but the deadliest portion mingled in his cup of baleful care and sorrow was the sad news which awaited his touching the shores of his adopted country. The son of his old age, the child of his prayers and hopes, was no more! Wyckliffe Campbell had been drowned at his father's mill! It is said by those who were near him, that Alexander Campbell never was equal to himself after this stroke; but it was long before the admiring world perceived any change.[1]

The closing statement, "It is said by those that were near him, that Alexander Campbell was never equal to himself after this shock," particularly impressed Lipscomb and was often used by him.

Still another fact that helped Lipscomb form the conviction that Campbell had changed was a statement made by Tolbert Fanning a few years after the Society was formed. Lipscomb was then a young man, an admirer of Fanning who had tutored him. Fanning grew distressed at the course Campbell was taking in favor of the Society, and made a visit to him at Bethany. Speaking of Fanning's return, Lipscomb years later wrote:

I remember well, on his return he stated that he was shocked to find his (Campbell's) mind was so shaken that he could, with difficulty, keep it on one subject; that he could converse in general terms on things he had studied in the past, but that all power of close, connected reasoning was gone; that he had to be continually prompted to keep up an ordinary conversation.[2]

Thus Fanning helped mold Lipscomb's conviction.

Frequently in years to come advocates of the Society quoted Campbell as favorable to their position. When it happened, Lipscomb usually met the challenge and answered it. The *Old Path Guide* in 1884 began running a series of articles showing Campbell's support of the Society. The *Guide* was edited by F. G. Allen, who took the position popular for many years in central Kentucky, that instrumental music was unscriptural but that the Society was scriptural. When the *Old Path Guide* first showed Campbell favorable to the Society, Lipscomb replied with a number of quotations from the *Christian Baptist,* showing Campbell to be apparently against Societies then. After these quotations, Lipscomb writes:

We might greatly multiply quotations showing his conviction of the unlawfulness of all associations or conventions or representative connections of the church, that they, inimical to the pure character and destruction of the work of the churches, were robbery of both God and the church of God. This reaches over seventy years of his most effective advocacy of the supreme authority and supremacy of the word of God for all religious ends. That he afterward

---

[1] Charles V. Segar, *Familiar Lectures on the Pentateuch* (Cincinnati: Bosworth, Chase & Hall, Publishers, 1871), pp. 37, 38.

[2] David Lipscomb, "A. Campbell and the Societies," *Gospel Advocate,* Vol. XXVI, No. 23 (June 4, 1884), p. 358.

worked in Societies we have no disposition to conceal, that in doing it, he violated his own principles, built again the society he destroyed and destroyed that supreme and undivided respect for the word of God, and his appointments which he had vindicated is beyond doubt, true. It represents another case, so pregnant in the history of the church, opposing others, substituting the appointments of the institution of God, yet doing them himself.[3]

Lipscomb goes on to point out that in later years Campbell's mind and will power lost much of their force and that his friends convinced him that these organizations were harmless, so he submitted.

F. D. Srygley, who in later years became a strong opponent of the Society, was in his earlier life in favor of it. Srygley wrote articles in the *Old Path Guide* in 1884 favoring the Society, and frequently answered Lipscomb's charges of Campbell. Srygley accused Lipscomb of saying that Campbell in 1849 was a "fool," and defended Campbell by showing he was an editor, college president, lecturer, and preacher. Lipscomb, however, was not to be shaken from his conviction. He asserted that Campbell still was a great preacher, but that in some respects he had declined.

Until the end, he could make speeches abounding in the general truths and principles he learned in his early manhood, but his power of applying them to present facts and theories, was gone. Srygley, at this time, followed the practice generally followed by advocates of the Society, compiling the names of great pioneer preachers who favored the society. But the weight of great names did not sway Lipscomb. He continued:

That appeal is a setting aside the authority of God by the wisdom and numbers of men. I am constrained to believe that no man ever made it except from a consciousness that the position could not be maintained by Divine authority. At what period of the world's history, have the learned, the institutions of learning, the wise, the scholars, the big preachers, the great popular crowds and currents, even in the church, been on the side of maintaining in its purity the word of God? Was it in the days of the Saviour? The doctors, they learned, the wise were against him. . . . The learning and wisdom of the world, the educational centers, the professors, the preachers of earth, the great papers, are all against the whole movement back toward the apostolic ways.[4]

On May 4, 1887 J. W. Higbee of Mexico, Missouri began a

---

[3]David Lipscomb, "Solid Thoughts by Earnest Men," *Gospel Advocate,* Vol. XXVI, No. 17 (April 23, 1884), p. 262.
[4]David Lipscomb, "A. Campbell and Missionary Society," *Gospel Advocate,* Vol. XXVI, No. 24 (June 11, 1884), p. 374.

series of articles on "Christian Unity." Higbee stressed three kinds of unity: (1) Unity of fellowship which is the recognizing of one as a member of the church. (2) Unity of thought and purpose. (3) Unity of plan or of method. Under the third head he advocated the principle of liberty, and went on to gently upbraid those who stood in opposition to the society. In Lipscomb's answer there were many things said about the society and especially of the attitude men favorable to the society took. Lipscomb wrote:

Bro. Higbee never makes a protest against division, to those who introduce the occasion of this strife, so far as we can see, this impresses us all that the protest is more in the interest of building up the society than in peace. So it destroys the force of the appeal for peace with us.

Then again these Society brethren have always said they would be glad to see us at work without the Society. We have a long while doubted this. We have been at work all the time, but as it has been at home, it has not been open to view. Since we have begun work by sustaining the Indian mission, and are making preparations to do other work at a distance, the bitterness toward us seems greatly increased—Brothers Garrison and Spencer —the two 'sweet-tempered' men, compare us to the hypocritical Pharisees who crucified the Saviour. They can assign no reason for this charge than that we are trying to work in the way approved by God, and insist to depart from his way is to reject his authority. Hence, Brother Garrison says we are legalists, we dishonorably represent the brotherhood, remind him of the hypocritical Pharisees who persecuted the Saviour.

Accept God, Brother Higbee, as the only legislator in the church of God, and discussion and division will cease. Till then God demands the battle shall go on . . .[5]

Higbee was surprised to see his article answered. In his reply he politely accused Lipscomb of being old and of being reared in those dark and gloomy years of the 1840 decade, and therefore, blamed those years for giving to Lipscomb the attitude of seeing controversy in everything. In those early days the pioneers were fighting sectarianism so hard that they didn't have time to teach on missions. Higbee was thankful that he was a young man and therefore filled with the spirit of optimism. All who opposed the society were to Higbee skeptical and covetous. Lipscomb replied to Higbee by saying:

---

[5]David Lipscomb, "Brother Higbee's Article," *Gospel Advocate,* Vol. XXIX, No. 18 (May 4, 1887), pp. 278, 279.

Any society that takes from the churches of God, the work committed to them, or that transfers the control from the earnest, devoted elders to the young, the rich, who chiefly give their money to be seen of men, and disfranchises the poor from a voice in the work of spreading the gospel, is sinful in all shapes, principles and works.[6]

Before long, in these articles, the subject of Alexander Campbell's change came up. Reference was made to W. K. Pendleton's speeches on this subject, which shall later be studied, and Lipscomb replies that he can see but two explanations to Pendleton's denial that Campbell had changed:

First, Mr. Campbell denounced these societies when used by others in all their shapes and forms "as the man of sin, the son of perdition." When managed by him and his friends, they were all right. That is, he was so intoxicated by the idea he was president of one and it promoted his glory, that it blinded him to his lifelong work and he from selfish motives approved what he had all of his life condemned, and he had not the candor to acknowledge this, but denied it. This is discreditable to his moral character. I am unwilling to believe it is true.[7]

There were others who shared Lipscomb's conviction that Campbell had changed his conviction on the Society. L. F. Bittle for about fifteen years was one of the most forceful writers in the *American Christian Review*. He wrote considerably when Ben Franklin edited this journal and received the highest commendation from Franklin. Bittle wrote under the name B. F. Leonard, and at times contended for the view that Campbell changed. John F. Rowe, who followed Franklin as editor of the *Review,* likewise believed Campbell had changed. Rowe wrote:

Alexander Campbell favored the Society as simply representing the cooperation of the congregations; but he never went beyond that, as his writings in the *Harbinger* show. He was opposed to missionary societies composed exclusively of the clergy. He was opposed to complicated machinery. He was absolutely opposed to societies which assumed to dictate to congregations; which assumed to assess them; which assumed to try preachers and pronounce upon their fitness to preach; which assumed to take the control of colleges and other secular institutions; which assumed to read out preachers and congregations who would refuse to acquiesce in the measures and policies of the societies; which assumed to the as-

---

[6]David Lipscomb, "Brother Higbee's Article," *Gospel Advocate,* Vol. XXIX, No. 23 (June 8, 1887), p. 359.
[7]David Lipscomb, "Higbee Reviewed," *Gospel Advocate,* Vol. XXIX, No. 33 (August 17, 1887), p. 518.

senting editors; which assumed to sequestrate church property, and to appoint courts of inquiry. Alexander Campbell, while he had complete possession of his mental faculties, never wrote a syllable in favor of such ecclesiasticism. He was in favor of the absolute equality of the brethren, and opposed to a system of things that would estimate the moral standing of a Christian in proportion to the amount of money he contributes to the society.[8]

With these quotations one side of this great controversy has been unveiled. Led by David Lipscomb, in the main, there was a group of brethren thoroughly convinced that Campbell had, from the days of the *Christian Baptist,* changed his views on the Society. He was, in his older days, less the mental giant of his former and was therefore, an easy victim of younger men who influenced him in favor of the Societies, according to their point of view. The other side, of course, had its champions who vigorously held to the conviction that Campbell had not changed. On this side were many men, but the leader of the group was doubtlessly W. K. Pendleton. Pendleton was called upon to defend the Society and Campbell's position at two periods of crisis. In 1866 Ben Franklin threw the *American Christian Review* for the first time against the Society. The *Review* was at this time the most popular paper in the brotherhood, and its weight against the Society all but annihilated it. The following year Pendleton was called upon to deliver an address before the Society in its defense, which address was printed in the *Harbinger.* In 1869, as an appeasement policy to stop the opposition of the *Review,* the Society adopted the *Louisville Plan.* The *Review* backed the Society then for about a year under this plan, but then again opposed it. By 1874 the Society had reached another low point, and Pendleton was called upon again to defend it. Pendleton's speeches, especially that of 1866, give considerable attention to the subject of Campbell's so-called change. It will be right to notice some of his remarks at this point.

There is a class among us, who have a sort of bibliolatry toward the Christian Baptist, and, as is usual in such cases, they imagine that it has uttered many oracles, which upon a more careful study it will be found, are not to be discovered on its pages. This is especially the case, with reference to this subject of missions. Early in the issue of this work, in the second number, the Editor declared that he did not intend to dwell much on this topic—and every one

---

[8]John F. Rowe, "Reminiscences of the Restoration," *American Christian Review,* Vol. XXIX, No. 19 (May 6, 1886), p. 148.

familiar with its pages, knows that this purpose was strictly ad-
hered to. Not only is the measure of interest which was given to
this subject greatly exaggerated, but the spring and main motive
of it, are almost universally misunderstood. . . . . It must be remembered that in his early writings, he was engaged almost inces-
santly in the fiercest and closest conflicts with the various forms of
sectarianism, which surrounded him, and was as organizations,
both in their theory and their practice, he was deeply convinced,
were injurious to the highest interests of the church, and incum-
brances upon the primitive power of the Gospel. As such he
attacked them. 'Their missionary *plans*' was but one feature of
many, and this, as a *plan*, not as legitimate *purpose*, he criticised,
with a moderation and caution, however, which showed that he
desired to touch it but gently. His arrows were directed against
the *scheme*. . . .'⁹

It will be seen at once that Pendleton asserts that Campbell did
not change his views from the days of the *Christian Baptist.*
Campbell's objection to the missionary society, as voiced in this
early publication, Pendleton says, must be understood in the light
of the fact he was attacking the *abuse* and not the institution. This
appears to be the thought Pendleton was driving at, for his use of
the words, "plan," "purpose," and "scheme" might be misleading.
Nobody ever accused Campbell of opposing missionary *work,* but
only the *plan* of doing it through the society.

Pendleton proceeds in the speech to which reference has been
made to point out Campbell's part in the early society. He says:

When this Society was first formed, he was made its President,
and in this relation he continued, by the partiality of its members
and with his own consent, till he was called to join the congregation of the first-born in Heaven. From the first, he threw his
mighty influence in its favor. During the earlier months of 1849, in
the autumn of which year it was organized, he gave his pen and
the pages of the *Harbinger* liberally to prepare the way for its
adoption.

Having now the testimony of W. K. Pendleton before us, that of
Charles L. Loos also is worthy of some consideration. Loos, for
several years was president of the Missionary Society as well as the
College of the Bible at Lexington, Kentucky. In 1891 Loos printed
a series of articles in the *Apostolic Guide* on the general theme of
the first missionary society, which articles were later compiled

---

⁹W. K. Pendleton, "Address by W. K. Pendleton," *Millennial Harbinger,*
Vol. XXXVII, No. 11 (November, 1866), pp. 497, 498.

into a book entitled, "Our First General Convention." Speaking of Alexander Campbell's part in the Society, Loos writes:

For years preceding the convention of 1849, this eminent man had been impressed with the urgent need of such national meetings, representative of the churches, their desires, their best intelligence and piety. He felt that the time had come for the church to enter, in full cooperation, on such enterprises as were necessary to execute its great mission of extending the kingdom of the Messiah to the ends of the earth. He held, in deepest conviction, that any enterprise of importance, which concerned the entire brotherhood and required and solicited their support—such, for example, as the gospel mission for the whole world at home and abroad—should only be established and directed by the combined will and wisdom of this same brotherhood, as far as such united action was possible and practicable. This man of far-seeing judgment, whose heart was filled with the purest and deepest concern for the triumphant success of the great cause to which he had given his life, was intensely troubled when he saw, here and there, the lack of a spirit of union and cooperation among us in matters of vital moment. The manifestations of a tendency to separate action, where unity was wisdom and was absolutely necessary for large success; to distrust, where generous confidence only was right and only could be blessed; the revelation of a morbid, narrow prejudice that hindered and resisted the free, legitimate development and action of the power of the church in great undertakings—a prejudice based upon ignorance of the law of liberty with which Christ has endowed his church—all this brought sorrow to his great heart, and stirred him up at times to strong remonstrance. . . .[10]

Loos proceeds to quote lengthy passages from the *Harbinger,* many of which are the same as the reader may find in the preceding chapter of this work.

In the long debate which lay ahead over whether or not Campbell had changed his position, there were many others to enter into the discussion on both sides. Pendleton and Loos have been sided [*sited*] on the one side and Lipscomb and Rowe on the other. Neither to be sure, ever seriously influenced the other. Pendleton and Loos considered Lipscomb and Rowe as ignorant and prejudiced; while Lipscomb states his views on Pendleton's speech as follows:

But what of President Pendleton's assertion? During the years 1842-44 A. Campbell wrote sixteen articles on 'Christian Organization.' In them are found the sentences quoted by President Pendleton, referred to be the *Old Path Guide.* We read the

---

[10]C. L. Loos, *Our First General Convention,* pp. 17-19.

speech of President Pendleton when it was delivered; and we now say that speech was intended to convince the world that A. Campbell had changed his position on the subject, before the shock to his mental and will power came; and the investigation to which it led me, satisfied me of the very opposite.

. . . I esteem President Pendleton as a scholarly and conscientious man, but on this subject a prejudiced juror. I accept all he states as a witness. His conclusions, drawn from the facts I doubt.[11]

Having set forth the views of representative men pro and con as to Campbell's attitude toward the society, it is in order now to turn to some of the writings of Campbell, as found in the *Christian Baptist,* and other sources, to see if there is a discrepancy in his attitude. Campbell says; speaking of the apostolic church:

The *order* of their assemblies was uniformly the same. It did not vary with moons and with seasons. It did not change as dress nor fluctuate as the manners of the times. Their devotion did not diversify itself into the endless forms of modern times. They had no monthly concerts for prayer; no solemn convocations, no great fasts, nor preparation, nor thanksgiving days. Their churches were not fractured into missionary societies, bible societies, education societies; nor did they dream of organizing such in the world. The head of a believing household was not in those days a president or manager of a board of foreign missions; his wife, the president of some female education society; his eldest son, the recording secretary of some domestic Bible society; his eldest daughter, the corresponding secretary of a mite society; his servant maid, the vice-president of a rag society; and his little daughter, a tutoress of a Sunday school. They knew nothing of the hobbies of modern times. In their church capacity alone they moved. They neither transferred themselves into any other kind of association, nor did they fracture and sever themselves into divers societies. They viewed the church of Jesus Christ as the scheme of heaven to ameliorate the world; as members of it, they considered themselves bound to do all they could for the glory of God and the good of men. They dare not transfer to a missionary society; or bible society, or education society, a cent or a prayer, lest in so doing they should rob the church of its glory, and exalt the inventions of men above the wisdom of God. In their church capacity alone they moved. Their church they considered 'the pillar and ground of the truth'; they viewed it as the temple of the Holy Spirit, and the house of the living God. They considered if they did all they

[11]David Lipscomb, "Alexander Campbell and Missionary Societies," *Gospel Advocate,* Vol. XXVI, No. 31 (July 30, 1884), p. 487.

could in this capacity, they had nothing left for any other object of a religious nature.[12]

The above article is a part of the first article written in the *Christian Baptist,* and is one which Lipscomb frequently quoted on the subject. The second issue of the *Christian Baptist* reveals, in part, the following:

The New Testament is the only source of information on this topic. It teaches us that the association called the church of Jesus Christ is, in *propria forma,* the only institution of God left on earth to illuminate and reform the world. That is, to speak in the most definitive and intelligible manner, a society of men and women, having in their hands the oracles of God; believing in their hearts the gospel of Jesus Christ; confessing the truth of Christ with their lips; exhibiting in their lives the morality of the gospel, and walking in all the commandments and ordinances of the Lord, blamelessly, in the sight of all men. When spiritual man, i.e., men having spiritual gifts, or, as now termed, miraculous gifts, were withdrawn, this institution was left on earth, as the grand scheme of heaven, to enlighten and inform the world. An organized society of this kind, modelled after the plan taught in the New Testament, is the consummation of the manifold wisdom of God to exhibit to the world the civilizing, the moralizing, the saving light, which renovates the human heart, which elevates human character, and which prostrates in the dust, all the boasted expedients of ancient and modern times. The church of the living God is therefore styled the pillar and ground of the truth; or, as Macknight more correctly renders it, the pillar and support of the truth.[13]

Robert Richardson, Campbell's biographer, quotes Campbell's definition of the church, and those definitions bear directly upon the theme. Richardson quotes Campbell as having said:

I am taught from the Record itself to describe a church of Christ in the following words: It is a Society of disciples professing to believe the one grand fact, the Messiahship of Jesus, voluntarily submitting to his authority and guidance, having all of them in their baptism expressed their faith in him and allegiance to him, and stately meeting together in one place to walk in all his commandments and ordinances. This society, with its bishop or bishops, and its deacon or deacons, as the case may require, is perfectly independent of any tribunal on earth called ecclesiastical.[14]

---

[12]Alexander Campbell, "The Christian Religion," *Christian Baptist,* Vol. I, No. 1 (August 3, 1823), pp. 6, 7.

[13]Alexander Campbell, "How, Then, Is the Gospel to Spread Through the World?" *Christian Baptist,* Vol. I, No. 2 (September 1, 1823), pp. 15, 16.

[14]Robert Richardson, *Memoirs of Alexander Campbell,* Vol. II, p. 58.

Campbell saw in ecclesiastical tribunals a transferring of the glory of the church to human organizations. So he wrote:

> Every Christian who understands the nature and design, the excellence and glory, of the institution called the *church of Jesus Christ,* will lament to see its glory transferred to a human corporation. The church is robbed of its character by every institution, merely human, that would ape its excellence and substitute itself in its place.[15]

Thus Campbell speaks out against human organizations which rob the church of its glory.

Great pains have been taken to compile the many quotations which bear on the subject of Campbell's proposed change. Lipscomb and Rowe, with a host of others, on one side claimed he had changed his views since the days of the *Christian Baptist.* Pendleton and Loos, with another group on the other side, denied he had changed. From their remarks on the subject we have gone directly to see what Campbell did say in the *Christian Baptist.* These are the tools that are now before us. What conclusion shall we reach? Did Campbell change his position? What was the attitude of Campbell toward the Missionary Society?

Fortunately the student of restoration history can afford to be entirely objective in his approach. Members of the churches of Christ are creed-bound to no man's views. Strong and weak points held by her pioneer preachers in no sense alter the convictions which members hold, nor does the fact a weakness is admitted in any pioneer reflect upon the intelligence, honesty or character of that individual. The objective historian must be always in search of Truth. Truth, to him, must be the Pearl of Great Price. The Truth cannot be dishonored in our quest to honor great pioneers. As honestly and objectively as we can, we shall seek only after the Truth.

In seeking to determine Campbell's attitude toward the Society, let us itemize some irrefutable facts that our conclusions may be drawn from these:

(1) *Alexander Campbell was active in the Society and defended its existence.* This fact is denied by no one. It is a matter of historical record that Campbell was the Society's first president, and that he defended the society until his death as a scriptural in-

---

[15]Cf. Alexander Campbell, "Mr. Robert Cautious," *Christian Baptist,* Vol. I (1823), p. 33.

stitution. On September 12, 1849, six weeks before the convention met, Campbell was sixty-two (perhaps sixty-one) years old. It is admitted by all that from this time to his death Campbell was a firm believer in the Society.

(2) *Alexander Campbell never himself believed that he had changed his conviction on the Missionary Society.* This fact must certainly bear some weight. A man sixty-two years old is not ordinarily in his dotage. It is most reasonable to expect that if he had changed Campbell would have been aware of it. If Campbell had been aware of it, he would have doubtlessly admitted it.

The first person to accuse Campbell of having changed his views from the days of the *Christian Baptist* was Jacob Creath, Jr. In 1850 Creath wrote to Campbell:

Now, permit me, my dear brother, to say to you in all kindness and candor, that your brethren who now oppose conventions, and who have opposed them since they entered this Reformation, are equally sorry to find you and others opposing conventions in the great platform you laid down for us in the *Christian Baptist,* and now to find you and them, advocating conventions as zealously as you then opposed them. If you were right in the *Christian Baptist,* you are wrong now. If you are right now, you were wrong then.[16]

Campbell, however, remarks:

This objection, and all this alleged antagonism between the *Christian Baptist* and the *Millennial Harbinger,* are disposed of, or, rather, annihilated, by one remark, viz.: *convention* indicates merely a coming together for any purpose. Such is its established meaning. Hence, a convention may be either scriptural or unscriptural, consistent or inconsistent with Christian law and precedent, good or evil, just as the end or object for which it is constituted, or for which it assembles.[17]

It is clear, then, that Campbell was not conscious of having changed his position. His statement above indicates that his opposition to conventions was not intended to be an opposition to any and all conventions, but to those that were improperly run and were abusing their own existence.

Yet, it must be admitted, that the reasoning of Creath, and later, of Lipscomb and others was certainly not far-fetched. A careful reading of Campbell's remarks in the *Christian Baptist* certainly indicates that he was opposing conventions, missionary

---

[16]Jacob Creath, "Conventions—No. V," *Millennial Harbinger,* Third Series, Vol. VII, No. 11 (November, 1850), p. 637.

[17]Alexander Campbell, *ibid.,* p. 638.

societies, etc. as such. If <u>lurked</u> away in Campbell's own mind was the thought that he was only opposed to their abuses, it may be fairly said that probably few of his readers got that idea. Nevertheless, it is fair to Campbell to understand his former statements in the light of his own explanation, and admit that he was only fighting their abuses.

(3) *Alexander Campbell favored the principle of the missionary society before 1847.* David Lipscomb, borrowing from Charles V. Segar, alleged that in 1847 Campbell's mind was affected so that he could never reason as closely after that as before. This was caused by his imprisonment in Scotland and the drowning of his son, Wycliffe. Yet, it must be admitted that before this time, Alexander Campbell favored the principle of human organizations such as underlay the missionary society. Campbell admits that he was displeased with the abandonment of the Mahoning Baptist Association in 1830. Beginning the following year, he wrote much favoring cooperation meetings which were but missionary societies on a smaller basis. Throughout his life Campbell showed himself to be a friend and advocate of organizations. He attended state and district cooperation meetings and at times held offices in them.

References in the preceding chapter will show that Campbell advocated a general organization for the churches. It is true that he did not use general organization as synonymous with missionary societies. Campbell thought that the general organizations should include more than missionary societies, and in fact that every phase of the interests of the church as a whole which could not be handled by local congregations should be handled by the general organization. Missionary societies were but one phase of this total organization. Nevertheless, the *principle* involved in a missionary society and the *principle* in the general organization were the same. This being true, it is unlikely that the happenings of 1847 influenced Campbell's thinking on missionary societies especially when the principle undergirding the society was a definite part of his conviction before this year.

(4) *Alexander Campbell did not criticize brotherhood organizations before 1847.* If Alexander Campbell had been against human organizations before the year 1847, it would be logically expected that he should lift his voice against them. Yet, with the exception of his articles in the *Christian Baptist,* Campbell did not

lift his voice against the human organizations arising all about him in the church. State organizations were being formed very early, yet Campbell failed to criticize these organizations. Almost his only criticism came against the American Christian Bible Society, but it is noticeable that this opposition was only on the ground that Burnet had not sufficiently consulted the brotherhood, not because Campbell thought the Society, as such, was unscriptural in its existence.

As fairly and honestly, as we can read Campbell's writings on the subject of human organizations, we are convinced that Campbell favored them even before 1847. His writings in the *Christian Baptist* are somewhat mystifying. Taken at their face value and for what they say on the surface they most certainly seem to oppose the missionary societies as unscriptural in their existence. Our only recourse is to take Campbell's own explanation as the answer, and if we err, let it be on the side of charity. However, the many articles which appear from his pen in the *Millennial Harbinger* from 1830 on down show a particular bias in favor of all human organizations in the church, and on this testimony, we base our conviction that Campbell did favor these organizations. Nevertheless, as previously stated, we feel no particular embarrassment for taking this position. Campbell is not our authority. He was a great man, but withal, a man, with the same tendency to err as others. That he was wrong in advocating these organizations, we believe most deeply, but that he nevertheless was friendly to them is a fact against which we cannot argue.

Campbell believed in them, but Campbell was wrong. This is our conviction.

Chapter XI

GROWING OPPOSITION

Scarcely had the American Christian Missionary Society been organized when a wave of opposition began sweeping over the brotherhood. This opposition came from various localities and for various reasons, but many, it seemed, looked upon the establishment of the society as a dangerous trend in the restoration, some avowing that it was definitely unscriptural. Some viewed with mild alarm the establishment of the Society and issued gentle warnings against it. J. B. Ferguson of Nashville, Tennessee, editor of the *Christian Magazine* comments at the close of 1849 that "the mails of the past week have brought to us letters from some of almost every class of laborers in the Lord's vineyard, and of every variety of talent and acquirement, urging us, by appeals to the highest and purest motives, to lift our voice against the *present dangerous tendency of the Reformation!*"[1] One brother wrote to Ferguson:

I consider our recent movements contrary to the teaching and usages of the Primitive Disciples; and so far as they are carried into operation, a trespass upon the free privileges of every Disciple of Christ; tending to a most hateful assumption of power; and that it is now the imperative duty of every sincere Disciple of Christ to throw himself in the breach if he would not lose everything that has been gained by our severest struggles.[2]

There were some during the early years who looked with suspicious eye upon the Society, who were not thoroughly convinced that it was scriptural, but who for the sake of peace gave in to the majority of brethren. James M. Mathes, one of Indiana's leading pioneer preachers, was editor of the *Christian Record*. Soon after the establishment of the Society, Mathes wrote:

A Missionary Society was formed for the spread of the gospel in our own and foreign lands. This is quite an important measure. We have always been in favor of sending the gospel to the destitute at home and abroad; but our own plan was to do all this through the church, as such. But as the brethren of the Indiana State

Opposed but acquiescent

---

[1] J. B. Ferguson, "Fear of Consolidation—Independence of Individual Churches," *Christian Magazine,* Vol. III, No. 7 (July, 1850), p. 207.
[2] J. B. Ferguson, "Fear of Consolidation—Independence of Individual Churches," *Christian Magazine,* Vol. III, No. 7 (July, 1850), p. 207.

196

Meeting, and those composing the general Convention, have thought proper to organize a Society for this object, we acquiesce.[3]

There were many brethren in the church who took the attitude of Mathes. They would not be the cause of contention or division, so they reasoned, and therefore, would not press their opposition. In years to come David Lipscomb declared that he believed that Ben Franklin would never have thrown his influence at first behind the Society except for the fact that he lived in the part of the nation where the Society was popular and therefore, acquiesced against his better judgment. That Franklin at first defended the Society is evident. In the years, 1858-59 Franklin conducted a discussion in the columns of the *American Christian Review* with D. Oliphant of Brighton, Canada West. Oliphant edited a paper called the *Christian Banner*. In years to come Franklin adopted many of the arguments of Oliphant and used against the Society, but during these years, he defended the Society's existence.

Nevertheless, it is plain that the core of Franklin's reasoning in these early years was sound. In years to come Franklin admits that he tried for the sake of peace to defend the Society even when in his own mind he was not sure of his position. Franklin shows that he is thinking along the right line when, shortly after establishing the *American Christian Review,* he writes:

We are perfectly aware that if we wish to put the Christian communities into the power of men, to control them, wield them, and make them engines to honor man, we need some kind of an organization, beyond the simple organization of the New Testament; but the simple, independent church, for keeping the ordinances, religious instruction, and saving the world, is all-sufficient for the good of the saints and the glory of God. Indeed, one of the principal reasons why this question of organization has perplexed the minds of so many is, that they are looking for, and trying to make out of something unknown to the whole New Testament. They overlook the simple, easy and common-sense arrangement of the New Testament, and complain that we have no arrangement. It is amusing to see the different routes by which brethren have attempted to arrive at the same conclusion, on this point. One brother sets out gravely to show scripture authority for such an organization as is desirable, and claims that he finds abundant authority for it. Another looks over the matter, and is satisfied that he has failed. He throws all that plan aside, and claims that the whole matter is left to human prudence and descretion, and that

[3]James M. Mathes, "The Great Convention," *Christian Record,* Vol. VII, No. 6 (December, 1849), p. 178.

we need no authority for it, any more than to build a house of worship, or send out a missionary to a certain field of labor.[4]

The last idea—that no more authority is needed than that to build a house of worship—is reminiscent of the attitude of Campbell, who placed such human organizations on the par of expediency. Consequently, Campbell wrote:

I do not place meeting-houses, pews or hymn books, on a footing with civil government or the church of God! The building of a meeting house is as conventional as a Bible Society or a missionary society; and he that opposes the one, should, on all his premises and logic, oppose the other.[5]

When the news of the establishment of the Missionary Society reached the churches, most of them concurred with the action, but some read carefully the constitution to see whether or not the Society was worth their backing. At once there was opposition from a few congregations on various grounds. (1) Some did not agree that membership should be contingent upon the payment of money. (2) Others thought the establishment of the society was, to say the least of it, a dangerous thing because of its possibility of disrobing the churches of their independence, and of its danger of becoming an ecclesiastical tribunal. (3) Some considered these societies a departure from the earlier restoration principles, and the very existence of them as sinful. The church at Connelsville, Pennsylvania seems to have objected on all three counts. A list of ten resolutions was sent by the Connelsville church to the various periodicals, declaring the congregation's convictions on the Society. Of the ten resolutions, articles four, five and six are especially significant.

4th. That, conscientiously, we can neither aid nor sanction any society, for this or other purposes, apart from the church, much less one which would exclude from its membership many of our brethren, and all of the apostles, if now upon the earth, because silver and gold they had not.

5th. That we consider the introduction of all such societies a dangerous precedent—a departure from the principles for which we have always contended as sanctioning the chapter of expediency —the evil and pernicious effects of which the past history of the church fully proves.

[4]Benjamin Franklin, "Clerical Organization," *American Christian Review,* Vol. I, No. 4 (April, 1856), p. 116.
[5]Alexander Campbell, "Conventions—No. III," *Millennial Harbinger,* Third Series, Vol. VII, No. 9 (September, 1850), p. 501.

6th. That we also consider them necessarily heretical and schismatical, as much so as human creeds and confessions of faith, when made the bonds of union and communion.[6]

In commenting upon their resolutions the Connelsville church agrees "that the church of Jesus Christ is; in constitution and design, essentially missionary, we conceive to be an axiomatic truth. Not *a* missionary society, but emphatically and preeminently *the* missionary society—the only one authorized by Jesus Christ or sanctioned by the apostles." In anticipating certain arguments the congregation further said:

We know it is thought by some, that these Societies are not separate and apart from the church, but part and parcel of her. But by a little reflection, it will be seen, that although they may be entirely composed of members of the church, (which is not often the case,) yet they are separate and distinct from her; as much so as any Free Mason or Temperance Society composed of church members. Her president is not the president of any of them; her constitution is not the constitution of any of them; her laws are not their laws; she has an initiatory *rite—they* have initiatory *fees;* and but comparatively few of her members are members of any or all of them. Hence, it follows that they are distinct organizations, separate and apart from the church.[7]

[margin note: Societies are separate from the church]

After the report of the convention of 1849 reached the ears of the churches in Detroit, a very similar action was taken there. Their report, signed by a committee, was dated January 6, 1850 and was forwarded to the *Ecclesiastical Reformer.* The report said in part:

That while we thus approve of the Preamble to the Bible Society, its objects and the objects of the Missionary Societies, yet we are sorry that we cannot also approve of the constitutions themselves, inasmuch as they create new organizations, distinct from, and in some respects, independent of the churches; which we believe to be contrary to the teaching of God's holy word, and also to the example of the churches under the guidance of the apostles; a returning to these being the express object, and avowed intention of those calling themselves the Disciples of Christ, in

---

[6] A. Shallenberger, L. L. Norton, E. Holliday, "The Christian Missionary Society," *Millennial Harbinger,* Third Series, Vol. VII, No. 5 (May, 1850), p. 282.

[7] Colin Campbell, Alexander Linn, John E. Dixon, "Action of the Church in Detroit, Michigan, Respecting Our Bible and Missionary Societies," *Ecclesiastical Reformer,* Vol. III, No. 2 (January 19, 1850), pp. 139, 140.

these latter days; the accomplishment of which is our heart's desire and prayer to God.[8]

Meanwhile in Virginia, a meeting was held May 4, 1850 at Emmaus in Caroline County to discuss cooperating with this new society. This general meeting of the churches found several objections to the Society. Their opposition was worded as follows:

. . . the principle of membership recognized by them, which admits members by virtue of *pecuniary consideration,* (the sum of one dollar,) and not by virtue of any appointment by, or authority from their respective churches; and secondly, on the ground that they admit Christians, Jews and Infidels, as members—thereby amalgamating the church and the world. We further object to the provisions for life-membership, which makes an invidious and unchristian distinction between the rich and the poor in the kingdom of our Lord; . . .

It may be seen that one of the strongest objections, voiced from many quarters to the Society, was the fact that membership was made contingent upon the payment of specified amounts of money. Some argued that this would immediately make it impossible for either the Lord or His apostles to have belonged to the Society since "silver and gold had they none." Anything that would exclude the Lord would exclude them, they argued. This particular objection to the Society was to be a source of worry to the Society for many years to come.

Advocates of the Society, however, did not take the objections without some struggle. D. S. Burnet accepts the challenge which the church ot Connelsville seemed to be hurling out by a strongly-worded answer. Burnet says:

I was born into the missionary spirit, and did not relinquish it when I associated myself with my present brethren. Before I was eighteen years of age, I was one of the Secretaries at the first session and at the formation of the Ohio Baptist Convention for missionary purposes; and the Bible and missionary causes have lain near my heart from before that time to the present.[9]

It was not without some foundation that in future years brethren who opposed societyism complained that the Society was born in the heart of D. S. Burnet, who, when he left the Baptist Church, was not thoroughly converted to the cause of restoration but

---

[8]P. Woolfolk, R. Y. Henley, "Missionary and Bible Societies," *Millennial Harbinger,* Third Series, Vol. VII, No. 7 (July, 1850), p. 415.
[9]D. S. Burnet, "Reply to the Connelsville Letter," *Christian Magazine,* Vol. III, No. 6 (June, 1850), p. 173.

brought with him a part of his Baptist practices. To the charge
that the preaching of the gospel must not be left to an organization
separate and apart from the church, Burnet says that this is a
lack of understanding of the *direct* and *indirect* influences of the
church. Burnet contended that Christians had an influence out- *This admits*
side the local church, and therefore, could work through such *that, the*
societies. He proceeds to lay down the charge, as others after him *societies are*
were so often wont to do, that those who oppose the Societies *not a part of*
but apart from
were those who wanted to do-nothing in the church. This charge, *the church.*
although often made, was generally recognized by the more thinking brethren to be a stronger appeal to prejudice than to reason. *Thus—*
No group of men established more churches, baptized more people,
than those who commonly objected to the societies. Their work
was generally of a less sensational nature, and consequently, got
less publicity. But they were anything else but men who did
nothing.

Even though objections were raised by these congregations, yet,
the chief war against the Missionary Society was fought by Jacob
Creath, Jr. in the months immediately following the society's establishment. At first Creath was evidently trying to be diplomatic.
His early articles were but lengthy quotations from Dr. W. E.
Channing of Boston, who had written much against Conventions.
These articles in addition to Creath's comments, furnished his first
objections. As time went on Creath become bolder and laid the
charges directly down himself. Creath's first quotations from
Channing served to point out the dangers and disadvantages of conventions. It was charged that the few did everything, and soon
had the tendency of becoming despotic. Campbell's reply was
that the abuse of a thing did not argue against the thing itself. By
this rule, Campbell reasoned, the church itself should be opposed
since it is a convention. Conventions, he pointed out, may err,
but do not necessarily do so.[10]

It has already been seen that some brethren who really in sentiment were opposed to the society, acquiesced because this was the
course the majority of the brethren took. Such an attitude did
James M. Mathes have, as already has been seen. Yet, Creath was
an independent thinker and actor. To sustain such societies be-

[10]Alexander Campbell, "Dr. William E. Channing's Opinions of Conventions," *Millennial Harbinger,* Third Series, Vol. VII, No. 7 (July, 1850),
pp. 408-412.

cause the brethren agreed to them meant little to Creath. Consequently, he writes:

As to the argument offered to sustain these associations— that they are acceptable to our brethren—we would say, that they have been *unacceptable* to them until recently. What has produced this change in them? What new light is this which has sprung up so recently upon this subject? I confess I have no more light now, upon the subject of associations, than I had twenty-five years ago. Will these brethren, who have been so recently and suddenly converted from their former faith upon this subject, furnish us with a small portion of this new light, that we may be converted too? I suppose the golden calf was acceptable to all the Jews, *except Moses.* I believe the calves set up at Dan and Bethel were popular with Jereboam and the ten tribes. The report of the spies was acceptable to all the Jews, *except Caleb and Joshua.* The pope is very acceptable to the Catholics; so are creeds and clerical conventions to all the Protestant parties. But does all of this prove that they are acceptable to God?[11]

Campbell had argued that the abuse of a thing does not argue against the thing itself. Creath says this is the same argument that the liquor traffic and that opium eaters have always put up. He writes:

Your saying that conventions have not *always erred,* is a tacit admission that they have *generally erred;* that they have done more injury than good to truth; that good men ought not to use them; that they are dangerous weapons, that safety is on the side of abstinence.[12]

Campbell had said that the church itself was a convention and therefore to argue against conventions was to argue against the church. Creath answers:

You place conventions on a level with the church of God and civil governments. From the Acts of the Apostles, we have authority for the organization of all the early Christian churches. Paul says the governments that exist are ordained of God—Rom. ch. 13. Now, if you will produce as good authority for conventions as I have for the congregations of God and civil governments, *I will yield* the controversy to you.

Creath is forceful in demanding of Campbell apostolic authority that authorized the use of conventions.

---

[11]Jacob Creath, Jr., "Dr. William E. Channing's Opinions of Conventions —No. II," *Millennial Harbinger,* Third Series, Vol. VII, No. 8 (August, 1850), pp. 470, 471.
[12]Jacob Creath, "Conventions—No. III," *Millennial Harbinger,* Third Series, Vol. VII, No. 9 (September, 1850), p. 496.

You say that our Saviour and the apostles did not denounce conventions, as such. Did they denounce Popery or corrupt Protestantism, as such? Did they denounce infant baptism, or creed making, or auricular confession, as such? It is for you to show where they *authorized* conventions.

The heart of Creath's argument lay in his insistence that there was no scripture authorizing the use of conventions. He writes again:

. . . it will be seen that, in this discussion, the advocates of conventions have *totally abandoned* the rule on which we and all Protestants set out—that the Bible alone is the religion of Protestants. They have not produced one passage of scripture, to countenance these assemblies from the New Testament.[13]

Again Creath argues in the same article:

Because God our Father *divinely commissioned* his Son to our world, and his Son sent the apostles as missionaries to the world, and they *divinely organized* individual congregations all over the Roman empire, in the first century, does it, therefore, follow, that we in the nineteenth century, without any *divine warrant,* and contrary to our own rule of faith, have the right to call conventions, from Bible, missionary, and tract societies, elect popes, and do all other things we wish? My logic does not run that way. They had divine credentials for what they did. We have none for what we are doing. That is the difference between them and us.

Society advocates had long argued that their idea of a society was not one that would disrobe the church of its own independent right of action. Societies were not to be legislative tribunals, but mere organizations through which the churches could work to do their missionary work. John T. Johnson had early favored the Society and had even introduced the resolution at the first convention saying the society was scriptural. Yet, Johnson was careful to oppose any type of organization that would be over the churches. Shortly before his death, Johnson wrote:

The congregation plan is the divine arrangement. It works best. It accomplishes most good, by calling forth all the energies and resources of each congregation, and the least injury is the result . . .

I am yet to learn that an ecclesiastical establishment, by its messengers, has the divine right to select and ordain evangelists, to sit in judgment on evangelists, on congregations and their difficulties; to try heresies, to declare fellowship, non-fellowship, etc., etc.[14]

---

[13]Jacob Creath, "Conventions—No. IV," *Millennial Harbinger,* Third Series, Vol. VII, No. 11 (November, 1850), p. 615.

[14]John T. Johnson, "Communication from Elder J. T. Johnson," *American Christian Review,* Vol. II, No. 1 (January, 1857), p. 28.

When Tolbert Fanning found himself in conflict with George W. Elley of Kentucky over the Society in 1857, Elley was quick to point out that the Kentucky State Society had no ecclesiastical powers whatever. Elley wrote:

The State Meeting of Ky. claims no authority over any congregation, nor do they exercise any control over any evangelist farther than to direct him to the proper field of labor, connected with such other objects as belong exclusively to the work of their voluntary agents. No church is bound either to send money or messengers, and consequently it can have no existence or executive rule only as they are pleased to give it.[15]

When, therefore, Jacob Creath argues that the Society possessed the potential danger to the church of becoming an ecclesiastical and legislative body, Campbell was quick to defend the independence of the church. He answered Creath by saying:

I have indeed, since I became a writer, always opposed, do now oppose, and I presume so far as to say, that I am likely always to oppose, all ecclesiastic, associational, conventional, or synodic meetings, to legislate for the church, or any form of sound words or sound doctrine, enacting new formulas of church ethics, church politics, or church enactments, or anything called morality or church polity. But because other men, in other times, have, in running out of Babylon, run past Jerusalem, I have endeavored till now, and will always, I presume, simply endeavor to run into Jerusalem. I am glad to opine and hope that our good, gifted, and well informed Brother Creath, will not, with Dr. Channing or any other popular and gifted man, run off into an extreme, or into inappreciable tangents, or into mere metaphysical disquisitions.[16]

The weight of Alexander Campbell's name served the purpose to subdue very great opposition to the Society for a time, and was a powerful recommendation for it to many people. The objections of Jacob Creath in addition to those of the Connelsville church and the Detroit church were about the only voiced for some time. The minutes of the Society's annual meetings and the addresses of the correspondent secretaries show that the Society was not receiving the financial backing that it needed. Several of the major addresses during the decade of the 1850's breathe an atmosphere of depression. To bolster its influence the Society tried

[15]G. W. Elley, "no title," *Gospel Advocate*, Vol. III, No. 7 (July, 1857), p. 213.
[16]Alexander Campbell, "Response to Dr. Channing—No. II," *Millennial Harbinger*, Third Series, Vol. VII, No. 9 (September, 1850), p. 495.

discarding the article from the constitution, making membership dependent upon the payment of stipulated amounts of money, but this availed little. It is evident, then, that much of the opposition to the Society made itself known, not by public remonstrance but through indifference and refusal to support it on the part of the churches.

Tolbert Fanning had for a number of years doubted the wisdom and scripturalness of human organizations. But while the doubt was, still rolling in his mind, and before it settled down to a stern conviction, Fanning gave at least lip devotion to these organizations. At times he even strongly defended them as he did in the case of the American Christian Bible Society. Fanning frequently attended the Cooperation Meetings in Tennessee, and apparently encouraged them. There is no question that Fanning wanted to be convinced that human organizations were right if he could be convinced conscientiously. He attended the great convention of 1849 in Cincinnati in the hope that he might see or hear something to settle his doubts in favor of the Society, but he came away as great a doubter as ever. His troubles in Nashville over the speculations of J. B. Ferguson occupied almost all his thought from 1852 to 1855, and he doubtless had little time to give the subject as thorough an examination as he intended. When, in July, 1855, he and William Lipscomb established the *Gospel Advocate,* he had hopes that the *Advocate* might be used for a free discussion of the subject of human organizations pro and con. Fanning had hopes that through this means the truth might be unveiled so that brethren might become settled either for or against and thus go forward on a united front. Consequently he writes:

In establishing 'The Gospel Advocate,' I determined by the help of the Lord, to give the subject of cooperation a thorough examination. I do not pretend to say how it has been brought about, but I have for years believed that a change must take place in our views of cooperation, before we can labor to each other's advantage, or to the honor of God.[17]

The *Gospel Advocate* began as a monthly in July, 1855. Throughout the first year and a half of its publication Fanning found nothing at all to ease his doubts as to human organizations.

---

[17]Tolbert Fanning, "Cooperation," *Gospel Advocate,* Vol. I, No. 4 (October, 1855), p. 110.

His observations upon the conduct of the brethren and the influence of the Society but more and more convinced him that the church was being pushed in the background for the Society and that advocates of the Society were depending and exalting more and more human wisdom in the place of divine revelation. His convictions were moulded and more and more he presented them through the columns of the *Advocate* to see if they would stand the test of critical analysis and argumentation. In February, 1857 he writes:

We regard the church of Christ as the only divinely authorized Bible, Missionary and Temperance Society on earth; and furthermore, we believe that it is in and by means of the church the world is to be converted, and Christians are to labor for the Lord. . . . In all the efforts to do the service of the Lord through human institutions, it has seemed to us that the church is degraded, and rendered indeed useless.[18]

Three months later he wrote again:

We believe and teach that the Church of Christ is fully competent to most profitably employ all of our powers, physical, intellectual, and spiritual; that she is the only divinely authorized Missionary, Bible, Sunday School, Temperance and Cooperation Society on earth. It is, has been, and we suppose always will be our honest conviction, that the true and genuine service of God can be properly performed only in and through the church. Hence, we have questioned the propriety of the brethren's efforts to work most successfully by means of State, district, and county organizations, 'Missionary,' 'Publication,' and 'Bible Societies' or 'Bible Unions,' 'Temperance Societies, Free-Mason and Odd-Fellowship Societies' to 'visit' the fatherless and widows in their affliction, or any other human organization for accomplishing the legitimate labor of the church.[19]

Still again Fanning goes on to say:

The church, as we have often said, is Heaven's missionary society to a suffering world, and the ministers commissioned, sent out and supported by the church, are God's missionaries to call sinners to life. We have not been able to see the necessity of a missionary society beyond the church. We ask the brethren, in all kindness, if it would not be better even to send our beloved, Brother, Dr. Barclay and his most amiable, intelligent and really accomplished family, to Jerusalem, by the agreement and cooperation of the churches than by another and strange body.

[18]Tolbert Fanning, "The American Christian Missionary Society at Cincinnati, Ohio," *Gospel Advocate,* Vol. III, No. 2 (February, 1857), p. 43.

[19]Tolbert Fanning, "Missions and Missionaries," *Gospel Advocate,* Vol. III, No. 5 (May, 1857), p. 130.

Fanning's purpose was to glorify the church instead of human organizations and to glorify divine revelation instead of human wisdom. It was only to be expected that he should have an influence far and wide, especially among the readers of the *Advocate*. One evidence of this was to be found in Tennessee itself. Up to this time the churches in the state had followed the general practice of organizations such as was characteristic of other states. Tennessee churches had their cooperation meetings, and finally, their State Meetings much as other states. By 1857 these meetings were beginning to lose some ground as brethren became filled with doubts as to their use. That year William Lipscomb attended the Mountain District Cooperation Meeting. After the meeting, he wrote:

While there was no special discussion of church cooperation, still we think that the disposition manifested by many of the brethren was clearly for the supremacy of the church of Christ in opposition to all other organizations. There are some few of the brethren I think who do not yet see exactly how they can get along without a little human machinery, but we hope that these will soon see the way clearly.[20]

Some were looking with less and less favor upon the usual arguments of society advocates stressing the need of better organization. S. B. Giles of Austin, Texas wrote in the *Advocate* in 1857:

Throughout the length and breadth of the land, there seems be a manifest desire for a better organization. All the delinquencies of churches and individuals, are charged to bad organization, or the want of organization. While I admit our organization is not perfect, still I think there are some other causes that retard our progress. . . . I think I see a manifest disposition with some, to adopt a system of organization that will create hireling priests and a clerical dominion. I venture the assertion that those who are loudest in their complaints and clamor most for organization, are those who have made the least sacrifices in support of Christianity, and would be the first to accept the gown and salary. Such are always deploring our lukewarmness and inefficiency, and lauding the order, zeal, and progress of some of the sects. That there is some departure from Gospel purity and relaxation in devotion by the brotherhood, I think requires but little sagacity to discover.[21]

---

[20]William Lipscomb, "Mountain District Cooperation," *Gospel Advocate*, Vol. III, No. 1 (January, 1857), pp. 26, 27.

[21]S. B. Giles, "Signs of the Times," *Gospel Advocate*, Vol. III, No. 1 (January, 1857), pp. 17, 18.

The *Gospel Advocate* during these early years of its existence very frequently discussed the issue of human organizations. Sometimes the issue dealt with the Society, sometimes with Cooperation Meetings, and at least once with an Educational Society. In all cases the very principle was the same: does a human organization have the right to usurp the work of the church? Fanning was answering, no. Early in the year, 1856, Fanning found himself in a controversy with George W. Elley, a popular Kentucky preacher. The churches in Kentucky had organized the Kentucky Christian Education Society. This society was to select worthy young men, pay their tuition, and send them to one of the colleges. To this Fanning objected saying, "Our experience is unfavorable to educating men in the schools with the view of making preachers of them."[22] It must be made clear that what Fanning was opposing was the existence of theological seminaries. He believed in the education of youth, and in teaching the Bible in educational institutions, but theological seminaries with him were different. At any rate, an unnamed Kentucky correspondent, noting the move on the part of the Education Society, saw a danger and wrote, saying:

We move in Kentucky with a steady step toward a hierarchy as unscriptural as that of Rome, or England, and the preachers who seek to make themselves the Church, appear to think all is well. It seems that some are endeavoring to degrade the Church into an auxiliary to the more than foolish societies of our age and country. [23]

This statement—which later was shown to be written by W. G. Roulhac of Hickman, Kentucky—drew the ire of Elley. Elley defended the organization by admitting it was a human organization and had the right to exist on the grounds of expediency. To this Fanning replied and went to the core of the trouble.

Bro. George W. Elley admits that the Kentucky State Cooperation is a human organization. It would be well for the brethren to decide the question as to the utility of such organizations to keep the church alive. Can she perform her mission on earth without the aid of human legislation? Can the churches of

---

[22]Tolbert Fanning, "The Kentucky C. M. Education Society," *Gospel Advocate*, Vol. II, No. 6 (June, 1856), p. 168.

[23]G. W. Elley, "Reply to Certain Remarks in Reference to Real or Supposed Errors in the Managements of Brethren in Kentucky by a Kentuckian," *Gospel Advocate*, Vol. II, No. 10 (October, 1856), p. 316.

Christ cooperate as churches without converting them into human establishments? This embraces all the controversies of the age. Settle this point and all sincere religionists will become one.[24]

This series of discussions between Fanning and Elley continued through the columns of the *Advocate* for some time. To Fanning's criticism that human organizations had no authority to assume to do the work of the church Elley replied by asking for scriptural authority for two or more congregations uniting their efforts to send the gospel to destitute places. Fanning cited such scriptures as 2 Cor. 8: 19, and Phil. 4: 16. On the whole Elley's articles show that he could not conceive of cooperative work taking place without the forming of a human organization.

The controversy over human organizations in the restoration movement shows the development of an attitude on the part of the advocates of these organizations that became a thorn in their side. Oddly enough those who favored human organizations generally managed to generate more enthusiasm and energy on behalf of these organizations than they ever had for the church. Of human organizations Elley had written: "They have been advocated as necessary to the increase of the number to be saved."[25] This led Fanning to make the charge that some men believed these organizations were necessary to keep the church alive. This is an error into which the over-zealous advocates of these enterprises have fallen into, not once but many times. Robert Milligan defended Societies as "institutions of necessity," and W. K. Pendleton, in the hope of subduing opposition, asked Fanning to suspend his judgment until some further time. But Fanning concluded by saying:

. . . but we say to these good brethren, and all others concerned, that we made up our mind long ago, and unless better reasons are shown, we shall consider all religious expedients unnecessary, and in opposition to the reign of Christ.[26]

As already noted, by the year 1857, Fanning had crossed the Rubicon. Beginning with the first edition of the *Advocate* in 1855, he stated his doubts on societies and was willing for his ideas to be

---

[24]Tolbert Fanning, "Notice of Brother Elley's Essay," *Gospel Advocate*, Vol. III, No. 2 (February, 1857), p. 54.

[25]Tolbert Fanning, "Notes on Brother G. W. Elley's Essay Regarding Cooperation," *Gospel Advocate*, Vol. III, No. 7 (July, 1857), p. 214.

[26]Tolbert Fanning, "Missions and Missionaries," *Gospel Advocate*, Vol. III, No. 5 (May, 1857), p. 131.

put to the test. More and more did he become convinced that there was no ground on which these societies could be defended. Consequently, in the spring of 1857 he states his position more boldly:

We think it due to ourselves, to the cause we plead, and to the brethren especially who seem to differ widely from us, to state our teaching in reference to cooperative labor—embracing missions and missionaries—in very plain terms. It was with much hesitation we brought ourselves to the conclusion, in 1855, to commence the publication of the Gospel Advocate. As expressed to our intimate friends, we were satisfied that we would be forced to attack existing institutions among the brethren, and we felt unwilling to have their opposition. But we have freely spoken, and now all we ask of our brethren is a fair discussion.[27]

In the year 1859 at the regular meeting of the Society in October, Fanning was invited to be present. He went and delivered a discourse. Later Fanning explains that his purpose in presenting this particular address was to elicit some discussion on the subject of human organization. Fanning complained that Isaac Errett, the corresponding secretary that year, carefully squelched any possibility of a discussion by directing the line of thought to something else, and thus defeated Fanning's purpose.

Fanning, in this address, directed attention to the way he believed missionary work, and cooperation work, should be conducted. He cited the example of the way they were then doing it. The church which met at Franklin College in Tennessee had sent out J. J. Trott as missionary to the Cherokee Indians. Two or three other congregations were assisting in the support of this work. This, Fanning defended as being scriptural and right. As to human institutions, Fanning remarked:

Touching, however, institutions not recognized in the Scriptures, as agencies to carry forward the good work of saving the world, many of us have staggered, and still entertain serious doubts as to the expediency of taking any part in them. Not that we doubt for a moment that there is something good in them all, but we have been impressed with the idea that the church of God, which is represented as 'the pillar and support of the truth,' fully covers all the ground which Christians should occupy in their labors of love.[28]

[27]Tolbert Fanning, "Missions and Missionaries," *Gospel Advocate*, Vol. III, No. 5 (May, 1857), p. 131.
[28]Tolbert Fanning, "Brother Fanning's Remarks," *Gospel Advocate*, Vol. VI, No. 1 (Jan., 1860), p. 8.

During these years, the position of the *American Christian Review* was somewhat dubious. Ben Franklin had founded and begun editing this periodical as a monthly in January, 1856. While Franklin, as already pointed out, was defending human organizations, especially the Missionary Society; yet, there were times when his articles completely condemned the principle upon which these Societies were founded. It should have been clear to readers of the *Review* that Franklin was headed for a crisis when he would swing one way or the other. A man with Franklin's independence of mind and fearlessness of spirit could not long try to defend two irreconcilable principles. Two years before, while editing the *Christian Age,* Franklin had written a series of articles on "Church Organization." In these he deplored the weakened condition of the brotherhood. He took note that many were blaming this upon the lack of organization. He challanged the men who favored a better organization to produce one. In the latter part of 1855, as an attempt to improve upon the organization, the "Central (Kentucky) Christian Union" was formed with H. T. Anderson as president. Some brethren, particularly Franklin, looked somewhat aghast upon this institution. One statement in its constitution said:

If there shall at any time arise any who shall teach things tending to the injury of the churches and the cause which we plead, such person or persons shall be subject to the discipline of the Union.

The nine churches which made up the Union seemed truly to have formed an organization that was synodical and denominational in its entirety. Franklin felt convicted to say something against it. As a result he writes:

We are truly sorry that this controversy has come up. It appears that schism among men is becoming so rife, that no great and good work can be prosecuted with general unanimity. Our power must constantly be weakened by jarring and opposing elements. I am truly sorry these brethren have made the move they have; because I esteem them, love them, and desire the most fraternal feeling between us; and I fear I cannot make the objections I solemnly entertain without producing unpleasantness.[29]

Franklin proceeds to sum up his objections in the following words:

We object to the organization formed by our brethren in Danville, not merely because it is not done to suit us, but because the

---

[29]Ben Franklin, "Organization II," *American Christian Review,* Vol. I, No. 2 (February, 1856), p. 79.

entire move is uncalled for, unwise, and wholly unauthorized. The thing is unknown to the New Testament. The New Testament records inform us of the organization or rather the institution of individual communities, or churches, and the appointment of officers in them. But these records know nothing of any organization of the churches in any given district into one body, under a new set of officers, who are officers not of the churches but of the district.[30]

Later, Franklin attempted to get at the very root of the weakened condition of the brotherhood. The most commonly-expressed cause of this weakness was the lack of organization, but Franklin took direct issue here. If the cause was languishing, it was so only because the preachers were not as fervent as they once were. He says, "If preachers lament that the cause languishes, let them cease scheming about some organization unknown to the New Testament, and go into the field and labor for the Lord's sake, and for the Lord's name, as brethren did years ago, and as we are doing now, and as certain as God is the author of the Bible, we shall prosper." The thing needed was better preaching, so Franklin adds: "Preaching is what is needed, fervent, soul-stirring preaching, exhortations, entreaties and impressive persuasions with the people to turn to God, and be saved." Unquestionably, Franklin was hitting at the real cause. The history of the restoration movement shows that the less devotion men have to Christ the more they stand in need of human organizations.

Thus we bring to a close the early objections raised against the American Christian Missionary Society and all human organizations. It will be noticed that these objections fell into three classifications. The first of these was based upon the Society's method of membership, viz., making membership depend upon the payment of stipulated amounts of money. The second of these stemmed from the potential danger the Society maintained of infringing upon the independence of a local congregation. The third objection came from the conviction that human organizations were unauthorized in the scriptures, and therefore, were unscriptural. The Society found it could overcome the first of these by changing its constitution; the second could be overcome by suggesting that the danger of a thing did not argue against the thing itself. The third ob-

[30]Ben Franklin, "Clerical Organization," *American Christian Review*, Vol. I, No. 3 (March, 1856), p. 115.

jection, the Society sought to answer by saying that human institutions were matters of expediency. Eventually this last objection became the core of the issue, although in years to come many churches who believed in societies found that the Society very little respected their local independence. But all of that is by way of anticipation; we shall leave it until later.

Chapter XII

ORGANIZED MISSIONARY EFFORTS

The activities of the American Christian Missionary Society forms an intrical part of the historical data on the restoration movement for those years before and during the war. It is of little concern whether one agrees with the existence of the Society or not; still it is a historical fact that the Society did exist and that it carried on certain activities which activities form a vital part of the study of the restoration. Certainly then, no investigation into the period can be complete without some comprehensive analysis of the activities of these years.

Scarcely had the Society been established until a matter of business came up relative to the sending out of foreign missionaries. But who should be sent and where? Early in the year 1850 Campbell began the publication of a series of articles on the American Christian Missionary Society. After a discussion on the Society, its place and purpose, Campbell came directly to this point.

But where shall we begin? Charity begins at home, as the old adage goes; but, as someone has said, 'it does not continue at home' . . . But whither shall we send our missionaries abroad? I am anticipated in the judgment and good sense of some of our brethren. They have named Jerusalem as especially worthy of a concentrated and protracted effort. The claims of Jerusalem are, with me, paramount to those of any other spot on the green earth.[1]

At the same time, Carroll Kendrick, editor of the *Ecclesiastical Reformer,* wrote: "How grateful the thought, that Jerusalem, which at the beginning gave us the gospel, should from our hands receive it back again."[2] Thus there was a sentimental cause for the selection of Jerusalem as the first place for a missionary. Few in the brotherhood needed to be convinced of this for there was a ready concurrence that the first site should be Jerusalem, the city of the Great King.

Moreover, there needed to be little argument as to who would go.

---

[1] Alexander Campbell, "The Christian Missionary Society—No. II," *Millennial Harbinger,* Third Series, Vol. VII, No. 2 (February, 1850), p. 86.

[2] Carroll Kendrick, "Jerusalem Mission," *Ecclesiastical Reformer,* Vol. III, No. 2 (January 19, 1850), p. 50.

As early as October 5, 1848 Dr. James T. Barclay had written to James Challen, offering his services as a missionary if the society were to be organized. Furthermore, he had the backing of Alexander Campbell who was vitally interested in his going abroad as a missionary. So significant is this first missionary of the American Christian Missionary Society that it might be of interest to note more about him.

Barclay Volunteers

Thomas Barclay, grandfather of Janie T. Barclay, was one of the very earliest settlers in this country. The Continental Congress appointed him in 1781 as the first American consul to France. Robert Barclay, son of Thomas Barclay and father of James T., was a moderately wealthy business man, who drowned, however, in 1809 as he crossed a swollen river in King and Queen County, Virginia. James T. was born on May 22, 1807 at Hanover Courthouse, Virginia. His early education was received at Staunton Academy, Virginia. Upon graduation from the school of chemistry in 1826, he entered the medical school of the University of Pennsylvania and stayed there for two years. At the end of this time he married Julia Ann Sowers of Staunton, Va.

Six years after the death of Thomas Jefferson, Barclay purchased the famous Monticello home from Jefferson's grandson, Jefferson Randolph, for $7,500. Barclay at that time lived in Charlottesville in a home valued at $4,500. He traded this and gave three thousand dollars extra for the Monticello home. Monticello, it will be recalled, was designed by Thomas Jefferson himself when he was but twenty-one years old. He completed the building of it in 1802 at a cost of $7,200. Bricks for the home were made on the ground, and the nails were made by Jefferson's own negro boys. The home was run down when Barclay got it, and he repaired it to make it look very much like a mansion. He was once offered twenty thousand dollars for Monticello, but turned down the offer. Later, when he finally did sell it, he lost over two thousand dollars on the sale.

The Barclays were Presbyterians, and James T. was very religiously inclined. His early ambition was to be a missionary to China, but his mother would never hear to it. About 1839, after the death of his mother, James T. and his wife heard the preaching of R. L. Coleman, one of Virginia's early gospel preachers, and were baptized by him in the James River near Scottsville. Barclay immediately used his influence to establish a church in Scottsville. Shortly afterward, he went to Washington, D. C., where in 1843, he succeeded in establishing the first congregation in this city. This congregation met first in his home, then in the fire station, and then in the city hall.

His decision to go to Jerusalem as a missionary came about in an interesting manner. One evening he returned from taking care of a patient. He was sitting on the front lawn of his Scottsville home. His daughter was sitting on a lawn stool by his side with her head on his knee. Mrs. Barclay was reading from the eleventh chapter of Romans. The two boys were some distance away, putting up a beehive. Barclay himself sat in a reflective mood as he listened to the scripture reading. The boys soon came to him. Then Barclay spoke thoughtfully to his family. "Our constant prayer is for the fulfillment of the promises contained in that chapter. I have been reflecting on the question whether we can pray with confidence for anything which we are not willing to lend our aid for the accomplishment of . . . We have all been praying for the conversion of the Jews; yet no one has stepped forward to engage in the work. If the end is to be gained, someone must commence the undertaking. Shall I, if I obtain the cheerful cooperation of my family?" Thereupon the family agreed to abide by his wishes.

Early in 1850 Barclay was selected to go to Jerusalem. John Boggs acted as a representative for the Society in collecting funds for the Jerusalem Mission. He met considerable opposition some of which came as a criticism of Barclay's attitude toward slavery. It was known that he had been a slaveholder, and northern churches were reluctant to back him. Nevertheless in time, the money was raised, and Barclay prepared to depart. On September 14, 1850 the Barclay family boarded the Devonshire, and sailed for Europe. The sea was rough, and Barclay was ill most of the way. He landed in London in twenty-one days. After some difficulty, he finally left London on board the Hebe, and sailed for Malta. From Malta the Barclays took a steamer to Beirut, and from there they went horseback through Tyre, Sidon, Ptolemais, and Joppa to Jerusalem where they arrived on February 10, 1851.

The Convention of 1850 met in Christian Chapel, corner Walnut

& Eighth in Cincinnati on Wednesday, October 23, at 2:00 P. M. Campbell was absent again and so D. S. Burnet took the chair. G. R. Hand was appointed secretary, *pro tem.* James Challen delivered an address, reviewing the year's activity. Since the first annual convention the year before, the Board had been meeting once a month. They were chiefly engaged in surveying the field, gathering resources and selecting men for the fields. The corresponding secretary in his report stated that they had much prejudice to all, much opposition to overcome, and much apathy and lukewarmness to encounter. The report complains of the lack of preachers to go. One thousand preachers were needed *Needs At Home* to preach along the states bordering on the Mississippi River. In Illinois alone, the report stated, there were thirty to forty towns on the river without preachers. Indiana had then a population of over a million, and yet preachers were sorely needed. The Society that year had in contemplation missions in New Orleans, Boston, Michigan, California, Oregan and Texas in addition to the mission already established in Jerusalem.

The opposition to Life Directorships and Life Memberships being contingent upon the payment of money came in for some consideration. As a result the constitution was changed so that any church in North America was entitled to one representative or member for the year. However, by giving twenty-five dollars any congregation or organization could have another representative. The proposal was made by James Challen and was incorporated into Article Three which now read:

Every Christian Church in North America, cooperating with this Society, and all associations of churches, shall be entitled to representations equally at the annual meetings.

Just what real change this meant is hard to see in view of the fact that by payment of the extra twenty-five dollars, increased representation could be had.

So went the Convention of 1850. The next year the Convention met on Wednesday, October 22, in Cincinnati. Alexander Campbell was present now for the first time and delivered an address which he got up on the impulse of the moment. The report of the Corresponding Secretary showed the progress within the past year. The Barclays had been paid $881.88 to start their trip and then, had been sent another five hundred dollars, making $1,351.88 for

1951 Convention

the Jerusalem Mission. The Secretary's report showed that little had been done for home missions, since the most of the funds had been going to the Barclays. The report likewise showed that the previous year's change in the constitution regarding Life Directors and Life Members was still a source of trouble. The controversy and dissatisfaction with them had not abated. John Shackleford decided that the controversy was useless and moved that the article be restored to its original reading which was done. Still there were two other items of business that were interesting. J. J. Moss moved that a paper be published by the Societies, both Missionary and Bible, to promote their cause, but this suggestion was not acted upon. James Challen proposed a mission on the Pacific coast in view of the rapid growth of California, but in view of the hard financial circumstances that the Society was feeling, no action was taken upon this proposal.

Barclay's Experience — Meanwhile, in Jerusalem James T. Barclay was not idle although the results of his work were not sensational. His first year in the city had resulted in twelve baptisms. His reports home showed that the general conditions of the so-called Christian section of the city were so deplorable that not one Mohammedan had been converted to Christianity but many Christians had been converted to Mohammedanism. By Christian as Barclay used the term here, he meant all types of sectarianism in opposition to Mohammedanism. Barclay not only preached in the city but acted also as physician. His report home showed that two thousand cases of sickness had come before him that first year.

In December, 1852 Barclay received word from Bethlehem that six hundred people wished to become Christians. They were prepared to come over "en masse" to the cause of New Testament Christianity. Barclay strongly objected on the ground that they hadn't been sufficiently taught. He went to Bethlehem, rented a room, and started a small school to thoroughly teach these people. Opposition soon grew against his school, and many of the people refused to attend. Miss Mary Williams, whom Barclay had met after his arrival over there, was placed in charge of the school while Barclay established a hospital over which he placed his son, Robert. The school did not last long because of enticements and threats from Jews and Catholics. The hospital for a time was successful, but the Catholics soon placed a trained doctor in the city with a hospital and threatened those who dared patronize Barclay. Soon the hospital closed.

Shortly after this, Barclay bought a piece of land from some Sheiks in the valley of the Wady Farah. When he went to take over the land, he found that the Sheiks had no title, so he had lost in the deal. His intention had been to erect a place of refuge for the poor among his converts. It seemed, then, that every effort of Barclays went wrong. In three years he had baptized only twenty-two persons and on every hand was checked in his advancement. In a letter to Alexander Campbell, dated August 27, 1853, he expressed his disappointment that results were not greater. Trouble also came on the home front for funds did not come to the Society fast enough for them to support Barclay. Not only so but Barclay's general physical condition was gradually getting worse. The shapening up of events pointed toward Barclay's coming home, and so during the summer of 1854, the Jerusalem Mission was closed, and Barcley was on his way home.

Barclays Withdraw Mission

Meanwhile, as interest had waned in this mission, another way was in the making, which was to prove to be equally as much a failure. D. S. Burnet, through the columns of the *Christian Age* had encouraged the brethren to think of sending a missionary to Africa. Campbell took up the plea, and in his address before the convention of 1853 said:

Convention of 1853

Plans for African Mission

That we should have an African mission as well as an Asiatic mission—a station in Liberia as well as in Jerusalem—missionaries peregrinating accessible portions of the land of Ham as well as of the land of Shem, appears to me like a duty, a privilege and an honor. We are abundant in means, and wanting, if wanting at all, only in will, in purpose or in liberality.[3]

In this speech Campbell told the convention of the fact that a certain Ephraim A. Smith had volunteered to visit Africa and survey Liberia and return and report conditions there. His going was to be no financial cost at all to the Society. With him was to go Alexander Cross, an emancipated slave, from Christian County, Kentucky.

Proposal

Early in the spring of 1853 D. S. Burnet had started pleading for a mission in Africa through the columns of the *Christian Age*. A member of the church in Christian County, Kentucky wrote to

[3]Alexander Campbell, "An Address," *Millennial Harbinger,* Fourth Series, Vol. III, No. 11 (November, 1854), p. 614.

Burnet that he had the man for the task. He had overheard a certain negro addressing his slaves sometime before on the subject of temperance. This negro showed an unusual amount of intelligence. Burnet wrote back to the brethren in that county, recommending that the freedom of Cross be purchased at once. This was quickly done. The church at Hopkinsville began putting the negro through a training course to help him to become more familiar with the scriptures. Meanwhile, a session of the Kentucky State Convention willingly turned Cross over to the Society, and along with him came four hundred and seven dollars from G. W. Elley and John G. Allen for his support. Besides this the church at Hopkinsville sent twenty-eight dollars.

Cross sailed from Baltimore on November 5, 1853 accompanied by his wife and his eight-year-old son. Early in January, 1854 he landed at Monrovia. Two months were spent in getting prepared to do this mission work, but during this time Cross showed little prudence relative to his own physical condition. In his zeal he went too far. He was warned to be careful of the hot tropical sun, and not expose himself too frequently or too long in the direct rays. But Cross was indifferent to the warning. In an effort to build himself a house at a certain point on the St. Paul's River, Cross poled a canoe fourteen miles up the river under the hot African sun. In a few days he fell down with a fever, and died. His little boy, James, who was along, also took the fever and he too, soon died. With this tragic episode the African mission came to an abrupt close.

There were other missions readily proposed. An Indian Mission was under consultation, awaiting the proper moment to send a man to the Cherokee tribe. A China Mission was proposed but delayed during this time for lack of funds and a missionary to go. Missions to Germany and France were also under consideration. Home Missions were in demand with the Society especially looking toward Chicago where a few members had more recently moved.

Attention during this time was also being given by the convention to the American Christian Publication Society. This Society was first called the Cincinnati Tract Society, having been founded through the joint efforts of D. S. Burnet and Ben Franklin. When the Convention first met in 1849, J. J. Moss recommended that the Sunday School Library, organized by certain brethren on the

Western Reserve be amalgamated with the Cincinnati Tract Society and the whole be the property of the brethren at large. There was a ready agreement by the Convention, and the constitution of the Cincinnati Tract Society was changed to read, Christian Tract and Sunday School Society. The objects of it were confined to tracts and Sunday School books. The next year, the title was changed to read, American Christian Publication Society.

This Society in the year, 1853 took over the publication of the *Christian Age* which was then being edited by Ben Franklin. The Publication Society also was publishing the *Sunday School Journal.* The circulation of the *Age* at this time was admitted to be over six thousand, and that of the *Journal,* eight thousand. During the year, 1854 the Publication Society published D. S. Burnet's "Jerusalem Mission" and a new edition of the biography of Barton W. Stone.

As has already been mentioned, James T. Barclay left Jerusalem during the summer of 1854 to come back to America. Soon after his arrival at home, he began gathering material for his book, "The City of The Great King," which was published in 1858. During the summer of 1856 Barclay approached Alexander Campbell with the suggestion of reopening the Jerusalem Mission. He found Campbell favorably impressed with the idea. This gave Barclay the encouragement to try further. The annual meeting of the American Christian Missionary Society met that year of 1856 in Christian Chapel, corner Walnut and Eighth in Cincinnati on October 21. Barclay attended and delivered an address before the convention suggesting the reopening of the mission. The measure was favorably received, and Barclay prepared for a return trip. It was not, however, until 1858 that he could find passage abroad, so on May 26, 1858 Barclay left Boston to finally arrive in Joppa in August. He found all of his converts except two gone, and living conditions deplorable. By December, he found a home, and also found it difficult to get around for he had contracted rheumatism. The next May a malaria epidemic hit Jerusalem, so Barclay left to make his home in Joppa. From here on, he had his hands full. His daughter married at this time and gave birth to twins. The twins died. Early in 1860 a revolt broke out between two tribes on Mt. Lebanon and, as a medical doctor, Barclay was again very busy. Then the Civil War in America broke out, and the Jerusa-

Jerusalem
Mission
Ends

lem missionary was forced to return because of low funds. Thus ended permanently the Jerusalem Mission.

The report of the Convention was read in 1856 by D. S. Burnet, who was then acting as Corresponding Secretary. His words were filled with discouragement. He remarked that during the past year little had been done in the way of mission work. He complained of a general want of concerted action, stating that he had received only two hundred and fifty-six dollars and seventy-five cents during the entire year. Burnet himself laid the cause of this to worldliness in the church and a general state of apathy regarding the salvation of men.

1857
Convention

The next year the report to the convention was read by Ben Franklin, then the Corresponding Secretary. Franklin held this position through the following circumstances: in 1856 Charles L. Loos left Somerset, Pennsylvania to become the preacher for the church at Walnut and Eighth Streets in Cincinnati, and shortly afterwards, was appointed corresponding secretary of the Society. But hardly had he arrived in Cincinnati until he was offered the position as President of Eureka College in Illinois, so Loos accepted and the job of Corresponding Secretary was turned over to Franklin. Franklin's report before the convention of 1857 stated that the Society was yet in a deplorable condition, although it had some improvement over the previous report. Its interests had been hindered by the deaths of such men as John T. Johnson, S. W. Irwin and H. W. Parrish who had died since the previous convention. Moreover, a severe drouth had hit the nation the previous year, producing a minor depression, which reflected in less money coming in to the Society. The trouble also lay, Franklin pointed out, in the fact that brethren were showing more of an interest in State Missionary Societies, and local missionary work, than in the foreign. Not one single man had been found who would devote all of his time to the Society. But Franklin thought he found some encouragement that the opposition to the Society was not having the effect as it formerly had. He reported that $1,752.45 had been given in the previous year.

Meanwhile, other missions were opening up. The Jerusalem Mission this year—1857—was not ready to be opened due to the lack of funds, but plans were made for another mission. J. O. Beardslee of Collamar, Ohio visited Cincinnati and talked to Ben Franklin about going to Jamaica. The Society agreed to send him, and so on January 20, 1858 Beardslee and his wife left New York harbor for the island of Jamaica where they arrived on the twenty-seventh of the same month. Ten months later Beardslee reported that eighteen had been baptized. When the Convention met in October, 1858, there was high enthusiasm over the Jamaica Mission, for it was looked upon as a stepping stone to the continent of Africa. David Livingstone was just opening the dark continent and the Society had visions of future work there themselves.

Jamaica Mission [margin note]

Still another mission was opened by 1858 in Nova Scotia. W. W. Eaton was the missionary there, and his written report sent to the convention indicates considerable progress. Forty-seven had been baptized there in fifteen weeks. But more encouraging to the Society perhaps in its days of financial stress, was the fact that the Nova Scotia mission was self-sustaining.

Nova Scotia Mission [margin note]

Isaac Errett became Corresponding Secretary for the Society in 1858. The next year his report to the Convention showed some reason for optimism by the Society. The church in Jamaica now had thirty-seven members. As to Nova Scotia, W. W. Eaton had been forced to return early in 1859 but William Patterson was sent in his place. Patterson by the first of October had baptized thirty-five persons. The Kansas Mission had opened up and John O'Kane had been sent there with a view of doing half-time work in Kansas and the other half with the church in Independence, Missouri. The Jerusalem Mission already by now had Barclay back, but the progress was almost non-existent.

Isaac Errett Becomes Cor. Sec. [margin note]

The Convention of 1860 met admidst troublesome times. In national affairs there was high political excitement over the election which was less than two weeks off. The Convention met, nevertheless, in Cincinnati, and for the first time met in the church located between Smith and Mound Streets and not in the building at Walnut and Eighth Streets. The general color of mission reports was about the same. Jamaica was encouraging, and Jerusalem was getting worse due to the intolerance of Turkish rule. John I. Rogers was preaching under the Society's supervision at Leavenworth, Kansas having C. G. Bartholomew as his helper.

This year of 1860 the Convention was the largest in point of attendance the Society had yet witnessed. Fifteen states were represented when the Convention met on Tuesday afternoon, October 23. The report of the Corresponding Secretary informed the

1860 Convention [margin note]

Society that over fifteen thousand dollars had been raised since the previous year's meeting and a total of one thousand three hundred and forty-four additions to the church had been made. D. S. Burnet was this year elected to be the Corresponding Secretary.

When the Convention met on Tuesday, October 22, 1861, at the Walnut and Eighth Streets church in Cincinnati, it probably had its most trying circumstances of it. The war had begun the previous spring, and in view of this attendance was off considerably. The report on mission work was not encouraging to the Society in any realm. The subject of the war was so much on the minds of the attendants that it was impossible to keep it from coming up. The sympathy of most men was decidedly toward the North, so it was difficult to keep northern bias away from the Society's activities. This fact was later to cause considerable criticism to the Society and probably helped southern churches considerably in their opposition in the years ahead. J. P. Robison of Ohio suggested the following resolution:

Resolved, That we deeply sympathize with the loyal and patriotic in our country, in the present efforts to sustain the Government of the United States. And we feel it our duty as Christians, to ask our brethren everywhere to do all in their power to sustain the proper and constitutional authorities of the Union.

When the Resolution was suggested, D. S. Burnet immediately questioned whether such a resolution was not contrary to the second article in the Society's constitution. The Chair, however, upheld the resolution. John Smith was present and asked that the decision pass from the Chair to the entire house for a vote. This was done and the decision to pass the Resolution was defeated. L. L. Pinkerton, who had ardently seconded the motion, suggested a recess of ten minutes. During this recess, D. S. Burnet was called to the Chair, and the resolution re-read. James A. Garfield, a Colonel at this time in the Forty-Second Regiment of the Ohio Infantry, was present, and made a few remarks. After which another vote was taken, and the resolution was passed with only one negative vote cast. This entire procedure was to prove a precedent for another similar action two years later.

When the Convention met the next year, 1862, Alexander Campbell was present for the last time. His presence at these meetings for the past several years had hardly accomplished much, for Campbell was old, and most action was taken by others. R. M. Bishop, one of the vice-presidents was present and leading a portion of the time. Burnet's report for this year indicated that $6,773.09 had been received. As to the Missionary work, the only report of encouragement to the Society came from Jamaica where J. O. Beardslee reported that he had immersed one hundred and seventy-two. The previous year, on October 11, 1861, Barclay had resigned the Jerusalem mission, and had already arrived back in the United States. For all practical intents and purposes the mission to Jerusalem had been a failure.

The Convention of 1863 might be termed the War Convention. *1863 Convention* Because of its resolutions in favor of the Northern position, considerable criticism, especially from the South, but from other sources as well were later cast against it. In the absence of Campbell, Isaac Errett, first vice-president, sat in the chair. The report of the Corresponding Secretary announced that Beardslee was planning to return from Jamaica the next spring. As to the funds received, the announcement was made that over eight thousand dollars—nearly nine thousand—had been received since the previous convention. The work in Kansas, Nebraska, and other Home Mission fields continued with about the same degree of success.

The report had apparently gotten around that the Society was indifferent toward the war. R. Faurot, accordingly, suggested three resolutions, placing the Society definitely behind the cause of the Northern army. Only the second resolution need be mentioned.

Resolved, That we tender our sympathies to our brave and noble *The War Resolution* soldiers in the field, who are defending us from the attempts of armed traitors to overthrow our Government, and also to those bereaved, and rendered desolate by the ravages of war.

Immediately the question was raised whether these resolutions were in order. Errett, who was on the Chair, replied that two years ago, the house had voted against adopting a similar resolution, and that he would be forced to uphold their decision, although such a decision was contrary to his own convictions. A vote was taken of the house, after considerable discussion, and the resolution was adopted.

W. K. Pendleton, because of sickness, was unable to attend this particular convention. The passing of Faurot's resolutions was, to him, a source of great displeasure as he learned about it later. He writes:

We have deeply regretted the unpleasant excitement which has been occasioned by the forced innovation in the last anniversary upon a long cherished principle among us, concerning the intro- duction of resolutions foreign to the objects of the organization.[4]

Still, while Pendleton regretted the lack of wisdom in writing up these resolutions, he nevertheless did not agree to abandon the Society because of them. He says,

Our Missionary Society must not be abandoned because of a single imprudence or unwarranted innovation upon its sacred principles. These things are human, and we must deal with them as such.

The passing of such Resolutions made some brethren realize what a dangerous instrument a Missionary Society could be. The confidence of many was shaken, and the Society entered into one of its black eras of unpopularity. Pendleton admits this by saying,

It ought not to be disguised, that the fortunes of the Am. Ch. M. Society have for a year or two been under a cloud. The confidence of many of her oldest and most liberal supporters has been in good measure withdrawn from her, and she has not been repaid for this loss by any correspondent accession of new friends.[5]

During the spring of 1864, D. S. Burnet resigned as Correspond- ing Secretary. Burnet's wife had been ill and besides, Burnet's own health had been gradually getting worse. H. S. Bosworth, the Recording Secretary, began immediately acting as Correspond- ing Secretary. B. W. Johnson then took the position but acted as secretary only a few months. O. A. Burgess then took it over, but one reads a year later that W. C. Rogers had the position.

Pendleton was doubtlessly right in saying that the attitude of brethren toward the Society had changed considerably. Truly, the Society was making enemies and few friends. Neither of the Conventions of 1864 or 1865, both of which were held in Cin- cinnati, displayed anything spectacular in the way of progress. The latter Convention had a note of optimism about it in that

---

[4]W. K. Pendleton, "Monthly Summary," *Millennial Harbinger,* Fifth Series, Vol. VII, No. 3 (March, 1864), p. 190.

[5]W. K. Pendleton, "American Christian Missionary Society," *Millennial Harbinger,* Fifth Series, Vol. VII, No. 9 (September, 1864), p. 419.

the war had ended, and there were great prospects of preaching facing them.

In accordance with the design of this first volume, we shall leave the Society here at 1865. We note, however, its condition. With the cessation of hostilities, the Society faced the world with a wave of unpopularity sweeping against it. The next ten years were to be crucial ones, but we leave these for a later time.

Chapter XIII

IMPRESSIVE LEADERS

While the Missionary Society must often come before us in our survey of the restoration movement, yet we must not linger too long on it. The drama that was the restoration movement had many impressive actors, men whose names today are revered as great pioneer proclaimers of the ancient order. As we move from step to step in recording events and analyzing discussions and controversies, we must first pause long enough to familiarize ourselves with the men behind the movements. In this chapter, therefore, we turn our attention to three impressive leaders of the pre-war years of the restoration—John T. Johnson, P. S. Fall, and "Raccoon" John Smith.

Exclusive of Alexander Campbell, there was probably no preacher in the days before the war so widely loved, highly admired, and so exuberantly eulogized as John T. Johnson. He was a man of great power and ability who succeeded in baptizing many hundreds in the twenty-six years he preached the word. He had not the wit of John Smith, and accordingly, was not the controversalist that Smith was. He was reserved, strongly emotional, progressive and active at all times. Still he had not the timidity of P. S. Fall. He had a lawyer's mind and a poet's heart and he preached with strong appeals both to logic and to emotions.

John T. Johnson at times was an editor. He never held a debate, in the popular sense of that term. It was preeminently as an evangelist that Johnson was known. It is as an evangelist that he is most widely remembered, and as an evangelist he gained his great reputation. To know John T. Johnson in the two-fold aspect of an evangelist and a man is to go a long way toward becoming acquainted with him as he lived in those early years.

W. K. Pendleton once called John T. Johnson the "Chevalier Bayard of the pulpit in Kentucky." Truly he was one of the few preeminently great preachers in that state in these earlier years. Alexander Campbell wrote of him,

The boldness, cheerfulness, vivacity, fluency, and perseverance of brother Johnson eminently qualify him for great usefulness. I wish Kentucky had a few persons equally gifted for taking care

228

JOHN T. JOHNSON

of the sheep, as brother Johnson is for marking them and putting them into the green pastures.[1]

Indeed, Johnson's ability to mark the sheep and put them into the pasture was almost incomparable. In the pulpit he was dignified, and yet simple in his presentation. Samuel Rogers, who heard him often, says of him:

As an evangelist, I have thought John T. Johnson the best model I have ever known. Perhaps, I ought not to speak of him as a model at all, for no man could imitate him. His style beggars all

---

[1]Alexander Campbell, "Incidents on a Tour," *Millennial Harbinger,* New Series, Vol. III, No. 6 (June 1839), p. 265.

attempts at description. I have read descriptions of him as a preacher, from the pens of those who are masters in the art of composition; but the best of them were tame in comparison with the real John T. Johnson as you saw and heard him for yourself. . . . He stood like a lord before the people, and yet no one was awed in his presence, for his dignity was blended with the sweet simplicity of a child. He did not wear the dignity of the world, but it was that of conscious rectitude and goodness. In coming before his audience, he had the appearance of a bold, fearless, and defiant champion, every nerve being fully strung, and his dark eye flashing fire.[2]

It was said of Johnson that he had the ability to make every theme something that lived in the present. In speaking on hell, his hearers were often made to think they were looking into the very abyss of torment. It was only natural that he could move people with such preaching.

A little boy sat beside his mother, listening to Charles H. Spurgeon speak. In a moment the boy looked to his mother and asked, "Mother, why does he keep preaching at me?" Spurgeon could make his sermons *personal*. Here was one phase of the power of Johnson as an evangelist. Accordingly, Jesse B. Ferguson once wrote of him:

Brother Johnson is known to our readers as one of the first, most zealous, indefatigable and successful advocates of Primitive Christianity. It has called him from the bar and from the halls of Congress, to plead the cause of life and salvation with his fellow-men.

Twenty years of unremitting labor has he devoted to this cause, and when we last saw him, although he had some of the marks of a war-worn soldier of the cross, we thought him as fresh and vigorous as many of the younger recruits . . .

The cause of his unexampled success in inducing his fellow-men to bow to the Sceptre of Prince Emanuel, has often been inquired into. No reflecting man would long be in doubt after hearing him address the world of the ungodly. His personal appearance and address are those of an honest, courageous man. His discourses are discursive in their character and marked by great vitality and energy; whilst his appeals are so various and happy that scarcely a man who hears him who does not feel that he is directing his address to his peculiar state. His manner is affectionate, earnest, intrepid and scriptural. And, well furnished with facts and truths drawn from every source and rendered tributary to the great themes of the gospel proclamation, he grapples with his audience,

---

[2]Samuel Rogers, *Autobiography of Elder Samuel Rogers* (Cincinnati: Standard Publishing Co., 1880), p. 200.

and that man must be pertinacious and obstinate indeed, who will not yield in the athlete struggle.[3]

The encomiums to John T. Johnson by brethren who knew him were characteristically superlative. He was a preacher without a peer; an evangelist incomparably successful. W. K. Pendleton found many things about Johnson analogous to those in the saintly apostle Paul himself. Pendleton writes:

The qualities which made Paul colossal in the world, were many of them shared in a pre-eminent degree by John T. Johnson. Unflagging zeal, golden purity, Christian charity, dauntless courage, indomitable energy, care for the churches, confidence in the power of the gospel, singleness of purpose, fidelity to Christ, reverence for his authority, trust in his sustaining aid, a restless ambition to be useful in his service, an unclouded vision of the things not seen, and an earnestness in all, that almost consumed his heart— these were some of the elements that made up his noble life, and put upon his brow the stamp of its nobility.[4]

In personal appearance Johnson was slightly under six feet tall. He was erect and slender. Early in life his hair had been the color of Walter Scott's—black as a raven's wing, but later it became very thin and sprinkled here and there with silver. He had a bilious temperament although he was never discouraged and even buoyant under the most adverse of circumstances. He had little time for clownishness. In his conversation, he was easy and somewhat familiar although always chaste, dignified and almost exclusively he dealt with things concerning the kingdom of God. In his speaking—whether public or private—he was always in earnest.

The birth of John T. Johnson takes us back to Scott County, Kentucky in the year, 1788. About three miles west of Georgetown, on the Owenton Road was a place called Great Crossings. It got its name from the fact that in the earlier days a main buffalo path had here intersected North Elkhorn Creek. Here on October 5, 1788 Johnson was born. He was the eighth of eleven children.

Johnson's family connections were very much related to the military which doubtlessly influenced him much in his earlier life. His father, Robert Johnson, was a colonel in the army. The name of his brother, Richard Mentor Johnson, became very familiar in

[3]J. B. Ferguson, "Encouragement—J. T. Johnson," *Christian Magazine,* Vol. I, No. 2 (February, 1848), p. 64.

[4]W. K. Pendleton, "Life of J. T. Johnson," *Millennial Harbinger,* Fifth Series, Vol. VI, No. 4 (April, 1863), p. 181.

military circles. Richard was a colonel in the army during the War of 1812. Later he became the ninth vice-president of the United States. Another brother, James, was a lieutenant-colonel in the Battle of Thames, and for several years, a member of Congress.

It was only natural that the mind of John T. Johnson should also turn toward the military, and that he should accept the first call that came his way. During the War of 1812 General William Henry Harrison commanded the North-western army at Fort Meigs. Harrison invited Johnson to become a volunteer aid. Johnson accepted, and joined the forces at the fort. During the spring of 1813, many of the volunteers found their time of enlistment was up, so they began returning to their homes. The Indians, sensing that the Fort was undermanned, began planning an attack. Harrison, unmindful of the planning, left for a visit to Cincinnati with his family. The battle with the Indians, fought at Fort Meigs on May 5, 1813, was very fierce. Johnson escaped the battle unhurt, although he had a fine gray horse shot from under him. After the battle, Harrison sent Johnson to join the forces of his brother, Richard M., but on the way, John T. got down with a fever and barely managed to get home alive. He was sick for some time but finally recovered.

Considering the educational opportunities of the times, John T. Johnson was a well educated man. He went to school at first to Malcolmb Worley who ran an acadamy near his home. Worley was a devout Presbyterian. Later he followed Barton W. Stone out of Presbyterianism, and after that, when Stone's followers were badly shaken by Shakerism, Worley was one to abandon the cause. At any rate, after finishing his schooling with Worley, Johnson entered Transylvania when this school was under Dr. James Blythe. Here he studied law. Upon graduation, he applied for and received his license to practice even though he was under twenty-one.

While Johnson was a student at Transylvania, he boarded with a family by the name of Lewis. Mrs. Lewis took a particular liking to John T. When the subject of girls would come up, she often commented to Johnson that he needn't worry about a wife, for she was rearing a daughter especially for him. The statement was truer than Johnson realized. On October 9, 1811, he married

Sophia Lewis, the fifteen year old daughter of the Lewis family. Johnson himself was now twenty-one, six years her elder.

Soon after marriage, Johnson settled on a one hundred and fifty acre farm on South Elkhorn, near Georgetown. He and his younger brother, Joel, built a mill and went into business. They continued this business for many years. In 1815 Johnson went into politics, running for the legislature of the state. He was elected each year for the next four. Meanwhile, with his farm, his business, and his politics, he managed to build up quite a wealthy position for one who lived in the backwoods of Kentucky as he did. But all of this was to be short-lived. In 1819 a severe panic swept the country. Johnson's tender heart had compelled him to sign many promissory notes for his friends and neighbors. When the panic hit, they couldn't pay, so the obligation fell upon him. Johnson gave up about fifty thousand dollars worth of his real estate to pay these notes.

In 1820 Johnson turned his attention toward national politics, and ran for Congressman. He was elected that year, and also, re-elected several times. In 1825 in the hotly contested election of Andrew Jackson, which finally had to be decided by Congress, Johnson voted for Jackson. In 1828 he was reelected to Congress, and immediately announced that he would retire from politics after this term. His busy life had caused him to neglect his family, and in deference to their wishes, he was determined to quit public life.

Johnson, even though busy with his thinking about politics, never entirely forgot thinking about religion. He was only a boy when the Great Revival of Cane Ridge took place in 1801, but he long remembered this event. In 1821 he joined the Baptist Church at Great Crossings. Of this, Johnson says, "Oh, it was a most glorious thing for me. It preserved me from a thousand temptations, and kept me a pure man."[5] In 1823 Alexander Campbell began publishing the *Christian Baptist* but Johnson was so busy thinking of politics that he had no time to seriously investigate it. But around 1830, while he was preparing to retire, Johnson found that he had more leisure to examine it. Moreover, there was a compelling urgency since the whole community around him was aroused over what it vulgarly called "Campbellism." He determined in his own mind that he would examine this teaching in the light of the

[5]John Rogers, *The Biography of Elder J. T. Johnson* (Cincinnati: 1861), p. 21.

Bible, and determine for himself what the truth was.   And so, he began an earnest investigation of the scriptures, and gradually the light began to dawn.   Of this he later says,

My eyes were opened, and I was made perfectly free by the truth. And the debt of gratitude I owe to that man of God, A. Campbell, no language can tell.[6]

Immediately after his conversion, Johnson set his goal to converting the Baptist Church at Great Crossings where he was a member.   In his innocency he did not take into account the power of religious prejudice.   They scorned him until he became convinced that they were beyond the realm of possible conversion.   On the second Saturday in February, 1831 he, together with B. S. Chambers, and W. Johnson, formed a separate congregation at Great Crossings worshipping after the ancient order.   Before long he had baptized his wife, his brother, Joel, and his wife.   In one year's time the number in this church increased to seventy.

It will be seen that Johnson's life had undergone a radical shifting of emphasis.   If his wife found him too busy in politics to give his time to his family, it is not likely that she found him less so in his preaching of the gospel.   In addition to his preaching, Johnson was soon called upon to do considerable writing.   In 1831 Barton W. Stone lived near Georgetown, and was editing the *Christian Messenger*.   He urged Johnson to become co-editor. Johnson continued this until Stone moved to Illinois in 1834.   The next year, Johnson, feeling that a paper was needed in Kentucky, collaborated with B. F. Hall in publishing a paper they called the *Gospel Advocate*.   This paper, however, continued only for a short time.

By and large the life of John T. Johnson, from his conversion to the principles of restoration in 1831 until his death in 1856 is connected with his preaching work.   Seldom was he away from it. In 1832 he led the forces of Barton W. Stone and Alexander Campbell into a union.   In 1836 he gave some assistance toward establishing Bacon College.   He attended the conventions of the American Christian Missionary Society and was an ardent support of it.   But withal, he spent the most of his time in preaching.   He traveled extensively, all over the south, and into the west—Arkansas and Missouri.   It is not necessary, nor would it be of great

---

[6]John Rogers, *The Biography of Elder J. T. Johnson*, p. 21.

profit, to list these excursions and preaching engagements. Needless to say, if it were done, the biography of John T. Johnson would read very much like a diary.

The death of Johnson came on December 18, 1856, and came as a sudden shock to the whole brotherhood. His health apparently had been good. No one suspected that death, even for one his age, was as close by as it was. Johnson had attended the annual convention of the Society in October, 1856, but had stayed only two days. During these two days, he was with Ben Franklin a good deal, and even spoke for the church at Covington, Kentucky, across the river, where Franklin then preached. He left Cincinnati early in order to take an extended tour into Missouri. After arriving in Missouri, he preached at Columbia, Fayette and Rocheport. Then he went on to Lexington, arriving there on the fourth Lord's Day of November, this day being the twenty-third. His arrival at this particular time was unexpected. It was Sunday morning when the steamer docked, and the church services were already under way. Johnson headed for the building to find Allen Wright already up preaching. Wright stopped in the middle of his sermon, and insisted that Johnson speak. Thus began a meeting in which Johnson preached twice a day, and which was destined to be his last such meeting.

On Sunday evening of the first Lord's Day in December, Johnson preached his last sermon. The night was cold, and the building was unusually warm. The sermon was entitled, "The Word." After the discourse was over, Johnson left the building, walked a little way, and pulled his coat up over his throat, complaining that he was cold. The next morning he slept late, but was still feeling ill. That afternoon, he was suddenly struck with a severe pain in his side, and had to be helped back to bed. He was staying in the home of Thomas C. Bledsoe, and from this bed, never walked away again.

He had an attack of pneumonia which was followed by other attacks bringing severe pain and suffering to him. Most of the time he was delirious. Five days before his death he had a severe hemorrhage of the bowels. It was seen that he could not live long. Bledsoe informed him of the news he was going to die. Johnson's reply was, "I did not think that death was so near, but let it come." Asked if he had any fears in dying, Johnson replied: "None, none whatever; I have lived upon Christianity, and can die upon it." In his delirious moments, Johnson would quote scripture or preach, his preaching consisting of thoughts on the sacrifice of Jesus for sin. A few hours before his death he asked Allen Wright and a Brother Duval to sing, "O Land of Rest For Thee I Sigh," a favorite song. Johnson tried to sing along, too, as they in their feeble way, sang the hymn. Only a few minutes after sunset on the evening of December 18, 1856 did John T. Johnson close his eyes in death. The time was 6:15 P.M.

PHILLIP S. FALL

The life of Phillip Sydney Fall was largely limited to three localities—Frankfort and Louisville, Kentucky and Nashville, Tennessee. P. S. Fall was not a controversalist, but by temperament was quiet and reserved. Yet, he was a man of strong conviction, pure and lofty ideals, and a deep and pure love for Christ. Consequently, his influence upon those around him was definite and uplifting. While his part in the restoration was not so public as that of others, yet, in his quiet and reserved manner, he served the Lord. Particularly is he important in a study of the restoration movement for two things: his early connection with Campbell's principles, and the progress of the church in Nashville, Tennessee.

Fall was born in Keloedon, England in September, 1798. His parents seemed to lean a little toward the Episcopalian beliefs. His maternal grandfather was an Episcopalian, while his paternal grandfather was a Baptist. Fall himself was educated religiously in the Episcopalian belief until he came to America. This trip to the United States occurred in 1817. His parents stopped for a short time in Pittsburgh, and then came on to settle near Russellville, Kentucky. But they had only been in their new home for about a year when they both died, leaving P. S. Fall to look out for himself.

The year, 1818, the year that his parents died, Fall established an academy near Louisville, Kentucky. That same year he united with the Baptist Church, and began to give his attention toward preaching. The next year, in December, 1819, he was licensed to preach in the Baptist Church.

In 1821 Fall married Miss Annie Bacon, who came from one of the illustrious families of the state. She was of great assistance to her husband in his preaching, and stood faithfully by him. That same year Fall was invited to visit Louisville once a month

P. S. FALL

and preach for a newly organized Baptist Church here. This church was meeting in the courthouse and stood badly in need of a preacher. Through Fall's monthly preaching, it grew until in 1823, he was invited to move to the city, and devote more of his time to the church. It was while here preaching for this church, most members of which he had converted, that P. S. Fall began to give his attention to the cause of the restoration movement.

After Alexander Campbell's debate with John Walker in 1820, considerable excitement was raised among the Baptists of Kentucky. It was easily apparent that Campbell was no ordinary man. In learning, in piety, and independence of thought he was already standing above the other preachers in the denominations. Yet, Baptists generally had mixed emotions over Campbell. They liked his emphasis upon immersion, but they questioned seriously his view of the two covenants, with his emphasis upon the abrogation of the old. Up to the time of the McCalla debate, Campbell had hinted very little as to his conviction upon the purpose of immersion. But when his debate with McCalla occurred, he was ready to declare his belief that immersion was for the remission of sins. Baptists now cocked an eyebrow. Accusations of heterdoxy began to rumble from various quarters. One of P. S. Fall's temperament,—who sincerely loved the truth for truth's sake, could not bring himself to defend party beliefs just for party's sake. He would examine the matter fairly in the light of the scripture, and determine the truth for himself.

In 1822, while still preaching monthly in Louisville, Fall read Campbell's sermon on the Law. He followed closely Campbell's reasoning. The next winter he openly preached these ideas himself, and received considerable criticism. The Baptist Church in Louisville was convinced and joined the principles of restoration. P. S. Fall himself became the first resident Baptist preacher in the state to accept the ancient order of things. He was not long in being cast into disfavor by most Baptists. He was secretary of the Long Run Baptist Association, and in 1824 was invited to write the circular letter to the churches. Fall did so, explaining that the New Testament was the only rule of faith and practice. But of course, the letter was finally rejected.

The Nashville Female Academy of Nashville, Tennessee issued an invitation for Fall to teach there. Accordingly, he moved to the city in 1825, and in addition to teaching, began preaching for the Baptist Church. He explained to the church his conviction, however, that he must be left free to preach only the Bible, and that he would reject all human creeds. The church acquiesced, and Fall began preaching. The Baptist Church in Nashville was a member of the Concord Baptist Association. Fall's insistence that the church take only the New Testament for its rule of faith and practice soon put it into disfavor with the Baptist Association. The minutes of the Concord Baptist Association for 1827 refer to P. S. Fall as "a thorough dyed Campbellite under a Baptist cloak." It is small wonder they thought so.

Fall and Alexander Campbell became the very closest of friends.

In November, 1824, while Fall was still in Louisville, Campbell paid a visit to the city. On a Friday night he spoke to the church. He spoke for two hours from the book of Hebrews. The house was crowded, and five Presbyterian preachers were present. Meanwhile, Fall was being invited to speak in those Baptist churches that leaned toward the restoration. In Cincinnati the Aenon Baptist Church was such a congregation. Its influence was extending far and wide. Jacob Burnet, one of its members, was mayor of the city. Fall went to preach for this congregation late in 1824. He visited in the home of Mayor Burnet, and had the privilege of seeing the latter's son, David S., a boy then only fifteen years of age, immersed into Christ.

Fall stayed in Nashville until 1831, and because of ill health was forced to move back near Frankfort, Kentucky. During his stay in the city, he had succeeded in getting the church to leave the Baptists and standing solely upon the Bible. Through his influence, too, Alexander Campbell first visited the city, and made many friends there which occasioned his return many times in the future. At Frankfort, Fall established the Female Eclectic Institute where many of the daughters of Kentucky's great families received their education. For twenty-six years Fall conducted this school. Meanwhile, Fall preached around the state, very frequently having skirmishes with the Baptists. Silas M. Noel was a prominent Baptist preacher. Through the *Christian Examiner,* Fall addressed a letter to Noel, criticizing certain attitudes Noel took. Noel replied by a sarcastic poem directed at P. S. Fall.

> Our little Phill, can ne'er be still,
>   From nestling and from hatching;
> 'Tis point look up, to Cam'mell'sville,
> 'Tis point no point, with little Phill,
>   And yet he will be scratching.
> Chorus—Twittle twattle, etc.[7]

Probably nobody took such remarks seriously, especially not P. S. Fall.

In 1852 the church in Nashville began having serious trouble over the teaching of J. B. Ferguson, which shall be recorded in our next chapter. Suffice it to say, the church was badly divided.

---

[7]Alexander Campbell, "The Holy Spirit, for Which Silas M. Noel Contends," *Millennial Harbinger,* Vol. II, No. 3 (March, 1831), p. 143.

The feeling generally was that only one man could remedy the unpleasant condition and that was P. S. Fall. They appealed to Fall to return to Nashville. In 1858 Fall came back, and preached here until 1877, when he felt that the work should be turned over to men younger than himself. Accordingly, he turned his attention again toward Frankfort, and here spent the remainder of his life.

In the fall of 1889 the Missionary Society held its annual meeting in Louisville. Fall attended. He by this time was quite feeble and very deaf. Fall went to the Convention, not because he agreed with the Society, for he never did. He was against human societies to do the work of the church. Fall had the feeling he would soon be dying, and he wanted this last opportunity to see some of his old friends. The *Louisville Times* on the occasion, gave Fall quite a write-up. But yet, time was about to catch up with him. On December 3, 1890 Fall died. He was ninety-two years old. His body was laid to rest near Frankfort where he had spent so many years.

"RACCOON" JOHN SMITH

Perhaps the most colorful character of the restoration movement was John Smith of Kentucky. More frequently he was referred to as "Raccoon" John Smith, this backwoods sobriquet being given to him after a sermon he delivered at the Tate's Creek Baptist Association at Crab Orchard, Kentucky around 1815. A vast audience, seeing his unkept appearance, started to leave as he stood up. He then called aloud:

'Stay, friends, and hear what the great Augustine said!' and they all stopped to listen.

'Augustine wished to see three things before he died,' continued Smith. 'Rome in her glory and purity; Paul on Mars Hill; and Jesus in the flesh.' A few now sat down, but many smiled, and started off again.

'Will you not stay,' he cried, in a still louder voice, 'and hear what the great Cato said?' Many returned and took their seats, and seemed willing to be amused.

'Cato,' he continued, 'repented of three things before his death: first, that he had ever spent an idle day; secondly, that he had ever gone on a voyage by water, when he might have made the same journey on land; and thirdly, that he had ever told the secrets of his bosom to a woman.'

The people continued to come back, and began to crowd close to the stand. A few acquaintances, who had not seen him for a long time, now recognized him, and passed the word among the crowd—'It is John Smith, from the Little South Fork!' Seeing groups of persons still standing in the distance, he called again with all the strength of his heavy voice:

'Come, friends, and hear what the great Thales thanked the gods for.'

'Let us go and hear the fellow', said one; 'there may be more in him than we suppose.' And they all, at last, sat down near by to listen.

'Thales thanked the gods for three things: first, that he was endowed with reason, and was not a brute; secondly, that he was a Greek, and not a Barbarian; and thirdly, that he was a man, and not a woman.'

'And now, friends, I know you are ready to ask: 'And pray, sir, who are you? What have you to say for yourself?'

'I am John Smith, from Stockton's Valley. In more recent years, I have lived in Wayne, among the rocks and hills of the Cumberland. Down there, saltpeter caves abound, and raccoons make their homes. On that wild frontier we never had good schools, nor many books; consequently, I stand before you today a man without an education."[8]

In a little while a man went to Jacob Creath, Sr., begging him to come and hear the sermon. "Sir," he said, "the fellow with the striped coat on, that was raised among the 'coons is up; come and hear him preach. His name is Smith." Reared among the 'coons of Stockton Valley and in Wayne County, Smith soon acquired the epitaph of "Raccoon" which has always stayed with him.

Kentucky had many great pioneer preachers. Jacob Creath, John T. Johnson and John Smith were among the more famous. Of these three John Smith's name is probably more familiar to the neophyte in restoration history. Who has not loved to tell— and to listen—to the countless stories of wit and humor coming out of Smith's life? Yet, who among those who have studied his life have failed to walk with Smith through the valley of despair? His life is one of humorous incidents on the one side and one of pathos and drama on the other. We laugh with him in the sunlight of his days, and weep bitterly with him in the many tragedies that marred his life, and darkened the sunless days. We stand in awe at his fearless independence, and watch with profound ad-

---

[8]J. A. Williams, *Life of Elder John Smith* (Cincinnati: The Standard Publishing Co., 1904), pp. 89, 90.

miration his unbounded zeal at work in bringing stubborn wills in subjection to the King of Kings. Smith was without education, knew little of human philosophy, never heard of modern comforts of life, but he loved the Lord and the cause of truth and everything else good and noble and pure with a heart that had no limitations for such love. Rustic, uncouth, and unlearned though he was, he was a good man, a noble man, a courageous man. His life reads like a legend of the sacrifices the early pioneers made for the cause of truth.

Smith was born on October 15, 1784 in what later became Sullivan County, East Tennessee, although at the time of his birth, it was called by the people the state of Franklin, in honor of Benjamin Franklin, the great American statesman. His father was George Smith, and was of German descent. His mother was Irish, and named, Rebecca Bowen. His father fought in the colonial struggle for independence, and then came back to his wife and eight children to provide a living on their farm. But the west was beckoning. Land was cheap, opportunities unbounded, so in this direction he turned his attention. With his large family he moved into the Valley of the Holston early in the year 1784. On the banks of this river, he erected a log cabin, and here in the middle of October, John Smith, the ninth of thirteen children was born.

The parents of John Smith were hardy pioneers quite capable of meeting the rigors of wilderness life. Smith's mother had none of the luxuries that wealthier women possessed, and toiled long hours each day for her family. George Smith, his father, worked equally as hard. By disposition he was quiet, grave and somewhat diffident. But his children loved his presence. Smith's parents held firmly to the teaching of the Philadelphia Confession of Faith, and accordingly, were members of the Baptist Church. They were thorough-going Calvinists in belief and felt that no one could be saved until a mysterious call came from the Holy Spirit. Smith's father sat in the log cabin on Sundays, while the farm work remained idle, and read aloud to his family from the Bible. In this kind of a home atmosphere characterized by godliness, and rigorous toil, the children of George and Rebecca Smith grew up.

Educational advantages in those early years didn't exist. Occasionally a schoolmaster would journey through the wilderness, visiting each log cabin and trying to convince the parents to release their children from the hard work to attend school. When John Smith was about eight years old, he managed in this manner to secure about four months' education, but in that time, he learned to read sufficiently that he could read with comparative ease the New Testament. Soon Smith's father was asking him to read the scripture to the family every Sunday.

In the fall of 1795 George Smith began to get restless to move his family into a different locality. He sold his farm on the Holston, and moved into the Powell valley. Here he erected a cabin and made suitable preparations for his family to live. Taking with him two of his sons, John and Joseph, he said goodbye to the rest of his family, and started across the mountains into Kentucky. He followed the trail to Crab Orchard and from there proceeded to the valley of the Cumberland River. He stopped in a valley at the foot of Poplar mountain, in what later became Clinton County. The little valley was called Stockton valley in honor of a pioneer who had preceded him. Here George Smith purchased two hundred acres of forest land and began immediately to build a home.

Before going back for his family, George Smith desired that the farm work be largely done. To plant the crops in the spring seed corn was needed, and yet the nearest place to buy this corn was in Danville, nearly one hundred miles away. John was now twelve. His father called him to his side and told him he was old enough to take this journey alone. Getting his horse, John set out. He crossed swollen rivers, traveled through thick wilderness trails, and spent the nights in log cabins along the way. He made the trip safely, returning with the corn. The spring crop was planted, and Joseph and John were left to tend it while George Smith returned to Powell's valley for his family. By midsummer the family was reunited in their new home in Stockton's valley.

The only religion John Smith knew during his childhood days in this valley home was the Baptist. Issac Denton, a Calvinistic Baptist preacher, moved to the valley, and Smith was often in his companionship. Calvinistic ideas were more heavily implanted in the young boy's mind, and he began to listen to every movement in the forest, every happening of his life, for some voice to speak to him, declaring that he was among the regenerated.

The older children in the Smith household began to marry and provide homes of their own. William moved into Wayne County, and George into the Green River country. Others settled down nearer their father. John paid occasional visits to see his brother, George. The first visit occurred when the rumor reached home that George had been captured by an outlaw band of murderers by the name of Harpes. George was safe, it was discovered, although he had a narrow brush with death. On Smith's second trip to see George, he witnessed for the first time the religious excitement led by James McGready such as occurred at Cane Ridge. Smith turned from these scenes in disgust, although he still held to his youthful impressions of Calvinism.

Smith began to think more and more seriously of his own salvation and waited more anxiously than ever the divine call. He tried to convince himself that he was totally depraved—worse than the Harpes brothers who had murdered so many. He underwent an inward struggle that was intense, but could feel nothing more than concern because he couldn't realize a call. After one such intense struggle to feel converted, he relaxed. The rolling sea of emotions gradually subsided and a calm swept over his soul. Then Smith told himself that this might be the sign that he was saved. His friends told him so, and urged him to go before the church with this personal experience. Finally he agreed and so on Saturday, December 26, 1804 he told the story to the Baptist Church in Stockton valley. He was voted in, and was immersed the next day in Clear Fork by Isaac Denton.

Denton felt that John Smith would be a preacher. He urged him to lead public prayer, and to read the scripture publicly. But yet, Smith awaited the call. In the meantime, he bought a farm near his brother, William, in Wayne County, and began to build it up. He attended social meetings in cabins and led in a study of the Bible, but still he felt no call to preach. At one of these meetings, he saw a beautiful young lady by the name of Anna Townsend. Smith had rarely noticed the opposite sex before, but now felt attracted to this one. He paid occasional visits to the Townsend household, and on December 9, 1806 was married to the first and only girl he ever loved. The next morning he and his new wife moved to Wayne County, to settle on Smith's farm.

But Smith continued to look for a call to preach. In everyday events he thought he saw a call that he wanted. He side-stepped a rattlesnake, and was prone to think this meant he had been spared to preach. But finally, in a struggle with an ox in which it looked for a moment that he might be killed, he suddenly vowed that if he got away alive, he would preach. He did escape, and this was interpreted as a divine call. In May, 1808 he took an examination for his ordination to preach, and passed. He was now a full-fledged Baptist preacher.

Two years went by, and Smith became convinced that a move would do him good. He had made the acquaintance of Jeremiah Vardeman, who was perhaps the most famous Baptist preacher in Kentucky, and Vardeman urged him to move into the Blue Grass region. Smith went up there, but didn't like it. The war with England came on, and Smith heard of land selling for $1.25 an acre near Huntsville, Alabama. He had visions of selling his Kentucky farm, and buying this in Alabama, and coming out ahead financially in a matter of time. Still he was undecided. The year, 1814, came, and he definitely decided to go. He sold his farm, and in the fall of that year, settled on a new farm in northern Alabama.

Misfortune frequently followed Smith, and the first of any serious consequence met him here. He was off preaching. His wife left the cabin to care for a sick neighbor. The children were left at home with Hiram Townsend, brother to Smith's wife. Suddenly, the cabin caught afire, and quickly burned to the ground. Two of the children were burned alive. The terror and horror that struck Smith's wife can only be dimly imagined. The sad news reached Smith, and he returned home as quickly as possible. His wife, like Rachel, would not be comforted. The days passed by and she sank lower and lower only finally to be planted beneath the soil beside the ashes of her two departed children. Smith himself got sick. He contracted a fever, and for days hovered near death. Slowly he improved.

In a matter of months he sold his farm, and started retracing his steps back to Kentucky. He headed back for Wayne County to talk to his brother, William, and get advice. When he arrived, he found a note from Vardeman, urging him to attend the Association meeting at Crab Orchard, and it was on this occasion that he spoke, as we have already narrated, of being reared among the 'coons' of Wayne County.

The meeting at Crab Orchard together with the kindness of so many friends seemed to inspire Smith to greater work. He continued his preaching tours. Before long he married Nancy Hurt and settled down again on a farm, trying to start anew with a heavy indebtedness hanging over him. Meanwhile, as he continued preaching, and studying his Bible, questions began to be raised in his mind. There was something wrong somewhere in their teaching that didn't match the teachings of the scripture, but he didn't know where. In March, 1822, he was preaching at Spencer's Creek, urging sinners to repent and believe the gospel. He got confused. Suppose the elect didn't believe, would they be saved? Suppose the non-elect did believe, would they be saved? He closed his address abruptly saying:

Brethren, something is wrong—I am in the dark,—we are all in the dark; but how to lead you to the light, or to find the way myself, before God, I know not.[9]

While Smith was thus pondering the subject of salvation, and of Calvinism's teaching, Alexander Campbell began publishing the *Christian Baptist.* Smith became a subscriber, and read eagerly every word. Campbell's reputation had followed his debates with Walker and McCalla, and many Baptist preachers looked upon him with great disfavor. Smith studied and waited. Meanwhile, news came that Campbell was going to visit Flemingsburg and Mt. Sterling. As an act of courtesy, Smith proposed that a delegation of Baptist preachers meet and accompany Campbell. The preachers turned it down, so Smith went alone. He arrived in Flemingsburg ahead of Campbell, and spoke to William Vaughn, a Baptist preacher. He inquired of Vaughn, who had heard Campbell, whether Campbell was a Calvinist, an Arminian, an Arian or a Trinitarian. Vaughn replied that Campbell had nothing to do with any of these things. When Smith inquired if Campbell knew anything about Christian experience, Vaughn replied that he knew everything.

Before meeting, Smith met Campbell, and desired just to sit

---

[9]John A. Williams, *Life of Elder John Smith,* pp. 115, 116.

and look at him. At the service, Campbell spoke on the allegory of Hagar and Sarah. When the meeting ended, Smith turned to Vaughn and said:

"Is it not hard, brother Billy, to ride twenty miles, as I have done, just to hear a man preach thirty minutes?"

"You are mistaken, brother John; look at your watch. It has surely been longer than that."

When Smith looked, he found Campbell had preached two hours and thirty minutes. Two hours were gone, and he knew not where.

During the months that followed, Smith continued to read articles from the *Christian Baptist,* comparing them to the Bible. He was sure there was something wrong with his own teachings, but still he remained unsure that Campbell was right. Gradually he became convinced that human creeds were wrong, and by 1825 was asking the churches to reject them. Soon he began to see that Calvinism was the great evil in the doctrine of Kentucky Baptists, and he began to urge that people be Christians by believing upon Christ as the Messiah and obeying Him in baptism. In taking such positions Smith was turning squarely against his early teachings. He had to turn down the influence of his aged mother in addition to a host of friends including Isaac Denton. But Smith could not preach a thing that he conscientiously believed to be wrong. He could not refrain from opposing something that he thought was standing in the way of the salvation of numerous souls, such as he believed Calvinism was doing. By the year 1826 Smith had joined the other preachers of Kentucky in proclaiming a return to the ancient order.

It was to be expected that Smith's preaching would excite the Baptists a great deal. When the North District Association held its annual meeting at Cane Spring on the fourth Saturday of July, 1827, Smith went, expecting the Association to take action against him. A letter was read before the Association, directed at Smith, although not calling him by name. It charged that certain ones were guilty of the following three heresies: (1) Of reading from Campbell's translation of the Bible instead of the King James version. (2) Of saying "I immerse you" instead of "I baptize you" when administering baptism. (3) Of allowing the communicants to break their own bread when partaking of the Lord's

Supper instead of having the preacher do it for them in advance. When Smith heard the charges, he jumped up and cried, "I plead guilty to them all." After considerable altercation, the Association decided that no action should be taken against Smith, but that such action should be postponed for another year. Smith's replies to the Association on the charges gained for him the sympathy of the people while securing the dislike of the clergy.

But Smith found himself with plenty of company. Jacob Creath, Sr., Jacob Creath, Jr., and John T. Johnson had joined the host of those pleading for a return to the apostolic order, and often stood beside Smith before the Elkhorn, Franklin, and North District Association. Together with him they received their anathema, and like him they counted it a joy to suffer for the name of Christ and for the cause of truth. The years that lay ahead were years that these men together planted the seed of the kingdom over the state of Kentucky. They saw hundreds immersed, and witnessed the establishment of congregations throughout the state.

During these years of experience as a gospel preacher, Smith found frequent use of his witticisms, but all of them were used to illustrate a point. Smith was never without an answer, no matter the unexpectancy of the occasion. Once when he had baptized several members of a certain family, he afterwards met the father, who had always been a close personal friend.

"Good morning, my brother," said Smith to him kindly.

But the old man fixed a scornful look upon him and said: "Don't call me brother, sir! I would rather claim kin with the devil himself."

"Go then," said Smith, "and honor thy father!"

Smith, in his preaching was hard on the false doctrines of his time, and especially was this true with Calvinism. His wife felt that at times he was too severe, and urged him to let up. One day Smith held up a glass of water before her and said, "Nancy, can I fill this tumbler with wine, till I have first emptied it of water? Neither can I get the truth into the minds and hearts of the people till I have first emptied it of water. Neither can I get the truth into the minds and hearts of the people till I have first disabused them of error."

Such illustrations but show the natural turn of Smith's mind.

He was fearless, positive, humorous and uncompromising in his presentation of the truth. He had strong convictions that money, position or prestige could not buy. These he continued to declare until those last hours of the year 1867 and early 1868 when the faint gallop of the pale horse and his rider could be heard approaching off in the distance.

In the fall of 1867 Smith went to Mexico, Missouri to spend the winter with his son-in-law and daughter. Although then in his eighty-fourth year, his mind seemed to have suffered little. His memory was yet clear and his wit remained undiminished. On Lord's Day February 9, 1868, while at the home of his daughter, Mrs. Emma S. Ringer, Smith stated that he would go to church and preach as usual. It was an unusually cold day, and Smith remarked to his daughter that he had never seen such a cold day before. Nevertheless, against the wishes of his daughter, he walked from her home to the church house. His discourse on this day was the last that he ever gave. He walked home again, his aging frame shivering in the cold. After a cup of hot coffee and a meal, he went to his room and went to sleep. He awakened in the afternoon and would have gone to meeting that night but his family was insistent that he stay home, so he complied with their wishes. The next morning he was suffering from inflammation. For nearly three weeks Smith lay in bed before passing to his reward at half-past eight in the evening on Friday, February 28, 1868. Three days earlier Smith had sent word by W. J. Mason to Elder Wright, editor of the *Christian Pioneer*. "Tell Bro. Wright," he said, "I am better and most home."[10]

Smith had already made plans for the body to be shipped back to Lexington, Kentucky for burial. It arrived at the depot at eleven o'clock in the morning on the next Wednesday, March 4th. J. W. McGarvey and a delegation of brethren with a hearse and carriages met the body when it came in, and reverently escorted it to the church building. Some of the brethren were asked to give short discourses and did so. John A. Williams, the biographer of Smith, and a very close friend, could not be present. He was especially wanted to deliver the funeral address, but since that could not be, on the third Lord's Day of May, Williams did

---

[10]W. J. Mason, "Elder John Smith," *Christian Standard,* Vol. III, No. 11 (March 14, 1868), p. 85.

preach a memorial discourse at Somerset, Kentucky. Following the short messages over the body at the church in Lexington which were delivered by J. W. McGarvey, Robert Graham, and George W. Elley among others, the body of Smith was borne to the cemetery and carefully laid away in the grave.

The next Sunday afternoon, George W. Elley wrote a letter to W. C. Huffman, his good friend, of Sumner County, Tennessee. This letter we now have in our possession. It is an interesting letter in the light of the events just recorded.

Lexington, March 8th, 1868

Dear Bro. Huffman,

This is the 'Lord's Day,' and a soft bright beautiful day it is. I have just returned from town and from hearing a discourse from Moses Lard, upon "As in Adam all die, so in the Christ shall all be made alive." His mind seemed to be unsettled and wandering, as are the mental visions of us poor preachers at times, and he did not show his usual clearness but said much that was good and cheering to us pilgrims. Generally he is instructive and profitable.

Last week our venerable John Smith was brought here from Mexico, Missouri and planted in our cemetery, a beautiful spot there to lay until our Lord comes. He was with one of his daughters in Mexico. He was in his 84th year and was seriously ill for only a few days. He was not only a good but an extraordinary man. What he knew to be truth he would teach anywhere and insist upon it. No man in Kentucky or the West has been more efficient for Christ than John Smith. In 1827 he immersed 700 persons. God has greatly blessed his ministry since he became an advocate for the whole truth.

I feel that my days are rapidly coming to an end, altho my health is better than for years. And as my time is short I feel more anxious to be at work and owing to my present situation I am unable to give myself to the work. We live one mile out from the city on a small farm, and no white person here but wife and myself. Consequently, it is difficult for me to leave home so as to do any good. . . .

G. W. Elley

The Lord had blessed the labors of Smith. To him largely the success of the church in Kentucky can be attributed.

CHAPTER XIV

TENNESSEE TROUBLES

It is not known for certain when the plea for a return to apostolic Christianity first entered the state of Tennessee. The Bethlehem church in Wilson County took its stand for the truth in 1816, and seems to have been the first in the state to do so. One reads of the old Liberty congregation in Marshall County separating from the Richland Association of United Baptists to take an independent stand for the Bible alone as early as 1823. By 1827 the church at Nashville had left the Baptists. By 1840 there were a large number of congregations standing on apostolic ground in the state. It can be stated for certain that by the time of the war between the states the cause in Tennessee had made great progress and was resting upon a substantial basis.

For a time before the war brethren took great pains to collect statistics about the church. Due to this effort, the strength of the church in the state can be fairly accurately known, as well as, in many cases, the origin of the various churches. An analysis of the information at hand may prove, not only interesting but profitable to our investigation of the progress of the cause of restoration.

In east Tennessee in the year 1844 there were but eleven congregations. The largest of these churches seems to have been at Boone's Creek in Washington County with two hundred and fifty members. In the same county were three other churches: Kibber's, with thirty-nine members: Limestone with fifteen and Buffalo with one hundred and twenty-one members. Four congregations were found that year in Carter County—Buffalo, Mt. Pleasant, Turkey Town, and Crab Orchard. Buffalo was the largest of these churches with one hundred and twenty-one members. There were two congregations—Liberty and Roan's Creek—in Johnson County, and the Concord and Fork churches in Sullivan County.

In 1846 A. G. Branham visited the churches in Wilson County to gather statistics of their strength. He found a number of congregations although in many cases, they were meeting only once a month. At Rutland's meeting house, where John Scobey was a deacon, the church was having only monthly meetings. This congregation separated from the Baptists in June, 1832, and by 1845 had forty-seven members. The church in Lebanon had a difficult time getting on a substantial basis during these early years. It was organized in October, 1836 with nineteen members, but many moved, and the church reorganized in December, 1842. By 1845 it had only forty-two members. As already mentioned, the oldest congregation in Wilson County, if not in the state, was the old Bethlehem church. Its first building was made of hewn logs and was located six miles from Lebanon on the old Trousdale Ferry turnpike. Calvin Curlee and John Bonner were among the first preachers at the Bethlehem church. Alvin Hobbs is said to have preached the first full gospel sermon at this congregation. Sandy E. Jones held the first meeting here, baptizing forty persons. Barton W. Stone, Jesse L. Sewell, Tolbert Fanning, J. M. Kidwell and E. G. Sewell did much of the first preaching here. W. C. Huffman preached for this church after the war. When the war broke out, Turner Goodall, a young preacher enrolled in Franklin College, visited the church regularly. When the war started, however, he joined the Confederate ranks and lost his life. Many years after the war C. M. Pullias and F. B. Srygley preached here.[1] Wilson County had another congregation called the Big Spring church which was organized in September, 1839.

At least ten congregations were found in Jackson County before the war. The church at Liberty was organized by John Mulkey as early as 1826. Ten years later a congregation was formed at Bagdad. Between 1840 and 1846 the following congregations were formed: Trace Creek, Salt Lick, Ridge Meeting-house, Pleasant Hill, Buckeye on Flynn's Creek and Meigsville.

A small congregation existed in Marshall County that shared the distinction with the Bethlehem church of being the oldest in the state. Wilson Hill on Globe Creek was also formed in 1816. The new church in the county was organized in 1828 by Joshua K. Speer. Soon there came along other congregations. Cedar Creek church was organized in 1831. The Long's House congregation was formed in 1840. Two years earlier the church at Lewisburg had been formed, and met in the Court House. There were

---

[1]John M. Hill, "History of Bethlehem Church, Wilson County, Tennessee," *Gospel Advocate*, Vol. XLV, No. 18 (April 30, 1903), p. 279.

churches formed on Richland Creek and Cane Creek in the year 1843.

In Warren County, there were three hundred and fifty members in 1848 divided among the following congregations: Ivy Bluff, Fountain Spring, Philadelphia, Irving College, Rocky River, and McMinnville. In Rutherford County the churches appeared to be rather numerous by 1850. There were congregations at Cripple Creek, Millersburg, Rock Spring, Murfreesboro, Fall Creek, Fayetteville, Woodbury. At Millersburg a large camp meeting was held in September, 1847. In Bedford County there were churches at New Hermon, Big Flat and Richmond. In Lincoln County there were congregations at Cane Creek and Lynchburg, and in Cannon County, the Brawley's Fork church had one hundred and twenty-eight members by 1850. A congregation with twenty-five members was organized at Dresden in Weakley County that same year.

The first congregation in Sumner County, Tennessee was organized at Sylvan Academy on March 30, 1834 by Professor Peter Hubbard. There were only nine members of the church. On the evening of April 22, 1837 W. C. Huffman was baptized here by John Mulkey. Sylvan Academy was the school house, owned and used by Peter Hubbard. Later, in 1838 there was a church organized at Electa Cyria. After this building burned, the name was changed to Union, and soon became known as "Old Union." Huffman worked with this church for several years. Through his efforts John T. Johnson and George W. Elley came from Kentucky on various occasions to hold meetings here.

At Chattanooga the church was late being established. J. J. Trott and J. Eichbaum visited here in the summer of 1848 and preached in the Presbyterian church house. When Fanning visited here in 1855, he says, "We found no church of the disciples, and heard of but few members in the vicinity."[2]

Turning briefly to the western side of the state, one finds the cause less flourishing. The church in Memphis was established in 1847 by B. W. Stone. (This was not Barton Warren Stone.) By the following summer, the congregation had about seventy members. There was a congregation at Union in Shelby County

---

[2]Tolbert Fanning, "A Tour Through Georgia, Alabama, and Mississippi," *Gospel Advocate,* Vol. I, No. 1 (July, 1855), p. 11.

which was organized in 1839. At Fayette there was a church with thirty-seven members. In Henry County there were about seven hundred members, the church at Paris, being organized in 1833, had by 1850 over a hundred members.

In middle Tennessee the church was not outstandingly strong. Fanning and Absalom Adams established the church in Franklin, in Williamson County, in 1832 with twenty members. Between the years, 1837 and 1839, Fanning conducted a Female Academy here and his influence helped the church to grow considerably. In 1846 W. J. Barbee, who was a physician, did the preaching for this church. At Columbia the church met in the court house in 1848. J. K. Speer conducted a meeting here that year with thirteen additions. There was considerable complaint that the church had poor leadership and many worldly and disorderly members. In Davidson County there were several other congregations besides the one in Nashville. The church at Franklin College was organized in 1846 with fifty members. The church at Sam's Creek, eighteen miles west of Nashville, had nineteen members. South Harpeth, twenty miles southwest of the city began in 1834, and the following year, a congregation was organized at Sycamore, twenty-five miles northwest of Nashville.

In other sections of the state a few congregations could be found. We have failed up to now to mention that a congregation of thirty-five members existed at Clarksville in 1844, but the church had no meeting house of its own. At Pikeville in Bledsoe County there was a church. W. D. Carnes in the year, 1848, ran "Pikeville Academy" in this vicinity. There was a church also at Athens, and at Lavergne, in Rutherford County.

The work of planting all of these churches fell on the great evangelists of the church who were so willing to sacrifice for the advancement of the cause. One of the earliest of these preachers was John Mulkey. He was the son of Jonathon Mulkey, a Baptist preacher. Mulkey was born in South Carolina on January 14, 1773, and began preaching in East Tennessee during his twentieth year. He had a brother by the name of Phillip, the two being among the strongest Baptist preachers in the community. In 1809 John Mulkey changed his mind on "unconditional election," and as a result, Baptist ire was aroused against him. On the 2nd Saturday of November of that year he and a few others decided to leave off creeds and take only the Bible. This was the same year that Thomas Campbell wrote his Declaration and Address. How significant that so many people, in widely separated areas, were thinking along the same line! Mulkey continued to preach until in 1841 he became too old and feeble. He died on December 13, 1844 at 12:45 A.M. In fifty-one years of preaching, he had delivered ten thousand sermons.[3]

Another of Tennessee's early preachers was Joshua Kennerly Speer. Speer was born in 1794 in Yadkin County, North Carolina. He was reared a Baptist. At the age of twenty-four he moved to Williamson County, Tennessee to live near Franklin. He was religious by nature and wanted to do the will of God. J. J. Trott, who was in those days a Baptist, taught him Baptist doctrine. On the fourth Lord's Day of November, 1823 Speer began preaching. But he wasn't satisfied with his beliefs. He studied his Bible, and also read the *Christian Baptist*. Before long he was converted to the restoration plea, and discarding all creeds and confessions of faith, he began to urge men to come back to the Bible. For thirty-five years Speer preached the gospel. He held meetings all over Tennessee, and baptized hundreds of people. He died at his home in New Hermon on May 27, 1858.

Jesse Londerman Sewell was another of Tennessee's leading preachers. He was an older brother to E. G. Sewell. He was born on Wolf River in Overton County on May 25, 1818 of Stephen and Annie Sewell. There were fourteen children in all, twelve of which lived to be grown. Jesse L. Sewell had but little education, although his younger brothers, Isaac, Caleb, and Elisha, got more after they were grown. He was religiously inclined and very early learned to read the Bible. Consequently, he became a member of the Wolf River Baptist Church at an extremely early age. He was not yet ten years old when he became a member on the third Sunday of December, 1827. Of him, David Lipscomb writes:

Jesse, when young, was small of stature and slender. He became fleshly as he grew older, but his bones and feet and hands were always small. His head was large, well balanced and full; his arms were awkwardly hung upon his body, he never learned what to do with his hands while preaching.[4]

---

[3]Isaac T. Renau, "Obituary," *Christian Review,* Vol. II, No. 5 (May, 1845), p. 120.

[4]David Lipscomb, *Life and Sermons of Jesse L. Sewell* (Nashville: Gospel Advocate Publishing Company, 1891), p. 49.

On July 21, 1839 he married Elizabeth A. Speer. Two years later he began devoting his life to preaching, although he was, at this time, still a member of the Baptist church. Jesse Sewell's older brother, W. B. Sewell, married a member of the church of Christ in 1840. Consequently, W. B. Sewell often attended these meetings. Finally, he was led to see the truth, and obey it. The Baptists turned him out of the church. Jesse L. Sewell was disappointed in his older brother, and so, began to search the scripture to convince him of his error. Instead of finding something to convict his brother of, Jesse Sewell himself was converted. He spent many years after this preaching the word, and died at his home at Viola, Tennessee while seated upon his front porch on June 29, 1890.

Still another Tennessee preacher was W. C. Huffman. He was born of German parents in Central Kentucky on May 4, 1802. Early in his life he became a blacksmith. He had a powerful physical constitution and an extremely quick mind. Religiously, he was nothing in his early years. He reacted to the religious divisions by going into Universalism. He moved to Cairo, Tennessee on the Cumberland River in Sumner County in 1825. Two years later he married Lucy A. Goodall, daughter of Charles Goodall. Meanwhile, he maintained his belief in Universalism until 1836 when he read the language of Jesus in Matt. 25: 46. His father-in-law was a Cumberland Presbyterian. Huffman went to their meetings and turned away in disgust. He decided to study the Bible for himself to see if it were true. He concentrated upon the study of the Messiahship of Jesus. He concluded the Bible was true, and went back to the meetings determined to take nothing the preachers said unless it was read from the Bible. He went to the mourner's bench, but found no consolation for his soul. At night, he couldn't sleep. Once he got up, put on a light, and read his Bible, and resolved to be immersed. The next morning early he went to an old man by the name of Wiseman, a Baptist preacher. The preacher asked Huffman for a personal experience, so it could be told to the church the next Sunday, but Huffman insisted that he wanted to be baptized for the remission of his sins. Wiseman refused but told Huffman that a man would be preaching that kind of doctrine the next week at Peter Hubbard's school house. Huffman went and heard John Mulkey. He was immersed on April 22, 1837. Huffman labored with the churches in Sumner County until after

W. C. HUFFMAN

the war. The last two years of his life he preached at Union City in West Tennessee. He died on February 19, 1880.[5]

With this background of the Tennessee churches our attention now turns to the city of Nashville where excitement and misfortune were frequently known in those early days before the war. In 1780 a party of forty families traversed the wilderness led by General James Robertson and came to the Cumberland River where they established what later became the city of Nashville. The

[5]A. Alsup, "Wilkinson C. Huffman," *Gospel Advocate,* Vol. XXII, No. 21 (May 20, 1880), pp. 328, 329.

church in Nashville was established in July, 1820 by Jeremiah Vardeman and James Whitsett. It wore the name of "Baptist Church of Nashville." The membership at that time included: R. C. Foster, Sr., H. Ewing, Dr. John O. Ewing, S. Whitsett, M. Fly. The women members were Sarah Ewing, A. Foster, Phereby White, H. Temple, S. Robertson, E. Boyd, P. McIntosh, L. Gibbs, S. Hays, P. Taylor, A. Goodwin, and L. Garner.

In December, 1820 Elder Richard Dobbs was installed as the first preacher for this congregation. Soon after its establishment, the church had applied for and received membership in the Concord Baptist Association. This Association had been formed in 1810 in Wilson County with twenty-one Baptist churches. But, while Dobbs was preaching for the church, the congregation withdrew from the Association. Dobbs died on May 21, 1825. The next year, the Nashville Female Seminary invited P. S. Fall to the city, and he accepted. Arrangements were made and Fall became the preacher for the church on May 20, 1826. The next year the church reunited with the Concord Association. A letter was addressed to the Association, written by R. C. Foster and P. S. Fall. The letter said:

Dear Brethren: When the church of Jesus Christ in Nashville sent us up to meet you, she vested us with authority to request to be dismissed from the Association, should circumstances render it proper. Our only object in uniting with you, has been to promote the welfare of the Christian cause, and the harmony of the disciples, and although we cannot approve the course some individuals have pursued in the present controversy, yet we do not wish to be considered as taking a part therein. We do not think there is authority in the New Testament for Association, at any rate, and much less is there any ground for supposing that it authorizes their existence for the purposes to which they generally apply. If we can meet you at any future time, merely for the purpose of worship and general edification, we will cheerfully attend. But until we think those ends can be gained, we request the privilege of continuing to ourselves.[6]

At this time the church in Nashville had one hundred and thirty-one members. It will be seen that the church went back into the Association thinking it was advancing the Christian cause. When it very readily became apparent that they were not, they withdrew. Of the membership, all except five went with the reformation.

---

[6]John Bond, *History of the Baptist Concord Association* (Nashville: Groves, Marks & Co., 1860), pp. 40, 41.

In December, 1830 Alexander Campbell, with Jacob Creath, Jr., came to Nashville. On Friday, the tenth, he spoke on the apostasy, and announced that the next night he would speak again. Questions were passed to him. It was during this time that Obadiah Jennings, a Presbyterian preacher, arose and disputed with Campbell. For the moment Campbell paid little attention to him. On Christmas Day, after returning from a trip to Franklin and Columbia, Campbell debated Jennings, after which thirty persons were baptized. Following this meeting in Nashville, Campbell wrote:

This Christian congregation is so far advanced in the reformation as to meet every Lord's Day, to remember the Lord's death and resurrection, to continue in the apostle's doctrine, in the fellowship, breaking of bread, and in prayers and praises. From its location, in the capital of the state, this society has already exerted, and is likely still to exert, a happy influence over the whole state.[7]

As we have already seen, P. S. Fall left Nashville in June, 1831 because of ill health. At this time the church had two hundred and fifty members, having enjoyed a remarkable growth during Fall's stay. For the next ten years the church was without a regular preacher. Tolbert Fanning came to the city in 1832 to enter the university, and helped to serve the church on various occasions. Early in 1835 Alexander Campbell returned to the city with his daughter, Lavina. During his stay, there were twenty additions, and by now the church was said to number six hundred members, although it is not unlikely that this figure is a little high, for in 1849 the church is said to have numbered five hundred and forty-three members, and in 1852, five hundred and fifty members. It is very probable that in 1835 the church had nearer three hundred than six hundred members. At any rate, it may be at once seen that the church during these years, up to 1852 enjoyed a remarkable growth.

From the time that P. S. Fall left in 1831 up to 1842 the church appears to have been without a regular preacher. The feeling began to be widespread in the church that a preacher should be secured to labor full-time with the congregation. As a means of talking over the work in general, and of discussing the issues then facing the church, in Nashville several leading brethren met. The subject of cooperation was discussed and then the matter of secur-

---

[7]Alexander Campbell, "The Church in Nashville," *Millennial Harbinger*, Vol. II, No. 3 (March, 1831), pp. 121, 122.

ing a preacher. Tolbert Fanning was present at the meeting. As
for himself Fanning was always opposed to the idea of a preacher
locating with a congregation. The woes which later came upon the
church Fanning could not help but lay to the fact that it had a
regular preacher. Of this meeting, Fanning remarks:

It was taught that the labor of an evangelist consisted in preaching the gospel to the lost, in planting churches and enabling the
members to do their work—to keep house for God. It was understood that the pastor's office devolved, of right, upon the older
members of the church, and upon no others. Then the idea of
beardless lads, flippant, and impertinent orators, taking the oversight of venerable sages and matrons, was regarded highly lu-
dicrous.[8]

Despite Fanning's objections, the church secured the services of
W. H. Wharton, then a popular southern preacher. But as time
went on, Fanning noted that Wharton got himself busy with other
things until his sermons grew stale. By the year, 1846, there was
a general feeling that a younger man was needed, and so in May,
that year, J. B. Ferguson cast his lot with this church as its pro-
claimer of the word.

In the meantime, other events had taken place around Nashville
that will bear some notice. Franklin College was organized in
1843, but more will be said of this in our next chapter. In January
1844 Fanning began the publication of a paper which he called the
Christian Review. His purpose for establishing this publication
he outlines in the first issue. Basically there were four reasons for
beginning. First, the sentiments and beliefs of the church, Fanning
believed, were woefully misrepresented and the truth needed to be
taught. While he conceded that there were other papers doing
this, yet, none of them enjoyed a very extensive circulation in the
"southwest." The second reason was that the Christian religion
was not being practiced by any party of the age, so Fanning felt a
responsibility to call men back to the word of God. In the third
place, Fanning felt that the churches of Christ were not yet fully
and scripturally organized, and consequently the disciples of Christ
were not as intelligent, spiritual and zealous as they needed to be.
Lastly, Fanning believed the *Review* would be in a better position

---

[8]Tolbert Fanning, "The Church in Nashville," *Gospel Advocate,* Vol. III,
No. 3 (March, 1857), p. 72.

to get brethren acquainted in different parts of the country, because it had reporting editors in many of the different states.[9]

With high hopes, then, Fanning started the *Review*. Its motto was "Union and Peace On the Bible Alone." For four years it continued its publication, and doubtlessly did much to advance the cause in the southland during those years. Yet, Fanning was always busy, and most of the time, too busy. He could not do the paper justice, so made plans to turn it over to someone else. In casting around for a new editor, his attention immediately centered upon J. B. Ferguson, who at this time had been in Nashville less than two years. He had arisen constantly in popularity with the people, and had all the appearance of being a man with great ability, soundness and judgment. So Ferguson was selected to be Fanning's successor.

Of Jesse Babcock Ferguson, H. Leo Boles has well said,

Like a meteor which flashes across the horizon, making a trail of glorious light behind it, and then suddenly disappearing and leaving nothing but darkness in its wake, so Jesse B. Ferguson came above the horizon and shone as a great pulpit orator in the church of Christ at Nashville, Tenn., and then as suddenly disappeared and dropped into obscurity. Perhaps no preacher of the gospel ever stood so high in the estimation of the people and received the plaudits of the populace and then dropped so low as did this man.[10]

Ferguson was born in Philadelphia, Pennsylvania on January 19, 1819. His father was Robert French Ferguson, who soon after Jesse B's birth moved into the Shenandoah valley in Virginia. When he was eleven years old, Ferguson attended Fair View Academy. He failed to get to attend William and Mary College and so turned his attention toward an apprenticeship in printing. When he was twenty-one years of age, he moved to Ohio, but stayed here only a short time, later moving to southern Kentucky.

In 1838 Ferguson began preaching the gospel. His fame spread far and wide in Kentucky. He was both eloquent and brilliant, and he knew it. Flattery fell abundantly upon his head, and he grew vain and proud, losing at the same time, his spirituality. His popularity reached Nashville, and in May, 1842, he was invited to con-

[9]Tolbert Fanning, "The Christian Review," *Christian Review*, Vol. I, No. 1 (January, 1844), p. 1.

[10]H. Leo Boles, *Biographical Sketches of Gospel Preachers* (Nashville: ʻpel Advocate Co., 1932), p. 186.

duct a gospel meeting. The meeting was a huge success, and he was urged to locate with the church. He declined the offer. Two years later he conducted another meeting, and again was begged to locate with the church, but he declined. He began regular wrok with the church in the spring of 1846 and continued this for several years.

Therefore, in 1847, when Fanning was looking for an editor for his paper, decided upon Ferguson. Ferguson accepted the invitation. He decided, however, to change the paper. The name of it now became *Christian Magazine*. It was somewhat larger, and a little more attractive. Ferguson introduced this new publication by saying:

We need a work suited to the times in size, spirit and matter. We have been often and earnestly solicited to commence such a work; but until recently, owing to the fact that we have so many publications, but meagerly sustained, we have hesitated and declined. But in our present enterprise this difficulty is removed; we enlarge and seek to improve an existing periodical, while we have thrown around us increased facilities for making a paper such as we desire . . .

To our friends in the South and South-west, especially, we look for support. Theirs is a somewhat new and uncultivated field of labor.[11]

The *Christian Magazine* continued publication until the end of 1853. At first B. F. Hall and Tolbert Fanning were associate editors, but this arrangement was brief. In 1850 John Eichbaum was chosen associate editor, but he continued in the capacity for only about two years. The Society belief was sweeping all the churches, and the Tennessee churches for a few years fell in line. In 1849 at a State Meeting, it was decided to start a Publication Society, and turn the *Christian Magazine* over to it. But Jesse B. Ferguson continued as the editor, and stipulated the policy of the paper.

The real woes for Jesse B. Ferguson and for the Nashville church began in April, 1852. At this time, in the issue of the *Christian Magazine* for that month and year, Ferguson set forth his views upon 1 Pet. 3: 18-20. He suggested that he had been requested to write on this, and, although he had held this view for eight years, he had refrained from saying so because he knew he

[11]J. B. Ferguson, "Introduction," *Christian Magazine*, Vol. I, No. 1 (January, 1848), p. 1.

differed radically from his brethren upon it. Then, in commenting upon this scripture, Ferguson wrote:

It is clear to our mind that the language of the apostle conveys the idea that Christ by his spiritual nature, or by the Spirit, did preach to the Spirits of the invisible world. And as if to include all, the apostle refers to those who died in disobedience in the days of Noah, which would make his language equivalent to all the dead; which he afterwards confirms by declaring that in order that Jesus Christ might be the judge of the dead and living, the 'gospel was preached to the dead'—to those now dead—not 'in the flesh,' 'now in prison.'[12]

When Alexander Campbell read the above article, he was somewhat stunned and took an immediate issue. To Ferguson's idea that when Christ died, he went to Hades and preached the gospel to those that had been disobedient, Campbell answered by calling it a "posthumous gospel." He pointed out that this interpretation contradicted the plain teaching of the scripture that "it is appointed unto man once to die and after this the judgment." Certainly, it would have been successful preaching to preach to the dead, for it would take little argument and no urging to get lost men out of Hades. But what did the passage mean? Campbell says,

The passage fairly construed is this—He warned the spirits in prison that once were disobedient, while the ark was preparing, in which few (that is, eight) persons were saved through the flood, or through the water, that unless they would repent they should all perish.

These spirits, then, were Noah's contemporaries, and were addressed by Noah, speaking through the Holy Spirit, which emphatically is, and ever was, dispensed officially by the WORD, which became flesh and dwelt among us. So that during one hundred and twenty years this great preacher of righteousness, through the Spirit which was in Christ, announced repentance, or ruin, to his contemporaries, then confined, or in prison bounds, during the time the ark was in building and furnishing.[13]

Ferguson's reply to Campbell was entitled, "The Rewards and Punishments of The Life." It was a vague answer, if any at all. Campbell later complains that he read this article five times and was never able to determine whether Ferguson believed in a punishment after death. Meanwhile, the brethren as a whole, were somewhat

---

[12]J. B. Ferguson, "Exposition of Scripture," *Christian Magazine,* Vol. V, No. 4 (April, 1852), p. 113.

[13]Alexander Campbell, "A New Discovery," *Millennial Harbinger,* Fourth Series, Vol. I, No. 5 (May, 1852), pp. 322, 323.

excited. Samuel Church of Pittsburgh complained that Ferguson had a "maggot in his brain." John Rogers wailed, "O, if I could blot out the lines he has written on this subject with my tears, most gladly would I do it."[14]

In line with Campbell's suspicions Ferguson soon let it be known that he did not believe in punishment after death. Heaven and hell, he argues, are not places but states. Ferguson exclaims:

Is Hell a dungeon dug by Almighty hands before man was born, into which the wicked are to be plunged? And is the salvation upon the preacher's lips a salvation from such a Hell? For ourself, we rejoice to say it, we never believed, and upon the evidence so far offered, never can believe it.[15]

From these beliefs Ferguson went farther and farther from the truth. Before long he began to teach that men could have communications with the spirit world, and thus went off into Spiritualism. The influence of these teachings around Nashville was disastrous to the church. Almost all of the church followed him in the belief. Many congregations went off with him. In Nashville there were some who tried to save the church from such teaching. In November, 1854, W. H. Wharton read a letter publicly to the church, objecting to Ferguson, but a large body of the brethren stood with Ferguson, so about fifty left to worship somewhere else. Late that same year, Campbell was called in to preach on this doctrine publicly. Meanwhile, Ferguson had had a spirit communication from Dr. William E. Channing, advising him to have nothing to do with Campbell, so he failed to show up at the meetings. Nevertheless, the meetings did, however, do some good, and a year later, Ferguson's popularity had declined some.

On the last Lord's Day in 1855 Ferguson read a letter, signed by five men, asking him to stay on as a preacher. Significantly, none of the five were members of the church. When the matter was put to a vote, only a third of the people now wanted him to remain. Bitter division now ensued, and the question of the legal right to the property came up. A lawsuit was planned, but on June 1, 1856 Ferguson resigned, and the brethren settled the difference without such legal procedures. The next February the elders of the church—James H. Foster, J. D. March, Frank

---

[14]Alexander Campbell, "The Spirits in Prison," *Millennial Harbinger,* Fourth Series, Vol. I, No. 7 (July, 1852), p. 414.

[15]J. B. Ferguson, "The Punishments and Rewards of the Future Life," *Christian Magazine,* Vol. V, No. 7 (July, 1852), p. 202.

McGavock—announced the property matter cleared up and back in the right hands. By this time, Ferguson had shown, even to many friends, his true color. He left the church completely and went off with a denomination.

It was to take a little time to completely revive the congregation after these disastrous events. The church had sold its old building and moved into a newer, much nicer one, on Cherry Street. But, on April 8, 1857 this building mysteriously caught fire, and burned to the ground. The church managed to rent its old building, and in a few months had repurchased it. Meantime, the church had been casting around for another preacher. Old timers remembered P. S. Fall and his good work twenty-five years before. They needed now an older man, one in whom they had confidence, and so Fall was urged to come. In 1858 he arrived, and then began collecting together the scattered flock. Forty-two white people and fourteen colored were snatched from Ferguson's influence. By 1860 the church numbered two hundred members, and was at peace once again.[16]

Fanning, in the meantime, watched the Ferguson fiasco with a heavy heart. He fought bravely and furiously to save the church from the wreck Ferguson had brought upon it. To make matters worse, so far as his own conscience was concerned, he felt he had helped Ferguson by giving him the *Christian Review*. But that mistake was past, and he could do nothing about it, save to make what amends he could. He resolved to try to off-set Ferguson's harm by again establishing another paper. Ferguson had closed the *Christian Magazine* in 1853, which was fortunate. By the spring of 1855 Fanning had fully determined to start another paper, and to have another partner in his work. This time he selected William Lipscomb to serve with him as co-editor of his new paper.

William Lipscomb was, by seventeen months, the older brother of David Lipscomb. He was born on June 20, 1829. His parents were Granville and Ann Lipscomb. Physically, William was a sickly child, lacking in physical vigor and activity common to youth. A great portion of his life he was semi-invalid, suffering from asthma and bronchial troubles. The sight of blood severly sickened him, and so weak was he that frequently during his life, he would bleed at the lungs, so that friends would never have been

---

[16]James Challen, "The Church in Nashville, Tennessee," *Millennial Harbinger*, Fifth Series, Vol. III, No. 4 (April, 1860), pp. 214-216.

surprised at his death at any time.   Yet, William lived a good long life.   There were twelve in his graduating class at Franklin College, yet he outlived them all except one.   He was the weakest member, physically, of the Franklin College faculty, but he outlived all of his fellow teachers.   Very often he was too weak to walk two hundred yards to his school room, and would ride the distance.

William Lipscomb was fond of school books, of reading and studying.   Studies never seemed difficult to him.   He entered Franklin College in January, 1846 and graduated at the top of his class two years later.   His proficiency in his studies made Fanning interested in making him a full time professor at the school.   Here he taught Greek and Latin.   Both teachers and students recognized him to be the most thorough scholar in the college, and no man exercised a greater influence.   He was at once an outstanding mathematician, a master of the English language, and unexcelled in Botany.

William confessed Christ in the summer of 1846 and was baptized by Tolbert Fanning.   He preached some, but his physical disabilities made it impossible for him to be a great preacher. When he was twenty-two, he married Anna Fulgham.   They lived together twenty-four years and had seven children.   When she died, William married Allie Hudson and they lived together for thirty years.   He died in East Nashville at the home of his daughter, Mrs. G. A. Davis, on February 7, 1908.

Self-assertion and aggressiveness were not traits that belonged to William Lipscomb, and consequently, he was never an outstanding leader.   He did, however, have his own convictions and never hesitated to stand for them.   He had a great, kind and good Christian soul, and his friends loved him greatly.

In July, 1855 William Lipscomb and Tolbert Fanning began publication of the *Gospel Advocate,* a monthly periodical.   As already mentioned, a chief purpose in starting this work was to make amends for the harm done through the *Christian Magazine,* which Fanning felt that his lack of proper foresight had partly caused. So, Fanning writes at the outset:

The history of the work substituted for 'The Review' is well known and bitterly regretted.   The error committed cannot be corrected—'there is no place for repentance.'   But we would gladly shroud the past in impenetrable night.   We once more appear before our brethren and the world as a religious journalist, and whilst we ask the indulgence of all, we are happy in the belief that our labor in the 'Gospel Advocate' will prove a blessing to many.[17]

As to the course the *Gospel Advocate* was to pursue, the editors wrote:

The 'Gospel Advocate' will be devoted to the interests of the church of Jesus Christ, and especially to the maintenance of the doctrine of salvation through 'the gospel of the grace of God.' It will be the careful study of the conductors to present, in an intelligible form, the great and distinguishing principles of the Christian institution, and affectionately enforce the observance of its heavenly practices; to give such reviews and notices of religious systems, speculations, books, publications, and sayings and doing of men, as may to them seem proper and useful, and to keep the reader advised of religious and educational progress. Their motto shall be, 'Open columns and free discussion of all questions calculated to advance the spiritual interest of society.'
While they feel not at liberty to compromise the least 'jot or tittle' of truth, they will regard it an honor to fraternize with all who fear God and respect His institutions, as developed in the Divine Oracles.[18]

Scarcely had the prospectus gone out until letters began to come in expressing best wishes for the undertaking. Campbell wrote:

We are of opinion that such a periodical is needed in Nashville, and in Tennessee. The condition of things in the city and state call for not only oral, but written and printed materials of thought and action. The press, well furnished and guided, is a powerful auxiliary of truth or of error. If evil spirits use it in the projects of evil, why should not good spirits use it against fraud and imposture? Under the editorialship of Elders Fanning and Lipscomb, we anticipate for it a large circulation and a liberal patronage.[19]

Ben Franklin wrote: "Respecting your proposal to publish a newspaper, I can say that I think the move a good one. I trust you will meet the new phases of unbelief in such a manner as to do great good. I will furnish you a few short pieces, and everything I can do to encourage your enterprise, I will cheerfully do. May you have abundant success."[20]

---

[17]Tolbert Fanning, "Reminiscences," *Gospel Advocate,* Vol. I, No. 2 (August, 1855), p. 27.
[18]Tolbert Fanning and William Lipscomb, "Prospectus for the Gospel Advocate," *Millennial Harbinger,* Fourth Series, Vol. V, No. 6 (June, 1855), p. 358.
[19]Tolbert Fanning, "Friendly Expressions in Regard to the Success of the Gospel Advocate," *Gospel Advocate,* Vol. I, No. 2 (August, 1855), p. 25.
[20]*Ibid.,* p. 25.

The name, *Gospel Advocate,* was not particularly new. A Baptist periodical in Virginia some ten years before had worn this name. In addition, as we have seen, John T. Johnson and B. F. Hall had published a paper in Kentucky with this name in 1835-36. Neither of these facts seemed to have influenced the name which Fanning and Lipscomb decided to give to their paper. Since it was the gospel that was to save the world, the paper should take that title. Moreover, since the avowed purpose of the editors was to advocate the gospel, and not the opinions of any man or party, it seemed fitting to call it, the *Gospel Advocate.*

The *Advocate* continued publication until the War Between the States began in 1861. During the war, when the mails were closed, the paper was discontinued. It started again in 1866 as a weekly and not a monthly.

Thus we bring to a close our survey of troubles in Tennessee before the war, and the influences resulting which deserve a place in a study of the restoration.

CHAPTER XV

EDUCATIONAL ENTERPRISES

The brotherhood has had from its very beginning a major interest in two types of work—the press and the classroom. As early as 1818 Alexander Campbell was running Buffalo Seminary in his own home at Bethany, and by 1823 was editing an influential religious periodical. Walter Scott, while running his academy at Pittsburgh, did not fail to teach the Bible along with teaching other subjects. P. S. Fall was running a female academy as early as 1831 near Frankfort, Kentucky, and Tolbert Fanning was running one at Franklin, Tennessee. Many members of the church had disinguished themselves in the classroom, and it was only natural that they should want to incorporate the teachings of the Bible in their curriculum as time went on. More and more, then, the minds of many turned in the direction of the school where the Bible could be taught.

This emphasis was occasioned largely by the need for the Bible and its teaching which was not and could not be given in the colleges and universities over the country. In addition to intellectual training, it was thought that an emphasis had to be placed upon "moral culture", the teaching of the principles of Christian living as outlined in the Bible. From 1835 until his death this great need was constantly upon the mind of Alexander Campbell. The *Millennial Harbinger* is replete with articles, emphasizing the need of a knowledge of the Bible, or spiritual teaching as well as intellectual. Campbell's long series entitled, "Conversations at the Carrollton House," which were purely fictitious conversations, were for the purpose of stressing the need of Bible teaching as well as other kinds.

Campbell's mind thought in terms of great principles. One of his favorite lines of thought was to divide his study of man into three important phases or states—the natural, preternatural, and supernatural—man as he was, as he is, and as he will be. Man is a physical, spiritual, and intellectual being, and no education can be complete that does not train man for all three. To train man to be a physical and intellectual giant while overlooking the spiritual is like putting a high-powered gun in the hands of a savage. He becomes a potential threat to the safety and progress of the community.

The many controversies which were later to arise over colleges were never thought of in these early years. Men who taught in these schools were for the most part school teachers by education and training. They desired to take their Christianity with them in their business, and while teaching other subjects, they would not neglect the greatest book of all—the Bible. Theological seminaries were for the most part tabooed. The idea was to give a general education, and along with it teach the Bible, for it was just as necessary to a complete education as any other phases of study. So, accordingly, Campbell writes to Tolbert Fanning, in answer to a query:

Colleges are not instituted especially for the benefit of qualifying men for preaching the gospel. Sacred history, and the Bible in colleges as a textbook, with regular systematic lectures thereon, are just as necessary to properly educate school teachers, lawyers, doctors of medicine, farmers, merchants, mechanics, etc., as to educate preachers. This question insinuates a doubt whether colleges are not primarily, in our esteem, got up exclusively for theological purposes. I judge not the intention of its propounder, but its relevancy to the question of moral culture in colleges. Colleges, as far as religion is concerned, must be a blight to any community, if irreligious; if conducted without religion and the Bible.[1]

No attempt is going to be made to trace the history of all the schools which the brotherhood had before the war, for if all of these are considered, large and small alike, it would occupy a large volume in itself. There were three schools that were destined to play a decided role in the future of the restoration movement. These were Bacon College, Bethany College and Franklin College. A more detailed consideration of these is to be given, but before closing the chapter some less detailed study of others will be included.

Bacon College was the first of the colleges established in the brotherhood. Its first session began on November 14, 1836 and was held at Georgetown, Kentucky, then the home of the school. The school owed its origin to dissention with the Baptists in that town, and to a man who otherwise played a very small role in future events in the restoration movement.

---

[1]Alexander Campbell, "The Bible a Textbook in Colleges," *Millennial Harbinger,* Third Series, Vol. VII, No. 9 (September, 1850), p. 511.

Thornton F. Johnson, a graduate of West Point, and a teacher of civil engineering by vocation, had gone to Georgetown, Kentucky in 1829 to become one of the faculty members for the Baptist college. Barton W. Stone lived near Georgetown, and soon became a close friend of Johnson's. In 1832 Stone was seriously considering a move to Jacksonville, Illinois and urged Johnson to accompany him and start a college in this vicinity. Johnson decided to go and view the possibilities. In 1834, while he was in Jacksonville, the Baptist college at Georgetown reorganized its faculty, leaving all teachers who were not sympathetic to their doctrine. Johnson then went about his plans of establishing the school in Jacksonville, but another reorganization at Georgetown took place, and Johnson was urged to return. Finally, he agreed to do so, and so for the next two years worked hard to build up the college.

In 1836 the Baptist college again began to tighten its grip on the school, and Johnson felt himself being pushed out. Nothing but a separation would do, so Johnson began planning for another school. Preferably, he wanted a Female Academy, and so urged P. S. Fall to move his school from Frankfort to Georgetown. Fall refused. Johnson built a large brick house on Clinton Street. He waited until after the opening of the Baptist college before opening his own to avoid the criticism of taking other students. On November 10, 1836 he met with the students, but because many faculty members had not yet arrived, the formal opening of the college was delayed until November 14. Nearly sixty students were present for the occasion, and so the college opened with high hopes.

The name attached to the school was Bacon College in honor of Sir Francis Bacon, the great philosopher. The first president of the school was Walter Scott, although, for some reason not stated, Scott never served beyond delivering an inauguration address. Scott was scheduled to teach Hebrew Literature. Besides him the faculty consisted of S. Knight, professor of moral and mental sciences; T. F. Johnson, professor of mathematics and civil engineering; S. G. Mullins, professor of ancient languages; C. R. Prczriminski, professor of modern languages and topographical drawing; Tolbert Fanning, professor of natural history; J. Crenshaw, teacher in preparatory department.

The first board of trustees consisted of Walter Scott, John T. Johnson, S. Hatch, John Curd, Henry Johnson, James Challen,

Samuel Mickolls, Asa R. Runyoun, J. H. Daviess, T. C. Flourney, George W. Williams. H. M. Bledsoe, John Duncan, P. S. Fall, S. W. Muckolls, Thomas Smith and John Bowman.

In Scott's place D. S. Burnet was elected as president. John T. Johnson was vice-president. T. F. Johnson resigned in 1837 to carry out his original design to establish a female school. Thus, the school carried on until 1839. A problem, not peculiar to Bacon College, had arisen relative to securing enough financial aid to run the school. Considerable opposition had been incurred in Georgetown. This opposition had been manifested even in getting the State Legislature to grant the charter. It was finally obtained with a vote of nineteen to thirteen in the senate, and sixty-one to thirty in the house of representatives. Now this opposition made the securing of the school financially even more difficult. By 1839 the situation for the school had entered a stage where something had to be done.

The trustees of the school made it publicly known that they would move the college from Georgetown to any town that would promise financial subscriptions equal to at least fifty thousand dollars. Major James Taylor, a lawyer of Harrodsburg, saw an advantage in having the school there. He went to work and raised one hundred subscriptions of five hundred dollars each, besides another ten thousand dollars for a building site. On May 2, 1839 the trustees of Bacon College agreed to move the school.

Although Alexander Campbell complimented the move, all of the problems were by no means settled. D. S. Burnet resigned as president and Samuel Hatch began to serve *pro tempore*. Meanwhile, the school moved in on the residence of James Curry in Harrodsburg, and opened its first session on September 2, 1839.

The need of a permanent president was seen. The next year the College had secured James Shannon to fill this office. Shannon was a prominent educator, a man of high qualities and noble bearings. He was born on April 22, 1799 in Ireland. In 1815 he entered the Royal University at Belfast and graduated three years later. A position was soon opened to him as rector of an academy at Sunbury, Georgia, and he accepted. Here he was immersed and became a member of the Baptist church. In January, 1830 he was professor of languages at the state university at Athens, Georgia. Five years later he became president of the College of Louisana at Jackson. He went from here to Harrodsburg.

In 1843 Bacon College moved into a building put on a ten acre tract which Major Taylor had purchased for this purpose in 1839. But now, the attendance began to decline, and again the school entered a financial distress. Shannon handed in his resignation in 1845. Immediately friends of the school got busy and raised some more money, so Shannon took back his resignation and agreed to stay for another five-year period. The College now had twenty thousand dollars worth of property and a fifteen thousand dollar endowment. But the income got worse. All of the scheming, begging and planning could not raise enough funds to keep the school going. What was wrong?

Carrol Kendrick, during this time, was editing the *Ecclesiastical Reformer* in Kentucky. Kendrick took up the battle, and for several months he and Shannon debated the issue before the brethren of the state. Kendrick charged that the brethren of Kentucky were refusing to support the school because Bacon College was not serving its cause. Shannon revealed to the brethren for the first time the utter misconception which he had of the restoration plea. Yet, Shannon's position was one that in later years was freely adopted by many of the schools. Shannon declared that their charter, which was borrowed from Centre College at Danville, had stipulated that the peculiar doctrines of no sect should be preached. Shannon defended the school by insisting they were teaching the Bible, but that they had consistently refused to teach the peculiar doctrines of the churches of Christ. For the first time, in all probability, many brethren learned that they belonged to a "sect," according to Shannon. It is not at all unlikely that Kendrick had struck at the basic trouble with the College, although there were many who agreed with Shannon in his viewpoint.

Nevertheless, matters continued to get worse for the school. When his time expired, Shannon resigned. This was in 1850. That year he became the president of the University of Missouri. On June 14, 1850 the trustees voted to close the college. Apparently, Bacon College had failed, but things were not as bad as they appeared, so far as the future of the school was concerned.

The buildings of the college continued to be used for a high school, conducted by Samuel Hatch. This prevented many legal technicalities from occurring. In 1852 at a state meeting of the churches it was voted to reopen the college, but to amend the charter so that the school would belong to the "Christians in the state of Kentucky." No action, however, came from this. Meanwhile, Hatch continued to teach here until 1855 when he closed down the high school. It was now urgent that something be done with the College, but what?

The solution was offered by John B. Bowman. At a meeting of the brethren held at Harrodsburg on October 22, 1855, Bowman suggested that a university be established upon the ruins of Bacon College. It doubtlessly occured to Bowman that the state needed such a university and the people would more likely support it if this could be done. The Board of Trustees approved the idea, and some plans went immediately ahead to raise the money. Thirty thousand dollars was immediately raised in Mercer County. By Nov. 7, 1856 Bowman was able to announce that a hundred thousand dollars had been raised, and soon after this, that number was one hundred and fifty thousand. On the first Wednesday of May, 1857 the donors to the project met to decide upon definite action. John Allen Gano was present and acted as chairman. A committee of seven was appointed to draw up another charter to be presented to the State Legislature.

The new charter was soon drawn up. It called for a self-perpetuating board of thirty curators, two-thirds of whom were to be members of the church in Kentucky. The Board of Trustees approved the charter and submitted it to the state legislature where it met approval on January 16, 1858. A Board of Curators was appointed and on September 19, 1859 the school began operation under the new name, Kentucky University.

The new president of the University was Robert Milligan, a man whose name was destined to be among the immortals of the church. Milligan was predominantly an educator, and as an educator, always was best known. He was born in Tyrone, Ireland on July 25, 1814, and the next year, came as a baby with his parents to settle in Trumbull County, Ohio. In 1831 he entered Zelienople Academy in Beaver County, Pennsylvania and two years later, entered the Classical Institute at Jamestown in Crawford County, Pennsylvania. His father had been an elder in the Associate Reformed Presbyterian Church, so in 1835 Milligan became a member of the same denomination. Milligan opened his first school at Flat Rock in Bourbon County, Kentucky. While

ROBERT MILLIGAN

he was teaching here, some of the students asked the meaning of certain passages in the Greek New Testament. Milligan set out to re-examine the New Testament and ended up by being immersed into the New Testament church at Cane Ridge by John Irvine in March, 1838. The next year, he entered Washington College in Pennsylvania, and by 1843 had received both his Bachelor of Arts and Master of Arts degrees. He taught English literature at this college, as well as chemistry and natural history. In 1852 he resigned this position and moved to Bloomington, Indiana where he taught mathematics in Indiana University for two years. In 1854 he taught mathematics at Bethany College and became co-editor of the *Millennial Harbinger*. He also served as an elder of the church in Bethany. He was serving in these positions until he went to Harrodsburg to become president of Kentucky University.

There were one hundred and ninety-four students at the opening session of the university, but this number rapidly decreased. The political excitement of the elections, and finally, the war, hurt the attendance considerably. School continued, however, during the war except for a brief time after the battle of Perryville which was fought October 8, 1862 when the Confederate army took over the university's buildings for a hospital.

On the night of February 16, 1864 a tragedy occurred to the school which affected its future course. The main building burned to the ground. Would it be more profitable to put up this building, or, since it is down, would it be wiser to move to a better location? There was the question. The trustees decided to move, and appointed a committee to investigate the possibilities. Four years earlier—in June, 1860, the trustees of Transylvania University in Lexington had made a proposition to turn over their property to Kentucky University if it would move there. Besides the citizens offered thirty thousand dollars. At the time the Trustees had turned down the offer. However, in 1864 when the offer was again made, it was readily accepted. The state legislature approved the move on February 28, 1865, and the University opened its doors in Lexington on October 2, 1865.

BETHANY COLLEGE

The opening of Bacon College in 1836 caused a delay in the plans of Alexander Campbell to establish a college at Bethany. Campbell had been planning such a school, and had made those plans known only to D. S. Burnet. For fear that he might be accused of working against Bacon College's interests, he had decided to wait until this school was well re-established before going ahead with his own plans. After three years of waiting, Campbell divulged to the public his plan for the first time in the October, 1839 issue of the Harbinger. He writes:

I am now about to divulge to this community, to philanthropists, to lovers of good order, to the Disciples of Christ a favorite scheme deeply impressed upon my mind; long cherished, and in the establishment and supervision of it, it is probable, *if the Lord will,* I shall close all my earthly project.[2]

With this announcement, Campbell proceeds with his statement of the establishment of Bethany College. With Campbell, keeping the Bible foremost, was a paramount interest. He continues:

We want no scholastic or traditionary theology. We desire, however, a much more intimate, critical, and thorough knowledge of the Bible, the whole Bible as the Book of God—the Book of Life and of human destiny, than is usually or indeed can be, obtained in what are called theological schools.

Campbell announced that the College would have the following buildings: (1) Stewart's Inn for the boarding and lodging of students. (2) The Family House where children, ages seven to fourteen, could live in a parental atmosphere. (3) Three Professor's Mansions or private dwellings for the faculty. (4) Primary School Rooms where children, ages seven to fourteen attend classes. (5) The College Proper for classes. (6) The church edifice.

With these announcements, the plans were formulated and action was brought to bear as quickly as possible. The charter for the College was procured by John C. Campbell for the Virginia State Legislature in the winter of 1840. The Board of Trustees consisted of the following men: Alexander Campbell, Albert G. Ewing, Samuel Church, Henry Longley, James T. McVey, Robert Y. Henley, Samuel Grafton, William Stewart, Josiah Crumbacker, Adamson Bentley, Robert Nicholls, Campbell Tarr, Matthew McKeever, John Andrews, Robert H. Forrester, Jacob Creath, Robert Richardson and John C. Campbell. The first donation was for a thousand dollars and came from Phillip B. Pendleton.

The first meeting of the trustees was held at Bethany on Monday May 11, 1840. Thomas Campbell was called to the chair. W. F. M. Arny was chosen secretary, and Alexander Campbell treasurer. A building committee was appointed consisting of William Stewart, Robert Richardson, Matthew McKeever, and Alexander Campbell.

----

[2]Alexander Campbell, "A New Institution," *Millenial Harbinger*, New Series, Vol. III, No. 10 (October, 1839, p. 446.

The second meeting of the board was held Friday, September 18, 1840. At this meeting Campbell turned over to the Board a deed for ten acres of land. The trustees authorized the building committee to erect any buildings they deemed necessary for the school. At this meeting, Alexander Campbell was elected president of the college. The third meeting of the Board was held on Monday, May 10, 1841. A report was read stipulating that $11,045 had been promised to the school, but ten thousand of that was only promised, not yet received. At this meeting other faculty members were selected. W. K. Pendleton, who had recently married Campbell's daughter, Lavina, was selected. Robert Richardson, Andrew F. Ross, and Charles Stewart were the others selected.

By the following October only Stewart's Inn was ready, but school opened nevertheless on the 21st of the month. Edwin W. Bakewell was the steward. There was considerable confusion getting started as both students and professors crowded into the same building. There were one hundred and two students that enrolled, coming from nine states and Canada. Twenty classes were formed, the first one meeting at 6:30 every morning. Alexander Campbell met this class and walked each morning to it from his home, three quarters of a mile away.

Regulations for the students were rather strict, and for our day a little unusual, but they were rigidly maintained in Campbell's day. Each student, upon entering the college, must submit testimonials of his good moral character that were at least ten years old. All students dressed alike in either dark gray or black color with cloth at a price not to exceed six dollars a yard. The Trustees recommended that each student wear Kentucky blue-jeans. The college bell was rung every morning at dawn, and each student was compelled to arise at that time. "Early to bed, early to rise . . . .," and they dare not forget it.

With the students as a whole Campbell was well pleased. Nevertheless, he found one disappointment, which doubtlessly every college official has seen. Campbell says,

Some it would seem, have either wholly mistaken the character of their sons or the character and intentions of our institution. They seem to have regarded it as a sort of pentitentiary institution, to which youth of either doubtful or desperate character may be sent in the hope of reformation.[3]

[3] F. D. Powers, *Life of W. K. Pendleton*, p. 63.

Campbell, therefore, had to make it clear that he was running a college, not a reform school. Many a parent has decided to send her wayward child to a "Christian College" with the hope he would be changed. When this child arrived at the school, he found many other parents with many other wayward children had the same idea. These soon got together in their wayward acts and the result has been that the college received a bad reputation over it. Even modern-day college presidents can sympathize with Campbell's problem.

The second year of the college started with more hopeful prospects for the future. There were one hundred and fifty-six students enrolled. Besides, Campbell had announced during the summer that over seventeen thousand dollars had been promised to the school. More buildings had gone up. The College Proper, four stories high, had been finished. So had Stewart's Inn. One wing of a mansion house had been completed. John Mendel, John Atkinson, Basil Wells, Samuel Muckols, and Joseph Wasson had been added to the Board of Trustees.

College commencements at Bethany were gala affairs. They were always held on July 4th, and lasted for hours at a time. The one held in 1843 may serve as an illustration. It was attended by one thousand, five hundred people. It opened by prayer and music at 9:30 in the morning. This was followed by a reading of the Declaration of Independence. Then followed seven speeches, among them a valedictory by Alexander Campbell and a Latin and Greek ode. The program continued without interruption for five hours.

The selection of a college emblem was left up to Robert Richardson. Richardson selected a tripod supporting two volumes— Truth and Science. Upon this was placed a quiver of arrows, and a bow with the motto inscribed above in Latin: *Pharetram Veritas, sed arcum Scientia donat.* The tripod was to indicate they were divine oracles. Truth was using the arrows to pierce her enemies.[4]

At the regular meeting of the Board of Trustees, which met August 13, 1845, a motion was made by John C. Campbell that

---

[4]Robert Richardson, "Seal of Bethany College," *Millennial Harbinger,* New Series, Vol. VII, No. 6 (June, 1843), p. 281.

"for the ensuing year it is expedient that there should be added to
the offices of the Institution a Vice-Presidency. . .."[5]
Accordingly, W. K. Pendleton was appointed to fill this office.

Alexander Campbell wanted Bethany College to keep the Bible
always first. He wrote:

Bethany College is the only College known to us in the civilized
world, founded upon the Bible. It is not a theological school,
founded upon human theology, nor a school of divinity, founded
upon the Bible; but a literary and scientific institution, founded
upon the Bible as the basis of all true science and true learning.[6]

Concerning the ideas he had in mind in establishing the college,
Campbell also said:

Not a feeling or thought of State pride or glory, of northern
or southern, eastern or western interest, spirit or character, had
anything to do with its conception, incipiency or design. It was
the cause of education—intellectual, moral, religious education—
the cause of Reformation, in its connection with literature, science
and art—the conviction that educated minds must govern the world
and the church—that God had made men of learning, talent and
character, his great instruments of human redemption, from the
days of Moses and Aaron to the days of Paul and Apollos—that
originated the idea of Bethany College. It was emphatically the
conviction, that pagan mythology, that Grecian and Roman idola-
try, fable and fiction, had supplanted the Bible; that college education, now-a-days, was more skeptical than Christian, more secular
than moral or religious, that induced me to add its burden to more
than enough before.[7]

Bethany College had many advantages over Bacon and never
had many of the problems of the other school. The best talent
in the brotherhood constituted its faculty. The dream of every
young man was to have the opportunity to sit under Campbell's
feet and be taught by this great man. Campbell's great reputation,
wide acquaintance among the wealthier people, made the securing
of finances with him less of a problem than with Bacon. Moreover,
Bethany's location among the hills of northern Virginia, in a
comparatively out-of-the-way place, gave it seclusion and protection
during the war, and the school continued without interruption.

---

[5]Alexander Campbell, "Bethany College," Third Series, *Millennial Harbinger*, Vol. II, No. 9 (September, 1845), pp. 417, 418.
[6]Alexander Campbell, "Bethany College," *Millennial Harbinger,* Third
Series, Vol. VII, No. 5 (May, 1850), p. 291.
[7]Alexander Campbell, "The Northwestern Christian University," *Millennial Harbinger,* Third Series, Vol. VII, No. 6 (June, 1850), p. 333.

Occasionally, a disaster struck such as it did on the night of December 10, 1857. A golden glow played across the windows of the professor's mansions and Stewart's Inn with its hideous message of fire. Before anything could be done, the college proper had burned to the ground costing the school nearly sixty thousand dollars. The library with its many valuable collections was gone. But classes were interrupted for only one day, and work immediately began on rebuilding the structure. But, aside from these rare occurrences, Bethany College continued right on through the war, and sent from her halls many of the greatest of the pioneer preachers.

FRANKLIN COLLEGE

Franklin College, near Nashville, Tennessee, was largely the product of Fanning's mind. Like Campbell, he believed that the educational institutions of the world had overlooked the need of the Bible and so, he proposed changing this. It was in devoting his life to this work that Fanning felt he was doing the most good. He once wrote:

Years since, I think I can say with a good conscience, I saw the folly of Christians toiling to heap together earthly dust; and although I had prepared myself in the profession of law, for practice, my final determination was to devote myself, with what ability I might possess, to the good of man. Many sincere friends advised me to give myself to the proclamation of the gospel; but with a hope of greater usefulness, I determined to spend my life, and be spent, in the education of youth. With a full knowledge of the difficulties of the profession, I was induced to attempt the establishment of a high school of learning.[8]

In the spring of 1844 Fanning gave considerable attention to establishing the college. By late spring, he was ready to make the following announcement in the *Christian Review:*

Perhaps it is not known to the readers of the Christian Review, that arrangements are in progress to establish by the beginning of another year, Franklin College, at Elm Crag, the residence of the writer. A charter was granted at the last session of the Legislature. . . .[9]

A farm belonging to Tolbert Fanning and B. Embry called Elm Crag, and located about six miles southeast of Nashville, was to

[8]Tolbert Fanning, "Education and Franklin College," *Christian Magazine,* Vol. II, No. 6 (June, 1849), p. 211.
[9]Tolbert Fanning, "Franklin College," *Christian Review,* Vol. I, No. 6 (June, 1844), p. 130.

be used for the college. By the summer of 1844 they had invested about fifteen thousand dollars, and needed about four thousand more. Their plans called for the erection of suitable buildings by the end of the year.

A Board of Trustees was selected consisting of the following: David G. Ligon, Moulton, Ala.; Dr. M. W. Phillips, Edwards Depot; Gen. Patrick Henry, Hinds Co. Mo.; Hon. J. A. Gardner Dresden, Tenn.; Col. Samuel Martin, Campbell's Station, Tenn.; Dr. John Shelby; Dr. John W. Richardson, Stewartsborough, Tenn.; W. G. Roulhac, J. J. Trott, Turner Vaughn, Ladoga, Tenn.; Tolbert Fanning; George W. Martin; W. H. Wharton; John Simpson; Thomas Martin; David King; Andrew Ewing; Beverly Nelson; John R. Wilson; Frank M'Gavock; B. Embry; James H. Foster; and Edward Trabue.

Franklin College opened its first session on Wednesday, January 1, 1845. The school was divided into three departments: Juvenile, Preparatory, and College Proper. The following constituted the first faculty: Tolbert Fanning, President; J. N. Loomis, professor of mathematics and chemistry; John Eichbaum, professor of languages; E. S. Chandler, professor of Music; A. J. Fanning, Principal of Preparatory Department; P. R. Runnels Principal of Juvenile Department; and B. Embry, Steward of the Boarding House. When school opened, Loomis couldn't fill his position, so J. Smith Fowler of Ohio took his place. School opened with forty-five students, and this number soon increased to seventy.

In certain respects Franklin College was unlike any other school. Fanning divided education into physical, moral and intellectual. His ideal was to combine all three. For the intellectual the regular college courses gave this education. The Bible furnished the moral, and so the word of God was regularly studied. But, in addition, every boy who attended the College spent a portion of each day working on a farm, which was run in connection with the school. This supplied the physical education. Still in another respect was the college different. It had no endowment, wanted none and argued against them. Alexander Campbell had something to say about both of these unusual features. Concerning the first, Campbell wrote:

There is Franklin College, not far from Nashville, Tennessee, under the presidency of Elder Fanning, also rising into notoriety and increasing in the number of its students. The energy and enthusiasm of brother Fanning are equal to almost any undertaking, and by his industry and perseverance this institution has been built up within a few years to a respectable seminary of learning, combining some of the useful arts of social life, usually called trades, with a literary and scientific education thus putting it in the power of young men to work their passage aboard the ship trade into a liberal and practical education.[10]

Concerning the endowment feature, Campbell had some other ideas. He writes:

The Franklin College asks for no endowment, and argues against endowment. It asks for aid to get up its buildings, and will have no fund. In this, it is our opinion, and in the history of all Colleges, decidedly in error. Not a College in the world has existed one century without endowment; nor can they. This fact is worth a thousand lectures. Can any one name a college that has seen one century without other funds than the fees of tuition?. . . .[11]

The average number of students in Franklin College for the first four years was one hundred and thirty. The faculty consisted of the president, four regular professors, and a teacher in the juvenile department. Around Tennessee, people were slow to come to the rescue of the school financially, for many were under the impression that it was a money-making scheme. In reality Embry and Fanning sank fifteen thousand dollars of their own money in it, and obligated themselves for a debt of five thousand more. With no endowment, and an extremely low tuition price, they were dependent upon the contributions of brethren. Fanning was a man of great faith, fully determining to do the will of God and depending upon God to look after him. With Franklin College he would undertake to please God and do good. He wrote:

Colleges and schools have sprung up with remarkable rapidity, amongst the disciples, within a past few years. . . . In a Christian point of view, there are few things more vain and corrupting than the idea that colleges give denominational respectability; and it is not altogether clear, that the kind of training most popular is, at the same time, most favorable to true piety. . . . If personal aggrandizement, or sectional and sectarian pride, have influence with us, our colleges will prove a curse instead of a blessing to the world.

---

[10] Alexander Campbell, "Our Colleges," *Millennial Harbinger,* Third Series, Vol. III, No. 6 (June, 1846), pp. 386, 387.

[11] Alexander Campbell, "Our Colleges," *Millennial Harbinger,* Third Series, Vol. II, No. 9 (September, 1845), p. 420.

The honor of God, and good of man should be our exclusive study.[12]

From its humble beginning in 1845 until the opening of the war Franklin College continued to exercise considerable influence in the south. Her roll of graduates includes many of the southland's outstanding preachers in later years. Fanning continued to act as its president. No great changes were made in the school until the summer of 1857. Fanning had by now concluded that he was too busy and absent too much from the college. He proposed a reorganization of the Board of Trustees together with the faculty to give the school added strength. When college opened that fall, there was a new board. One now finds on the board for the first time David Lipscomb, who that year resided at McMinnville, Tennessee; James E. Scobey of Lebanon, Tennessee and Joshua K. Speer of Lavergne, Tenn.

A change also was made in the general administration of the faculty. Before this, smaller children in the preparatory department had been forced to be thrown with the older students of the college, making teaching extremely difficult. A separate department was created and F. M. Carmack was placed in charge. The business management of the college was also changed so to relieve Fanning from this burden.

Fanning, however, apparently found the work too arduous even yet. After serving sixteen years as president, he proposed that he step down. W. D. Carnes, president of East Tennessee University became the next president. That year, 1860, the college was bought by an association of friends who did so with a view to establishing two colleges—one male and one female. A Board of Managers, with David Lipscomb as secretary was selected to look after the school. The buildings were repaired and put in first class condition and by the fall of 1860, the future of Franklin College looked brighter than it had ever been.

Then came the political election of 1860 followed by its rumbles of war. War came upon the south, and the boys from Franklin College quit school to bear arms. W. D. Carnes went back to his home, and Franklin College closed its classrooms. For the next months the soldiers of first the south and then the north used it for barracks.

---

[12]Tolbert Fanning, "Colleges Under Christian Influence," *Christian Record*, Vol. III, No. 2 (February, 1846), p. 48.

There were other schools to be established during those years before the war but anything like a complete history of all of them would make almost an endless volume. On the Western Reserve, the Western Reserve Eclectic Institute was born on November 27, 1850. This school was established through the joint labors of many Ohio brethren. In the fall of 1844 A. S. Hayden was conducting a school in Callamer, Ohio in a copper shop. At a yearly meeting of brethren in June, 1849 in Russell, Ohio, Hayden suggested to the brethren that some consideration be given to establishing a school among them. Another meeting was held at Ravenna on October 3. Then another followed in November at Aurora where thirty-one churches were represented. At this meeting it was agreed to establish a college and that it should be located at Hiram in Portage County. Another meeting was held in December at which a board of trustees was selected. The name, Western Reserve Eclectic Institute, was suggested by Isaac Errett. Shares of stock were sold at twenty-five dollars each to raise five thousand dollars. A farm of fifty-six acres was purchased, and by the summer of 1850, construction of buildings was well on its way. The school opened that fall with A. S. Hayden as president. There were one hundred and two students.

At Indianapolis there was yet another school that began during these years. At a state meeting of brethren held in Greensburg in October, 1847 the business committee reported "that the brotherhood in this state ought to make some special effort in the cause of education." During the discussion that followed, brethren from Lawrence County promised to raise eight to ten thousand dollars if the school would be located in their county. George Campbell made a similar proposal for Rush County. A committee was appointed to meet in Indianapolis in December to hear proposals from other places. The committee met and heard that Lawrence County would raise five thousand dollars if the school would be located at Bedford. But the committee decided to submit the matter to the brotherhood of the state. The next May another committee was held at which there was reluctance to agree upon locating the school in Bedford despite the insistence of Elijah Goodwin. However, they pushed the decision of location upon the next state meeting which was to be held in October, 1848.

At this meeting the Lawrence County brethren went up in arms, severely reprimanding the committee for a strong sectional bias against locating the school in Bedford. Nothing could be done except to appoint a group to visit every church in the state to get their views. At the next meeting the following year, it was decided to establish North Western Christian University at Indianapolis, and a committee of seven was appointed to take the steps necessary to found and endow the college.

The charter, which was granted by the state legislature in January, 1850 stipulated that the college was to be a joint-stock company with a capital of seventy-five thousand dollars in shares of one hundred dollars each. One-third of the capital was to be used on the erection of buildings and the rest was to go into a permanent endowment. Accordingly, the college opened in 1855 for classes.

There were many other schools. In Missouri was to be found Christian University at Canton, and the Female Academy which was run by L. B. Wilkes and W. H. Hopson at Palmyra. In Tennessee there were Minerva College, Burritt College and Hope Institute. In Kentucky there was Popular Hill Academy; in Indiana Fairview Academy. So it was all over the brotherhood, a multitude of academies and schools all of which did good in many respects but which can only be mentioned here in passing along.

Chapter XVI

LARD AND McGARVEY

We are gradually approaching the period of the restoration when the names of two individuals stand out prominently before us. These men are Moses E. Lard and John W. McGarvey. Both men were scholarly, pure men, and good preachers. They stood together on the major issues which came to face the brotherhood, although in temperament and disposition were different. Our attention turns first of all to Lard.

The full story of Moses E. Lard is yet to be written. One rarely reads a biography of this man from anybody who seemed really to understand him, and probably there is a reason for this. Lard was a difficult person to understand. He was a man of extreme nervous temperament, and of extreme moods. His blood circulated vigorously, causing his face always to be aglow. His mind worked rapidly; his feelings were always intense. After great mental exertion, he would have times of deep despondency. He was very often of a melancholy nature, and brooded for days over matters that no one could help.

Lard passed through life from one mood to another. As he grew older, he tended to reflect upon his past, and hard days were there, too. He found himself losing faith in humanity. His restless intellect made him search into things he could not possibly understand. He would labor at great ends to understand those scriptures which deal with life after death. He had a hard time reconciling eternal punishment with the nature of God. And so, he brooded frequently over the mysteries of the future. He was given much to speculation about the future, and one of the few just criticisms given to him, even by his friends, was on this point.

Never could Lard do anything he conscientiously thought was wrong. He found it impossible to cooperate with brethren who were using the instrument of music. This fact added to his despondecy. In the whole affair about Kentucky University, which shall be recounted in our next volume, Lard found himself placed in a false light before the brethren, and he could do little about it. More than anything else he wanted the College of the Bible to

287

MOSES E. LARD

serve the brotherhood. During the last year that John Bowman was regent of the University, Lard served as president of the College of the Bible. The brotherhood thought Lard had sold out to Regent Bowman, for whom they had little confidence. But Lard had taken the position only with the understanding that Bowman would resign after a year. But this fact, he could not tell to the brotherhood. His position and influence in his last days became narrowed. He became a lonely man, and out of sympathy with most of the brethren.

Too, Lard's family contributed considerably to this despondency which he had in his last days. His wife and children were continually afflicted. This was a continual drain on both his time and energy, while at the same time, his own health was gradually getting worse. He moved about in silence, seldom in contact with the brotherhood. All the while he continued to study the mysteries of the scriptures and ponder the whole thought of life and of death.

Yet this was but one side of Moses E. Lard, a side which is necessary to be known if Lard is to be understood. To ignore this side might be more charitable, but certainly less truthful, for a partial picture is only partially the truth. But Lard had many, many noble qualities about himself. There was in the man a sense of loyalty that seemed to be unlimited. Woe to the man that assailed one of his friends! Woe to that man who proved a traitor to to the truth of God! Lard seemed to be able to dip his pen into the fires of hell and belch out anathemas that would melt the whole field before him. Lard loved a good debate. He loved to get into a discussion, and the hotter the better. He once wrote:

I am so sorry Bro. Shepherd is averse to controversy. Were he not, what a nice time he and I could now have. I like controversy. I like it all the better the hotter it grows. I like to see it leap up even to a white heat. Give me a foeman over on the other side deeply entrenched in great banks of error. Only let the truth be with me; and then let the battle rage. I like sharp practice at short range. What if error shoots up high, and hisses and blazes like rockets? There is no cause for alarm. The rainbow with its soft, blending colors, lifts its arch high over the storm that rages below. So with truth. Gentle and bright as the star that hung over the cradle of the infant Saviour, it will still shine on, and bring the feet of the weary to the fountain of life. But two conditions are essential to make even controversy lovely: Let the end sought be truth, and the Spirit shown be Christian.[1]

It is as a preacher of the gospel that Lard is especially remembered. Unquestionably, he was one of the most eloquent speakers to come out of the whole restoration. Yet, there were times when Lard did not measure up to expectations. In this respect he was similar to Walter Scott. Lard, as we have said, was a man of mighty emotions. When those emotions were aroused, he would pour forth a stream of eloquence that would sweep an audience away. Once when he finished an eloquent discourse, he called suddenly on the audience to stand and sing. Not a word was uttered. It took several minutes for that great sea of emotion to

---

[1]Moses E. Lard, "Church Independence," *Apostolic Times*, Vol. III, No. 49 (March 14, 1872), p. 388.

calm down enough that the people could sing. On another occasion, Lard was preaching near Winchester, Kentucky shortly after the war. Two old men sat in the front listening. One was William Azbill, and the other was "Uncle Si" Collins. "Uncle Si" was an eccentric but devoted old man. He loved to hear Lard preach. On this occasion Lard was at his best. The music of his eloquence floated out like enchanted whispers. Higher and higher in a heavenly crescendo swept his eloquence until finally it seemed that the whole host of heaven had broken loose in one grand anthem of praise. Collins sat nodding his approval, clapping his hands, and slapping his knees. Finally when he could hold himself no longer, he jumped up in the air, slapped old William Azbill on the back and shouted: "Brother Bill, isn't he a sugar stick?"

Yet, Lard was not always at his best. Much of the time he was in evangelistic work. He had some thirty or forty sermons that were incomparable. The labor which he put on this was colossal. Such thoroughness of preparation and complete mastery of material few preachers ever knew. Beyond these sermons, he was sometimes disappointing. Dr. Winthrop H. Hopson was perhaps Lard's closest rival for pulpit supremacy. When someone asked him which was the greater preacher, himself or Moses E. Lard, Hopson replied: "Up to thirty sermons Lard can beat anybody, after that, up to two hundred and fifty, I can beat him." Sometimes Lard entered the pulpit moody and despondent, and his sermons were below par, but Lard at his best had no equal in his day. Concerning Lard as a preacher, a close friend of his once wrote:

The flashing activities of his intellect and imagination opened the fountain of his soul, gave it strong and daring wings, and it soared away to other worlds and into the light of other suns; and how often it brought back to the heavy atmosphere and dull days of earth dust of gold and gleaming splendors of celestial jewelry on its starring wings, ten thousands of living men and women can proudly testify. I have heard him form word pictures in his ecstatic moments that were unutterably grand, and at the same time clothed with a shimmering robe of beauty which seemed to have been woven in the looms of heaven by angelic fingers.[2]

The life of Moses E. Lard began at Shelbyville, in Bedford County, Tennessee on October 29, 1818. His Scotch parents

---

[2]J. W. Cox, "Moses E. Lard," *Christian Standard*, Vol. XV, No. 31 (July 31, 1880), p. 241.

joined in the migration westward in 1829 toward Missouri. His father, Leaven Lard, went to Missouri because of the plentifulness of game. He was poor. When therefore in a few years he died of smallpox, his widow found the burden too great for her. She had six children and no means of support. At a very early age, then, Moses E. Lard and a brother had to leave home to make their own way. His mother gave to each her blessing and a New Testament. Of this scene Lard in later years wrote:

As my brother and myself stood beneath the little cabin eaves, just ready to take leave of the only objects on earth dear to us, and thus close the saddest scene of our lives, my mother said: 'My dear boys, I have nothing to give you but my blessing and these two little books.' Her soul was breaking, and she could say no more. She then drew from her bosom two small testaments; and as her tears were streaming, and lips quivering, she screamed as if it were her last, and placed them in our hands. We all said good-by, and that family was forever broken on earth. . . . To that little book and the memory of that scene my future life owes its shaping. I never neglected the one, thank Heaven, nor forgot the other.[3]

By 1835, when Lard was seventeen years of age, he could not read or write. During these years he lived in Clinton County. He had taken up the trade of being a tailor, but he determined to learn to write. Around the village where he lived, he tore down the advertising and used the letters to learn to read and write. Thus Lard became what might be called a "self-educated" man.

During the next few years, Lard's mind experienced the vagaries common to youth with only imperfect knowledge on the subject of religion. He listened to denominationalism, and heard the pleas of Calvinistic preachers, urging sinners to get an experience. From these Lard turned away in disgust. Feeling that there was nothing to religion, he finally turned toward infidelity. Finally, however, he began to hear of preachers who were advocating a return to the ancient order. Into his hands there was placed a copy of Walter Scott's *Gospel Restored,* and Lard literally devoured it. A number of years after this, Walter Scott made a trip to Missouri, and for the first time met Lard. Immediately Lard threw his arms around Scott and said: "Bro. Scott, you are the man who first taught me the gospel."

[3] W. T. Moore, *The Living Pulpit of the Christian Church* (Cincinnati: R. W. Carroll & Co., 1868), p. 229.

"How so?" asked Scott.

"It was by your Gospel Restored," answered Lard.[4]

But Lard was twenty-three years old in 1841 when the first pro-
claimer of the ancient gospel came his way. This man was Jerry
P. Lancaster. Lancaster had at one time been a Methodist
preacher. His life later proved to be unfortunate in some respects.
He migrated to Missouri from Kentucky, and began to preach the
true gospel. Most of his preaching was done in the upper counties
of the state. Lard went to hear Lancaster, and accepted the gospel,
later being immersed by this same man. In years to come
Lancaster fell away from the truth, and consequently, his name is
little known today. In 1849 rumors flew in Missouri that he was
a Universalist. That same year Lancaster moved west to
California in the gold rush. In California he made shipwreck of
the faith and became a very bad man in many ways. There is a
happier end to the story in that several years later, when the war
was over, Lancaster came back to Missouri, friendless, penniless,
and in need of assistance. He went to a meeting being conducted
by T. M. Allen, one of Missouri's oldest pioneers. Allen had
talked to him privately before. During the meeting, Lancaster
came forward and back to the Lord. He was always faithful
afterwards. Though Lancaster was criticized heavily by other
preachers, yet Lard always had a tender feeling toward him, and
spoke kindly of this man who had immersed him.

It was in Clay County that Lard was immersed. It was in this
county also that he preached his first sermon. Soon he was
doing some preaching in Richmond and Lexington, also practic-
ing his trade as a tailor at the same time. At Lexington, he made
the acquaintance of Jacob and Ruth Riffe, who had a daughter,
Mary, in whom Lard was interested. Very shortly Lard married
her. By 1845 he was a married man with two children.

For Lard to think seriously of going to school at this time was
almost out of the question. He had little education, was married,
and the father of two children. Education was costly. To go to
school, and support a family at the same time, was something Lard
could only dream about. Nevertheless, circumstances were paving
the way in his favor. At Richmond Lard had become the good

---

[4]William Baxter. *Life of Elder Walter Scott* (Cincinnati: Bosworth,
Chase & Hall, 1874), p. 314.

friend of General Alexander W. Doniphan, one of Missouri's leading citizens, and an ardent and faithful Christian. Doniphan saw the potentialities in Lard and encouraged him to make the sacrifice to go to Bethany College. Lard determined to try and on March 4, 1845 enrolled in the school.

In its organization Bethany College had one feature that particularly proved advantageous to Lard. Students in the college, one discovers, "are not restricted to a fixed routine of classes requiring attendance at College a certain number of years, without regard to age or proficiency."[5] The classes were so arranged that the more mature minds could make the most rapid progress without being held longer because of class organization. In other words, a man who entered college late in life, could by proper application of his time, take a full four-year course in much less time, the time being determined only by how much he might apply himself and advance. This arrangement helped Lard. He completed a four years' course in three years. Even though he worked at physical labor while going to school, he graduated as valedictorian in his class.

Out of the gratitude of his heart, Lard wrote to Alexander Campbell, expressing his appreciation for what was done for him:

Four years and four months ago, strange, homeless, penniless, and untaught, I landed a stranger at Bethany College. It was my fixed purpose, though encumbered with the responsibilities of of a family, to qualify myself for more extended and enlightened usefulness. This object, the first and nearest to my heart, I wanted the means to accomplish.[6]

Lard goes on to tell of the letter from Campbell that brought him out to Bethany. "For which, and for the disinterested and cordial manner in which you have so often aided me when want bore heavy on me, I owe you the feelings of gratitude which I have no power to express." He continues:

To my tried friends and brethren in Christ, W. K. Pendleton and J. O. Ewing, I am under the strongest obligations. Friends, they proved themselves to me when I needed friends. They have untied their purse-strings and tendered me their gentlemanly aid at times and in ways of which I cannot think without the tear of grateful remembrance starting in my eye.[7]

[5]Anonymous, "Circular—Bethany College," *Christian Review,* Vol. II, No. 3 (September, 1844), pp. 69-72.
[6]F. W. Powers, *Life of W. K. Pendleton,* p. 135.
[7]F. W. Powers, *Life of W. K. Pendleton,* p. 135.

Upon graduation from Benthany College on July 4, 1848, Lard took his family and moved back to Missouri, locating at Independence. For the next few years only occasional notices tell us of Lard's activities. From Independence he moved to Liberty. From Liberty he moved to Camden Point where for a short time he was president of a Female College. From Camden Point he later moved to St. Joseph. In the spring of 1850 the church at Lexington divided, and one finds Lard taking an active part in trying to bring about peace.

Meanwhile, Lard was developing as a preacher. At first, like all young preachers, he had made many blunders, received many criticisms. Jacob Warrinner had often proved a tried friend. Warrinner would pat him on the shoulder and say, "Go on, my son, you have done well, be thoughful and persevere; and when I am gone, you will be a man."[8] Almost every preacher can contribute a part of his success, no matter how great or small it may be, to the encouragement of older preachers. No man had farther to go than Lard, yet he traveled the road with the help of the Lord, the determination of his own spirit, and the encouragement of those who saw in him great possibilities for the Lord.

Lard's first gospel meeting was held at Hainesville church in Clinton County. Perhaps his most famous meeting was held at South Point, where through the influence of Dick, a colored slave he baptized the boy Thomas, Dick's master. Lard was a masterful story teller. This story he tells in his first issue of *Lard's Quarterly,* and those who have access to it would find it interesting reading. The South Point Church was located five miles above Camden on the road to Liberty. It was established in the summer of 1853 by Lard with eighty-four members. Three years later a new meeting house was constructed here.

In 1857 J. B. Jeter, a Virginia Baptist preacher, decided to examine "Campbellism." Campbell, although giving the examination some notice in the *Millennial Harbinger,* decided that a more thorough notice should be given to it. He himself was too busy, and Moses E. Lard was selected for the work. This indicates the high opinion that Campbell had of Lard by this time.

There is no record of a great number of debates that Lard ever held. If he ever held many, they must have been too insignificant

---

[8]Moses E. Lard, "Dick and South Point," *Lard's Quarterly,* Vol. I, No. 1 (September, 1863), p. 17.

to be recounted. The one public discussion that he did have was conducted at Brunswick, Missouri in October, 1860 with W. G. Caples, presiding Elder of the Methodist Church. It was a lengthy discussion, beginning on Monday, October 8 and closing on October 18, Thursday. There was no debate on Saturday or Sunday. The audiences ranged from one thousand and five hundred to three thousand. Many outstanding preachers were present, among the number being, John Smith, W. H. Hopson, T. M. Allen and J. W. McGarvey, and John R. Howard. Howard, reporting on the discussion, said of Lard's part:

Such were the purity and chasteness of his language and diction, and his great earnestness, seeming ever to be properly impressed with his subject and with the importance of the great and solemn topics of the Christian religion, throwing his whole soul into what he was uttering, that he came nearer possessing the character of the real orator, the true Christian orator than almost any man I ever heard. His words generally fell from his lips, like coins from the mint, correctly struck and properly impressed by the organs of speech, and seemed to be ready for the press without any correcting or revision.[9]

Just exactly when Lard conceived of the idea of publishing a Quarterly may never be exactly determined. Nevertheless, by the year 1859 his plans were beginning to materialize themselves into action. In the spring of this year Lard announced to the brotherhood his intentions of publishing a periodical to be called *The Christian Quarterly,* from St. Joseph, Missouri. The first issue was to be sent out on the first Monday in January, 1860 provided two thousand paid-up subscriptions could be received by this date.[10] A month before Lard made this announcement the Central Pennsylvania Cooperation Meeting, on February 18, 1859 passed the following resolution:

Resolved; That the issuing of a quarterly, edited by Brother M. E. Lard, meets our hearty approbation.[11]

After making the announcement of his intentions to publish the *Quarterly,* Lard waited for the response. Two thousand sub-

[9]J. R. Howard, "Debate Between Lard and Caples," *Gospel Advocate,* Vol. VI, No. 11 (November, 1860), p. 338.

[10]Moses E. Lard, "Prospectus of the Christian Quarterly," *American Christian Review,* Vol. II, No. 14 (April 5, 1859), p. 55.

[11]Jesse H. Berry, "Central Pennsylvania Cooperation Meeting," *American Christian Review,* Vol. II, No. 10 (March 8, 1859), p. 39.

scriptions didn't come in.   On January 10, 1860 Lard wrote to
W. K. Pendleton:

Allow me to say that as the required number of Subscribers for
the Quarterly has not been obtained the work will not be published.[12]

Probably many brethren, as well as Lard himself, were disappointed
that the subscribers didn't respond.   The reason may be hard to
give.   The uncertainty of political affairs at this time probably
influenced the people.   If they subscribed, could the paper continue?   In addition, the brotherhood has shown over a number of
years a general reluctance to accept *Quarterlies*.   People with a
limited supply of money would rather receive a weekly than a
Quarterly or even a monthly.   The *American Christian Review*,
a weekly, was the most popular paper in the brotherhood, exceed-
ing even the *Millennial Harbinger,* a monthly.   But, up to this
time no one had tried to publish a *Quarterly,* and someone had to,
by bitter and disappointing experience, discover this fact.   It
was left up to Lard to do so.

Lard, although disappointed, was not inclined to give up.   He
still believed in a quarterly periodical, and the fact that there was
a war on, with mail service limited, and a large portion of the
brotherhood cut off from him, didn't discourage him.   Perhaps, for
his own good, he was overanxious.   In the spring of 1863 Lard
wrote:

To our brethren especially in Kentucky and Missouri, I have a
word to say.   You frequently write me to inquire whether I have
wholly abandoned my purpose to publish the Christian Quarterly.
Be patient, brethren, and if God will spare my life and open for
me a door in the future, you shall yet look in the pages of the
Quarterly.   I have four numbers of it lying in my drawer awaiting
the favorable moment to visit you.   Again I say, be patient and you
shall not be disappointed.[13]

On August 5, 1863 Lard wrote to Ben Franklin:

I have this day placed in the hands of the printer the manuscript
of the first number of my Quarterly, now so long delayed.   The
work will be printed in Frankfort, Kentucky; and each number
will contain 112 pages.   Cost of the work per year, $2 *in advance*.

[12]Moses E. Lard, "The Quarterly Not to Be Published," *Millennial Harbinger,* Fifth Series, Vol. III, No. 2 (February, 1860), p. 103.

[13]Moses E. Lard, "Correspondence," *American Christian Review,* Vol. VI,
No. 18 (May 5, 1863), p. 71.

The first number will be ready for delivery by the first of September following.

These are perilous times in which to commence the Quarterly. But now, more than ever before in this country, should the whole strength of every true man be exerted, and every legitimate means be used, to unite the hearts of Christians and spread the truth. A deep desire to work for these grand ends is both my reason and apology for commencing the work now.[14]

The name of the new periodical was not *Christian Quarterly,* as apparently had been the intention up to the very last, but *Lard's Quarterly.* On the opening page Lard states the purpose of the paper.

The chief of these certainly was the strong desire felt to increase our facilities as much as possible, for laying before the age in which we live, the claims of *Primitive Christianity.* With us these claims were paramount; hence the desire to give them the widest possible circulation swayed us in our decision, more than every other consideration besides. The highest distinction, then, to which the QUARTERLY aspires, is to contain a clear, true statement, and just defense of Christianity as taught in God's holy word. Should it, even in a small degree, prove to be successful in this, its highest aim will have been realized. On its opening page, then, we dedicate it to the uncorrupted Gospel of Christ, and to that noble body of saints who, for the last forty years, have been laboring for its restoration to the world.[15]

Into the *Quarterly* Lard put some of his greatest works. Despite this fact, the periodical was not widely received. At the close of the year, 1866, it had only one thousand five hundred subscribers —not enough to pay for its publication. The editor, because of the lack of funds, was preaching out of Lexington, Kentucky, very frequently which caused the paper to appear irregularly. Lard continued to beg for subscribers. Finally, in the summer of 1868, unable to go farther, he announced that publication would cease. Earlier in the year, February 23, 1868, Lard had written the following letter to the brotherhood:

Dear Brethren: Up to this date I have not felt sufficiently encouraged to place another number in the hands of the printer, nor even now am I sure that it is right to do so. Still hoping better things

---

[14]Moses E. Lard, "M. E. Lard's Quarterly," *Millennial Harbinger,* Fifth Series, Vol. VI, No. 8 (August, 1863), p. 378.

[15]Moses E. Lard, "Preface," *Lard's Quarterly,* Vol. I, No. 1 (September, 1863), p. 1.

for the future, I at once place No. 1 in the press. You may, therefore, expect it as soon as it can be printed. How far I can proceed with the work will depend on you.[16]

The *Gospel Advocate* printed the above letter, and urged the brethren to subscribe. While David Lipscomb admitted there were many things in the *Quarterly* with which he could not agree, he says, ". . . we have long since learned that it is a very narrow and selfish bigotry that refuses to sustain a paper because every thing in it does not suit ourselves." Lipscomb had on other occasions complimented the paper.

It is conducted with marked ability. Brother Lard, as a writer, in his own peculiar style, has not a superior among us, for point, pungency and force. His sentences are always pointed, not unfrequently barbed. There is a piquancy and an air of independent thought, that in this age of tame, sterotype styles and matters of thought in religion, are refreshing. There is an earnestness of thought and feeling manifested that exhibits hearty faith and decided convictions of truth, that stand in marked contrast with the almost universal time-serving, policy-ruling spirit of even the Church of Christ.[17]

But why, it may be inquired, did the *Quarterly* fail to get subscribers? Two reasons have already been suggested. There was a marked uncertainty about national life during these days of the war. People living as close as most of them did to the conflict, were thinking of it more than of trying to help a religious periodical live. Secondly, people with limited supplies of money would much prefer to spend it upon weekly papers like the *Review* or a monthly like the *Harbinger,* than upon a Quarterly. There was yet a third factor that entered in. The editorial policy of the *Quarterly* on the major issues was a middle-of-the-road one. Lard was strictly against the use of instrumental music and advocated that preachers refuse to preach where it was being used. It was, in and of itself, sinful. With regard to the Missionary Society, Lard took the belief, then so popular around Lexington, that it was a matter of expediency. There was nothing wrong or unscriptural about it, in and of itself. Yet, he went farther and admitted that while it was an expedient, it was an unnecessary expedient. Lard wrote:

---

[16]Moses E. Lard, "Lard's Quarterly," *Gospel Advocate,* Vol. X, No. 12 (March 19, 1868, page 276.

[17]David Lipscomb, "Lard's Quarterly," *Gospel Advocate,* Vol. VIII, No. 21 (May 22, 1866), p. 326.

The right of Christian men to have them is a right we by no means call in question; but a claim to have them based on any really necessary ground is a claim the force of which we must in candor say we have not felt.[18]

The general policy of the paper pleased but very few in the brotherhood. Friends of the Society, who were by far in the majority, did not appear anxious to support a paper that condemned them as this one did. The opposers of the Society did not altogether agree with the ground on which Lard objected. These, then, are the chief reasons why, in our opinion, the *Quarterly* was not supported, and why, in the summer of 1868, it had to come to a close.

After the close of the *Quarterly*, Lard threw his editorial fortunes in with the *Apostolic Times*. More about this shall be noted in our next volume. Suffice it to say, the *Times* likewise, proved not to be successful. Lard found himself among that number occupying positions which made him stand quite alone in the brotherhood. Although Lard was not an old man when he died in 1880, yet he had been sickly, disappointed, and was growing despondent. Physically, he was a large man, six feet and three inches, with a bony frame, black hair and small piercing eyes. That body began to give way under the strain, and Lard died. His body was borne from Lexington back to St. Joseph, Missouri where he had labored and preached so long, and was laid to rest in the Mount Mora cemetery.

JOHN W. McGARVEY

David Walk attended the convention of the American Christian Missionary Society in October, 1862 as an observer. John William McGarvey was there and spoke. Walk thus describes him:

He is probably three-and-thirty years of age; about 5 ft. 6 inches in height; has light brown hair and hazel eyes; head disproportioned to the size of his body, being very large and striking in appearance; countenance of the most radiant and innocent expression; with as pleasant and agreeable a contour generally as one would be likely to meet with in a day's travel. It will be seen from this description that he is not a man whose person would attract attention in a crowd. The plain, simple truth is, Brother McGarvey is a ten-fold greater man, intellectually, than any one would be led to suspect on merely seeing him. . . . We hail him

---

[18]Moses E. Lard, "Missionary Societies and Our Hymn Book," *Lard's Quarterly*, Vol. II, No. 2 (January, 1865), p. 136.

J. W. McGARVEY

as one of the 'coming men' of the age. Nay, more, *he is even now here.*[19]

It is highly interesting to note that one like David Walk would describe the J. W. McGarvey of 1862 as one of the coming men of the age, and then say, "nay, more, he is even now here." How absolutely right Walk was probably he himself did not fully realize.

---

[19]David Walk, "Brief Sketches of Noticeable Characters at the Late Missionary Meeting in Cincinnati," *American Christian Review*, Vol. VI, No. 3 (January 20, 1863), p. 1.

For in the years to come the name of J. W. McGarvey was to be household wherever the cause of the ancient order had gone.

There are yet a few older persons who sat at the feet of McGarvey in the College of the Bible at Lexington, who can appreciate to some extent Walk's description of McGarvey. In later years, however, some changes, brought out with time and labor, occurred. McGarvey was five feet, seven inches tall, of medium weight, with blue-gray eyes. Those who remember him now will recall that he was a little round-shouldered, although this was not true in his youth. When Walk saw McGarvey, his hair was a dark brown, but those now who will remember him, will remember it as sprinkled heavily with silver. He wore a beard all of his adult life, and in later years was rarely seen without a long ear trumpet in his hand, for McGarvey was very deaf. In personal appearance he was always neat. In disposition his most outstanding attribute seemed to be his kindness. He was rarely angry, never known to lose control of himself. In the presence of women he was always chaste and chivalrous and that made him many friends among them.

J. W. McGarvey was a man of deep convictions for truth, and kindly feeling for men. He believed the Bible most implicitly and could not tolerate men who cast a reproach upon it or rejected any part of it. His enemies called him a "legalist" and a "conservative." When he noted a man forsaking the scriptures, McGarvey would attack with a relentless barrage of criticism and argument, often becoming very bitter. Yet, personally he felt no bitterness. In a measure this was characteristic of the age. During the last half of the previous century, men fought furiously for their ideals. They took no offense at criticism and expected no one else to. Men born of a more modern spirit have often found this hard to understand. McGarvey loved the truth, and spoke accordingly. Men always knew where to find him.

The life of McGarvey is, in itself, an inspiration. He was born at Hopkinsville, Kentucky on March 1, 1829. His father was an Irishman who had migrated to Hopkinsville a short time before. Here, he had made the acquaintance of Miss Sarah Ann Thomson, daughter of John Thomson, and married her. They were married only four years when he died, but during this time, he ran a dry goods store in Hopkinsville. John W. was the second child of four born to this union. He was thus four years old when his father died.

Something rotten here

The child life of J. W. McGarvey was, therefore, spent under his step-father, Gurdon F. Saltonsall. Saltonsall's father had died when he was a young man, and he lived with an uncle in Connecticut. He fled his uncle's home and came to Georgetown, Kentucky where he secured a job working for John Thomson. Later he married Polly Thomson, McGarvey's aunt, who was the sister to his mother. Polly died leaving Saltonsall with nine children. Saltonsall then married McGarvey's mother and this made them have thirteen children. To this new union six more children were born, making a nice, quiet little family of nineteen children, quite a sizeable congregation in itself.

In 1839 Saltonsall moved his family to Tremont, Illinois. He had scruples against slavery, and thought this would benefit his family to move. Here, McGarvey's young manhood was spent. He was now ten years old and lived here until he was seventeen. He worked on the farm, and learned the fine arts of manufacturing hemp. Meanwhile, he had an unusual opportunity for going to school under James K. Kellogg. Kellogg was far in advance of most teachers of that day, and under him McGarvey got a good start in the fundamentals.

Saltonsall himself had been converted to the cause of restoration. He was a successful business man, and therefore, was a donor and a trustee for Bethany College. He had by 1848 given $2,500 to the College with but one stipulation and that was that any son or sons that he might send there would be educated off the income received from this money. Later, when he died, Saltonsall made Bethany College the twentieth child in his will, and it shared equally with the rest. McGarvey by his own choice determined to enroll in Bethany. Consequently in March, 1847 he entered school. He himself tells us that it was on March 17, 1847 that he first took his seat in chapel at Bethany College.[20]

While he was enrolled at Bethany, McGarvey determined to become a Christian. He made up his mind that at the first opportunity, he would confess Christ and be immersed. He listened to Campbell preach much, but it was not Campbell's custom to extend an invitation after each sermon, so McGarvey waited two weeks after he made up his mind before he had the opportunity of stepping forward and making the confession. It was, as Mc-

---

[20]J. W. McGarvey, "W. K. Pendleton," *Christian Standard,* Vol. XXXV, No. 37 (September 16, 1899), p. 1193.

Garvey would describe it, "an ordinary service." McGarvey confessed Christ, and was baptized in Buffalo Greek at Bethany by W. K. Pendleton.

School ended for McGarvey on July 4, 1850. He was graduating with honors, and was selected to give the Greek oration. As yet, he had not fully decided his future life. He wanted to preach, but by temperament, he was naturally diffident, and lacked, therefore, the full confidence in himself he needed. So McGarvey turned his attention toward home, not yet fully decided upon what to do.

His family had moved from Illinois to Fayette, Missouri. They wrote to their son, not to come down the Ohio River, as was generally done, for fear of cholera, but to come by the Great Lakes. McGarvey had quite an excursion on this trip, but he finally arrived at his new home in Missouri. His fortunes for the next twelve years were to be cast here. He did nothing great or outstanding, but McGarvey took full advantage of these years to use them for his own advancement and strengthening.

Soon he had fully decided that he wanted to preach. Yet he realized that he was not ready, for he needed more knowledge of the scriptures. He opened a private school for boys at Fayette, and on the side, studied the Bible as he found time. He reviewed his Greek, and became very adept at this subject. He continued this way until September, 1852 when the church at Fayette invited him to preach for them. He was ordained, according to the custom of the day, by the laying on of the hands of T. M. Allen and Alexander Proctor.

Young preachers frequently need the help of old preachers. T. M. Allen proved to be a counsellor and helper for young J. W. McGarvey in these early days. Allen himself was a great preacher. His one strong point was McGarvey's weak point. Allen's exhortation to sinners was mighty, eloquent and moving. McGarvey never possessed this power. Once when Allen and McGarvey were together in a protracted meeting, it was understood that Allen should preach in the morning and McGarvey in the afternoon. Just before McGarvey got up, Allen reached over and whispered one day, "Now John, come out and under whip and spur, head and tail up." McGarvey did his best to oblige.

In 1853, about this time, Alexander Campbell visited Missouri. G. F. Saltonsall had died recently and Campbell visited one evening with his widow, McGarvey's mother. James T. Saltonsall,

McGarvey's half-brother had attended Bethany a year before Mc-
Garvey, and was now a prominent lawyer in Fayette. But, concerning, McGarvey, Campbell wrote:

His brother, J. W. M'Garvey, is, however, as we are assured,
devoting his life to a higher usefulness, and a more honorable rank
in the Christian army. He was also one of our best and most gifted
students, and no one left the College, during his years there, with
a higher or more enviable reputation, for all the elements essential
to a learned, useful, and exemplary man. He has not disappointed
the expectations of his *alma mater* or his friends, but is yearly
growing in favor with the church and all the people of his acquaintance.[21]

In the fall of 1852 McGarvey, together with Proctor, held a
meeting at the church in Dover. McGarvey received an invitation
to locate. In January, 1853 he began his lengthy ministry for this
church. While here, McGarvey married Otwayana Frances Hix
on March 23, 1853. Alexander Proctor officiated at this wedding.
Their first child was born in April of the following year.

McGarvey was preaching at Dover when the war broke out.
As was customary with him on all points, he was positive and
straightforward. He believed it was wrong for Christians to go to
war, and maintained this idea throughout his life. The church at
Dover became divided in sentiment, and many criticisms were made
of him. Moreover, McGarvey met once a month with a large
gathering of negroes to teach them the Bible, and opposition came
because of this. His work at Dover therefore, was not as pleasant
as before. McGarvey was, therefore, prepared for a move when
the right invitation should come.

That invitation came in the spring of 1862. W. H. Hopson was
the preacher for the Main Street Church in Lexington. Because of
his pronouncedly sympathizing viewpoint for the South, several in
the Lexington church were antagonized. Hopson saw that he
needed to move. He recommended J. W. McGarvey of Dover,
Missouri as the proper man for the place. Hopson showed great
wisdom. McGarvey was neither northern or southern politically.
He taught both sides to lay down arms and settle their troubles
without bloodshed. He could antagonize neither. When therefore,
McGarvey arrived in Lexington, the church ranked fourth in size

[21]Alexander Campbell, "Notes of Incidents in a Tour Through Illinois and
Missouri—No. III," *Millennial Harbinger*, Fourth Series, Vol. III, No. 3
(March, 1853), pp. 130, 131.

of all churches in the city, but in a short while, it was first. His work was relatively uninterrupted by the war, except during the battle at Richmond, at which time the Main Street church building was used for a hospital.

Very soon McGarvey's fortunes were being cast with the College of the Bible. McGarvey had received invitations on two different occasions to teach mathematics at Bethany College and he refused both times. When he arrived in Lexington, Robert Milligan, president of Kentucky University offered him a position as teacher of English literature. Again he refused. McGarvey wanted to study the Bible. If he ever taught, he would teach the Bible, and he stayed dogmatically with this determination.

In 1865 Kentucky University moved to Lexington. McGarvey helped plan the curriculum for the College of the Bible. He himself agreed to teach two hours a day a class in Sacred History, which was a survey of the Bible. In a year, however, he was devoting too much of his time to the school to be able to do adequate work for the church, so he resigned to work entirely for the school.

In the years that lay ahead McGarvey found himself in the very center of most of the brotherhood activities. Upon the death of Alexander Campbell, Bethany College virtually surrendered the sceptre to Lexington, and here the center of activities was to be found. McGarvey then played the central role. In the regrettable conflicts over the College of the Bible which occurred between 1872-1875, McGarvey was in the middle. Later, when liberalism began sweeping the brotherhood, and frequent denials were heard of the inspiration of the Bible, McGarvey wrote prolifically in the *Christian Standard*. In sentiment, McGarvey was bitterly opposed to instrumental music, and refused to worship where one was used. He was, however, an ardent supporter of Missionary Societies.

It is not necessary for our present purpose and object to go into detail with McGarvey's life with his activities from 1865 to his death on September 12, 1912. We shall find frequent occasion to do this in our next volume, and therefore, we leave our analysis at this point, anticipating a closer analysis of his future activities in our next.

Chapter XVII

INSTRUMENTAL MUSIC

Destined to play an important role in the future struggle over instrumental music was the *American Christian Review* edited by Ben Franklin. The recognition of this importance is at once the apology for introducing this chapter with a brief analysis of the origin of this periodical.

The first issue of the *American Christian Review* was sent out in January, 1856, just six months later than the first issue of the *Gospel Advocate*. It appeared as a monthly for the first two years of its existence. Reference to the biography of Ben Franklin will show that this was by no means the first paper he published. He had either edited or partially edited the following papers: *The Reformer, Western Reformer, Proclamation and Reformer,* and the *Christian Age*. This last periodical he was publishing with D. S. Burnet when it was turned over to the ownership of the American Christian Publication Society. This arrangement did not meet with Franklin's approval at all, and in 1854 he resigned as editor with but one stipulation, viz., he would not edit another paper for at least two years. By January, 1856 that two-year agreement was up, and Franklin launched out again as an editor with an entirely new periodical, the *American Christian Review*.

In his introduction Franklin wrote:

Dear Reader: In the good providence of our most gracious and heavenly Father, we are again before you in the capacity of an editor; and desire to introduce to your acquaintance 'The American Christian Review' . . . In looking over our history for the last six years, the reader may conclude we are addicted to change, and that our operations are not as reliable as could be wished . . .[1]

Franklin goes on to state that these changes were beyond his control, and that they could not be fully explained or understood "till all the works of the children of men are manifest." He states that any failure now would be entirely his fault since the *Review* is now entirely under his control. Franklin is anxious too, to get the cooperation of the brotherhood at large:

---

[1] Benjamin Franklin, "Introductory Address," *American Christian Review,* Vol. I, No. 1 (January, 1856), p. 1.

In entering the field again, we wish the friendship, the fellowship and cooperation of all those great and good brethren of the same calling. We enter the list, not as a competitor or rival, of any one of them, but a cooperator with them in the same great work, and we wish them all possible success.

Franklin's ability was widely recognized and compelled the brethren to entertain great hopes for the future of the paper. After the January issue was off the press, reactions from various readers began to pour in. Aylette Raines of Paris, Kentucky wrote:

I have read, I think, nearly all that you have written, from the beginning, and I am glad to see you again on the arena, with a broad space, within which to battle it for the truth, and I trust a good supply of ammunition. You are, in my estimation, one of the few suited to the editorial chair. Clear, cool, strong, discriminating, balanced!—without these characteristics a writer cannot succeed, to any great extent in the advocacy of apostolic Christianity. Hence, many have made such havoc, both of themselves and of the cause of truth.[2]

Carroll Kendrick, now in Texas, writes:

Most heartily do I unite with brethren Raines, Rogers and others, in rejoicing that you are again at the helm of so good a vessel. The times demand such men. I mean not to praise you; but you have given evidence of good common sense strong, and so intelligent that you can afford to speak in God so strong, and so intelligent that you can afford to speak 'the truth, the whole truth, and nothing but the truth,' without fearing what man can do to you. You seem, too, to look all around a question, and from one end to the other of it, before speaking; to consider its bearings, general and special, in connection with its comparative or its absolute importance. Hence you are not a *hobby rider* . . .[3]

When the Prospectus of the *Review* was sent out, Tolbert Fanning wrote:

We call attention to the Prospectus of Brother B. Franklin's paper under the caption. Without the least disposition to flatter, we assure the brethren that Brother F. is one of our best thinkers on all matters connected with the Christian economy.[4]

With the January 5, 1858 issue, the *American Christian Review* became a greatly enlarged paper published now weekly. The

---

[2]Aylette Raines, "Letter," *American Christian Review,* Vol. I, No. 2 (February, 1856), p. 83.
[3]Carroll Kendrick, "Letter from Texas," *American Christian Review,* p. 189.
[4]Tolbert Fanning, "The American Christian Review," *Gospel Advocate,* Vol. I, No. 4 (October, 1855), p. 128.

editorial corps reached out to gather in the greatest name in the
brotherhood.   Those included were, Moses E. Lard, John Rogers,
C. L. Loos, Isaac Errett, and Elijah Goodwin.   Alexander Campbell now wrote:

Brother Franklin is an eminently *practical* man.   He discards
all metaphysical speculation in matters of religion: and pleads able
and earnestly for the Bible as the only infallible rule of faith and
practice among all Christians.[5]

It was only natural that the *Review* should become the brotherhood's leading paper.   It was a large weekly with an eminent
man at its head.   Franklin was a man of the people; he spoke
their language, knew their problems, and moreover, was unsurpassed in his knowledge of the scriptures and his ability to apply
it.   Even the veteran paper of all, the *Millennial Harbinger,* gave
evidences of yielding the sceptre to it.   The paper was edited from
Cincinnati, in those days the very heart of the brotherhood.   It
had easy access to Kentucky, Ohio and Indiana where a large bulk
of the disciples lived.   The resolution passed by the Central Pennsylvania Christian Cooperation in February, 1859 was perfectly in
line with the feelings of a vast number of brethren.   The resolution read:

Resolved, That we recognize the *American Christian Review*
the paper for the times—that we regard it all sufficient as a weekly
for the brotherhood, and that we urge upon the brethren of the
"Keystone State" to lend it their patronage.[6]

Many of the more liberal preachers to arise in the future found
the *Review* very much against their liking, and because the paper
was so popular with the people, they found it difficult to wean the
people away from it to their more liberal ideas.

The origin of the controversy over instrumental music, however,
really antedates the origin of the *Review*.   There was a brief flare-
up of the issue in Kentucky as early as 1851.   This affair, while
it was brief, yet it was intense.   Thoughtful men might have taken
it as an omen of things to come, but most men were too glad to see
it die down to raise the question for at least eight years after that.
On February 22, 1851 a man who signed his name "W" wrote to

---

[5]Alexander Campbell, "The American Christian Review," *Millennial
Harbinger,* Fifth Series, Vol. I, No. 2 (February, 1858), p. 92.
[6]Jesse H. Berry, "Central Pennsylvania Cooperation Meeting," *American
Christian Review,* Vol. II, No. 10 (March 8, 1859), p. 39.

J. B. Henshall, associate editor of the *Ecclesiastical Reformer,* the following letter:

Brother Henshall—What say you of instrumental music in our churches? Should not the Christian Church have organs or Bass Viols that the great object of Psalmody might be consummated? Would not such instruments add greatly to the solemnity of worship, and cause the hearts of the saints to be raised to a higher state of devotion while the deep toned organ would swell its notes of "awful sound"? I think it is high time that we awaken to the importance of this subject. We are far in the rear of Protestants on the subject of church music. I hope, therefore, that you will give your views in extenso, on this much neglected subject.

Henshall replied by saying,

In proportion as men become worldly minded, provided they have not entirely lost the fear of God, do they begin to require *helps* to their devotion. That they could require such helps under a dark dispensation where they were rather lead into the use of symbolic rites, than inwardly illuminated by God's word and spirit, is not at all astonishing; but to say that we need them who live in the full light of the gospel privileges, and enjoy God's mercies and providence over us, is to say that we have no gratitude in our hearts, and that we are every way unworthy of these benefits.[7]

While these were not the only articles to appear in the *Ecclesiastical Reformer* on the subject of instrumental music, they are enough to show the drift. On the one side, there were those who felt that the denominations were using them, and that the brethren were allowing themselves to get arrears of them by not using the instrument. Others felt that instruments in worship belonged only to those destitute of real spirituality.

John Rogers read with great disappointment the articles in the *Reformer,* advocating the use of the instruments. Rogers was a devotee of the old paths. He was baptized by Barton W. Stone at the age of eighteen in Wilmington, Ohio in the year, 1818. Most of his preaching career was spent around Carlisle, Kentucky. He baptized over a thousand people here in the twenty-five years from 1823 to 1848. When he read of the use of instruments in the churches of Kentucky, he wrote to Alexander Campbell: "But my brother, (would you believe it?) a popular preacher has come out in two numbers in the 'E. Reformer,' in favor of instrumental

---

[7]J. B. Henshall, "Instrumental Music," *Ecclesiastical Reformer,* Vol. IV, No. 6 (March 15, 1851), p. 171.

music in churches and social dancing in our families!"[8]   Rogers begged Campbell to make a statement on the subject at this early date.   After some delay, Campbell wrote a short essay on the subject.   He says:

The argument drawn from the Psalms in favor of instrumental music, is exceedingly apposite to the Roman Catholic, English Protestant, and Scotch Presbyterian churches, and even to the Methodist communities.   Their church having all the world in them—that is, all the fleshly progeny of all the communicants, and being founded on the Jewish pattern of things—baptism being given to all born into the world of these politico-ecclesiastic communities—I wonder not, then, that an organ, a fiddle, or a Jews-harp, should be requisite to stir up their carnal hearts, and work into ecstasy their animal souls, else 'hosannahs languish on their tongues and their devotions die.'   And that all persons who have no spiritual discernment, taste or relish for their spiritual meditations, consolations and sympathies of renewed hearts, should call for such aid, is but natural.   Pure water from the flintly rock has no attractions for the mere toper or wine-bibber.   A little alcohol, or genuine Cognac brandy, or good old Madeira, is essential to the beverage to make it truly refreshing.   So to those who have no real devotion or spirituality in them, and whose animal nature flags under the oppression of church service, I think with Mr. G., that instrumental music would be not only a desideratum, but an essential prerequisite to fire up their souls to even animal devotion.   But I presume, to all spiritually-minded Christians such aids would be as a cow bell in a concert.[9]

Aylette Raines, in 1851, was preaching at Millersburg, Kentucky. Raines was in a habit of keeping a diary, and on April 27, 1851 made the following entry: "Brother S(aunders) wishes to introduce the melodeon into the church."[10]   Raines, however, bitterly opposed it, and it did not get in at Millersburg at this time.

The subject of instrumental music did not come up again before the brotherhood until 1860.   At this time, a letter was sent to Ben Franklin, asking him to express his views on the use of the instrument.   Franklin's opposition was worded in an ironical vein. He said there might be occasions when the instrument would be permissible, such as the following:

---

[8]John Rogers, "Dancing," *Millennial Harbinger,* Fourth Series, Vol. I, No. 8 (August, 1851), p. 467.

[9]Alexander Campbell, "Instrumental Music," *Millennial Harbinger,* Fourth Series, Vol. I, No. 10 (October, 1851), pp. 581, 582.

[10]A. W. Fortune, *The Disciples in Kentucky* (Published by Convention of Christian Churches in Kentucky, 1932), p. 373.

1. Where a church never had or has lost the Spirit of Christ. . .

2. If a church has a preacher who never had, or has lost the Spirit of Christ, who has become a dry, prosing and lifeless speaker, so as to be entirely incapable of commanding and interesting an audience, it is thought that instrumental music would draw out and interest the people . . .

3. If a church only intends being a *fashionable society,* a mere place of amusement and secular entertainment, and abandoning all idea of *religion* and *worship,* instrumental music would be a very pleasant and agreeable part of such entertainment.[11]

After the appearance of the above article, Franklin heard from L. L. Pinkerton of Midway, Kentucky. Pinkerton was the preacher at Midway. His whole life had been spent in central Kentucky. At Midway he had been instrumental in establishing the Female Orphan School.

Pinkerton replied:

So far as known to me, or, I presume, to you, I am the only 'preacher' in Kentucky of our brotherhood who has publicly advocated the propriety of employing instrumental music in *some* churches, and that the church of God in Midway is the only church that has yet made a decided effort to introduce it. The calls for your opinion, it is probable, came from these regions.[12]

Thus the use of instrumental music and the church at Midway have been connected in the thinking of persons acquainted with restoration history from that day to the present. The facts about the introduction of the instrument at Midway may be gleaned from various sources which, when collected together, reveal an interesting story. The suggestion to use the instrument did not come from Pinkerton himself, although the persons responsible undoubtedly knew his opinion and that he would not oppose its introduction even before it was brought in.

The introduction of the instrument owed its inception to the deplorable singing the congregation did. This singing had degenerated into screeching and brawling that would, as Pinkerton said, "scare even the rats from worship." At first it was suggested that a meeting be held on Saturday night to practice the songs. Shortly afterwards, someone brought in a melodeon to be used in getting the right pitch. Before long, one of the sisters was ac-

---

[11]Ben Franklin, "Instrumental Music in Churches," *American Christian Review,* Vol. III, No. 5 (January 31, 1860), p. 19.

[12]L. L. Pinkerton, "Instrumental Music in Churches," *American Christian Review,* Vol. III, No. 9 (February 28, 1860), p. 34.

companying the singing with her playing on the melodeon. The group observed that the effect of the use of the melodeon was good on the singing, and so it was decided to try to use the instrument on the Lord's Day worship. Thompson Parrish, son of James Ware Parrish, one of the founders of the Midway Female Orphan School, played the instrument at the worship.

The presence of the instrument caused considerable friction. The most effective opposition came from Adam Hibler, one of the elders. Late one night Hibler pushed one of his colored slaves by the name of Reuben through a window. Reuben passed the melodeon through, and Hibler took it home with him. But another instrument was afterwards brought in, and continued in use by the church.

The church at Midway is the first congregation *on record* to use the instrument. It is not entirely accurate, however, to say that it was the first congregation among the pioneers to do so. It is evident that as early as 1851 some churches had put in the instrument to cause the flare-up to which allusion has already been made. Just which congregations these were remains unknown. To the church at Midway, then, must go the distinction—if it is a distinction—of being the first of the congregations on record to adopt the use of the instrument.

After the 1860 episode the subject of instrumental music again died down for about four years. The occurrence of the war immediately turned the attention of the brotherhood to other more immediate problems. In 1864 the question was renewed, and this time it was raised in the *Millennial Harbinger*. Early that year a brother, signing his name "Ancient Order," sent W. K. Pendleton the following question:

Will you inform me whether it is in accordance with the Scriptures to use in the churches organ or other instrumental music connected with the worship?

To this question Pendleton replied by giving a lengthy history of the use of instruments, and then setting forth his own ideas.

With respect to instrumental music, I presume that no one at all acquainted with ecclesiastical history will pretend to claim for its introduction in the church any pretence of primitive authority or warrant. . . The best authorities seem agreed that the first introduction of the organ, or any other instrumental music, (for the organ was the first form used,) was after the time of Thomas Acquinas, for this eminent man himself declares, (A.D. 1250)

'Our church does not use musical instruments as harps and psalteries, in the praise of God, lest she should seem to Judaize . . .

We confess to a fondness for good music of all kinds; and find it no offense to our own feelings of piety or praise to hear the grand and majestic swell of the organ rolling forth, laden with the strains of our sacred music; yet like Paul with respect to meats, I would rather never hear one again, than to have them interfering with the free, full, grateful, heartfelt singing of the whole congregation . . .

But this does not settle the question after all—for there are many things established and right, in the practical affairs of the church in this 19th century, that were not introduced in the days, nor by the authority of the apostles—questions of mere expediency, that involve neither moral nor spiritual principle or teaching . . . We have no evidence that in the apostolic days, the disciples owned houses, such as we would now call churches, at all . . .[13]

This lengthy quotation is given because of the gist of the argument it presents. In sum substance this was to be the apology that advocates of the instrument were to use in the years to come. It will be observed that Pendleton admitted that the early church, the apostolic church, did not use the instrument. As we have already seen in the case of the missionary society, so now in the case of the instrument, Pendleton did not consider the *silence* of the scripture on these points a sufficient reason not to use them. In both cases the silence is admitted.

The apology then for the instrument, Pendleton places on the plain of expediency, such as the eating of meats. To Pendleton it fell in the same classification as using meeting houses in which to worship. The scripture said nothing about a meeting house just as it said nothing about the instrument. That there was a fallacy in Pendleton's reasoning is easily apparent, but, lest we anticipate too much from the great controversy over this point which we shall notice in our next volume, we pass with only a review of Pendleton's argument.

Late that year, 1864, the controversy over the instrument gained momentum when J. W. McGarvey entered the battle. He writes:

In the earlier years of the present Reformation, there was entire unanimity in the rejection of instrumental music from our public worship. It was declared unscriptural, inharmonious with the Christian institution, and a source of corruption. In the course

---

[13]W. K. Pendleton, "Pew-Renting and Organ Music," *Millennial Harbinger,* Fifth Series, Vol. VII, No. 3 (March, 1864), pp. 126-128.

of time, individuals here and there called in question the correctness of this decision, and an attempt was occasionally made to introduce instruments in some churches.[14]

McGarvey went on to say that at first the newness of the thing caused the brethren to shrink from it, so men would refrain from pushing it on the ground that it was offensive. Now brethren had gotten to the point where they didn't care. McGarvey pled that brethren would lay aside all feeling pro and con, and start anew with the inquiry: Ought we to make use of musical instruments in public worship? He asked brethren to come out with their views on it, concluding, "Let us, then, have the question fully discussed and finally settled."

McGarvey himself began this discussion by an examination of the ground instrumental music apologists generally covered. If instrumental music were in the Bible, and if God by his written word approved it then, let us have the scriptures, McGarvey would say. If it is not in the Bible, McGarvey pled that the whole ground of expediency be given a thorough examination. He proceeded then to discuss the first question by examining the scriptures commonly used by those declaring the word of God favored it.

The first to answer McGarvey was A. S. Hayden. Hayden lived and preached on the Western Reserve, formerly being the president of the Western Reserve Eclectic Institute. Hayden made it clear that he was not advocating the use of the instrument, which meant, as such statements have always meant, that with him it was on the plain of expediency. He replied only because he thought he saw weaknesses in McGarvey's argument, Hayden maintaining that the silence of the scripture was not sufficient ground for rejecting it.

Advocates of the instrument frequently, when and if they believed the written word upheld the instrument, referred to the Old Testament scriptures. McGarvey, as well as many other pioneers, saw that the very fact that the church, when established, rejected the use of the Jewish worship of the Old Testament, was proof enough that the instrument was not suited to the worship in the church. The worship of the Jews was particularly fitted for the economy under which they lived. Their worship consisted of offering sacrifices, ceremonial washings burning of incense, and

---

[14]J. W. McGarvey, "Instrumental Music in Churches," *Millennial Harbinger*, Fifth Series, Vol. VII, No. 11 (November, 1864), p. 510.

the use of instruments of music, among other things. The church on the other hand is the realization of an entirely different economy, fully spiritual in scope. Here God chose a worship where the worshipper, directly from his heart worshipped the Lord without the aid of incense, animal sacrifice or mechanical instruments. McGarvey then, after reasoning upon the differences in the two economies and of musical instruments being out of place under the Christian dispensation, closed by saying,

Now, Brother Hayden, if this argument is valid, I again repeat, that every man who bows to the authority of God's word, must oppose the use of instrumental music in the church. If it contains any fallacy, please to point it out, for I declare to you, I am unable to see it.[15]

This same argument had been substantially made earlier in the *American Christian Review* by Z. F. Smith. He wrote:

It is very clear that musical instruments were used by the Jews in their praises to God. It is equally clear, to every one familiar to the New Testament, that not one evidence, either in precept or example, of such practice, is found in the appointed orders of Christian worship. This omission must be esteemed a consideration of great importance in solving the question of its right; and especially when viewed in the light of those circumstances which marked the change from one dispensation to another. Whatever was peculiar to the genus and character of both, was preserved; what was peculiar to the former alone, was omitted. Paul says of the Tabernacle services, that they 'stood only in meats and drinks, and divers washings, and *carnal ordinances;* imposed on them until the time of reformation.' While the types and shadows of the Temple service were *carnal* (addressed to the senses) in some respects, such is not the case with the appointments of Christian worship. While the magnificence of the temple-building and the costly splendor of its furnishings, the rich odors of incense, the official trappings of the priesthood, etc., entranced and gratified the senses of the worshiper, enjoined by the Saviour, *there is not the least shadow of an effort made to gratify carnal man!* What is it? The religion of Jesus Christ is purely spiritual; as such, its genius and character forbade the introduction of a carnal element.[16]

Early in 1865 S. Salisbury of Mumford, New York wrote, advocating the use of the instrument. He pointed to the fact that it was used both in the Old Testament, and, according to the book

---

[15]J. W. McGarvey, "Instrumental Music," *Millennial Harbinger,* Vol. XXXVI, No. 2 (February, 1865), p. 94.

[16]Z. F. Smith, "Instrumental Music in Worship," *American Christian Review,* Vol. I, No. 5 (February 2, 1858), p. 17.

of Revelation, in heaven. McGarvey seems to have paid little attention to these arguments, as the answers should have been self-evident.

In the main, the discussion on the subject through 1865 took place between McGarvey and A. S. Hayden. Moses E. Lard was not long in getting into the discussion either. Early in 1864 he wrote:

> . . . what defense can be urged for the introduction into some of our congregations of instrumental music? The answer which thunders into my ear from every page of the New Testament, is none. Did Christ ever appoint it? did the apostles ever sanction it? or did any one of the primitive churches ever use it? Never. In what light then must we view him who attempts to introduce it into the churches of Christ of the present day? I answer, as an insulter of the authority of Christ, and as a defiant and impious innovator in the simplicity and purity of the ancient worship.[17]

It could be denied that the churches were in isolated places putting in the instrument at this time. What action should those who opposed its use take? Lard raises the same question.

But what shall be done with such churches? Of course, nothing. If they see fit to mortify the feelings of their brethren, to forsake the example of the primitive churches, to condemn the authority of Christ by resorting to will worship, to excite dissension, and give rise to general scandal, they must do it. As a body we can do nothing. Still we have three partial remedies left us to which we should at once resort.

1. Let every preacher in our ranks resolve at once that he will never, under any circumstances or on any account, enter a meeting house belonging to our brethren in which an organ stands. We beg and entreat our preaching brethren to adopt this as an unalterable rule of conduct. This and like evils must be checked, and the very speediest way to effect it is the one here suggested. 2. Let no brother who takes a letter from one church ever unite with another using an organ. Rather let him live out of a church than go into such a den. 3. Let those brethren who oppose the introduction of an organ first remonstrate in gentle, kind and decided terms. If their remonstrance is unheeded, and the organ is brought in, then let them at once, and without even the formality of asking for a letter, abandon the church so acting; and let all such members unite elsewhere. Thus these organ-grinding churches will in the lapse

---

[17]Moses E. Lard, "Instrumental Music in Churches and Dancing," *Lard's Quarterly*, Vol. 1, No. 3 (March, 1864), p. 331.

of time be broken down, or wholly apostatize, and the sooner they are in fragments the better for the cause of Christ.[18]

Of course, both McGarvey and Lard were beginning to be looked upon by some brethren as extremists, but they were men of firm and deep conviction as it respects this issue.

It will be easily apparent that the issue of instrumental music did not occupy as large a role in the thought of the time as it came to much later. After the war, the instrument began to be used more and more and the issue became more warmly contested. We shall see a little later a greater conflict over the use of the instrument.

---

[18]Moses E. Lard, "Instrumental Music in Churches and Dancing," *Lard's Quarterly*, Vol. 1, No. 3 (March, 1864), pp. 332, 333.

CHAPTER XVIII

THE CHURCH DURING THE WAR

Never had the nation faced greater peril than it did through that decade from 1855 to 1865. A political upheaval had been fomenting for some time, and was now reaching its climax. The passing of the Kansas-Nebraska Act by Congress dealt a death blow to the Whig party and provided the way for establishment of the new Republican party. In the election of 1856 James Buchanan of Pennsylvania, a Democrat, was able to defeat the first Republican presidential nominee, John C. Fremont of California. But his four years in office served to prove to many people that the Democratic party was not prepared to settle the national strife. The Supreme Court, on March 6, 1857, announced that Dred Scott, a Missouri slave, was not considered a citizen for that honor belonged only to the white race. Chief Justice Roger B. Taney and his associates went on to announce that the Missouri Compromise "had all along been void for Congress lacked the constitutional right to enact a law which arbitrarily deprived persons of their property, slave or otherwise, in the territories of the United States."[1] Democratic efforts at compromise were availing little. Stephen A. Douglas of Illinois, in his debates with Abraham Lincoln, found himself in dilemmas from which he sought escape by the famous Freeport Doctrine, which was so obnoxious to southern Democrats that they called it the "Freeport Heresy." Meantime, the nation looked forward to the crucial election of 1860.

Early that year the political parties began to prepare for the fall presidential election. The Democrats met at Charleston, South Carolina, on April 23rd, and chose Stephen A. Douglas as their champion. Southern Democrats were not satisfied and so elected John C. Breckinridge of Kentucky as their candidate. In May the Republican party met in Chicago, declaring that "the union of the States must and shall be preserved." Abraham Lincoln was chosen as their standard-bearer. The Constitutional Union party which met that same month nominated John Bell of Tennessee as their

---

[1]Homer Carey Hockett, *Political and Social Growth of the American People, 1492-1865* (Macmillan Company, New York, 1940), Third Edition, p. 699.

presidential candidate, and so, after the customary campaigning, the nation waited tensely to see the outcome of the November balloting.

The electoral count showed that Lincoln had received 180 votes, and all of these came from free states. Breckinridge had received 72 votes and these had come from the south. Douglas received 39 votes and Bell, 12, both of the latter receiving all votes from the border states. The popular vote showed that Lincoln had received only forty percent, Douglas, twenty-nine percent, Breckinridge, eighteen, and Bell, nearly thirteen. After the vote was known, tenseness in the nation only increased. No one hardly knew what the next step would be.

Southern statesmen for the most part were reluctant to be too hasty. They now wanted to wait and see what the new president would do, most apparently feeling that he would take some definite action shortly against the south which would give them justifiable reason to take further steps. There were extremists, however, who were found mostly in the seaboard states from South Carolina to Texas that were ready for secession. The state of South Carolina took the lead. Having received the news of Lincoln's election, the legislature called a special state convention. The convention met and on December 20, 1860, formally announced a dissolving of the union and the state of South Carolina. Six weeks later Mississippi, Florida, Alabama, Georgia, Louisiana and Texas had followed suit. On the fourth of February, 1861, delegates of the several seceding states met at Montgomery, Alabama, and organized a new federal government, electing Jefferson Davis as president. The new name chosen was Confederate States of America. Optimism and enthusiasm was in a gradual crescendo arising to a higher pitch. Excitement was everywhere.

In the closing days of his office, President James Buchanan was at a loss to know what to do. Again, as was customary, he chose a compromise position. He denied emphatically the constitutionality of secession, but at the same time declared that the nation had no right to force a state to stay in the union if it didn't want in. He placed the blame almost entirely with the north. While his intentions were good, yet numerous questions were demanding an answer, one of which was: "What shall become of Federal property, such as forts, which resided within the Confederate States?" In the harbor at Charleston, South Carolina, Major Robert Anderson and a small body of men occupied the Federal Fort Sumter on the small island in the middle of the harbor. Early in January Buchanan sent an armed steamer, *Star of the West,* to the fort with military supplies. Confederate batteries on the shore opened fire and drove her off. While this was really an act of war, Buchanan ignored it. Other forts in Confederate territory with the exception of Fort Pickens at Pensacola, Florida, capitulated without bloodshed to the South.

Adding greatly to the perplexity of the days was the arrival of the new president in Washington for the inauguration. To the vast majority of the nation he was an uncouth backwoodsman, certainly unfit for the White House. Homely to the verge of ugliness, awkward in manner, his actions often shocked the dignified statesmen of his time. His jokes were not always in good taste and often led to his being accused of being flippant on grave occasions. A neophyte in politics, the nation at first felt a little apprehensive under his leadership. He was the butt of many cartoons, but the plain people, one of whom he was, loved him dearly. As events proved, he was providentially the man of the hour.

No sooner had Lincoln taken office than word came from Major Anderson that he would have to surrender unless help was forthcoming immediately. All the members of his cabinet except two —Chase and Blair—recommended that Anderson evacuate the fort. Lincoln very much disagreed. To evacuate looked to him like recognizing the Confederate government. Besides it would seriously impair the morale in the North. He pitted his judgment against his cabinet and ordered supplies to be sent to the garrison. At the same time he notified the Confederates that he was sending provisions without adding to the garrison or supplying it with ammunition. His move proved to be a show of superior judgment, for he avoided a warlike move and left that decision up to the South. If the Confederates now fired, they would immediately gain the reputation of being the aggressors. Upon receipt of the information, the Confederates ordered Major Anderson to surrender, but the latter refused. Southern batteries opened up on the 12th day of April, firing those first shots of the war. From their blazing guns thundered in fire and smoke, in death and devastation, a declaration of war more dramatic than any ritual in Washington could make it. North and South now pitted their respective strength against each other, and for four long, weary years Mars was to rule America.

The attempt to reconstruct the story of what took place among the churches of the restoration movement during this period can only be summarily told, for the reason that our sources are too inadequate. How, in a material way, did the war affect the members of the church? To what extent did they take part, and to what extent did they suffer? What were the issues raised by the war and what position did the brethren take on them?

From the time of Lincoln's election in November, 1860, until the guns sounded at Fort Sumter in April, 1861, there was intense excitement the like of which was never seen in the land before. During this period Tolbert Fanning was on a journey through Mississippi, Louisiana, Alabama and Georgia. Leaving Nashville at six o'clock on the evening of November 27th, he went to Corinth, Mississippi, and then on down to Jackson, the capital of the state. The Mississippi state legislature was then in session and Fanning confesses that while he thought on other occasions that he had seen political excitement, now he knew that he really hadn't. He went into the legislative halls and heard the speeches of Mississippi's southern orators. The only question before them was, "When, and how, shall Mississippi secede from the Union?" Significantly enough, the veteran preacher of the South, T. W. Caskey, was among the number chosen to draw up the document of secession and present it to the legislature. What a difference this spirit of war made in the church! Fourteen years before, Fanning had preached in Jackson to audiences that nearly filled the chamber of the House of Representatives in the State House. Now he preached for two days, and the audiences were very small.

From Jackson, Fanning went to Vicksburg and then on down to New Orleans. His searches revealed only two or three Christians worshipping after the New Testament order. From New Orleans, Fanning went on to Mobile, Alabama, and from there visited brethren throughout the state. Arriving in Montgomery, the capital of the state, he found the city in such a turmoil that no one had time or thought about the Lord. No brethren could be found, so Fanning went on to Atlanta, Georgia. He arrived here December 21st. He visited in the home of Dr. A. G. Thomas, but was disappointed. Fanning says, "Dr. A. G. Thomas is a brother of fine address, superior talents and learning, but we saw him with a

feather in his hat and a glittering sword in his right hand, and
doubted if he would be able to hold the sword of Georgia in one
hand and the sword of the Spirit in the other."[2]   The impressions
made upon Fanning's mind were very solemn.   He expresses regret that so many brethren had gotten excited over political affairs,
and mildly castigated his brethren who were forgetting the Lord
over affairs in the state.

During this period of excitement Alexander Campbell was on
a tour of the North.   As the 21st of December had found Fanning
in Atlanta, it found Campbell in Indianapolis.   Here he met with
his most recently appointed associate-editor of the *Millennial Har-*
binger, Isaac Errett, whose work with the *Harbinger* was really
to begin with the January issue of 1861.   Errett had turned down
the offer to teach at Bethany College but had accepted the invitation
to be traveling agent for the school to raise funds.   It was in this
capacity that he and Alexander Campbell were now visiting the
churches in the North, especially in Indiana.   Their journey began among the cities and churches of the state, New Year's day
finding them in Crawfordsville, visiting in the home of S. M.
Huston, who was then faithfully serving the cause here.   Campbell
spoke here before a large audience, a member of which was former
Indiana Governor Lane, who was then a United States Senator
from Indiana.   Lane was a Methodist, although both his parents
were connected with the restoration.   This journey took Campbell
and Errett on to Greencastle, Terre Haute, Washington, Vincennes,
Bedford, Bloomington, New Albany, Madison, and then via
Columbus back to Indianapolis.   At Vincennes they met D. S.
Burnet, who accompanied them on the rest of the journey.   At
Indianapolis Campbell preached to a large crowd on Lord's Day
morning, and Burnet spoke at night.   Burnet also spoke before
the assembled student body of Northwest Christian University
that afternoon.   Scholarly S. K. Hoshour was then its president.
By the middle of February, 1861, Campbell and Errett had arrived
back at Bethany College.[3]

Errett was at this time preaching in Detroit, Michigan.   After
returning from his Indiana tour, he held a short meeting at Ionia

[2]Tolbert Fanning, "Tour Through Mississippi, Louisiana, Alabama, and
Georgia," *Gospel Advocate,* Vol. VII, No. 2 (February, 1861), p. 39.
      [3]P. S. Fall, "Letter from Elder Phillip Fall," *Millennial Harbinger,* Fifth
Series, Vol. IV, No. 9 (September, 1861), p. 530.

which proved very successful in spite of the political turmoil. He went next to Monmouth, Illinois, for a short meeting and then prepared for an extended tour into Virginia in the interests of Bethany College. But Errett had little success. The excitement of war was too great. Dispatches were passing between Washington and Fort Sumter, and hourly men were expecting the worst. Then came the news of Anderson's surrender. Madness ruled the hour as men in the South feverishly cursed the North, and those in the North did the same to the South. Errett prepared to leave Virginia at once, and on his return trip to Detroit, passed through Washington, D. C., Wheeling, Cleveland, before getting home. Every town, large and small, was filled with shouting, milling people. Flags were unfurled in the breeze, banners were streamed across public places; shouting, hurrahing, screaming were heard everywhere. No man could possibly describe the excitement then heard over the nation.

On April 5, 1861 W. H. Hopson began a very hopeful gospel meeting for the church at Walnut & Eighth Streets in Cincinnati. During the meeting news of the fall of Fort Sumter came across the wires. Streets were filled with crowding, milling, shouting people. The music of fife and drum whipped the excitement up to near frenzy. R. M. Bishop, one of the elders of the church was mayor of Cincinnati. Only a month before he had entertained Abraham Lincoln who was on his way to Washington for the inauguration. On this day Bishop drove Hopson through the streets in his carriage. They talked of the meeting and the war, and both agreed to close the meeting abruptly that night.

In both the North and the South members of the church joined in with the excitement. Preachers of the restoration stepped down out of the pulpit and joined the cause of both sections. Young men in "our colleges" left school to join with the army of their respective sections. James A. Garfield at the opening of the war was president of Western Reserve Eclectic Institute at Hiram, Ohio. When news of the struggle came to him, he petitioned Governor Dennison to give him an appointment. He was soon commissioned a Lieutenant-Colonel, and given permission to raise a regiment. Garfield went back to Hiram, and among the young men in the student body, he formed the forty-second Regiment of the Ohio Volunteer Infantry. Garfield was soon made a full colonel, and placed in full command of the regiment. By November 26, its eleven companies were fully outfitted at Camp Chase near Columbus, Ohio. On December 14, they moved toward Louisville. Early in January, the next year, they fought their first battle near Paintsville, Kentucky and proved the victors. They joined the Union army of General Grant at Shiloh, Tennessee, and fought there. They drove on to Corinth, driving the Confederate army out. They proceeded across northern Mississippi and Alabama, stopping to make temporary headquarters at Huntsville. Garfield's fame was recognized by the Union. He was recalled to Washington, then committed as aid to General Rosecrans at Murfreesboro. Rosecrans pushed from Murfreesboro to Chattanooga, and led the Union army to its defeat at Chickamauga. Here Garfield was made a Brigadier-General, but soon resigned to enter into Congress as representative from Ohio.

There were two hundred and fifty boys from Hiram College in the Union army, most of whom fought under Garfield in Co. A of the 42nd Ohio Regiment. J. S. Ross led this company in the last campaign as a captain. Major F. A. Williams, a very faithful member of the church, was killed early in the war. Charles P. Bowler, another member, was killed at Cedar Mountain. Wallace Coburn, also a member of the church, was killed at Winchester, Kentucky in 1862. Both belonged to the 7th Ohio Regiment. Major Delos R. Northway, a faithful Christian, was killed in the Wilderness in 1864.

The opposite of Garfield in some of these struggles was a young man doing scout duty who was destined to become one of the foremost proclaimers of the ancient order. T. B. Larimore joined the Confederate army the first year of the war and reported for duty to Colonel McClellan at Knoxville. At the battle of Fishing Creek in Kentucky, he was present on special duty. With General Buckner under a flag of truce he went to get the body of General Zollicoffer, his commanding general who fell in the battle. After the battle, Larimore rejoined his command at Murfreesboro, and from here went to Shiloh. He was in charge of a group of guards above Pittsburg Landing, whose duty was to watch for a possible Federal landing higher up the point. Larimore wrote the dispatch that went to Albert Sidney Johnson, notifying him of the passage of the first Federal gun-boat up the river. Larimore was in the retreat to Corinth, and from here fell back with the Confederate army along the south bank of the Tennessee river. He was on scout duty in the Sequatchie valley and was captured at McLemore's Cove.

At Franklin College W. D. Carnes fought frantically to keep the issue of war out of the classroom. When, however, Lincoln issued his first call for volunteers, almost the whole student body left school to join the Confederates, many of whom never came back. Carnes closed the school and went back to Pikeville.

Meanwhile, the brethren in what was then the west—Arkansas and Missouri—were severely influenced by the conflict. Missouri was at first southern in sentiment. But her southern governor was dismissed and the state legislature voted to go with the Union. Not so with Arkansas for she, like Texas, voted to go with the South. Most of the people of these states felt that since they were out of reach of the North and East, that little warfare would ever reach her borders, but in this, they were badly mistaken. War came and when it did, it hit the church there as much as anywhere.

William Baxter was at this time president of the college at Fayetteville, Arkansas. Robert Graham, who had founded the school, resigned a position he was holding at Kentucky University at the request of the brethren in Arkansas and returned to work among them.

The fall of 1860 opened at Arkansas College, looking to be the most prosperous yet. Almost all of the students were members of the church. Baxter kept down the political discussions, although among the student body there were persons of both sentiments. As the spring semester wore out and Fort Sumter fell, the call of Lincoln was issued for volunteers and several of the young men came to Baxter to announce the fact that they were to enlist. Baxter, seeing it was of little use to try to persuade them not to, got them together and talked with them kindly before leaving. Some of the boys fought for the Union and some for the South. When the last gun of the war was fired, many of this same group were sleeping silently on the battlefields from Gettysburg to Prairie Grove.

The battle of Pea Ridge and the battle of Prairie Grove were both fought at the outskirts of Fayetteville, Arkansas. The college was occupied at different times by Southern and Northern troops, but once, on retreat by the Confederate army, was burned to the ground. Fayetteville was overrun frequently by the armies of both sides. After the long battle of Prairie Grove, the city became one large hospital where Confederate and Union soldiers cried in agony. Graham had been forced to escape the city secretly because of too pronounced Union sentiments but Baxter remained. He went to the buildings where the sick were, saw the doctors cutting off legs and arms without the use of antiseptic, heard the *anesth* terrifying screams of soldiers in pain, viewed the dead and bloated bodies of soldiers placed in the streets until workers could bury them. This was a part of the aftermath of war. The sadder part came when the bodies of young men, members of the church in Fayetteville, were brought in from the battlefield and placed in the church building. It was terrible to watch the mothers cry over them and kiss so fondly the lifeless lips of their boys whose bullet-ridden bodies now lay before them.

Many members of the church fought in the war on both sides. The names of some who did can be known, but most will remain to us unknown. Several lost their lives. Nothing would be gained by recounting all of the names of boys who went to war, for to most of us they would be just names without much meaning. On the other hand, there are some whose names are more or less familiar who might well be noticed. At the battle of Pea Ridge in Arkansas a regiment of the Texas Rangers joined the ranks of General M'Culloch. This regiment was led by Barton Stone, a son of the renowned Barton W. Stone. Chaplain in the regiment was B. F. Hall of whom we have made previous mention. Hall, it will be recalled, moved from Kentucky, his native state, to Texas, preaching for a short while in Memphis, Tennessee, on his way. The influence of B. F. Hall was never so great after the war as before it and the reason can be well seen.

Before the battle of Pea Ridge, when the Confederate army was encamped at Fayetteville, Arkansas, William Baxter and Robert Graham decided to pay a visit to Hall and talk to him. Never was any visit regretted so much. Hall had changed completely. He was advocating strongly the Southern cause and, all in all, acted more like a fiend than a Christian gentleman. He rode a fine mule, had a splendid rifle, and expressly requested of all friends that if a "Yankee" appeared, please let him get his share. During the conversation with Graham and Baxter, Hall mentioned not one word about the church, about the gospel, or what one might ordinarily expect of a preacher, but spoke only of his rifle and how many Yankees he hoped to kill. Graham had never met Hall before and he sat speechless at the violence of Hall's attacks against the North. The Texas chaplain told of a friend, Alf Johnson, who had gone over the battlefield after the battle of William's Creek and who, when seeing a wounded Federal soldier begging for medical assistance, instead ruthlessly shot him. Hall would tell this story and then laugh as though he thoroughly enjoyed and approved of such conduct. Graham, ordinarily an even tempered man, struggled to keep from expressing his views. Hall advocated catching every Yankee soldier, cutting off their right hands and sending them back home with the hand tied to the saddle. Graham asked Hall how he could feel this way toward his brethren in the North, and Hall replied that he had no brethren in the North; they were all infidels.

Going outside, Graham asked Baxter how he liked Hall and what he thought of the conversation. Baxter replied that he felt as though he had been in the presence of a highwayman instead of a Christian. Human nature being what it is, men who brag the most of doing something great will seldom do much. When the battle of Pea Ridge came off, B. F. Hall went to the front as chaplain for the Texas Rangers. About the only activity he ever saw was running, when the shattered columns of General M'Culloch's army poured back through Fayetteville on their way south. Baxter and Graham stood by and watched B. F. Hall, looking tired and worn, head back in retreat.[4]

The feeling in both the South and North reached great heights and dark deeds were done. Members of the church did not altogether escape disaster. Andrew Allsman, a member of the church in Palmyra, Missouri, was taken out and shot by Confederate General Porter. As members of the church go, he wasn't much, but yet the killing of him was wholly unwarranted. When news of the deed reached General McNiel, Union general in the same area, he selected ten men of his Confederate prisoners who would

---

[4]William Baxter: *Pea Ridge and Prairie Grove* (Cincinnati: Poe & Hitchcock, 1864), pp. 113-123.

be shot in retaliation. These men were placed in a cell and the day for their execution set. Jacob Creath, Jr., was called in to speak to them. As he stepped into their cell, he saw ten different men. One or two were silent, others were crying bitterly, begging for pardon. One tall youth with blond hair was a lieutenant. He was brave but despondent. His girl back home was waiting for his return so they could marry. Creath could do nothing to cancel their execution but begged them to have their heart right before God and be prepared. The morning came and all ten fell before a firing squad.[5]

When the army of General John Sherman swept across the South toward Atlanta, pillage, rapacity, plunder followed in its wake. The South suffered much because of this. In this army was the fourth Kentucky Regiment and in this regiment was one John B. Vawter, later to become one of the great preachers of the restoration in Iowa. While camped outside of Atlanta, General Sherman sent two thousand men around the city to cut off the supplies and cut the rail and telegraph lines. Vawter was among the number to go. But his regiment was attacked and almost all of the men were either destroyed or captured. Vawter was captured and sent to the Andersonville prison where misery and suffering reached its height.[6]

In Missouri, A. H. F. Payne was one of the first located preachers in the state. He spent most of his life in Clay County. He was born in Mason County, Kentucky on April 14, 1807. He moved from Lexington, Kentucky to Missouri in 1836 and preached in Clay County until 1854 when he moved to Plattsburg. He was strongly for the north in his political sentiment. He was ruthlessly murdered by a group of bush-whackers who came to capture him under the pretense of an order from a commanding general.

And so went the war! Men everywhere were affected by it. Churches in some places divided; others became discouraged and ceased to meet. The condition of the churches in Kentucky may be best seen in a report sent to the general convention of the Missionary Society in October, 1862 by J. W. McGarvey. McGarvey wrote:

---

[5]P. Donan, *Memoirs of Jacob Creath, Jr.* (Cincinnati: Chase & Hall, 1877), p. 179.

[6]Sergeant Oats, *Prison Life in Dixie* (Chicago: Central Book Concern, 1880), p. 1ff.

But a storm of human passion, seldom equaled in the history of our sinful world, is raging around us, and we have caught the infection. The results are such as human passion must always produce. Many brethren have been swept into hopeless apostasy; the zeal of many has been chilled; distrust prevails among many who were once bosom friends; the evangelical labors of nearly all have been much contracted; churches languish; congregations dwindle, and there is a fear that such divisions as have distracted the religious sects of the day, may yet disgrace our history.

The above report is taken from the original minutes of the Society for their meeting of 1862.

Our sources are inadequate to present anything like a complete picture of the activities of brethren in and during the war, so therefore, our minds must be contented with a partial picture. In this case a partial picture is better than none for it at least gives some information as to what was happening to the churches during those dark and dreadful days.

Yet there is another side of the whole picture at which we must now look and this side concerns itself with the issues that were raised by the war. Fundamentally, there were two. The first antedated the war. It was the issue of slavery—of whether or not a Christian could scripturally own slaves. The second issue was raised during the war. It asked, Does a Christian have a right to go to war and kill his fellowman? Both of these were highly important. Our attention now turns to the first one.

The question of Christians holding slaves was first raised among the brethren early in 1845. Both Thomas and Alexander Campbell expressed their views upon the subject and dropped it. The first article to appear came from Thomas Campbell in January of that year. He determined to thoroughly examine the Bible on it. Taking up all the scriptures on the subject one by one, he then drew certain conclusions. He decided, first, that God has allowed slavery at certain times as a punishment for sin. The descendents of Ham, therefore, were being punished by those of Japheth and Shem down to this day. Second, to hold slaves was divinely permitted. Slavery, while an evil, was one which God at times permitted.[7]

---

[7]Thomas Campbell, "Elder Thomas Campbell's Views of Slavery," *Millennial Harbinger*, Third Series, Vol. II, No. 1 (January, 1845), pp. 1-8.

Alexander Campbell spoke on the subject in the next issue. He stressed the need of such a discussion by saying,

Any one of much sagacity must see that the controversy between the North and the South has commenced. . . . Already, indeed, has it come into our American ecclesiastical courts, and distracted the councils of one of the most imposing communities in our Protestant ranks.[8]

But Campbell had the greatest confidence in his brethren in that he believed the principles to which they held would never allow a division in their ranks over slavery. Significantly enough, Campbell proved to be a true prophet, for the churches of Christ were among one of the very few that did not, in the war, divide over the question of slavery. At any rate, Campbell wrote that "we are the only religious community in the civilized world whose principles (unless we abandon them) can preserve us" from a division.

The position Alexander Campbell took toward slavery showed his deep knowledge of the scriptures. In a day when there were fanatical extremists on every side, Campbell taught that the issue was not a moral one, but a political one. That is to say, slavery was neither right nor wrong in and of itself so far as the scriptures taught, but that the settlement of it was to be left up to political discretion. He found many passages in the scriptures *regulating* slavery, but none prohibiting it. There was Biblical teaching to tell a slave how to conduct himself toward his master, and the same for the master toward the slavery. The scriptures neither condemned nor upheld slavery; therefore, it must be left to the political government as their peculiar issue. Campbell then concludes:

To preserve unity of spirit among Christians of the South and of the North is my grand object, and for that purpose I am endeavoring to show that the New Testament does not authorize any interference or legislation upon the relation of master and slave, nor does it either in letter or spirit authorize Christians to make it a term of communion . . . .

Every man who loves the American Union, as well as every man who desires a constitutional end of American slavery, is

---

[8]Alexander Campbell, "Our Position to American Slavery," *Millennial Harbinger*, Third Series, Vol. II, No. 2 (February, 1845), p. 51.

bound to prevent, as far as possible, any breach of communion between Christians at the South and at the North.[9]

Campbell had struck boldly at the heart of the issue. While there were those in the church who took both extremes, Campbell's influence and his stand prevented anything like serious conflict ever arising over slavery.

In 1850 the question of slavery arose again. Congress passed that year the Fugitive Slave Law, making it compulsory by law for a person who captured a fugitive slave to return him to his owner. A heavy fine was imposed upon any who refused. The law caused tremendous excitement. Those brethren in the North who held it was sinful to own slaves, believed it violated the scriptures for them to return a slave. Campbell, however, disagreed. He pointed out that the government was ordained of God, and that therefore, any Christian who disobeyed the Fugitive Slave Law was disobeying this stricture from God. As to his position Campbell declared:

So far, then, as editors in general are presumed to act, I stand on neutral ground. But, as I judge, I owe it to myself and to my readers, North and South, to place myself before them in my true and real position on this very interesting and exciting subject.[10]

Samuel Church substantially agreed with Campbell. Church preached in Allegheny City, and was one of the most highly respected preachers in his day. He wrote:

Slavery, be it good or bad, is not the voluntary choice of the present generation in the South. They inherit it, and all their established habits of thinking and acting, individually and socially—morally, politically and religiously—are, more or less, identified with it. If its existence be sinful, they are not conscious of it, and are unlikely to be enlightened by calling them thieves and villains.[11]

In the main, these positions were recognized as logical although a few disagreed. Occasionally a man was found like John Kirk of Palestine, Ohio who wrote to Campbell:

I have come to the conclusion that I will neither patronize

---

[9]Alexander Campbell, "Our Position to American Slavery—No. V," *Millennial Harbinger,* Third Series, Vol. II, No. 5 (May, 1845), p. 195.

[10]Alexander Campbell, "Slavery and the Fugitive Slave Law," *Millennial Harbinger,* Fourth Series, Vol. I, No. 3 (March, 1851), p. 171.

[11]Samuel Church, "Our Position on American Slavery," *Millennial Harbinger,* Fourth Series, Vol. I, No. 2 (February, 1851), p. 106.

priest nor paper that is not strictly anti-slavery. Your position to American slavery I very much dislike.[12]

Another extreme abolitionist in the church was Nathaniel Field. When Campbell visited Louisville, Kentucky in April, 1835, he met Field whom Campbell described as "body, soul, and spirit opposed to American slavery." At that time Campbell wrote:

There is, indeed, a healthy, rational, and scriptural reform of this great and growing evil much wanted, and which I am of the opinion would be satisfactory to the Doctor and many other good men, which as an incipient measure, is certainly practicable, and absolutely necessary to our pleading of reformation. No Christian can, on the principle of humanity or the gospel, sell a wife from a husband, or a husband from a wife; an infant from its parents, or parents from their infant offspring, under any pretense whatever. And no laws of any state can justify any Christian man in keeping his servants ignorant of God, of Jesus Christ, or of the Bible facts, any more than the laws of Greece or Rome could have compelled the first Christians to have worshipped idols, or to have called Jesus anathema, or sanctioned them in so doing. Of all this I have no more doubt than I have that Jesus is the Messiah.[13]

Tolbert Fanning in the meantime, plead that warfare was not the way to handle slavery, but peaceful means should be pursued. He says:

I regret exceedingly that the brethren of the North or South should be suspicious of each other. True, many of the north look upon slavery as a great evil; but as to the abstract question of good or evil, ninety-nine hundredths of the disciples of the south will have no controversy. If it be a destructive sin, it is our misfortune in the south,—we could not prevent the state of affairs, and now we must make the best of the subject we can.[14]

Some, like Walter Scott, were perplexed upon the subject. They did not know what to say, and thought silence in this case the lesser of two evils. Scott wrote:

The manumission of our slave population can be accomplished now only by a means which heaven only knows—I know it not. . . . I am no friend of slavery, I deprecate its commencement. I deplore its continuance, and tremble for its issue; but I am silent because I

---

[12]John Kirk, "Our Position on American Slavery," *Millennial Harbinger,* Fourth Series, Vol. I, No. 1 (January, 1851), p. 49.

[13]Alexander Campbell, "Sketch of a Tour of Seventy-Five Days," *Millennial Harbinger,* Vol. VI, No. 7 (July, 1835), pp. 331, 332.

[14]Tolbert Fanning, "Christian Bible Society," *Christian Review,* Vol. II, No. 11 (November, 1845), p. 234.

think to speak would be folly. What ought to be said I cannot say, and what ought not to be said I will not say.[15]

Ben Franklin took substantially the same position as Alexander Campbell. Franklin, as an editor, learned what many an editor soon learns, viz., he receives many inquiries to answer certain questions which the querist asks, not because he wants to find out anything, but because he wants to agitate an issue, and would use the editor as a tool. Franklin received inquiries on the slavery question, and for the most part paid little attention to them. However, in the spring of 1859 he brushed the question aside by answering that neither Jesus nor Paul had ever stated whether slavery was right or wrong. Who, then, was he to do something they didn't?

Did the Lord and the apostles do right in never deciding the question, whether slavery is right or wrong, discussing and never saying one word about that question in any form? If they did, we do right when we treat it in the same way. If they did wrong, we do wrong when we treat it the same way.[16]

We turn now from the question of slavery to one that far outweighed it in importance, the question of the Christian's right to take arms for his government. Early in 1861, when it became obvious that a war was seriously threatening, Tolbert Fanning began to answer these questions. After admitting that there had never been a time when the nation had suffered so much or was threatened so much as then, Fanning went on to say that it was not his duty to tell politicians what to do, but since the church of Christ was innocently involved, he must needs speak plainly to his brethren. He expressed the belief that the religion of Jesus Christ could prosper under any form of government and reminded the brethren that the kingdom of Christ was not of this world. He referred to the fact that Jesus was the Prince of Peace and His preachers, messengers of peace. He pled that it was only right for North and South to settle their differences, not on the field of battle, but through discussion. The politicians of both sides did not fear the Lord and should not be followed in this matter. He laid the blame for the agitation of war at the

---

[15]William Baxter, *Life of Elder Walter Scott* (Cincinnati: Bosworth, Chase & Hall, 1874), p. 360.

[16]Ben Franklin, "Our Position Called For," *American Christian Review*, Vol. II. No. 11 (March 15, 1859), p. 42.

feet of such men as Theodore Parker, Wendell Philips, Ralph Waldo Emerson and Henry Ward Beecher. He called the policy of southern preachers unchristian who were trying to excite the Southland to action.[17]

Later, getting more to the point, he argued that wars all came from the passions of men and did not meet the approval of God. He stated his firm conviction that Christians have no business fighting in them. He says:

Our conclusion of the whole matter is, that the wars of heaven, are moral conflicts between the church of Christ and the opposing world powers; and the wars of earth are struggles in the world without by men of the world, inaugurated by wicked men for wicked purposes, but which God may overrule for good. The history of the world sustains us in these conclusions, but the church of Christ is composed of "a peculiar people," separate from others, are not of the world, engage not in its bloody conflicts, and yet the Lord has promised to sustain them to the end.[18]

Some years earlier Fanning had expressed himself on the same question. Franklin College was reputed to have "military exercises," which were nothing but physical exercises, but someone had carelessly used the wrong word, and the school was receiving some criticism. Some thought training for war was being given. After explaining the exercises, Fanning wrote:

This was far from my view, for I have long been satisfied war, in every shape, is unsuited to civilized governments and opposed in all its bearings, to the Christian religion. The grand distinguishing characteristic of Christianity is, men shall not return evil for evil.[19]

The brotherhood had been divided into two different camps respecting the issue of war. There were those who favored a Christian's participation, and those who opposed it. We shall set before ourselves first of all the attitude of those opposing war and their reasons and then, the same for those who felt Christian participation was permissible.

Alexander Campbell had been opposed from very early to a

[17]Tolbert Fanning, "Duty of Christians in Reference to the Political Crisis of 1861," *Gospel Advocate,* Vol. VII, No. 2 (February, 1861), p. 33.

[18]Tolbert Fanning, "Wars of Heaven and Earth," *Gospel Advocate,* Vol. VII, No. 7 (July, 1861), p. 205.

[19]Tolbert Fanning, "Gymnastic Exercises in College," *Christian Review,* Vol. II, No. 6 (June, 1845), p. 127.

Christian's participating in war. In the first issue of the *Christian* /823
Baptist, Campbell said:

And, stranger still, see that Christian general, with his ten thousand soldiers, and his chaplain at his elbow, preaching, as he says, the gospel of good will among men; and hear him exhort his general and his Christian warriors to go forth with the Bible in one hand and the sword in the other, to fight the battles of God and their country; praying that the Lord will cause them to fight valiantly, and render their efforts successful in making as many widows and orphans as will afford sufficient opportunity for others to manifest the purity of their religion by taking care of them!!! If any thing is wanting to finish a picture of the most glaring inconsistencies, add to this those Christians who are daily extolling the blessings of civil and religious liberty, and at the same time, by a system of the most cruel oppression, separating the wife from the embraces of her husband, and the mother from her tender offspring; violating every principle, and rending every tie that endears life and reconciles man to his lot; and that, forsooth, because *'might gives right,'* and a man is held guilty because his skin is a shade darker than the standard color of the times, adverting to these signs of the times, and many others to which these reflections necessarily lead, will you not say that this prophecy is now fulfilled—2 Tim. 4: 3, 4—'There will be a time when they will not endure wholesome teaching; but having itching ears, they will, according to their own lusts, heap up to themselves teachers. And from the truth, indeed, they will turn away their ears and be turned aside to fables!" Chap. iii. 1-5. 'This also know, that in latter days perilous times *will* come. For men will be *self-lovers, money-lovers,* boasters, proud, blasphemers, disobedient to parents, ungrateful, unholy, without *natural affection.* covenant-breakers, slanderers—*having a form of godliness but denying the power of it.* NOW FROM THESE TURN AWAY.' Christian reader, remember this command and 'from such turn away.'[20]

In 1846 when it looked as though war would come again, Campbell /846
to set forth his position reprinted the above article, and expressed that from these views he had "subtracted nothing," but that his convictions were then even stronger.

Shortly after the first guns were fired in the war, Campbell wrote:

Civilized America! Civilized UNITED STATES! Boasting of a humane and Christian paternity and fraternity, unsheathing your swords, discharging your cannon, boasting of your heathen bru-

---

[20]Alexander Campbell, "Christian Religion," *Christian Baptist,* Vol. I, No. 1 (August 3, 1823), p. 8.

tality, gluttonously satiating your furious appetites for fraternal blood, caps the climax of all human inconsistencies inscribed on the blurred and moth eaten pages of time in all its records.[21]

Shortly after war broke out, W. K. Pendleton pled with brethren to have no part in it. He wrote:

O, my Christian brother think of it! When you shoulder your musket and equip yourself with all the instruments of death, ask yourself have you the right thus to take the life of your fellow? Who gave you the right? What has your brother done that you may shoot him?—Has he stolen your property? Can you murder him for that? Has he differed with you about political governments? Can you not part in peace?. . . .
I am anxious for the peace of Zion. Let not brother meet brother in battle. Let not two Christian souls perishing by mutual violence, going down to death, frantic with the rage of mortal combat, hope to rise to the climes of celestial peace from such a struggle.[22]

T. M. Allen, the veteran of Missouri, expressed himself tersely in these words: ". . . . I would sooner go to the grave being killed for not killing my brother, than to go to the tomb with my brother's blood on my hands."[23]

At the outset of the war, Benjamin Franklin, editor of the *American Christian Review,* took a decided stand against the Christian's participation in it. He wrote:

We cannot always tell what we *will,* or *will not do.* There is one thing, however things may turn, or whatever may come, that *we will not do,* and that is, *we will not take up arms against, fight and kill the brethren we have labored for twenty-one years to bring into the kingdom of God.* Property may be destroyed, and safety may be endangered, or life lost; but we are under Christ, and we will not kill or encourage others to kill, or fight the brethren.[24]

Again Franklin wrote:

We have never felt the value of our position, since we have been a people, as we have done during the political excitement that has swept over our country, and as we do now while such exciting things are occurring. We have been actively engaged every day

[21]Alexander Campbell, "Wars and Rumors of Wars," *Millennial Harbinger,* Fifth Series, Vol. IV, No. 6 (June, 1861), p. 348.
[22]W. K. Pendleton, "A Plea for Peace," *Millennial Harbinger,* Fifth Series, Vol. IV, No. 7 (July, 1861), p. 410.
[23]T. M. Allen, "Progress of Reform," *Millennial Harbinger,* Fifth Series, Vol. IV, No. 8 (August, 1861), p. 478.
[24]Joseph Franklin and J. A. Headington, *The Life and Times of Benjamin Franklin* (St. Louis: Christian Board of Publication, 1879), p. 287.

during this long political conflict, in directing the attention of the people to the one great center of attraction—the Lord of life and glory. We have had no time to turn to the right or to the left, to discuss the merits or demerits of exciting political issues of the times. We have left them to the men of the world—to the statesmen . . .

While the eyes of the men of the world are red with political strife and rage, and while their feet are swift to shed blood—while rapine and violence are stalking abroad in open day and threatening to destroy the peace and safety of the country, the children of God are assembling to hear the gospel of peace and to worship the God of their fathers. While sectarian preachers are haranguing their audiences on the question of political strife, and thus adding fuel to the flame, the preachers of the Cross are preaching peace by Jesus Christ; He is Lord of all.[25]

Benjamin Franklin goes on to say that not a preacher in the brotherhood had preached politics but had continued to preach Christ.

Seeing that war was inevitable, J. W. McGarvey, just a few days before Fort Sumter was fired upon, wrote his views:

I know not what course other preachers are going to pursue, for they have not spoken; but my own duty is now clear, and my policy is fixed. I shall vote, when called upon, according to my views of political policy, and whether I remain a citizen of this Union, or become a citizen of a Southern Confederacy, my feelings toward my brethren everywhere shall know no change. In the meantime, if the demon of war is let loose in the land, I shall proclaim to my brethren the peaceable commandments of my Saviour, and strain every nerve to prevent them from joining any sort of military company, or making any warlike preparations at all. I know that this course will be unpopular with men of the world, and especially with political and military leaders; and there are some who might style it treason. But I would rather, ten thousand times, be killed for refusing to fight, than to fall in battle, or to come home victorious with the blood of my brethren on my hands.[26]

McGarvey, furthermore, worked to get the leading preachers to use their influence to prevent other brethren from participating in the war. He wrote to Isaac Errett, whose Union sentiments were very pronounced, and tried to get his support.

It is absolutely necessary in a time like this, that our leading men—preachers, professors, and editors—should take no active partisan

[25]Benjamin Franklin, "Our Position in These Troublesome Times," *American Christian Review,* Vol. III, No. 49 (December 4, 1860), p. 196.

[26]Ben Franklin, "Our Position in These Troublesome Times," *American Christian Review,* Vol. III, No. 49 (December 4, 1860), p. 287.

position. The more prudent brethren ought to speak out plainly for the benefit of the more rash.[27]

Errett's answer to McGarvey on this point is not accessible. However, there can be little doubt as to the way his sentiments went, for McGarvey wrote again to him, saying:

Your favor is received and carefully perused, and although we differ as widely as ever, I am glad to be assured that you have no disposition to push your views forward in such way as to injure the cause. I have no doubt that you could easily produce a serious division in the churches of the North.[28]

McGarvey was tireless in getting the support of brethren to the neutral position in the war. He got up a large circular on the duty of the Christian to stay out of war and sent it to the *American Christian Review* signed by many of the outstanding preachers of the state of Missouri.

On the side of those who felt Christian participation permissible, there were a few leading brethren. B. W. Johnson was one, although he preferred to pursue a cautious course. His article on the subject was printed in the June 25th issue, 1861, of the *Review*. It was generally misunderstood and even McGarvey wrote Johnson, congratulating him on his anti-war stand. Johnson came back, expressing regret that he had been misunderstood. His belief was that the issue should not in such times of stress be argued in the pulpit. He tended toward the belief that the question was political, not religious. While deploring war, he yet held that the government was ordained of God and that it was the Christian's right to belong to that government. He argued that if government was right, the means to sustain that government is also right. He cites scriptures in the New Testament where men belonged to or held political offices. He furthermore declared that there is no proof that the soldiers of the New Testament times ever were told to cease being soldiers after becoming Christians. Relative to a Christian's duty to his government, Johnson concluded:

Either he can sustain it, or he is an incubus to his country; a State is weak in proportion to its Christian element and the conversion of a majority of the people would result in national ruin.[29]

[27]J. S. LaMarr, *Memoirs of Isaac Errett* (Cincinnati: The Standard Publishing Co., 1893), Vol. 1, p. 242.

[28]*Ibid.*, p. 243.

[29]B. W. Johnson, "Should Christians Go to War?" *Millennial Harbinger,* Fifth Series, Vol. IV, No. 10 (October, 1861), p. 586.

On the same side, the *Harbinger* presented a letter from Jacob Creath, Jr., on the subject which had been addressed to Benjamin Franklin. Creath suggested that he had been asked on various occasions to preach on the subject but had declined. He had nothing to do with the war and wanted nothing. Yet, if a Christian did go to war and did kill, Creath could only see that the guilt would fall upon the rulers of the country, not upon the individual. In the final analysis, he left the decision up to the individual to make for himself.

Thus we see two sides of an issue. Both sides admitted that war was an evil. The question of whether a Christian could engage in this evil practice was seen differently. Those who felt that it was allowable for a Christian to participate in carnal struggles based their conclusions on the fact that government was ordained of God, and that the God-ordained government had a right to protect, by bloodshed if necessary, its interests. The only question was, did a Christian have a right to consider himself a part of this government? If so, the Christian was not held *individually* responsible for killing, but he was acting as an official of his government, doing what the government was ordained of God to do. Johnson says,

My kingdom is not of this world; *if it were,* then would my servants fight.

Johnson reasons that since the kingdom of Caesar *is* of this world, and since it is right for a Christian to be a part of this kingdom, then it is right for him to fight for the kingdoms of this world.

On the other hand there were others who believed that warfare was intended for the kingdoms of man, and not for the kingdom of Christ. If the world would kill and murder, it must do so; but let the Christian maintain his allegiance to a higher kingdom. They looked upon war as basically conflicting with the Christian economy, maintaining that the Christian was to do good to his enemies, love those that despitefully used him, and return good for good instead of evil for evil.

Suffice it to say the problem has always been the occasion of much strife among brethren, especially during times of war. It is not likely that all men in the church will ever see eye to eye. Good men, consecrated men see differently, and at times, in the heat of passion, express themselves unkindly toward the other. For our part we admit that there are many angles to the whole question we have been unable to answer. But that a Christian can take up arms, kill his fellowman, make widows and orphans and cripples of innocent people, is in our opinion wholly incompatable and irreconcilable with the very genius and nature of the Christian economy.

CHAPTER XIX

TRENDS OF THE TIMES

When Phillip Henry, father of the famous author of the set of Bible commentaries, was thinking of marriage, he asked the hand of a certain young lady from her father. The father was unwilling, and later remarked to his daughter that this man who had proposed to her was but a poor preacher. He was young, had little guarantee of a large-enough income to support her, and withal had some particular weaknesses which he singled out. She replied that she knew all of this but still she had confidence in him for she knew "the direction he was going."

abrupt.

What direction was the restoration movement going up to 1865? Can we say we like this direction? Was the church drifting away from her mooring or standing more solidly for the earlier principles? Generally speaking what was the state of the church as we find it at the end of the war?

needs a transitional sentence or paragraph

In one sense of the term this is the most important chapter of all and yet it undoubtedly is the most difficult. The physician looks at the symptoms, carefully analyzing these, before applying the remedy for the disease. We are here looking at symptoms, carefully analyzing them to see if we can discover the disease. In the science of physics we are told that every action must have a reaction. We are studying reactions, trying to discover the actions that produced it. We are watching the movement of the windmill to determine the direction of the wind. There is something intangible, yet dangerous, about it all. The doctor can view the symptoms and mistakenly doctor the wrong disease. We are taking the events of the time and analyzing them, not for their significance as events, but in the fact that they show the direction in which the restoration movement was traveling.

In the late summer of 1856 Robert Milligan began setting forth a series of articles in the *Millennial Harbinger* on the "Permanent Christian Ministry." Tolbert Fanning took exception to this, and printed his reply in the *Gospel Advocate*. For several issues in both periodicals the discussion was carried on. Respecting the subject for discussion, there is very little that needs to attract our attention. Fanning was tremendously interested in the subject of

"Church Organization." In fact upon no subject did he write more often. Fanning's view of "Church Organization" was briefly this: The logical teachers, and overseers of the church were the elders. The elders were but the elderly men in the church. They "kept house for the Lord," and edified the saints. All the teaching was done by this group. They had no office, but each elder (old man) in accordance with his ability, taught and edified the church. The evangelists went from place to place, preaching the gospel, establishing churches, and encouraging them to meet regularly. With Fanning located preachers were but pastors and were taboo. So with salaried ministers. Milligan's articles as they respect this subject were accordingly much nearer the truth than Fanning, although Fanning was ready always to defend himself on this issue. Yet, out of the discussion, Milligan presents an attitude, a symptom of a disease that was creeping over a large portion of the brotherhood.

In the course of the discussions Milligan wrote:

In our present independent, weak, and distracted condition, we can, *as a church,* do but little for the salvation of the world. If we want to supply our own country with Bibles, or to send out a missionary to Jerusalem, or Liberia, we cannot do it *as a church;* in this capacity we have no means of cooperating: but we must form a Bible society, and a missionary society, to deprive the church of the glory of converting the world.[1]

Fanning missed no opportunity to pick this up and note it to be a symptom of a certain type of thinking. It is little wonder that Fanning saw in this a reflection upon the church, upon the wisdom of God, as well as upon the Bible. God had ordained that the church should preach the gospel to save souls. But, according to Milligan, the church could not do this, and must form itself into human societies before the work can be accomplished. Not only so, but the wisdom of God declared and instituted the church for the purpose of saving the world; but since the church couldn't do this, and since human societies had to be formed, man in his wisdom was wiser than the wisdom of God.

Here, then, was a strong objection that more and more came to be raised against missionary societies. Their very existence was a reflection upon the wisdom of God, the adequacy of the church, and

---

[1]Robert Milligan, "The Permanent Orders of the Christian Ministry," *Millennial Harbinger,* Fourth Series, Vol. VI, No. 9 (September, 1856), p. 499.

the Bible as the necessary guide. Their origin came, not from divine revelation, but from human planning; therefore, there was a subtle implication that the Bible was not a sufficient guide, but that something beyond it was needed. In years to come this was to be a forceful argument, especially with David Lipscomb. The whole program, he would point out, upon which the societies worked was a setting aside of the scriptures. It was not strange to him that in the years to come friends of the society became the most ardent advocates of liberalism and modernism, for they *began* by setting aside the word. How else could they *end?*

In the earlier days of the restoration movement Thomas Campbell had voiced the famous motto: "Where the Bible speaks, we speak; where the Bible is silent, we are silent." Milligan also pointed out in the discussion that a "thus saith the Lord" could not be found in the New Testament for all things regarding the church, its work and organization, for the New Testament was not a code of specific precepts. Milligan asserted that God made the New Testament to furnish us with a book of motives, and so the church is governed today by generic laws, examples, and motives. This was the forerunner of the viewpoint which later came up that the Bible was not to be obeyed in the *letter,* but only in the *spirit.* If man had the *spirit* of obedience in his heart, although he didn't obey the letter of the law, he was acceptable to God.

Fanning viewed Milligan's assertion with alarm. To him such a program deprecated the entire New Testament, not to mention the earlier platform of the restoration. Fanning referred to such commands as to believe, repent, be baptized, observe the Lord's Supper, etc. These were specific, not general. Milligan's position, Fanning asserted, was the next-door neighbor to the one Protestant bodies and infidels alike took, viz., if a man's *motives* were good, if he were sincere, nothing else mattered.

In fairness to Milligan it must be admitted that he did not mean to go this far, nor would he have been among the number to deny the necessity of any of these. Milligan admitted these specific commands, but cited other commands, as, "Honor thy father and thy mother," "whatever you do in word or deed, do all in the name of Christ," etc., as general commands. Fanning, however, was not wrong in seeing a danger to such assertions from Milligan, for led to the logical end, they would have said what Fanning argued they did.   It was only a question of a very short time that they did lead this far.

Fanning's discussion with Milligan probably did not accomplish the aim Fanning had for it.   There was some general prejudice against Fanning's idea on Church Organization to begin with. Many doubtlessly thought he was seeing symptoms of a disease that didn't exist.   But with Fanning this was far too serious to be taken lightly.   He was confident that friends of the society were leading the church in a general departure from the Bible.   This was the disease, and the symptoms became more and more numerous as he watched anxiously the passing of time.

Less than a year after his discussion with Robert Milligan, Fanning found himself at odds with Robert Richardson.   Richardson was one of the favorite teachers at Bethany College.   He was a very pious and deeply spiritual man.   His greatest fame, perhaps, was gained a few years after this when he wrote the Memoirs of Alexander Campbell.   In the March, 1857 number of the *Harbinger* Richardson began a series of articles on "Faith versus Philosophy."   The gist of the articles was this : The restoration movement had been launched upon some great principles that had been tried and tested.   Yet, Richardson went on to assert, it had not gone on to perfection.   The movement had fallen down as it respects true spirituality and the real practice of the teachings of Christ.   The reason for this Richardson ascribed to an introduction of human philosophy into the fundamental teachings of the restoration.   This philosophy is oftentimes held without the person holding it, knowing it, he went on.   Here, in his third number, he introduced the example of Tolbert Fanning, who had only recently run articles against human philosophy.   Fanning had, in those articles, denounced Natural Theology, and made the claim that man could not know God from the works of nature, but only through the revealed word. Furthermore, the popular philosophy of intuitive knowledge, or a knowledge of God *a priori,* that man was born with certain intuitive capabilities to know God, Fanning also rejected.   Richardson went out of his way to show that Fanning, while deriding philosophy, yet held a philosophy, for this was his own.

About the whole discussion, there is an atmosphere of misunderstanding and mystery.   Jacob Creath, Jr., was no doubt right when he wrote to Alexander Campbell complaining against Richardson's articles. He said if what Richardson was writing were the gospel, he himself had been preaching for years, and had been ignorant of it. He went on to beg Campbell to stop Richardson or he would ruin the *Harbinger*. Richardson's essays on this subject were lengthy and extremely wordy. Surely he was capable of clearer writing. At times he had a venomous pen, hardly characteristic of one with the reputation of piousness that he had. One finds himself disappointed with these articles from Richardson's pens. Again some allowance must be made for Fanning's position, for few today would hold today as tenaciously as he did that there was not, in the works of nature, some evidence of the existence of God. Nevertheless, there was a symptom apparent that Fanning was quick to see.

Fanning had the utmost confidence in the Bible, and would strongly object to those who indicated a lack of such confidence. He was undoubtedly right that Richardson, perhaps unconsciously, was putting too much confidence in philosophy himself, and too little upon the Bible. There was definitely a tendency in this direction, and the Bible was being partially shelved in favor of the more learned theology and philosophy of the times.

It has been remarked on various occasions that Ben Franklin up to the war days was following pretty much with the general drift of the brotherhood. He supported missionary societies, and meanwhile, watched anxiously the passing of the years, with the apparent refusal to believe that a drift from the truth could ever come. But by 1859 he began to have a definite feeling that all was not right within the walls of Zion. Unknowingly, the Trojan horse had been rolled into the mighty fortress, and now Zion was beginning to boil with internal dissention. There were enemies on the inside, and he was just awakening to the fact. Consequently, he writes:

We have tried to construe things we have seen among us in a favorable light, and to keep up the conviction that no evil was intended. But it was all in vain; the conviction is *there, deep* and *strong,* and though we desire to remove it, have tried to have it removed, it only becomes deeper and still deeper, that *evil, most ruinous and mischievous evil is intended.*

Franklin goes on,

It is now wisely discovered that the terms of pardon laid down in the New Testament, as advocated, propagated, and defended with such unprecedented success by the Disciples, for the last thirty years, as one man expressed it, 'have rendered us ridiculous in the eyes of the world,' and that we must 'go on to perfection.' But where have these men gone to, in 'going on to perfection'? Some of them have gone so far as to reach the silly, the anti-evangelical practice of praying for the conversion of sinners at the mourner's bench! Others of them have progressed so far as to make the remarkable discovery that the voice of conscience is the voice of God. Again, it has been discovered, that man can not believe the testimony of God till the Spirit quickens him and gives him life. It is again maintained that men in our time speak by inspiration, and that miracles should be performed in the church! What use have such men as these for the Bible?"[2]

Tolbert Fanning copied the above from the *American Christian Review,* and inserted it into the *Gospel Advocate* with the following additional note:

Fear not Brother Franklin, the cause we are advocating is the Lord's. We have felt confident for years that you have seen the storm cloud rising. The trifling matter with J. B. Ferguson, in Tennessee, is not to be compared with the evils still threatening the brethren, particularly in your latitude.[3]

Particularly should the student of restoration history ponder well those last words from Fanning. The battle was coming, "particularly in your latitude"—particularly in the North where the *Review* was being published. What a marvelously accurate prophecy of things to come!

Fanning's outspoken remarks against the symptoms that were rapidly increasing around him got for him the reputation from his enemies of being "ambitious," and of desiring to "lead a party." On many of the particular points that Fanning emphasized, he was not always right. Some of his very closest friends recognized this. Yet, in the main, Fanning was on the right track, and men closest to him knew it. Ben Franklin, therefore, came to his defense against such attacks by saying,

We have some personal acquaintance with Brother Fanning, and have read nearly everything he has written, and, while we do not precisely agree with him in everything, we do not believe there is a fairer man in investigation in the Christian ranks than he, one freer from misrepresentation, or less ambitious, or one who has less intention of heading a party. There is no man in our ranks possessing a higher sense of honor, a stricter respect for and devotion to

---

[2]Ben Franklin, "The Defection Again," *American Christian Review,* Vol. II, No. 15 (April 12, 1859), p. 58.
[3]Tolbert Fanning, "The Defection," *Gospel Advocate,* Vol. V, No. 6 (June, 1859), p. 169.

the oracles of God than he. He is unquestionably, in the main issues he has had with brethren, maintaining the very soul of what we have, as a body, struggled for from the beginning, and the brethren are with him. He is a full-grown man, now of mature years, deliberate, decided, and determined, and is not to shrink, nor to be put down by the charge of 'ambition' and the desire to 'head a party,' on the part of those who can never answer him.[4]

In December, 1861 in the *Millennial Harbinger* and the *American Christian Review* there arose another controversy that might be taken as a symptom. This particular discussion more than anyone up to date, showed particularly the different attitudes that brethren had toward the Bible. The subject matter under discussion was, "Communion With The Sects," but the basic attitude the whole discussion revealed was the underlying conception which various men had of the church, and toward the Bible as the proper guide in matters of faith and practice. We, at the present time, are more interested in this attitude than in the issue, although a brief notice of this seems necessary.

Richard Hawley, one of the leading members in the church at Detroit, Michigan, wrote to W. K. Pendleton, deploring the rise of Phariseeism and exclusiveness in the church with relation to the sects. Actually, what he called "phariseeism" and "exclusiveness" had been there, but there was arising a liberalism of which he apparently was unaware. At any rate, his letter caused W. K. Pendleton to invite various leading men to express themselves on the question of having communion with the sects.

Isaac Errett was one to accept the invitation to express his views upon the subject. Errett laid down four propositions as follows:

(1) In primitive times all who partook of the Lord's Supper were immersed believers.

(2) Corruptions have crept into the church because of Popery and have scattered the people of God into various sects.

(3) Our plea is for a reunion of the people of God. While our plea does not recognize these sects as of divine origin, yet it recognizes a people of God among them.

(4) "We are compelled, therefore, to recognize as Christians many who have been in error on baptism, but who in the *spirit* of obedience are Christians indeed."

---

[4]Ben Franklin, "President Fanning," *American Christian Review*, Vol. II, No. 22 (May 31, 1859), p. 86.

As to whether or not it was right to invite the sects to a communion around the Lord's table when they attend on Lord's Day, Errett's reply was: "Our practice, therefore, is, *neither to invite nor reject* particular classes of persons, but to spread the table in the name of the Lord, for the Lord's people, and allow all to come who will, each on his own responsibility."[5]   On the same point, Robert Richardson replied, "We simply leave each individual to determine it for himself."[6]

W. K. Pendleton's answer was,

We have ever most cordially approved the general, I may say almost universal, custom of our churches, in disclaiming all authority to exclude from the Lord's Supper any who, by their walk and conversation, and in their own hearts, approve themselves as the Lord's people. We have never known any evil to result from the practice, but on the contrary, much good.   Such is the influence of passion and prejudice upon the actions and opinions of men, that it is next to impossible to influence any one for good whilst we treat him with distance and distrust.   To plead for union, and at the same time exclude the really pious from the communion of the body and blood of the Saviour, is, in the very nature of things, to destroy the practical power of our plea.[7]

This controversy ran for not less than two years, and at times became bitter.   Before it had run its course the whole question of the "pious unimmersed" received a thorough discussion.   Could a pious man, who had not been immersed, be saved eternally?   The question tended to renew another controversy of former years, raised in Campbell's famous Lunenburg letter of 1837, and on which many brethren then did not find themselves in agreement. But, before drawing conclusions from this controversy, it is best to see now the other side.

George W. Elley of Kentucky was the first to give a reply to Pendleton's answer.   There appeared to be real alarm in his heart as he viewed the replies in the *Harbinger*.   He asks, "Is not such a practice the breaking down of all the landmarks separating Christ's from human kingdoms?"[8]   Elley clings tenaciously to the

---

[5]Isaac Errett, "Letter from I. Errett," *Millennial Harbinger,* Fifth Series, Vol. IV, No. 12 (December, 1861), p. 711.
[6]Robert Richardson, "Letter from Dr. R. Richardson," *Millennial Harbinger,* Fifth Series, Vol. IV, No. 12 (December, 1861), p. 712.
[7]W. K. Pendleton, "Remarks," *Millennial Harbinger,* Fifth Series, Vol. IV, No. 12 (December, 1861), p. 713.
[8]G. W. Elley, "Communion with the 'Sects,'" *Millennial Harbinger,* Fifth Series, Vol. V, No. 1 (January, 1862), p. 39.

principle that in New Testament time only those belonged to the
church, only those were Christians who had been immersed. What
right, then, do we have to declare that men today can be Christians
without immersion, as Errett and Pendleton were declaring. Can
these men claim they are restoring the primitive order of things
and at the same time set aside the primary necessity of the act of
immersion?

Shortly after Elley's article appeared, Ben Franklin entered the
controversy on the same side. Franklin merely wanted to know
why, if it were admitted that no one but the immersed partook of
the communion in primitive times, how can we claim to restore the
ancient order, and today do it differently? And so he asks:
"Where is the use of parleying over the question of communing
with the unimmersed persons? Did the first Christians commune
with unimmersed persons? It is admitted they did not. Shall we,
then, deliberately do what we admit they did not do?"[9]

In the spring of 1863 Moses E. Lard wrote an article which he
held in reserve for publication in the first issue of *Lard's Quarterly*
in September, that year. Lard stood squarely beside Franklin and
opposed W. K. Pendleton. The Lord's Supper, he argued, belonged properly to the kingdom, and those out of the kingdom had
no right to it.

Basically there were two questions raised in the whole controversy. The first one was, can a man be a Christian without
being immersed? The second question was, does the church have
a right to refuse the Lord's Supper to the unimmersed? The value
in these questions is that they were revelatory of certain attitudes
toward the Bible.

On the first question both Isaac Errett and W. K. Pendleton
proved themselves to be true prophets of liberalism. While they
agreed that no man was a Christian in New Testament times without immersion, yet we live in different times, times when we are
compelled to admit that the good, pious men in all sects are Christians. It is not at all difficult to see why certain brethren thought
of them as completely departing from apostolic grounds. They
admitted that it took immersion in primitive time to make Christians. Why not now? If not now, what then was the value of
restoring New Testament Christianity? On what ground could

[9]Ben Franklin, "The Limits of Religious Fellowship," *Millennial Harbinger,* Fifth Series, Vol. V, No. 2 (February, 1862), p. 120.

they defend themselves that they were even *trying* to restore it? It was plain to men like Ben Franklin and Moses E. Lard that Errett and Pendleton had exalted their human opinions above the revealed word.

Errett and Pendleton's attitude was truly symptomatic. In years to come a large host of liberal brethren were to adopt the same idea. Lard and Franklin were to be looked upon as literalists and extremists, and some, like W. C. Morro, in his book, "Brother McGarvey," frankly say so. All it took to be a Christian was to have a pious character. Either immersion was essential to salvation or it was not. If pious character were all that was necessary, why not abandon this thing of telling men to be baptized "for the remission of sins", especially when they could secure this remission by having only good, pious characters?

For the most part the churches of Christ down through the years have maintained that immersion is essential to being a Christian. They have refused to try to substitute opinions for this plain declaration of scriptures. Let this be called "exclusiveness," "phariseeism," "literalism," and an "extreme" or come what may; still, it is loyalty to God's word, and shows a respect for the revealed will, and that's what counts.

The second question was, does the church have a right to refuse the Lord's Supper to the unimmersed? From a practical point of view Errett's conclusion on this point has been followed by the churches of Christ down through the years, viz., they neither invite nor reject others from coming. God has not made the church a police force to guard the Lord's table from the unimmersed. The whole tenor of New Testament teaching is each man partaking of the communion is to examine himself. Self-examination is the prerequisite for participation. By the very nature of the case, the church *could not if it tried* guarantee that only those partake of the Lord's Supper who should. Therefore, most gospel preachers follow the practice of teaching the truth on the subject, showing the Lord's Supper to be for Christians, those that have been immersed for the remission of sins. If, after the truth is taught, a member of a sect violates it, the responsibility is his, not the church's.

By 1865, the year at which we bring this volume to a close, the war between the states had ended. The church had weathered the issues created by the war without any serious disruption. But could she long continue without disruption with so many symptoms present, indicating serious trouble? What were those clouds on the far-off horizon? Were they dark or were they white? Those whose hearts were heavy and anxious over Zion, strained their eyes to see, and then, with a look of consternation, declared they were indeed dark. Then there were those who thought this was no time to look for dark clouds. The nation around lay bleeding and broken from four devastating years of submission to Mars. The Country's president lay dead, and every home, from the log cabin in the wilderness to the White House was draped in black, and thousands walked in mourning. In such an hour of desolation there had to be something bright somewhere, and if not in the future, then where? And so some refused to look for fear of what they might see. But no matter. There was but one thing to do: press on with renewed strength and zeal. The corresponding secretary of the Missionary Society on October 17, 1865, spoke truly:

As behind the cloud, the sun shines more brightly; or as through the rain drops only can we see the rainbow, so through the tears of the past we have at length beheld the gorgeous dawning of the rays of peace over our so lately war-scourged land. Terrible indeed were the sacrifices; bitter the tears, deep the flow of human blood, made not to cease until reddened yet again, from the heart of a murdered President, and yet through all these times, hath God brought us safely to this happy anniversary hour. A country saved, a race delivered and peace restored, may well fill us with a profoundest gratitude to God, and bow us humbly at His feet. Amid these blessings, with such joys around us; with such hopes before us we can well afford to extend a new the right hand of fellowship to each other, without regard to dividing lines, from Main to the Gulf, and from ocean to ocean. With this Spirit, let us strive to forget the past and enter with a new life and strength upon the labors of the future.

O God, thou hast taught me from my youth;
    And hitherto have I declared thy wondrous works.
Yea, even when I am old and grayheaded,
O God, forsake me not,
    Until I have declared thy strength unto
    the next generation.

                              —Psalms 71 : 17, 18.

BIBLIOGRAPHY

PERIODICALS

Campbell, Alexander, *Christian Baptist,* (1823-1829)

Campbell, Alexander, *Millennial Harbinger,* (1830-1870)

Fanning, Tolbert, *Christian Review,* (1844-1847)

Fanning, Tolbert; Lipscomb, David, *Gospel Advocate,* (1855-1861 ; 1866-1948)

Ferguson, Jesse B., *Christian Magazine,* (1848-1853)

Franklin, Ben., *Western Reformer,* (1843-1849)

Franklin, Ben, *American Christian Review,* (1856-1948)

Lard, Moses E., *Lard's Quarterly,* (1863-1868)

Loos, C. L., *The Disciple,* (1851-1853)

Mathes, James M., *Christian Record,* (1844-1866)

Stone, Barton W., *Christian Messenger,* (1826-1845)

HISTORICAL BACKGROUND

Barrett, John Pressley, *The Centennial of Religious Journalism,* (2nd ed.), (Dayton: Christian Publishing Co., 1908)

Baxter, William, *Pea Ridge and Prairie Grove,* (Cincinnati: Poe and Hitchcock, 1864)

Bennett, William W., *Memorials of Methodism in Virginia,* (Richmond: Pub. by the author, 1871)

Bond, John, *History of the Baptist Concord Association,* (Nashville: Groves, Marks & Co., 1860)

Campbell, Alexander, *Debate on Christian Baptism,* (Campbell vs. McCalla), (Buffalo: A. Campbell, 1824)

Campbell, Alexander, *Debate on Christian Baptism,* (Campbell & Rice), (Lexington: A. T. Skillman & Son, 1844)

Cauble, Commodore Wesley, *Disciples of Christ in Indiana,* (Indianapolis: Meigs Publishing Co., 1930)

Fisher, George Park, *History of the Christian Church,* (New York: Charles Scribners Sons, 1946)

Fortune, A. W., *The Disciples in Kentucky,* (Lexington: ———, 1932)

Garrison, W. E. *Religion Follows the Frontier,* (New York: Harper & Brothers, 1931)

Gates, Errett, *The Disciples of Christ: Story of the Churches,* (New York: Baker & Taylor, 1905)

Gates, Errett, *The Early Relation and Separation of Baptists and Disciples,* (Chicago: Christian Century Co., 1904)

Green, Francis Marion, *Christian Missions, and Historical Sketches,* (St. Louis: John Burns, 1884)

353

Haley, Thomas Preston, *Dawn of the Reformation in Missouri,* (St. Louis: Christian Publishing Co., 1888)

Hayden, A. S., *Early History of the Disciples in the Western Reserve,* Ohio, (Cincinnati: Chase & Hall, 1875)

Hockett, Homer Carey, *Political and Social Growth of the American People, 1492-1865,* (New York: MacMillan Co., 1940)

Lewis, John T., *The Voice of the Pioneers on Instrumental Music and Societies,* (Nashville: Gospel Advocate Co., 1932)

Loos, Charles L., *First General Convention,* (Louisville: Apostolic Guide, 1891)

Moore, William Thomas, *A Comprehensive History of the Disciples of Christ,* (New York: Fleming H. Revell Co., 1909)

Morrill, Milo True, *A History of the Christian Denomination in America, 1794-1911,* (Dayton: Christian Publishing Association, 1912)

Oats, Sargeant, *Prison Life in Dixie,* (Chicago: Central Book Concern, 1880)

Qualben, Lars P., *A History of the Christian Church,* (New York: Thomas Nelson & Sons, 1940)

Rogers, James Richard, *The Cane Ridge Meeting-House,* (Cincinnati: Standard Publishing Co., 1910)

Scobey, James E., *Franklin College and Its Influences,* (Nashville: McQuiddy Printing Co., 1906)

Srygley, Fletcher Douglas, *Seventy Years in Dixie,* (Nashville: Gospel Advocate Co., 1891)

Watters, A. C., *History of the British Churches of Christ,* (Indianapolis: Butler School of Religion, 1948)

Wilcox, Alanson, *History of the Disciples of Christ in Ohio,* (Cincinnati: Standard Publishing Co., 1918)

Young, Charles A., *Historical Documents Advocating Christian Union,* (Chicago: Christian Century, 1904)

BIOGRAPHICAL

Baxter, William, *Life of Elder Walter Scott,* (Cincinnati: Bosworth, Chase & Hall, 1874)

Boles, H. Leo, *Biographical Sketches of Gospel Preachers,* (Nashville: Gospel Advocate Co., 1932)

Campbell, Alexander, *Memoirs of Elder Thomas Campbell,* (Cincinnati: H. S. Bosworth, 1861)

Donan, P., *Memoirs of Jacob Creath, Jr.,* (Cincinnati: Chase & Hall, 1877)

Franklin, Joseph and Headington, J. A., *The Life and Times of Benjamin Franklin,* (St. Louis: John Burns, 1879)

Grafton, Thomas W., *Life of Alexander Campbell,* (St. Louis: Christian Board of Publication, 1897)

Haley, J. J., *Makers and Molders of the Reformation Movement,* (St. Louis: Christian Board of Publication, 1914)

Hanna, William Herbert, *Thomas Campbell, Seceder and Christian Union Advocate,* (Cincinnati: Standard Publishing Co., 1935)

Hopson, Ella Lord, *Memoirs of Dr. Winthrop Hartly Hopson,* (Cincinnati: Standard Publishing Co., 1887)

Lamar, J. S., *Memoirs of Isaac Errett,* (Cincinnati: The Standard Publishing Co., 1893)

MacClenny, Wilbur E., *The Life of Rev. James O'Kelly,* (Raleigh, N. C.: Edwards & Broughton, 1910)

Moore, Allen R., *Alexander Campbell and the General Convention,* (St. Louis: Christian Board of Publication, 1914)

Morro, W. T., *Brother McGarvey,* (St. Louis: Bethany Press, 1940)

Power, Frederick D., *Life of William Kimbrough Pendleton, LL.D.,* (St. Louis: Christian Publishing Co., 1902)

Richardson, Robert, *Memoirs of Alexander Campbell, Vols. I, II,* (Cincinnati: Standard Publishing Co., 1897)

Rogers, John, *The Biography of Elder J. T. Johnson,* (Cincinnati: ————, 1861)

Rogers, John I., *Autobiography of Samuel Rogers,* (Cincinnati: Standard Publishing Co., 1880)

Segar, Charles V., *Lectures on the Pentateuch,* (Cincinnati: Bosworth, Chase & Hall, 1871)

Smith, Elias, *The Life, Conversion, Preaching, Travels, and Sufferings of Elias Smith,* (Portsmouth, N. H.: Beck & Foster, 1816)

Srygley, F. D., *Larimore and His Boys,* (Nashville: Gospel Advocate Co., 1898)

Stevenson, Dwight E., *Walter Scott: Voice of the Golden Oracle,* (St. Louis Christian Board of Publication, 1946)

Stone, Barton W., *Biography of Elder Barton Warren Stone,* (Cincinnati: J. A. & U. P. James, 1847)

Tipple, Ezra Squier, *Francis Asbury, the Prophet of the Long Road,* (New York: The Methodist Book Concern, 1916)

Ware, C. C., *Barton Warren Stone,* (St. Louis: Bethany Press, 1932)

Williams, John A., *Life of Elder John Smith,* (Cincinnati: Standard Publishing Co., 1870)

RECORDS

Spencer, Claude E., *Periodicals of the Disciples of Christ and Related Groups,* (Canton, Mo.: 1943)

Minutes of Concord Baptist Association.

Minutes of Mahoning Baptist Association.

Minutes of Meetings of American Christian Missionary Society (1849-1865)

INDEX